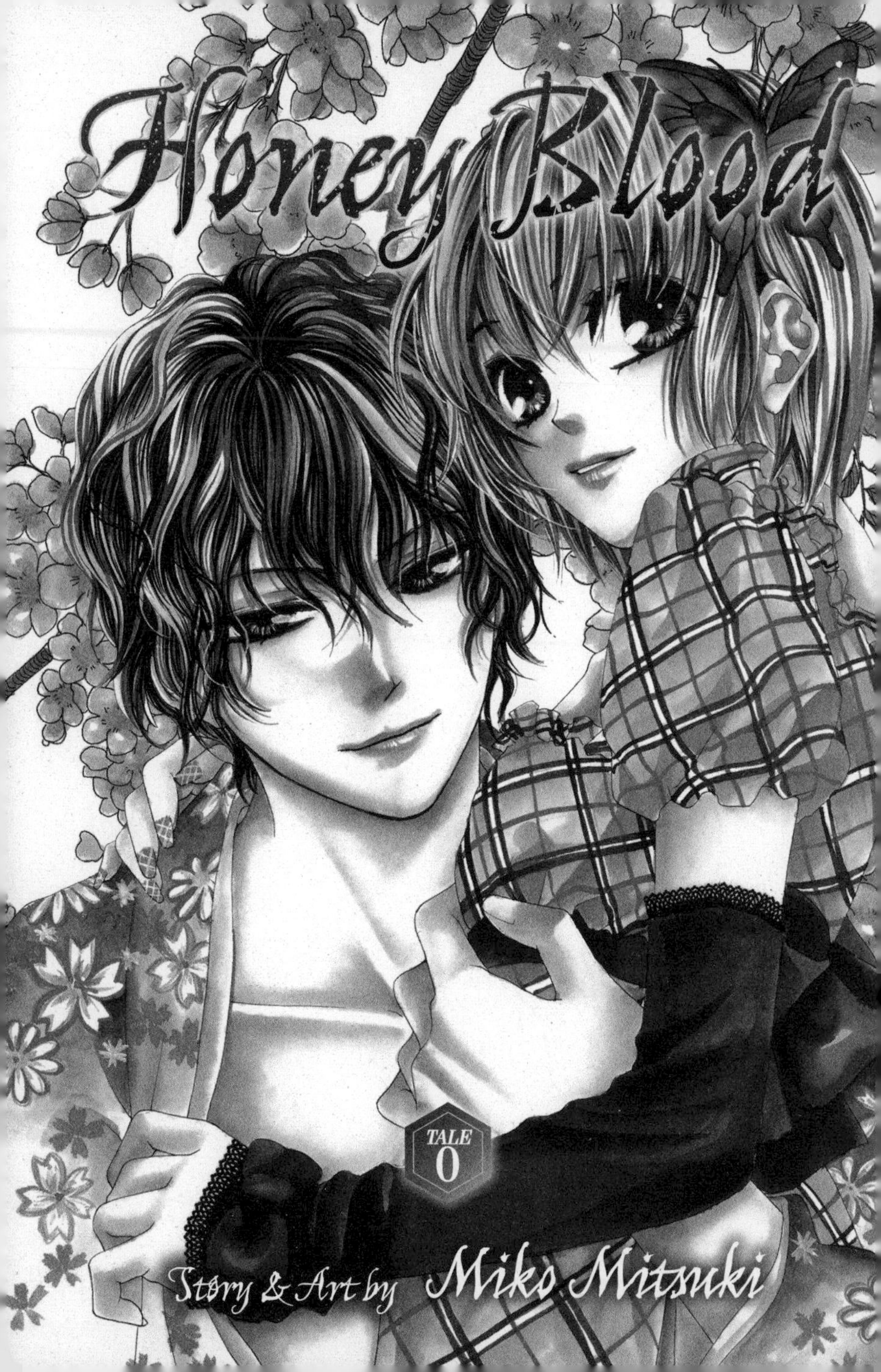
Honey Blood
TALE 0
Story & Art by Miko Mitsuki

Honey Blood

TALE
0

Contents

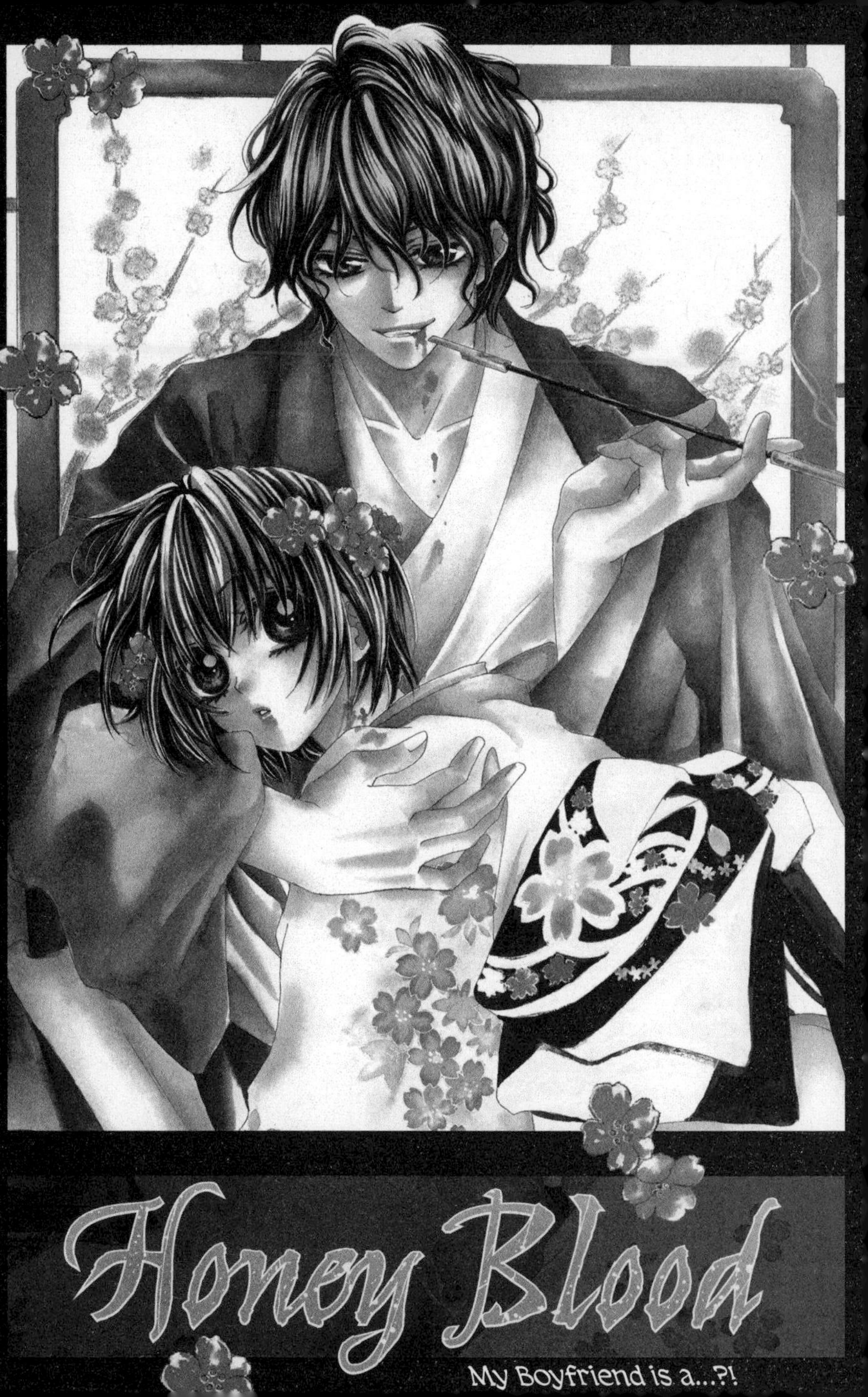
Honey Blood
My Boyfriend is a...?!

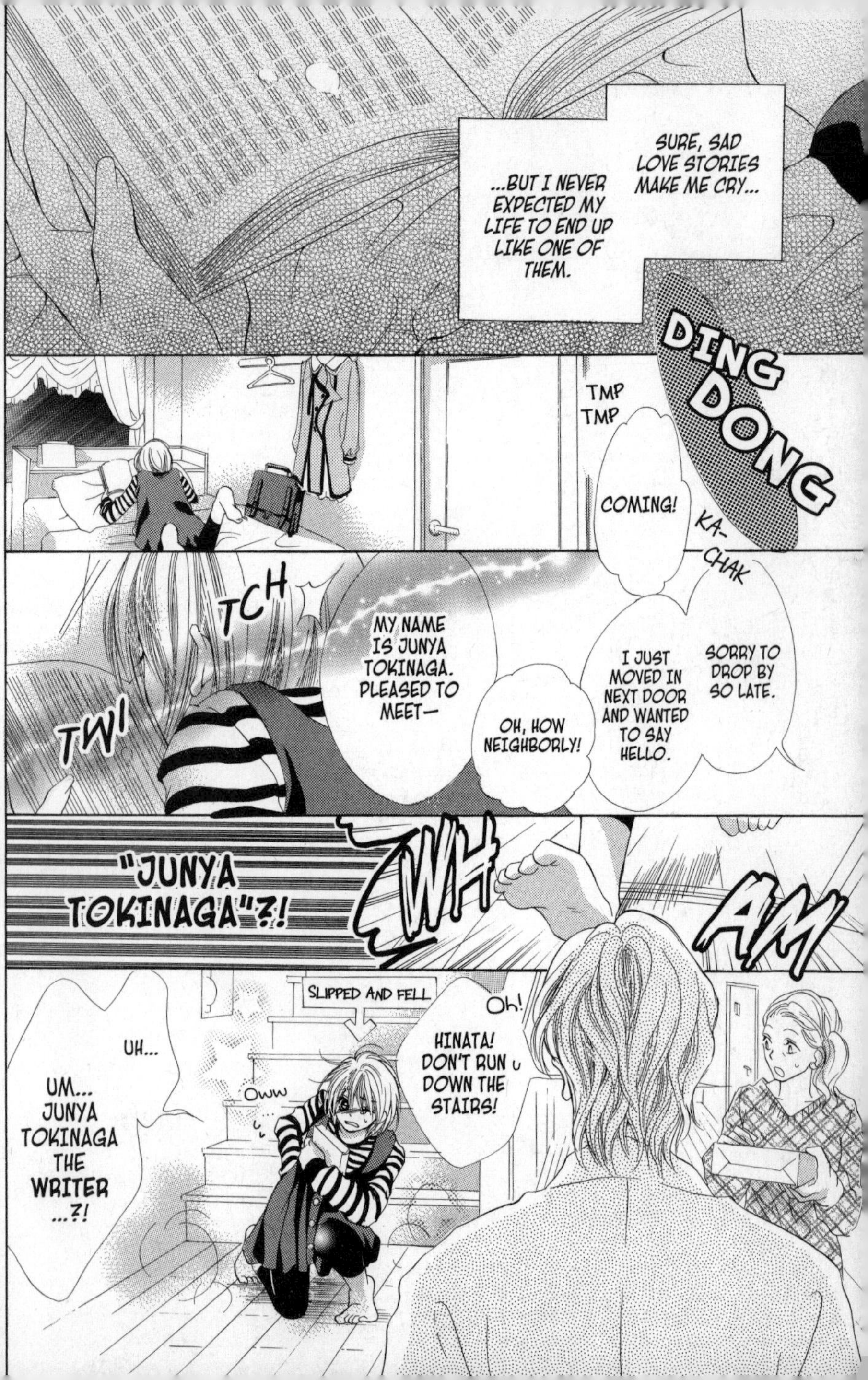
SURE, SAD LOVE STORIES MAKE ME CRY...
...BUT I NEVER EXPECTED MY LIFE TO END UP LIKE ONE OF THEM.
DING DONG
TMP TMP
COMING!
KA-CHAK
SORRY TO DROP BY SO LATE.
I JUST MOVED IN NEXT DOOR AND WANTED TO SAY HELLO.
OH, HOW NEIGHBORLY!
MY NAME IS JUNYA TOKINAGA. PLEASED TO MEET—
TCH
TWI
AM
WH
"JUNYA TOKINAGA"?!
Oh!
HINATA! DON'T RUN DOWN THE STAIRS!
SLIPPED AND FELL
Oww
UH...
UM... JUNYA TOKINAGA THE WRITER ...?!

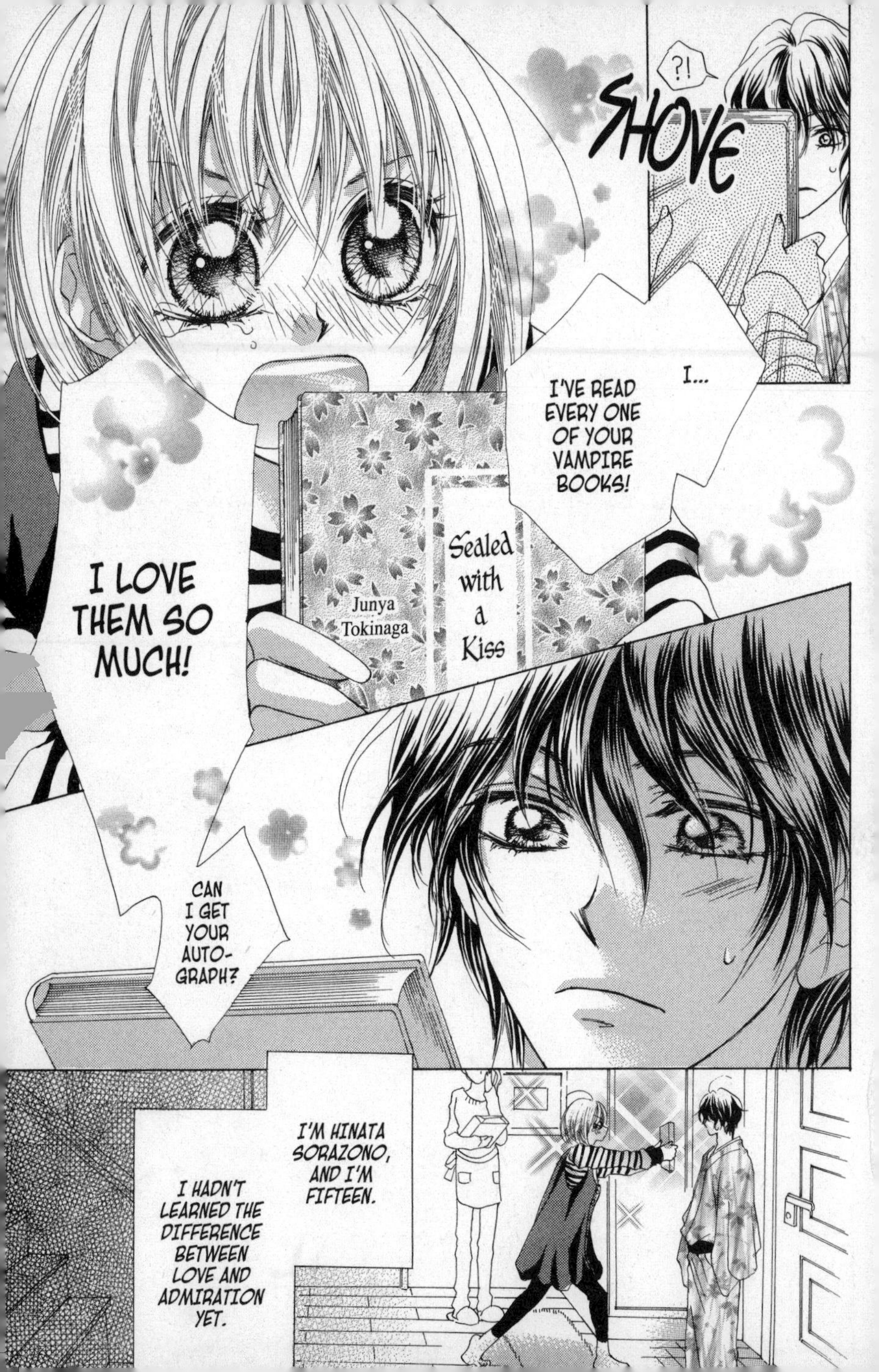
?!
SHOVE
I...
I'VE READ EVERY ONE OF YOUR VAMPIRE BOOKS!
Sealed with a Kiss
Junya Tokinaga
I LOVE THEM SO MUCH!
CAN I GET YOUR AUTO-GRAPH?
I'M HINATA SORAZONO, AND I'M FIFTEEN.
I HADN'T LEARNED THE DIFFERENCE BETWEEN LOVE AND ADMIRATION YET.

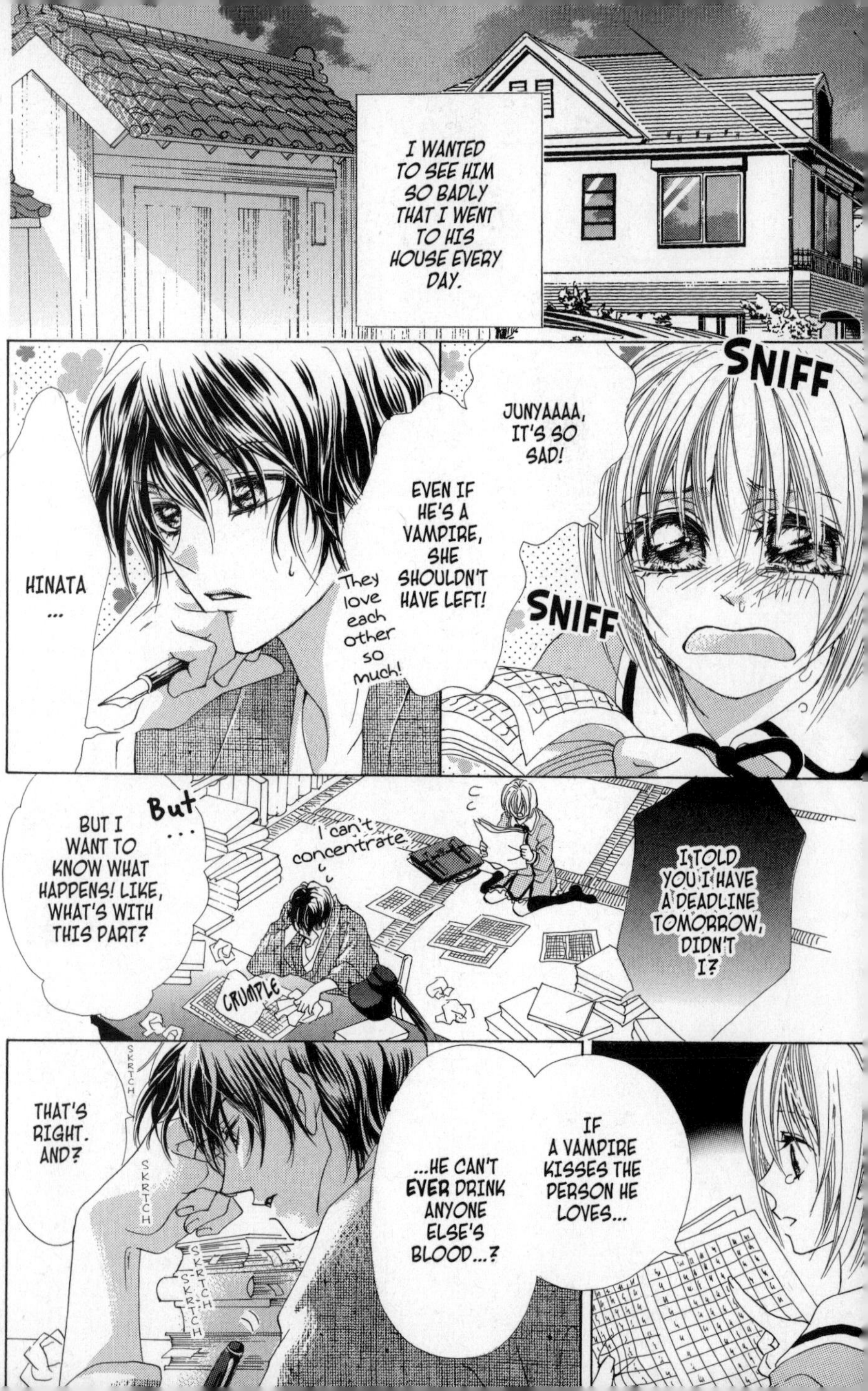
I WANTED TO SEE HIM SO BADLY THAT I WENT TO HIS HOUSE EVERY DAY.
SNIFF
JUNYAAAA, IT'S SO SAD!
EVEN IF HE'S A VAMPIRE, SHE SHOULDN'T HAVE LEFT!
They love each other so much!
SNIFF
HINATA ...
I TOLD YOU I HAVE A DEADLINE TOMORROW, DIDN'T I?
But ...
BUT I WANT TO KNOW WHAT HAPPENS! LIKE, WHAT'S WITH THIS PART?
I can't concentrate
CRUMPLE
IF A VAMPIRE KISSES THE PERSON HE LOVES...
...HE CAN'T EVER DRINK ANYONE ELSE'S BLOOD...?
THAT'S RIGHT. AND?
SKRTCH
SKRTCH
SKRTCH
SKRTCH

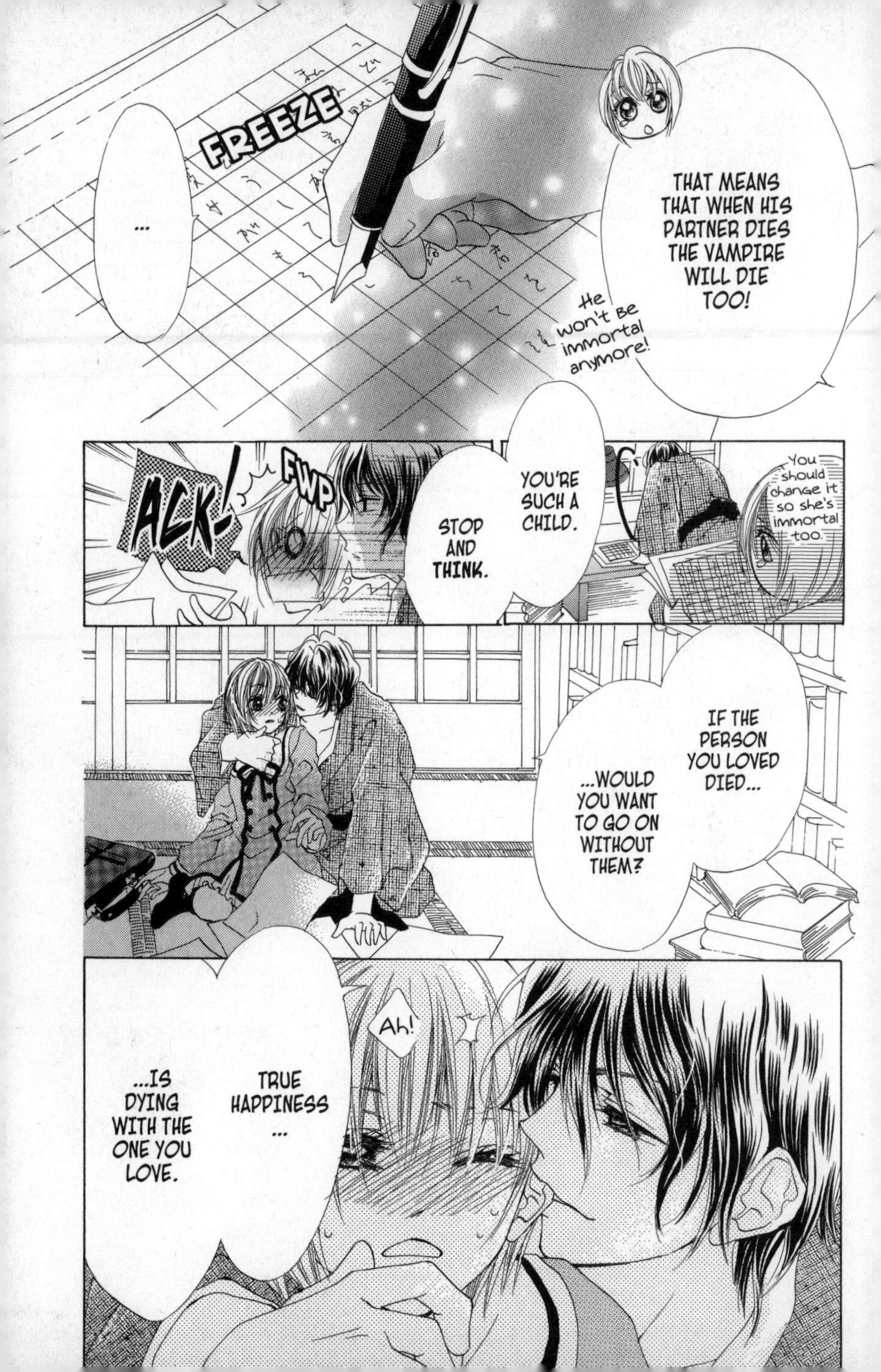
THAT MEANS THAT WHEN HIS PARTNER DIES THE VAMPIRE WILL DIE TOO!
He won't be immortal anymore!
FREEZE
...
You should change it so she's immortal too.
YOU'RE SUCH A CHILD.
STOP AND THINK.
FWP
ACK!
IF THE PERSON YOU LOVED DIED...
...WOULD YOU WANT TO GO ON WITHOUT THEM?
Ah!
TRUE HAPPINESS ...
...IS DYING WITH THE ONE YOU LOVE.

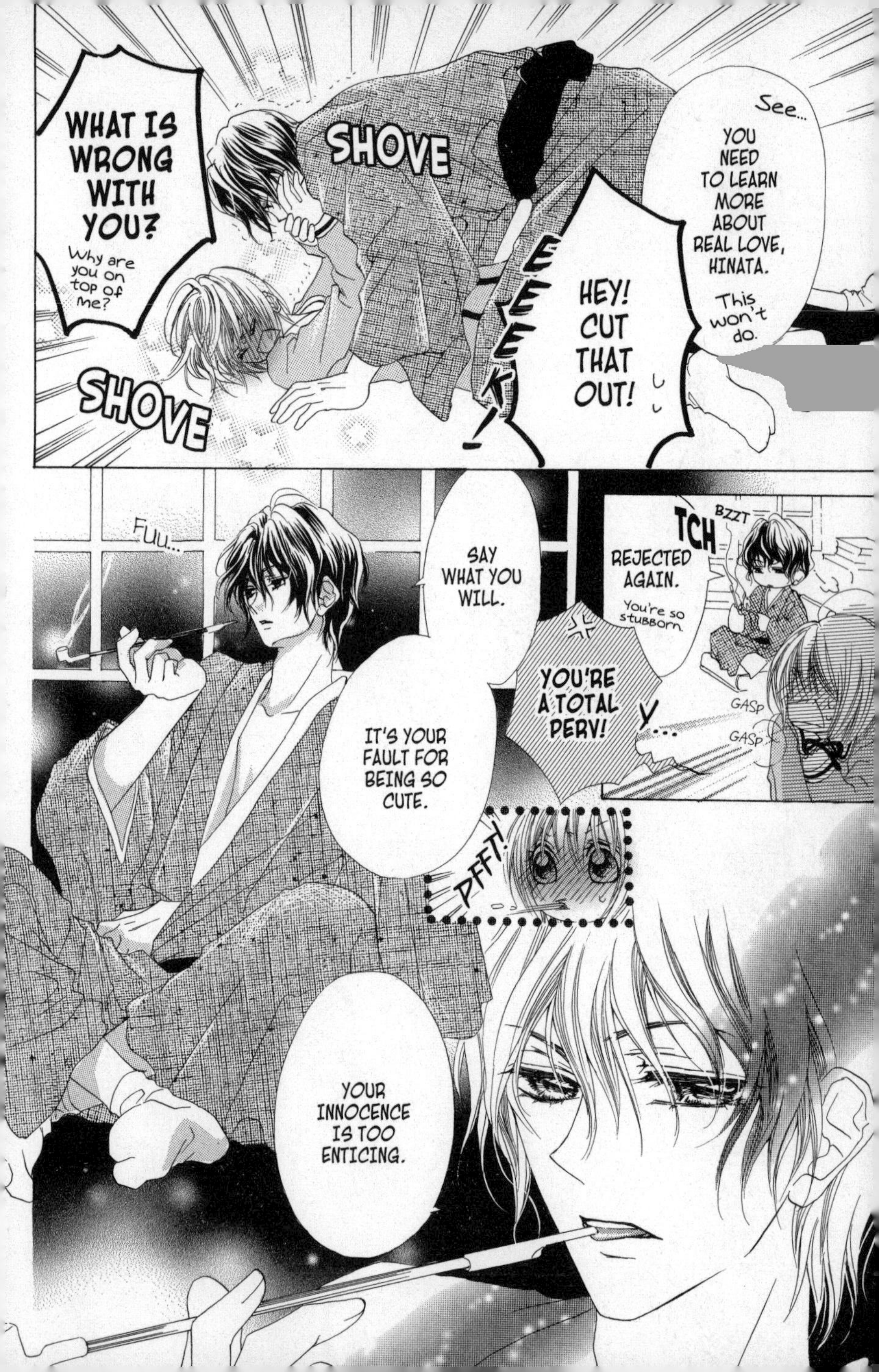
See... YOU NEED TO LEARN MORE ABOUT REAL LOVE, HINATA. This won't do.
HEY! CUT THAT OUT!
EEEEK!
SHOVE
WHAT IS WRONG WITH YOU? Why are you on top of me?
SHOVE
BZZT
TCH
REJECTED AGAIN. You're so stubborn.
YOU'RE A TOTAL PERV!
GASP
GASP
Y...
SAY WHAT YOU WILL.
Fuu...
IT'S YOUR FAULT FOR BEING SO CUTE.
PFFT!
YOUR INNOCENCE IS TOO ENTICING.

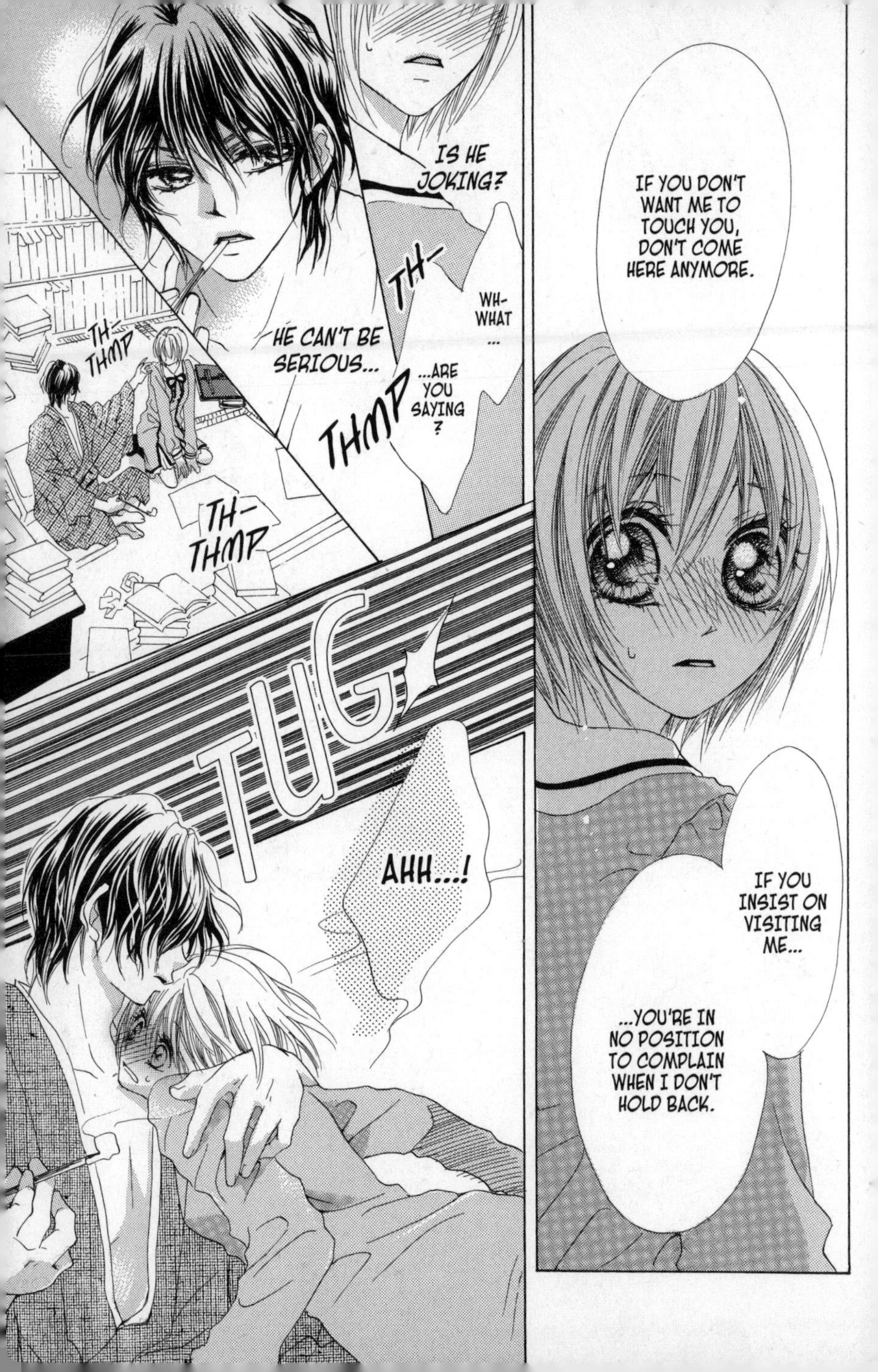
IF YOU DON'T WANT ME TO TOUCH YOU, DON'T COME HERE ANYMORE.
IF YOU INSIST ON VISITING ME...
...YOU'RE IN NO POSITION TO COMPLAIN WHEN I DON'T HOLD BACK.
IS HE JOKING?
WH-WHAT ...
...ARE YOU SAYING ?
TH-
THMP
HE CAN'T BE SERIOUS...
TH-THMP
TH-THMP
TUG
AHH...!

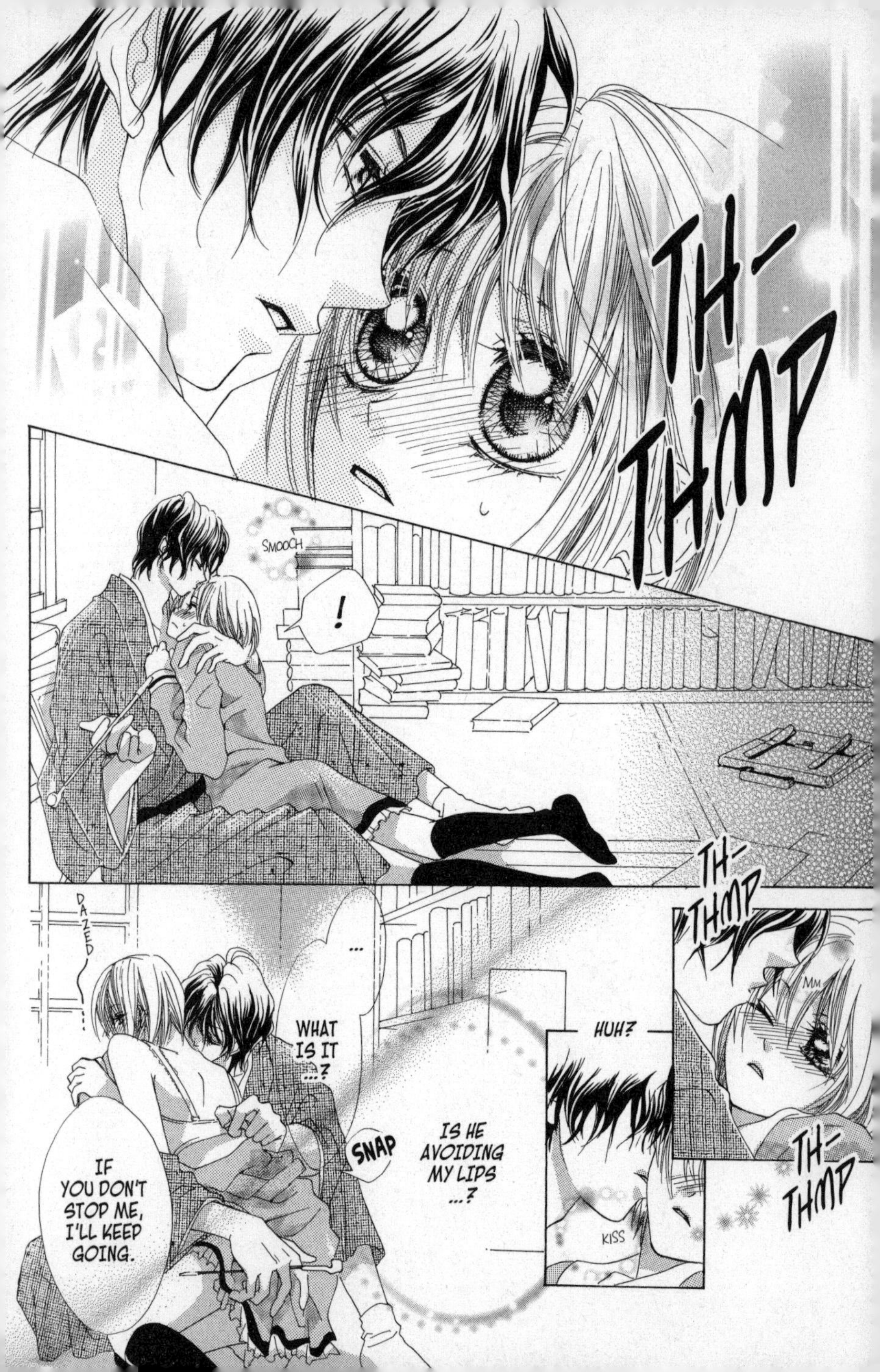
TH-THMP
SMOOCH
!
TH-THMP
MM
TH-THMP
HUH?
KISS
IS HE AVOIDING MY LIPS ...?
...
WHAT IS IT ...?
SNAP
DAZED
IF YOU DON'T STOP ME, I'LL KEEP GOING.

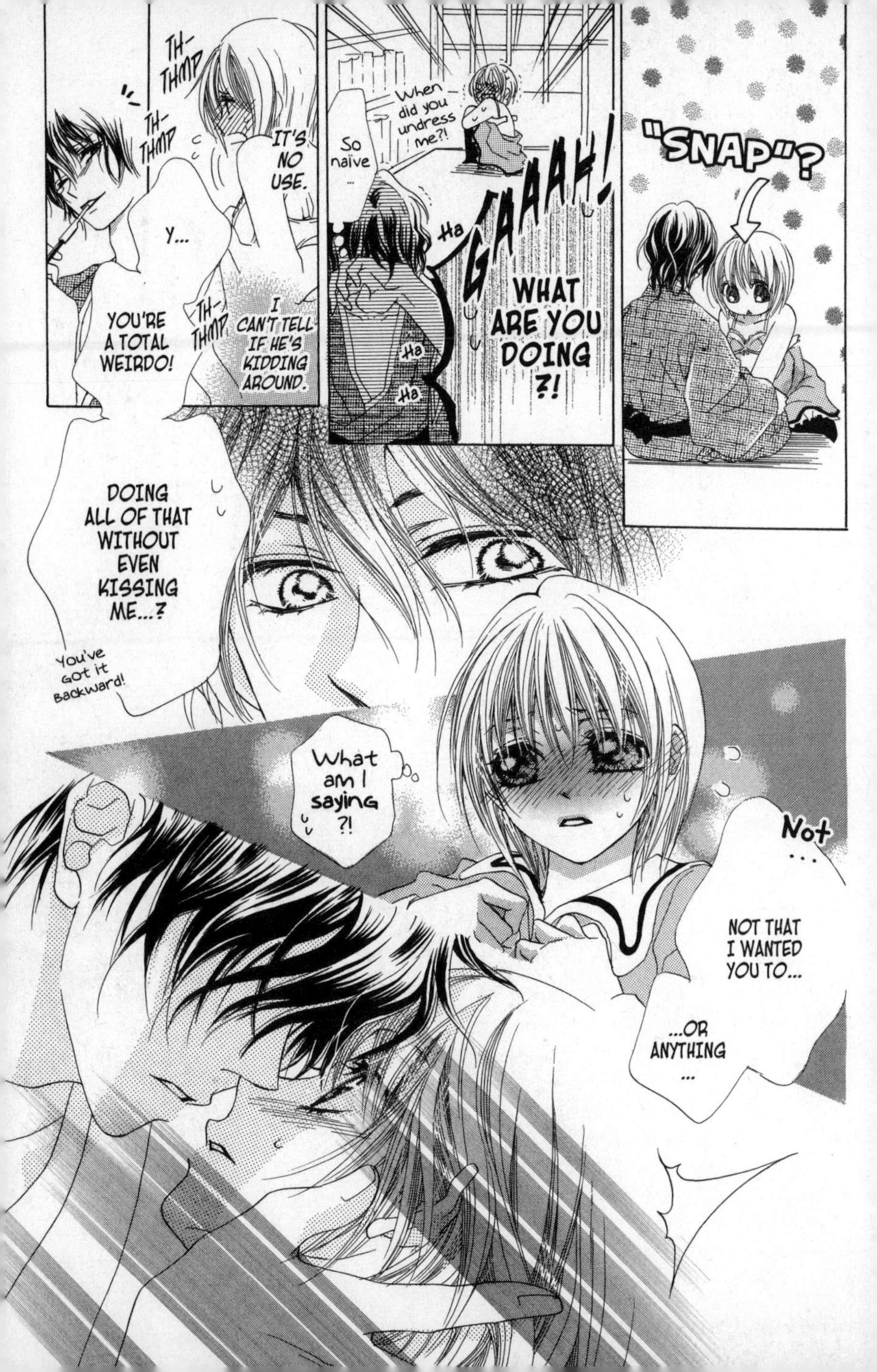
"SNAP"?
When did you undress me?!
GAAAH!
WHAT ARE YOU DOING?!
So naïve...
Ha
Ha
Ha
TH-THMP
IT'S NO USE.
TH-THMP
Y...
I CAN'T TELL IF HE'S KIDDING AROUND.
TH-THMP
YOU'RE A TOTAL WEIRDO!
DOING ALL OF THAT WITHOUT EVEN KISSING ME...?
You've got it backward!
Not...
NOT THAT I WANTED YOU TO...
...OR ANYTHING...
What am I saying?!

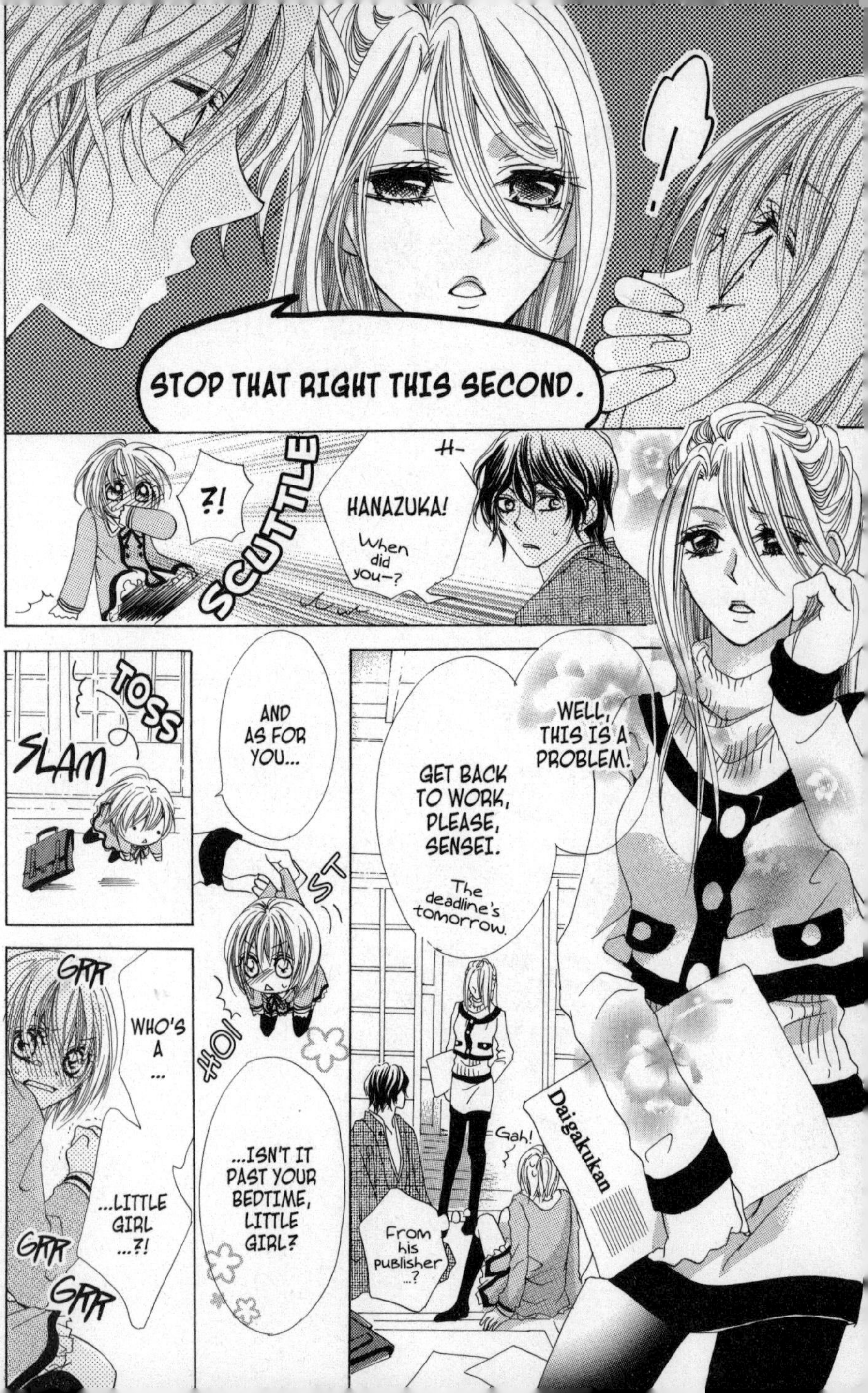
!
STOP THAT RIGHT THIS SECOND.
H-
HANAZUKA!
When did you–?
SCUTTLE
?!
WELL, THIS IS A PROBLEM!
GET BACK TO WORK, PLEASE, SENSEI.
The deadline's tomorrow.
Daigakukan
Gah!
From his publisher ...?
AND AS FOR YOU...
TOSS
SLAM
ST
HOI
...ISN'T IT PAST YOUR BEDTIME, LITTLE GIRL?
GRR
WHO'S A ...
...LITTLE GIRL ...?!
GRR
GRR

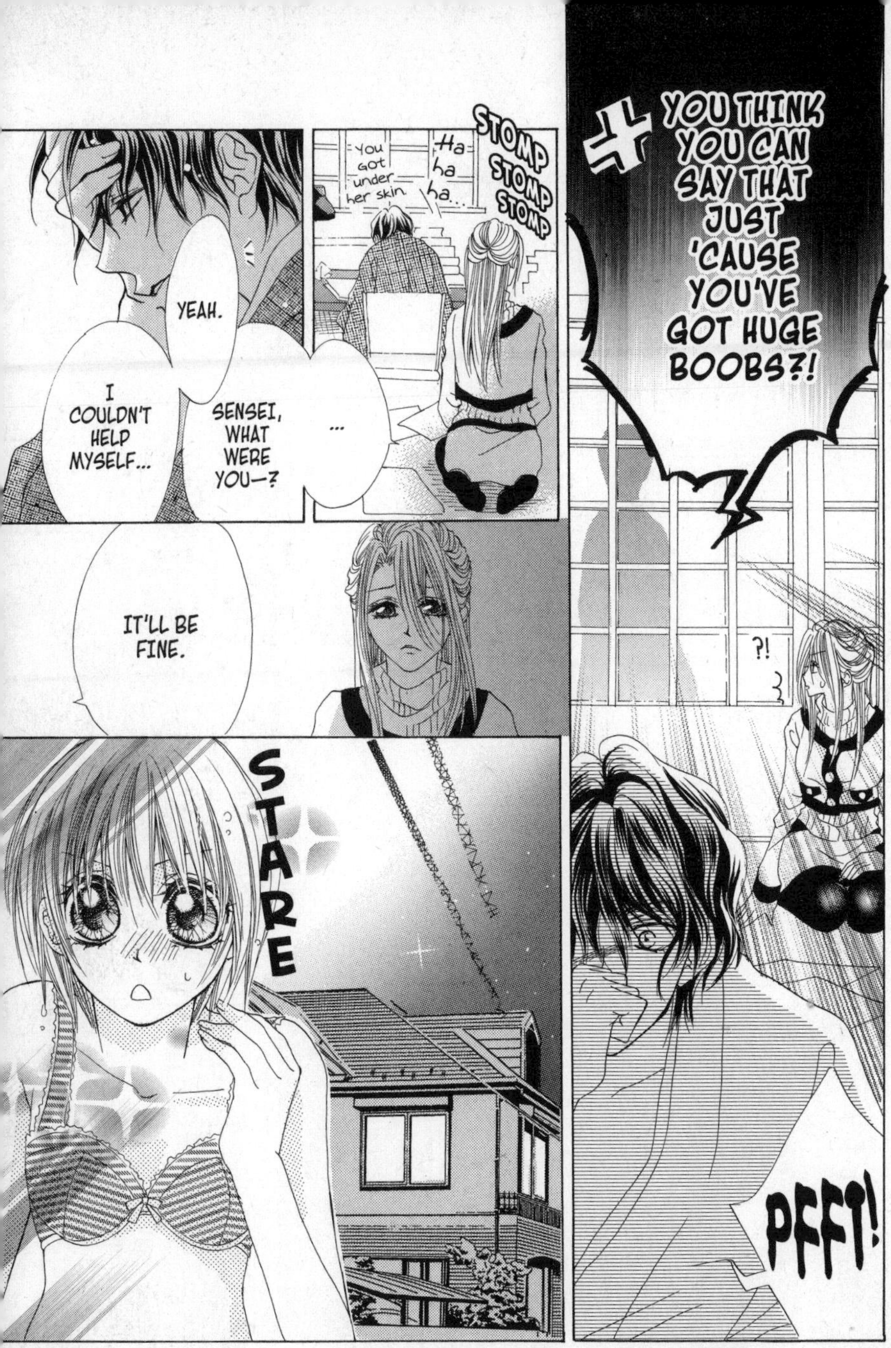
YOU THINK YOU CAN SAY THAT JUST 'CAUSE YOU'VE GOT HUGE BOOBS?!
?!
PFFT!
STOMP
STOMP
STOMP
You got under her skin.
Ha ha ha...
...
SENSEI, WHAT WERE YOU—?
YEAH.
I COULDN'T HELP MYSELF...
IT'LL BE FINE.
STARE

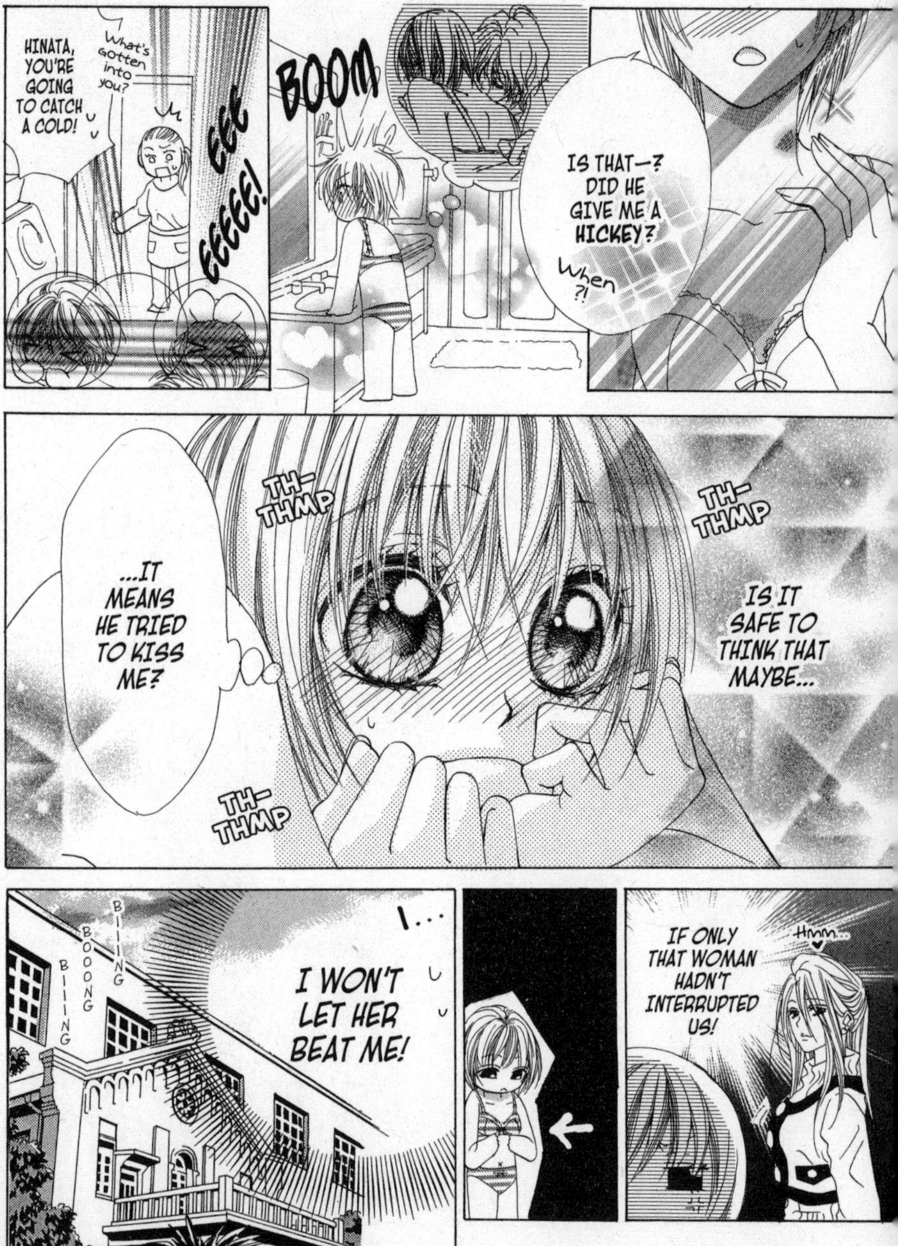
IS THAT—? DID HE GIVE ME A HICKEY?
When ?!
BOOM
EEE EEEEE!
What's gotten into you?
HINATA, YOU'RE GOING TO CATCH A COLD!
TH-THMP
IS IT SAFE TO THINK THAT MAYBE...
TH-THMP
...IT MEANS HE TRIED TO KISS ME?
TH-THMP
Hmm...
IF ONLY THAT WOMAN HADN'T INTERRUPTED US!
I...
I WON'T LET HER BEAT ME!
BIIING
BOOONG
BIIING

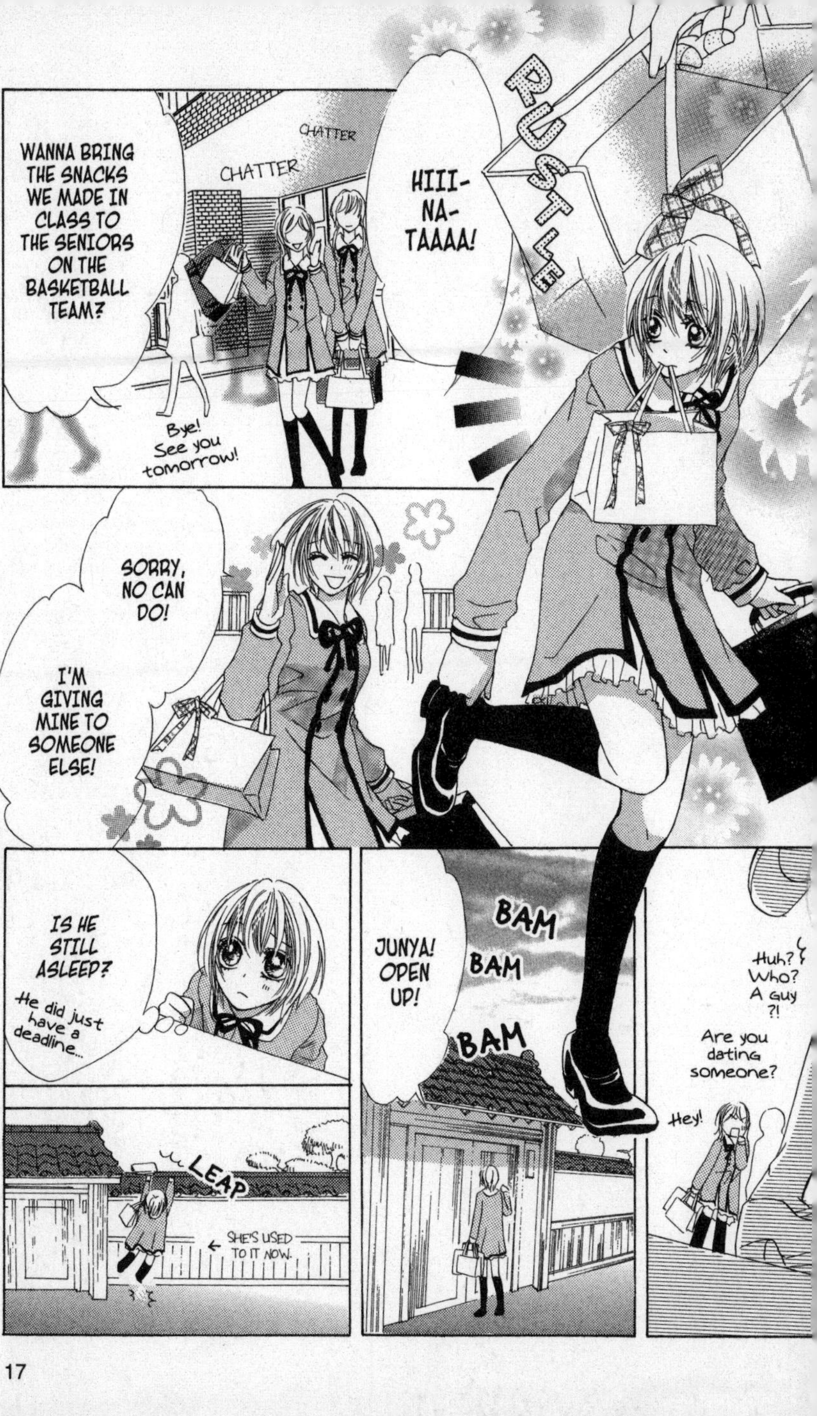
RUSTLE
HIII-NA-TAAAA!
WANNA BRING THE SNACKS WE MADE IN CLASS TO THE SENIORS ON THE BASKETBALL TEAM?
CHATTER
CHATTER
Bye! See you tomorrow!
SORRY, NO CAN DO!
I'M GIVING MINE TO SOMEONE ELSE!
Huh? Who? A guy?!
Are you dating someone?
Hey!
JUNYA! OPEN UP!
BAM
BAM
BAM
IS HE STILL ASLEEP?
He did just have a deadline...
LEAP
SHE'S USED TO IT NOW.

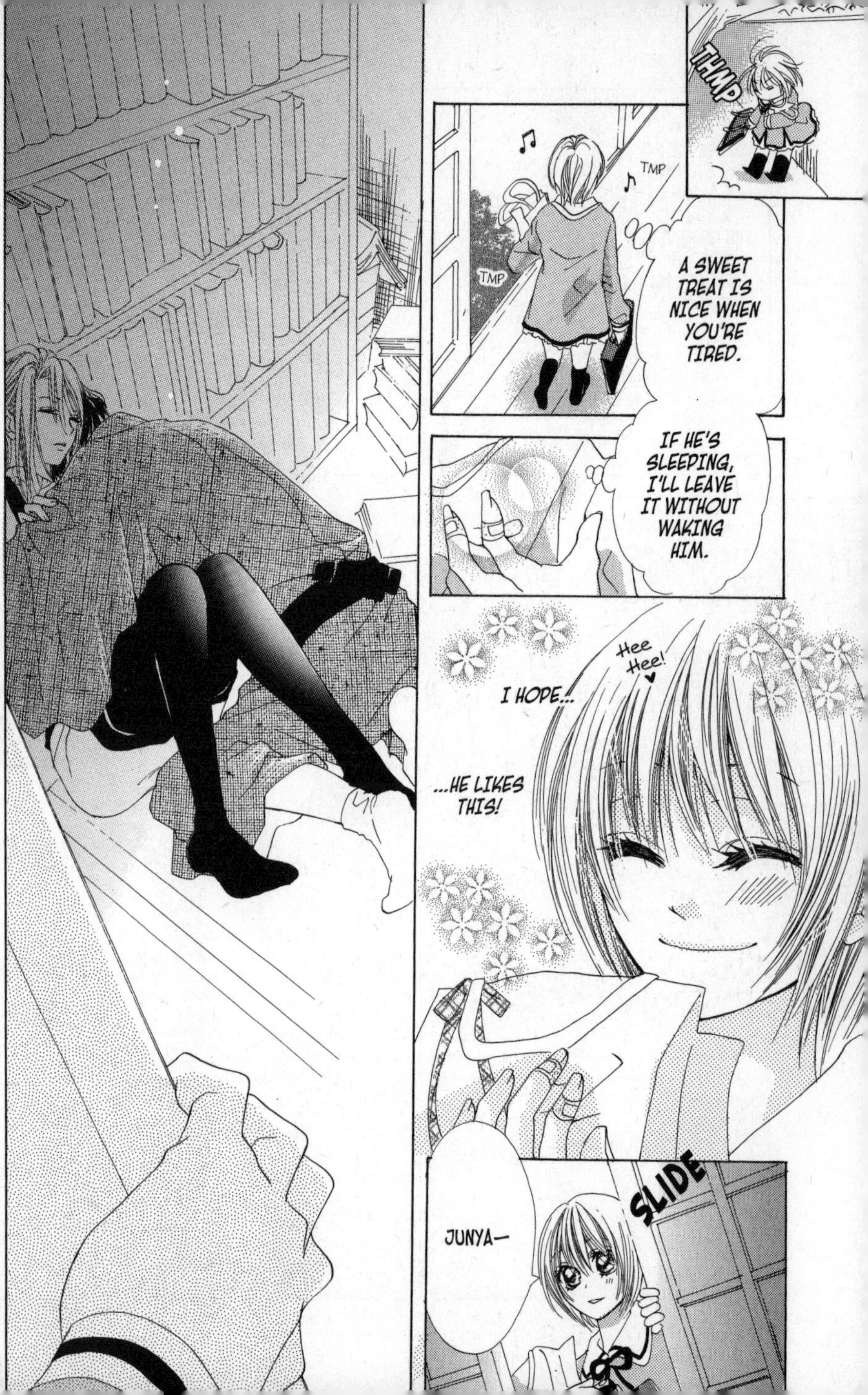
THMP
TMP
TMP
A SWEET TREAT IS NICE WHEN YOU'RE TIRED.
IF HE'S SLEEPING, I'LL LEAVE IT WITHOUT WAKING HIM.
Hee Hee!
I HOPE...
...HE LIKES THIS!
SLIDE
JUNYA—

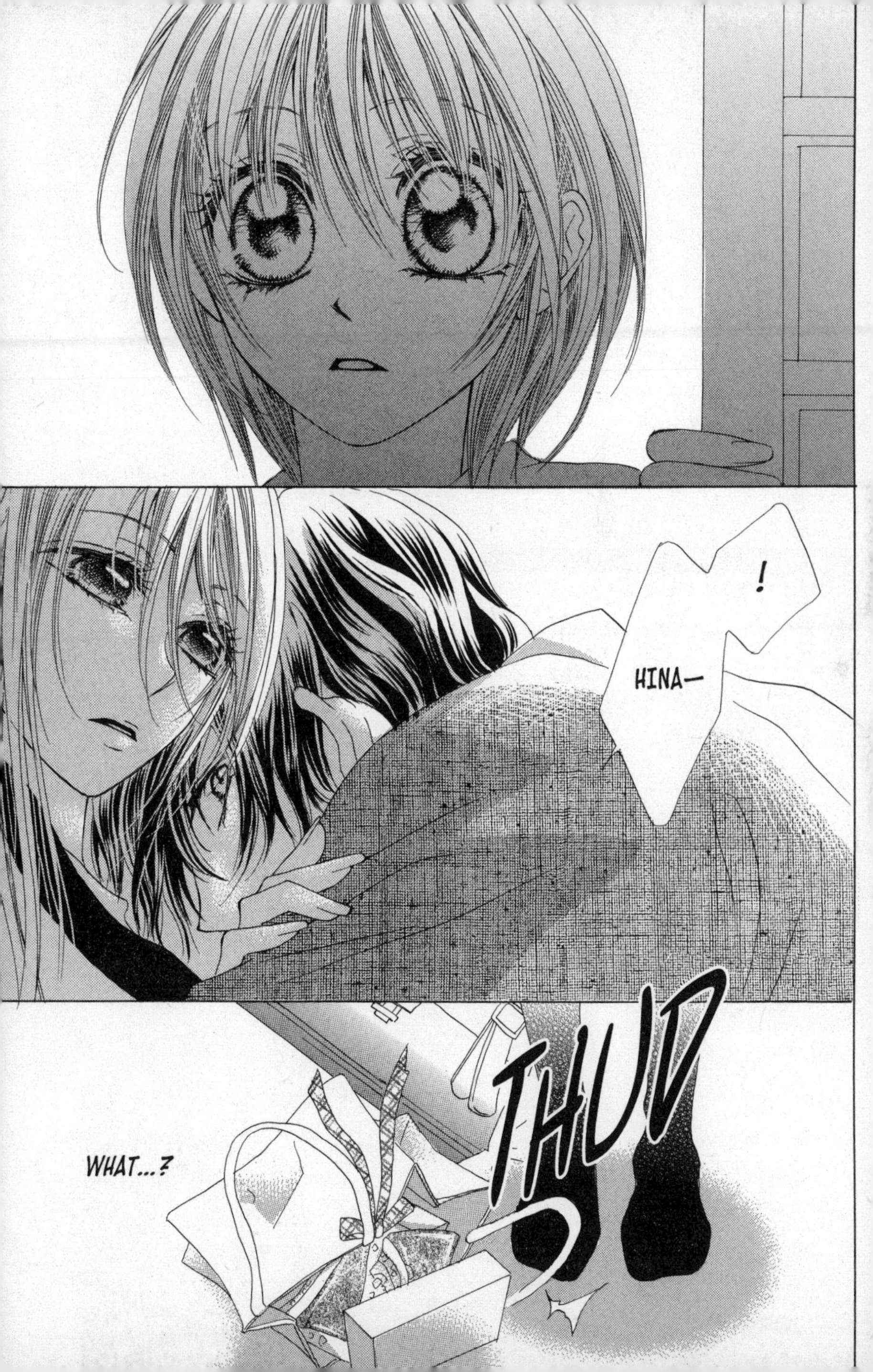

!
HINA—
THUD
WHAT...?

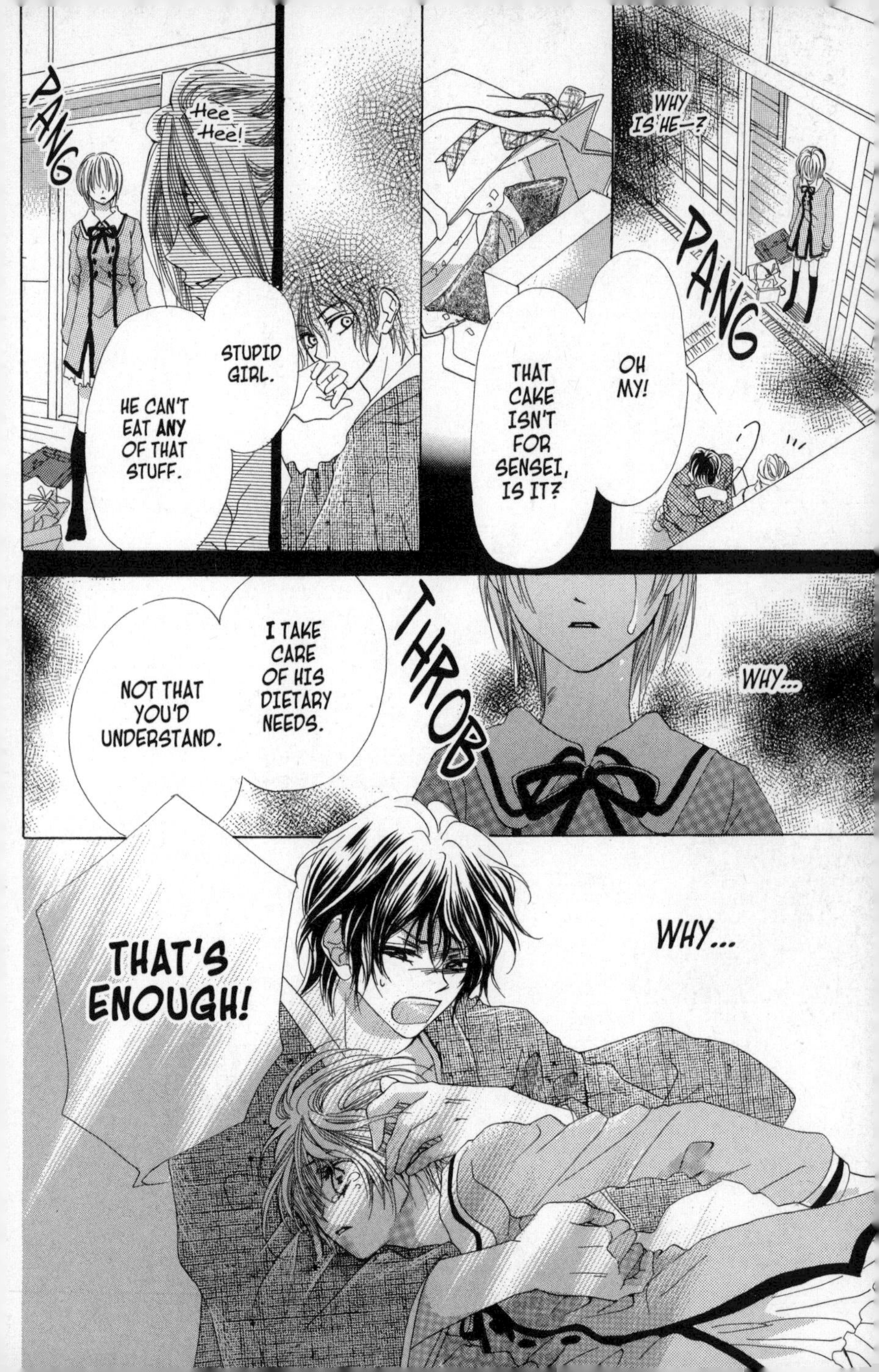
WHY IS HE—?
PANG
OH MY!
THAT CAKE ISN'T FOR SENSEI, IS IT?
Hee Hee!
PANG
STUPID GIRL.
HE CAN'T EAT ANY OF THAT STUFF.
WHY...
THROB
I TAKE CARE OF HIS DIETARY NEEDS.
NOT THAT YOU'D UNDERSTAND.
WHY...
THAT'S ENOUGH!

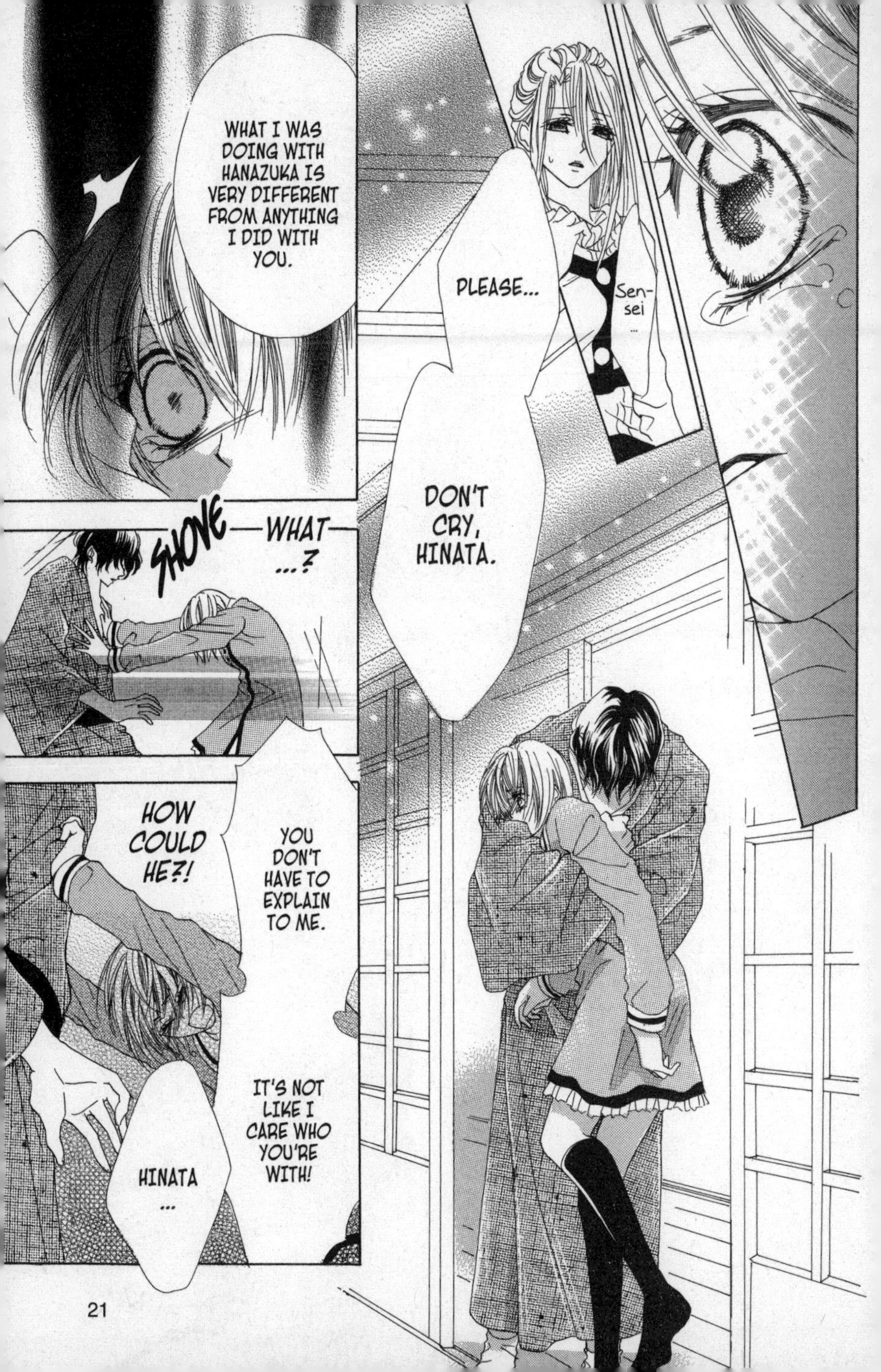
Sen-sei ...
PLEASE...
DON'T CRY, HINATA.
WHAT I WAS DOING WITH HANAZUKA IS VERY DIFFERENT FROM ANYTHING I DID WITH YOU.
SHOVE
—WHAT ...?
YOU DON'T HAVE TO EXPLAIN TO ME.
HOW COULD HE?!
IT'S NOT LIKE I CARE WHO YOU'RE WITH!
HINATA ...

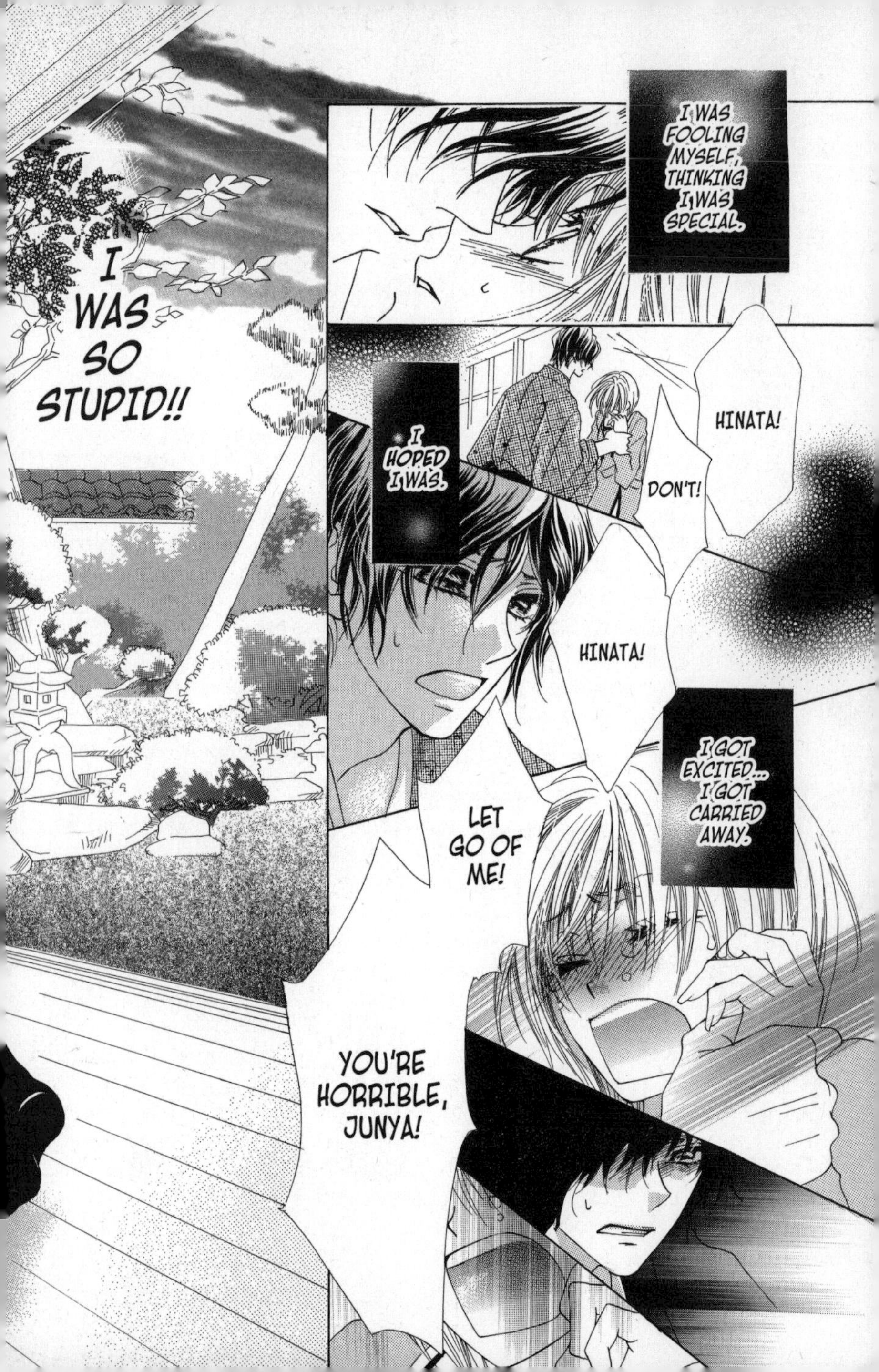
I WAS FOOLING MYSELF, THINKING I WAS SPECIAL.
HINATA!
DON'T!
I HOPED I WAS.
HINATA!
I GOT EXCITED... I GOT CARRIED AWAY.
LET GO OF ME!
YOU'RE HORRIBLE, JUNYA!
I WAS SO STUPID!!

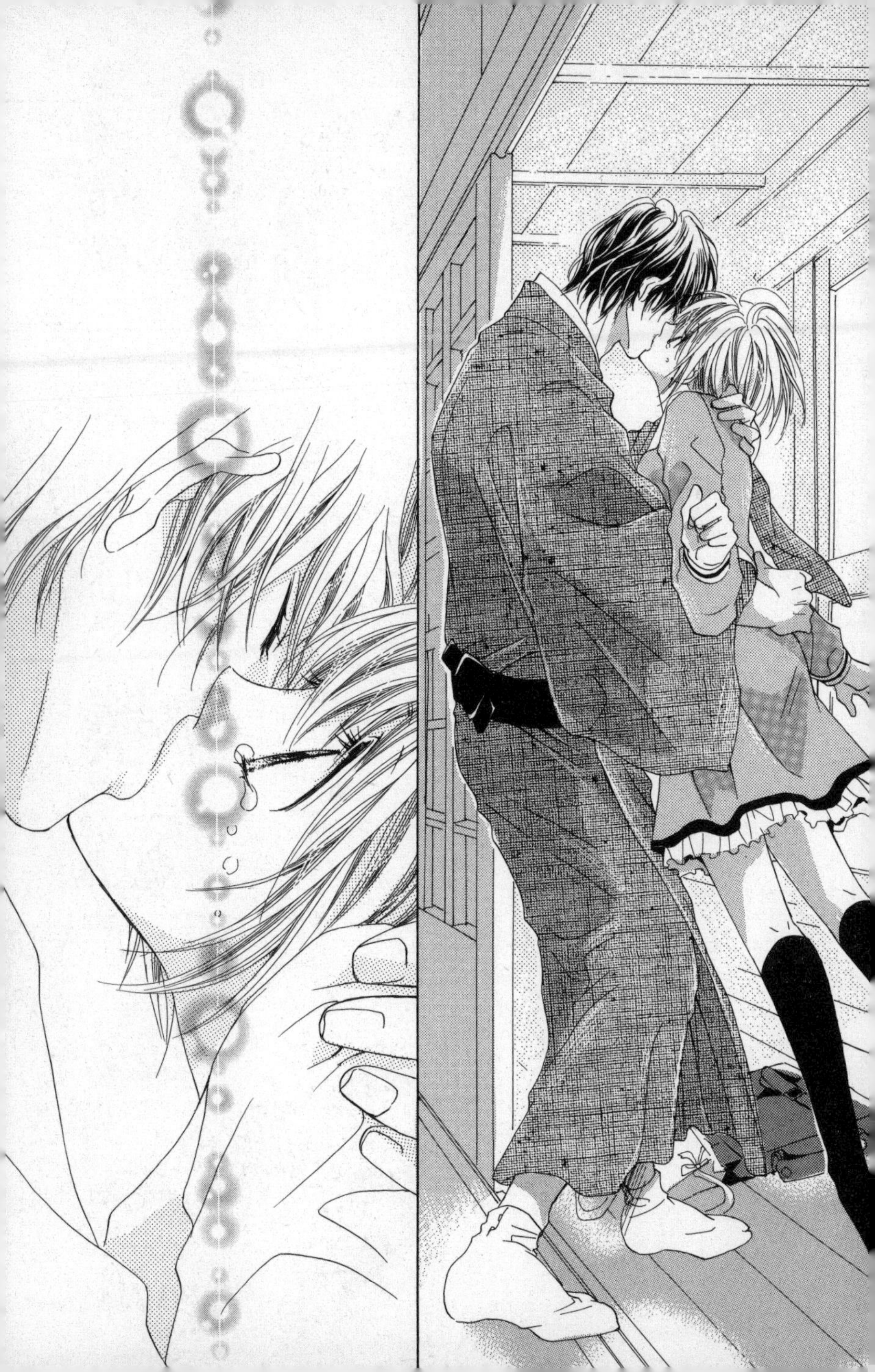

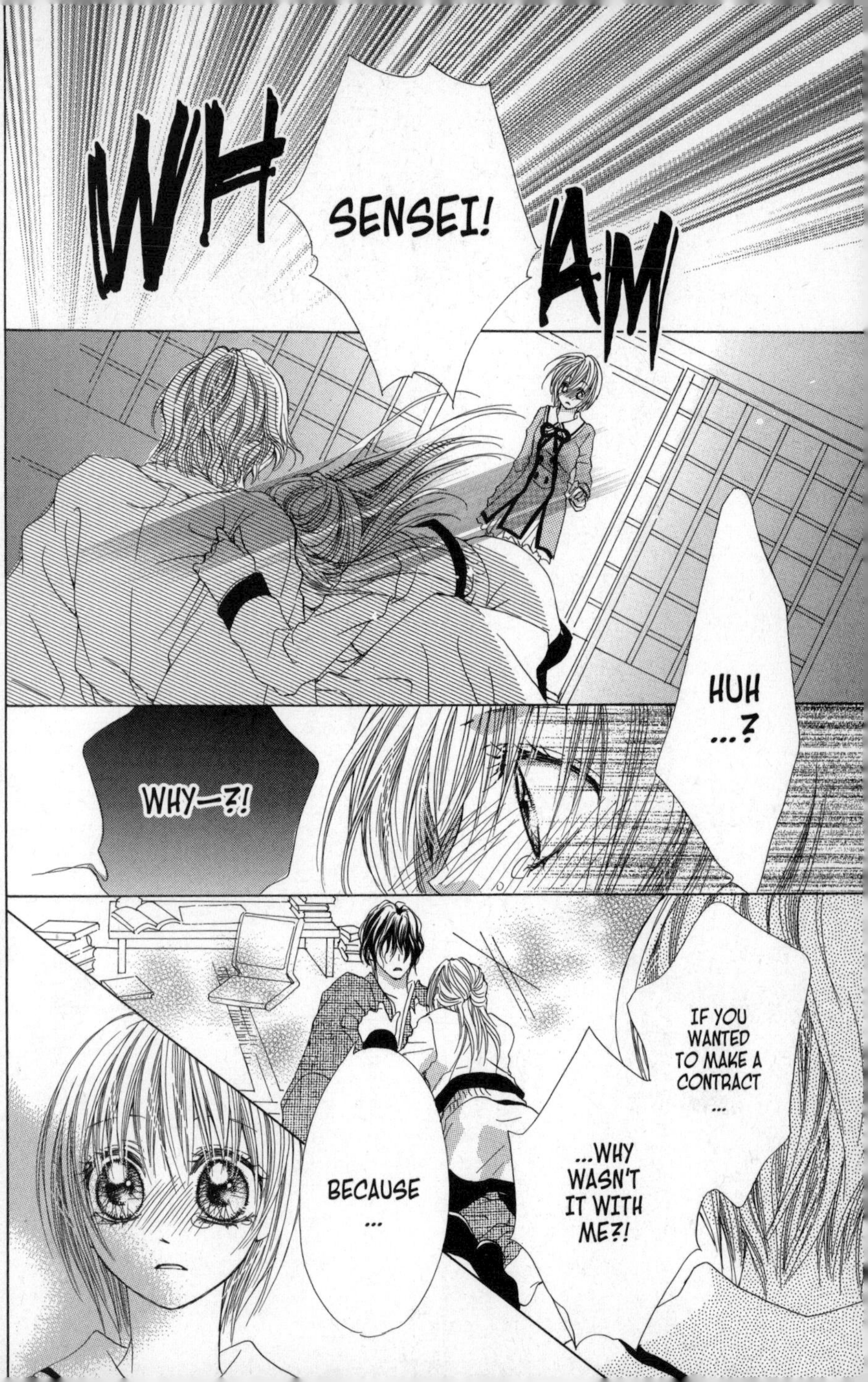
WH
AM
SENSEI!
HUH ...?
WHY—?!
IF YOU WANTED TO MAKE A CONTRACT ...
...WHY WASN'T IT WITH ME?!
BECAUSE ...

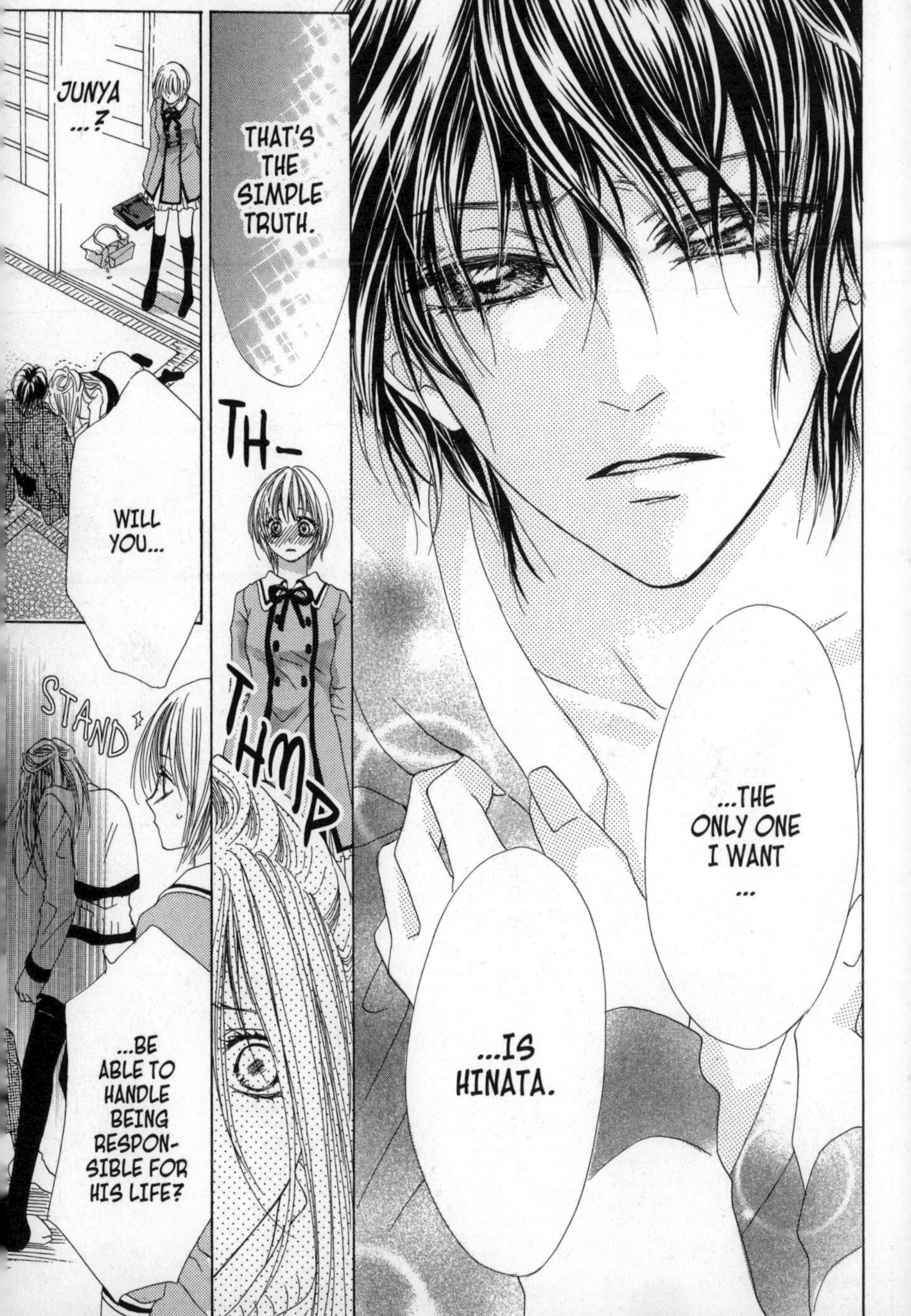
...THE ONLY ONE I WANT ...
...IS HINATA.
THAT'S THE SIMPLE TRUTH.
TH-
THMP
JUNYA ...?
WILL YOU...
STAND
...BE ABLE TO HANDLE BEING RESPONSIBLE FOR HIS LIFE?

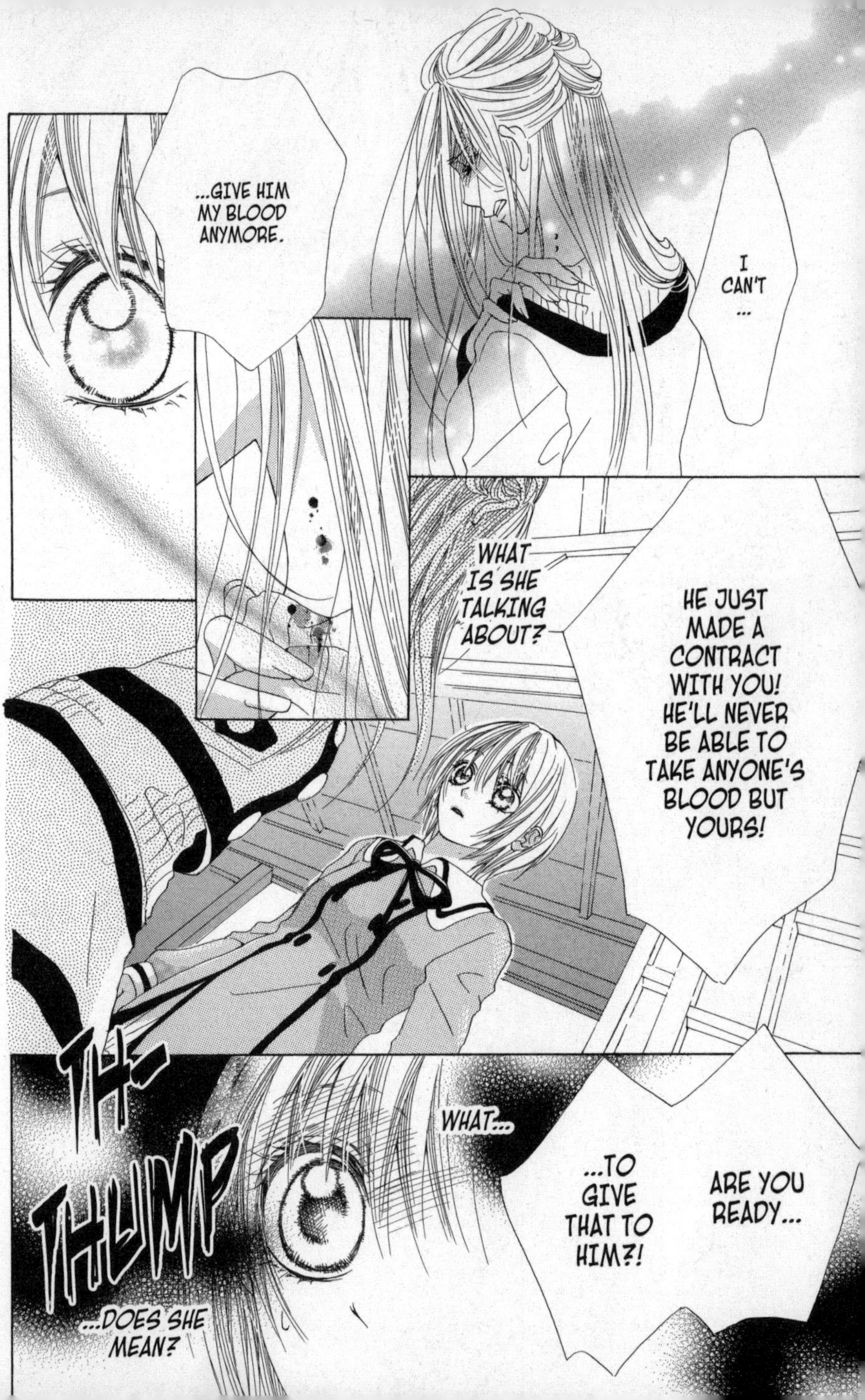
I CAN'T ...
...GIVE HIM MY BLOOD ANYMORE.
HE JUST MADE A CONTRACT WITH YOU! HE'LL NEVER BE ABLE TO TAKE ANYONE'S BLOOD BUT YOURS!
WHAT IS SHE TALKING ABOUT?
ARE YOU READY...
...TO GIVE THAT TO HIM?!
WHAT...
TH-THUMP
...DOES SHE MEAN?

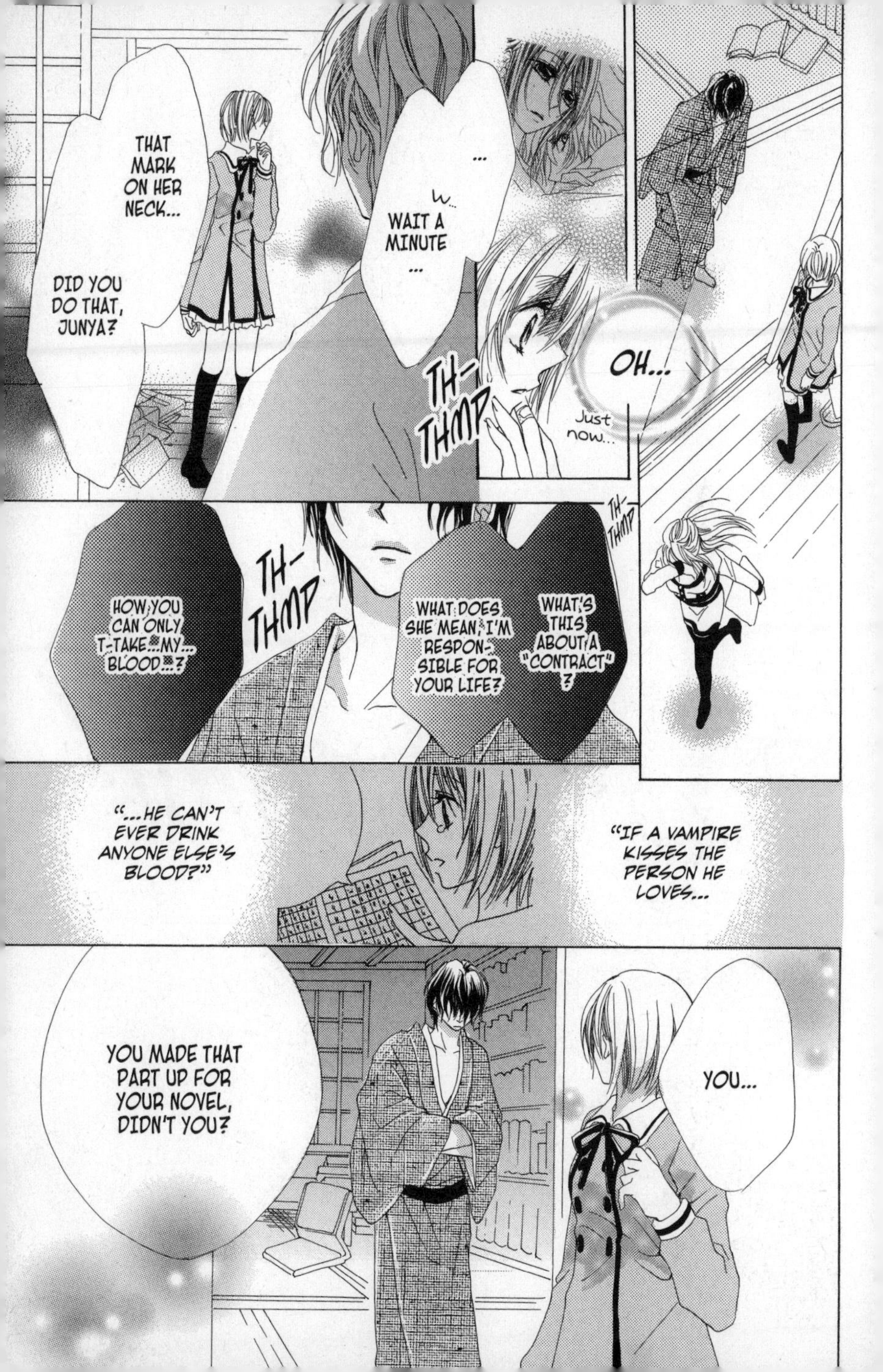
TH-THMP
OH...
Just now...
TH-THMP
... W... WAIT A MINUTE ...
THAT MARK ON HER NECK...
DID YOU DO THAT, JUNYA?
WHAT'S THIS ABOUT A "CONTRACT"?
WHAT DOES SHE MEAN, I'M RESPONSIBLE FOR YOUR LIFE?
TH-THMP
HOW YOU CAN ONLY T-TAKE... MY... BLOOD...?
"IF A VAMPIRE KISSES THE PERSON HE LOVES...
"...HE CAN'T EVER DRINK ANYONE ELSE'S BLOOD?"
YOU...
YOU MADE THAT PART UP FOR YOUR NOVEL, DIDN'T YOU?

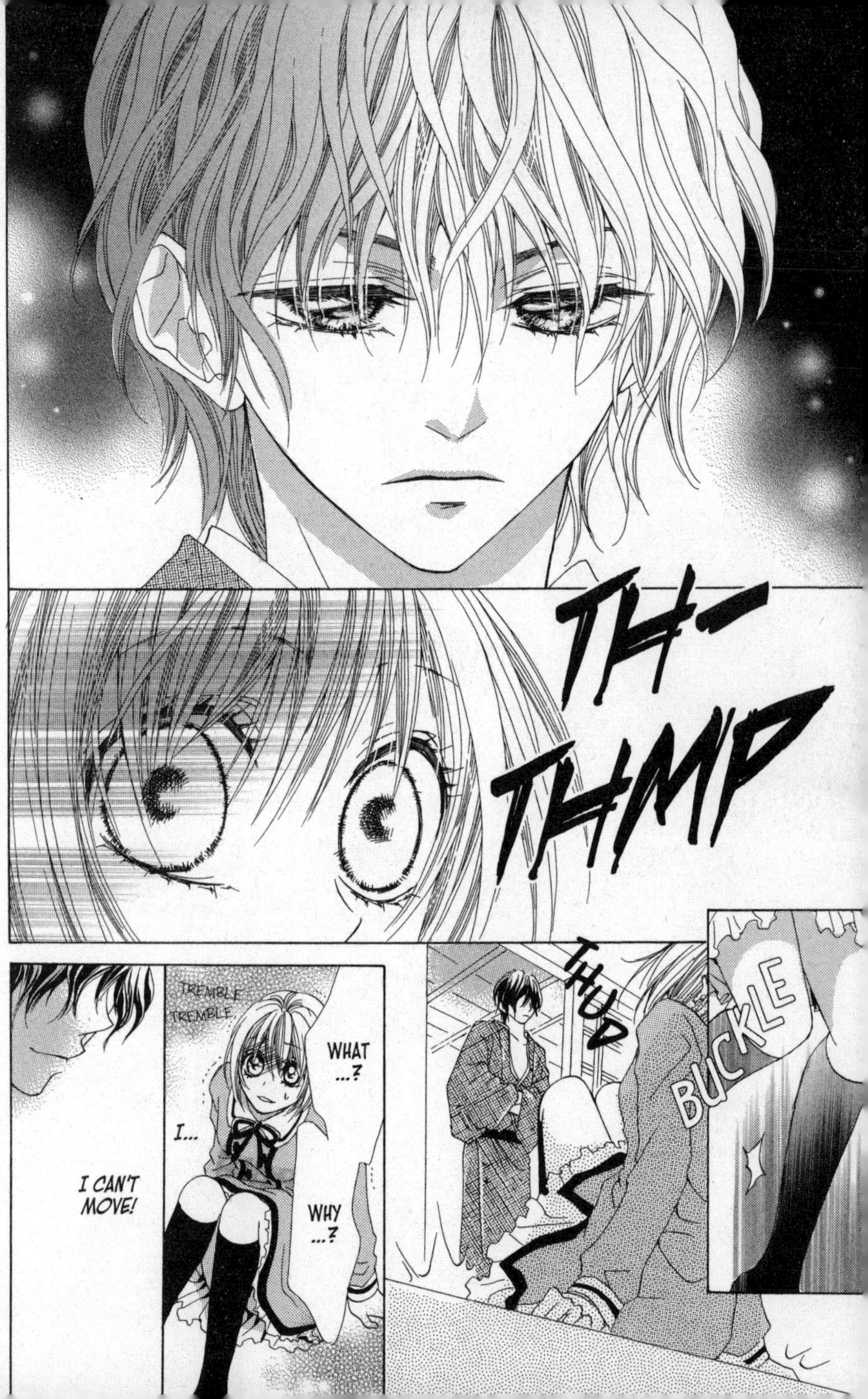
TH-THMP
BUCKLE
THUD
TREMBLE TREMBLE
WHAT ...?
I...
WHY ...?
I CAN'T MOVE!

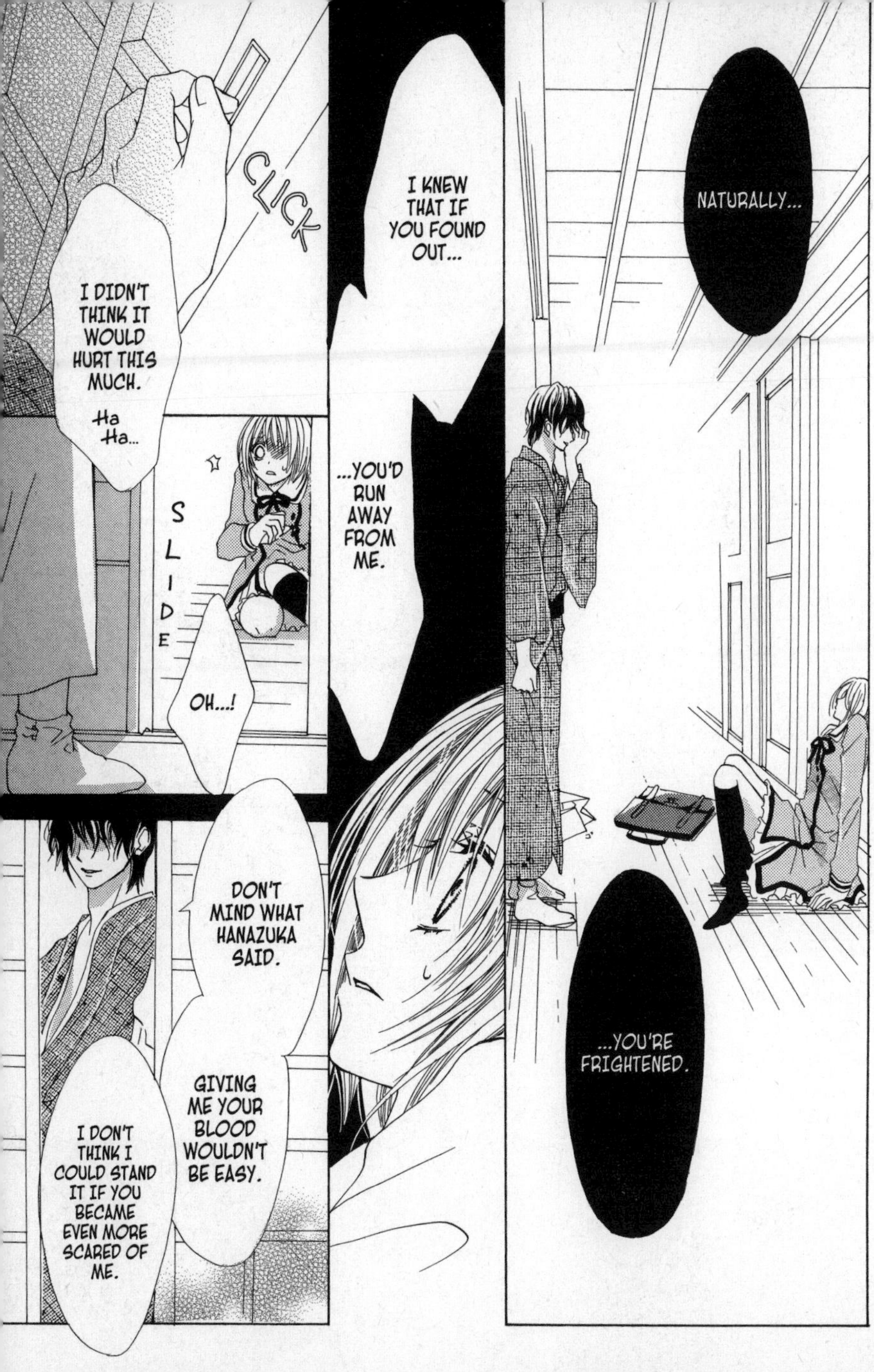
NATURALLY...
...YOU'RE FRIGHTENED.
I KNEW THAT IF YOU FOUND OUT...
...YOU'D RUN AWAY FROM ME.
CLICK
I DIDN'T THINK IT WOULD HURT THIS MUCH.
Ha Ha...
SLIDE
OH...!
DON'T MIND WHAT HANAZUKA SAID.
GIVING ME YOUR BLOOD WOULDN'T BE EASY.
I DON'T THINK I COULD STAND IT IF YOU BECAME EVEN MORE SCARED OF ME.

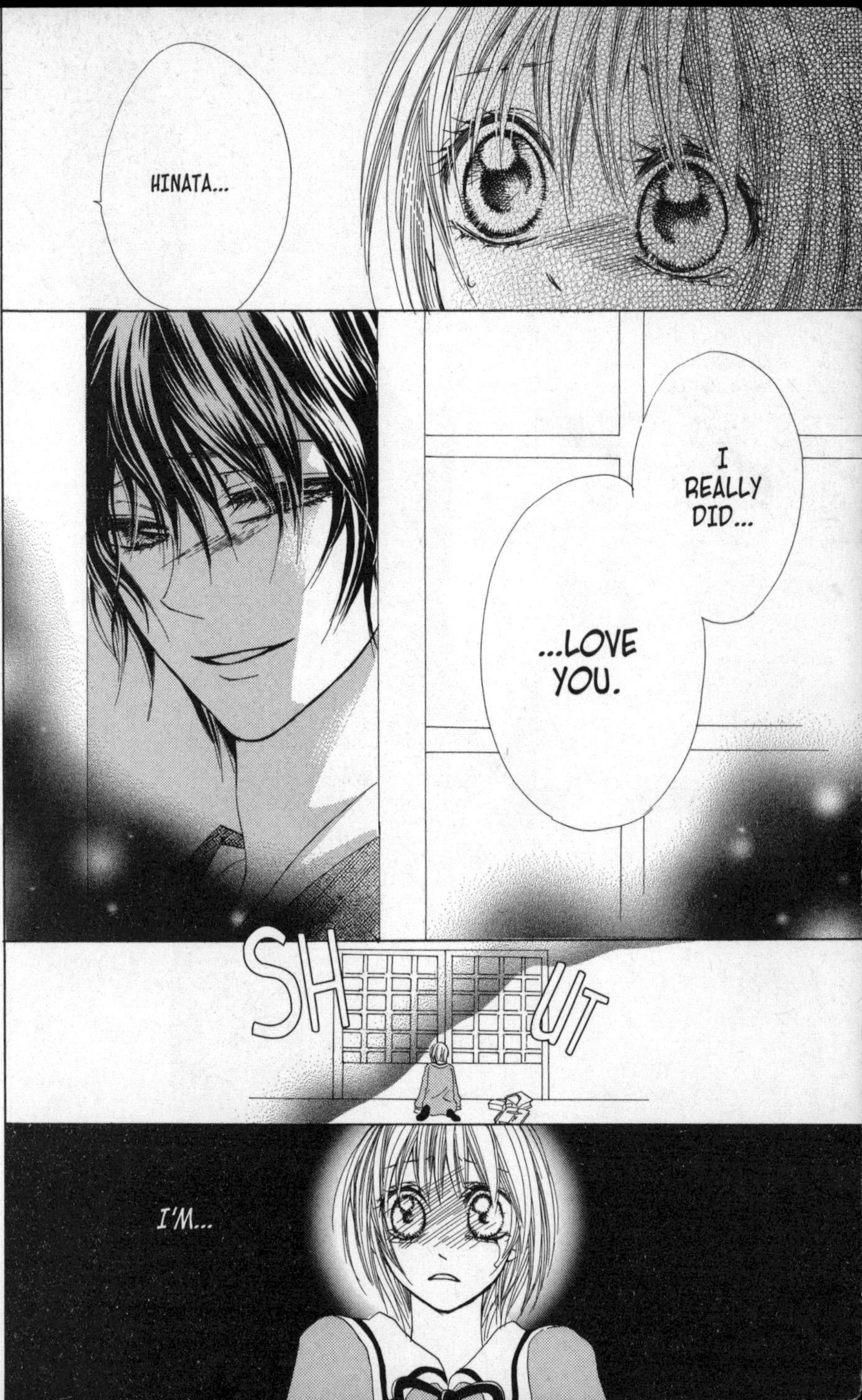
HINATA...
I REALLY DID...
...LOVE YOU.
SHUT
I'M...

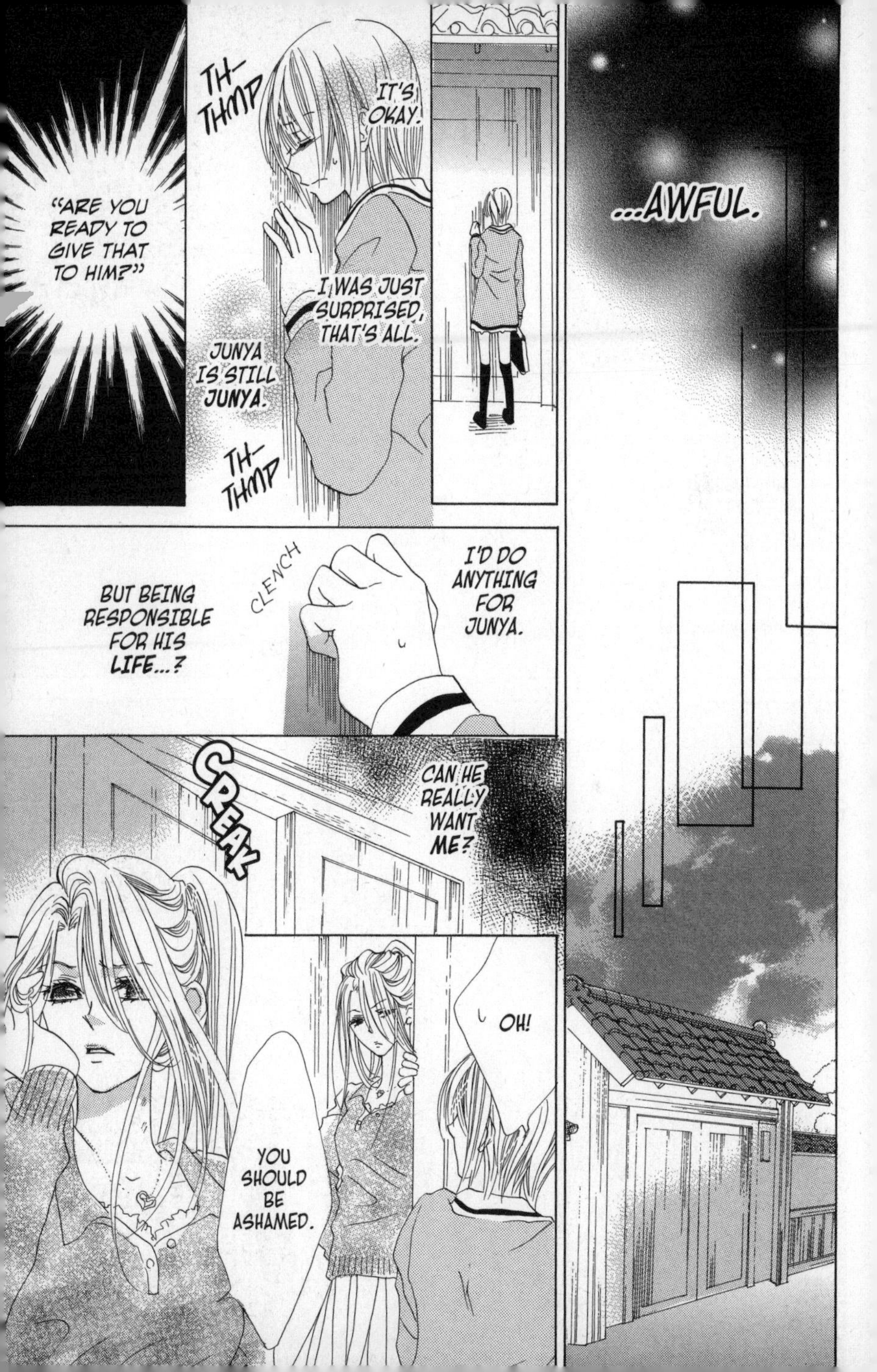

...AWFUL.
IT'S OKAY.
TH-THMP
I WAS JUST SURPRISED, THAT'S ALL.
JUNYA IS STILL JUNYA.
TH-THMP
"ARE YOU READY TO GIVE THAT TO HIM?"
I'D DO ANYTHING FOR JUNYA.
CLENCH
BUT BEING RESPONSIBLE FOR HIS LIFE...?
CAN HE REALLY WANT ME?
CREAK
OH!
YOU SHOULD BE ASHAMED.

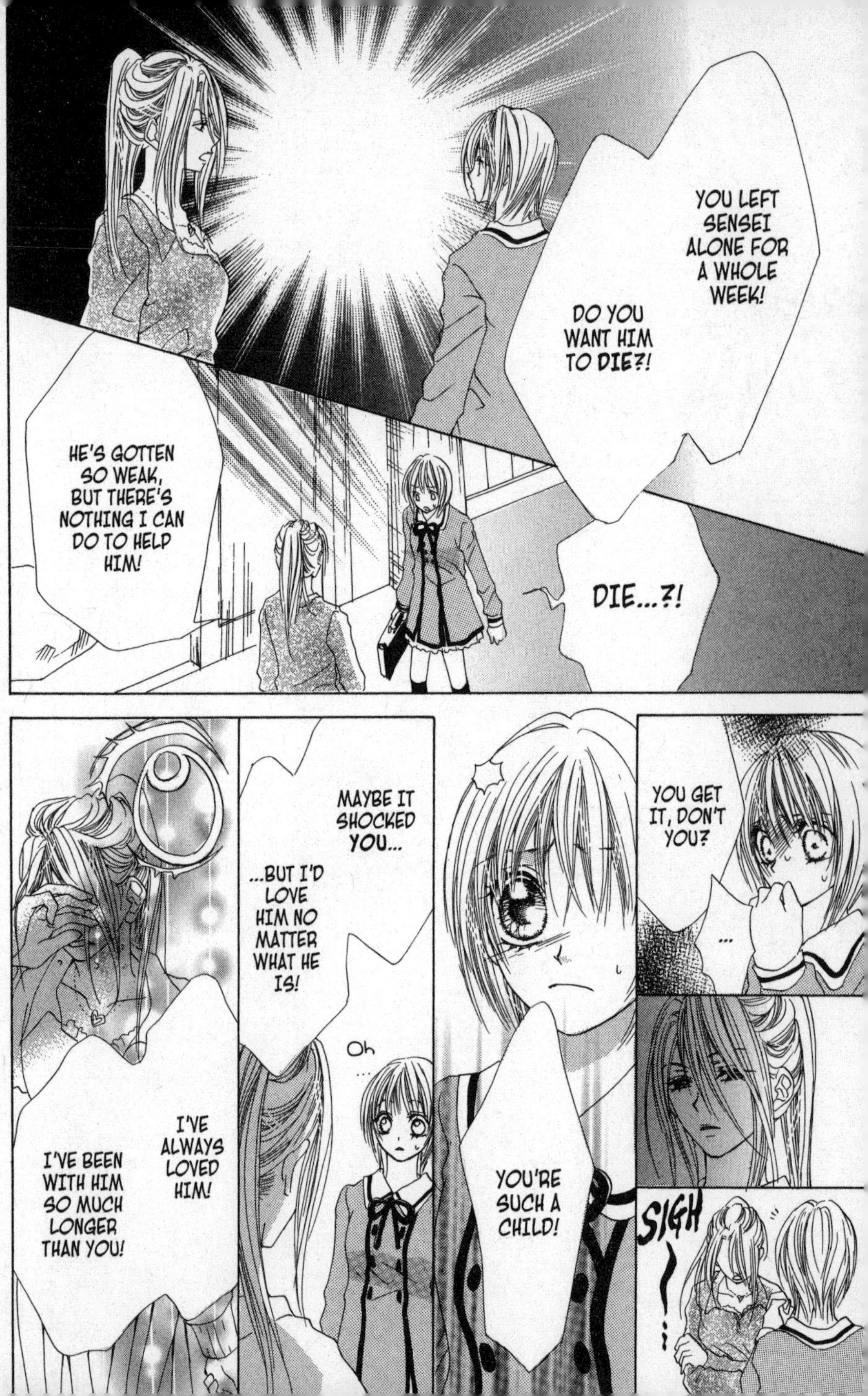
YOU LEFT SENSEI ALONE FOR A WHOLE WEEK!
DO YOU WANT HIM TO DIE?!
DIE...?!
HE'S GOTTEN SO WEAK, BUT THERE'S NOTHING I CAN DO TO HELP HIM!
YOU GET IT, DON'T YOU?
...
SIGH
YOU'RE SUCH A CHILD!
MAYBE IT SHOCKED YOU...
...BUT I'D LOVE HIM NO MATTER WHAT HE IS!
Oh...
I'VE ALWAYS LOVED HIM!
I'VE BEEN WITH HIM SO MUCH LONGER THAN YOU!

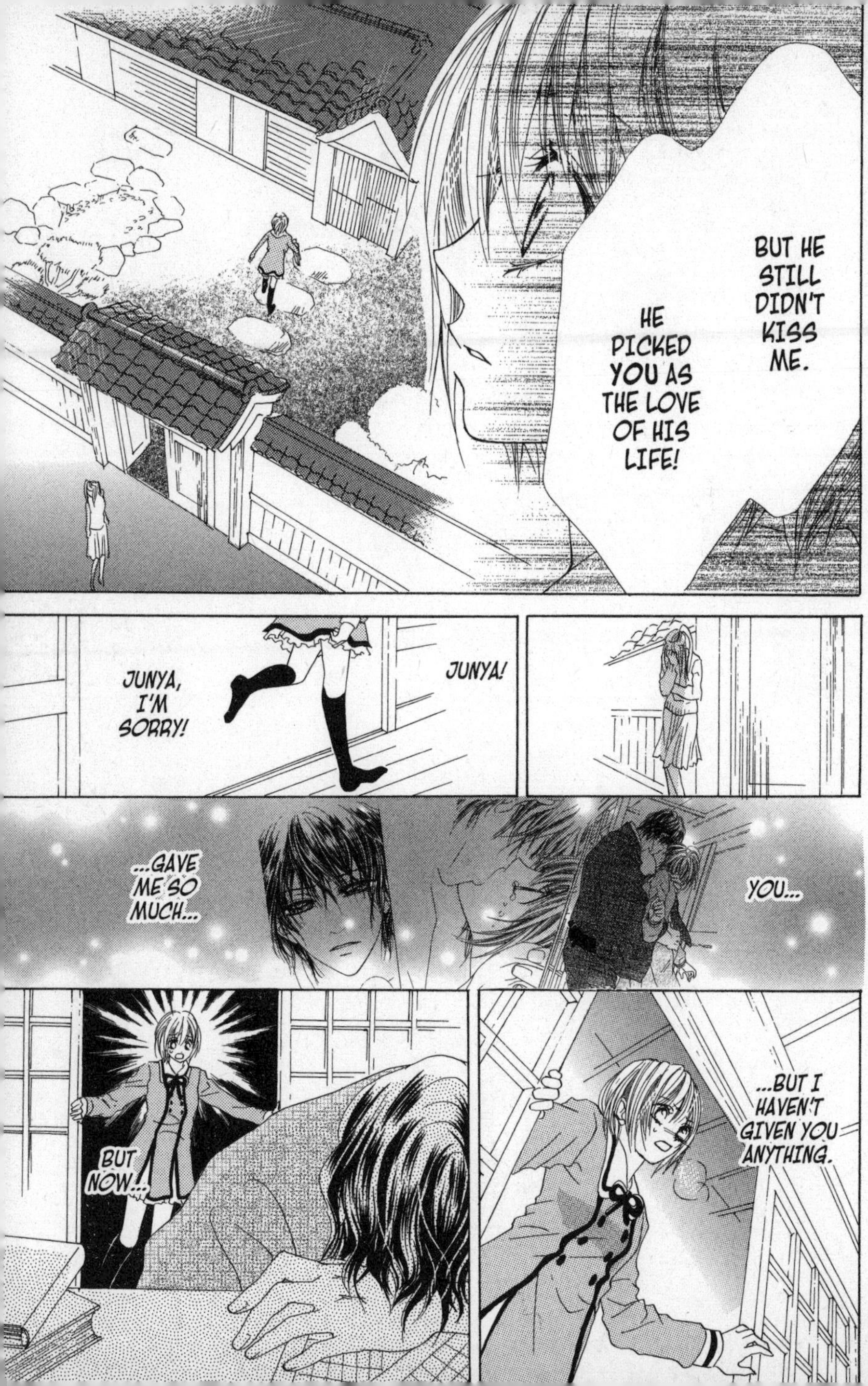
BUT HE STILL DIDN'T KISS ME.
HE PICKED YOU AS THE LOVE OF HIS LIFE!
JUNYA!
JUNYA, I'M SORRY!
YOU...
...GAVE ME SO MUCH...
...BUT I HAVEN'T GIVEN YOU ANYTHING.
BUT NOW...

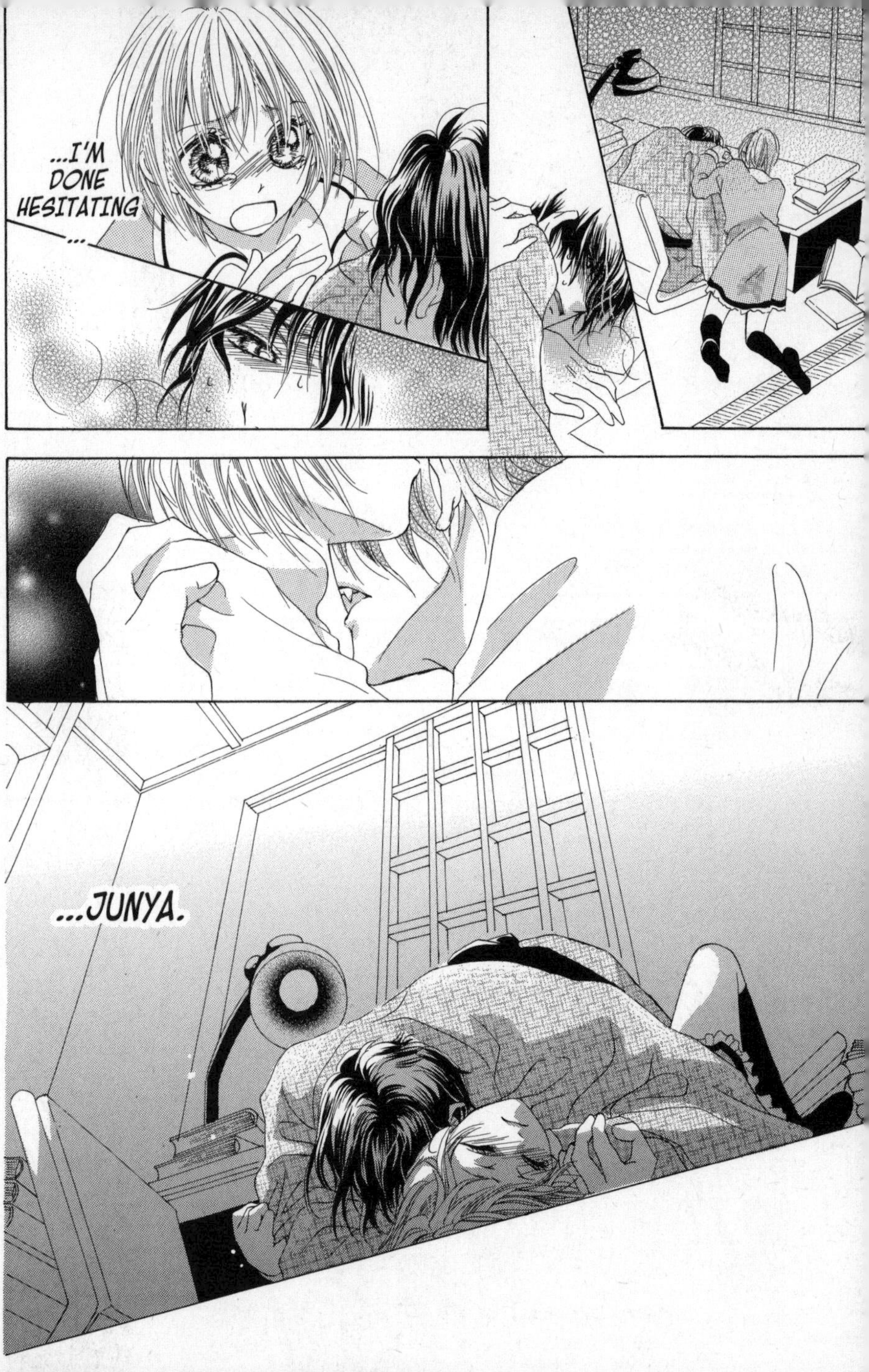
...I'M DONE HESITATING ...
...JUNYA.

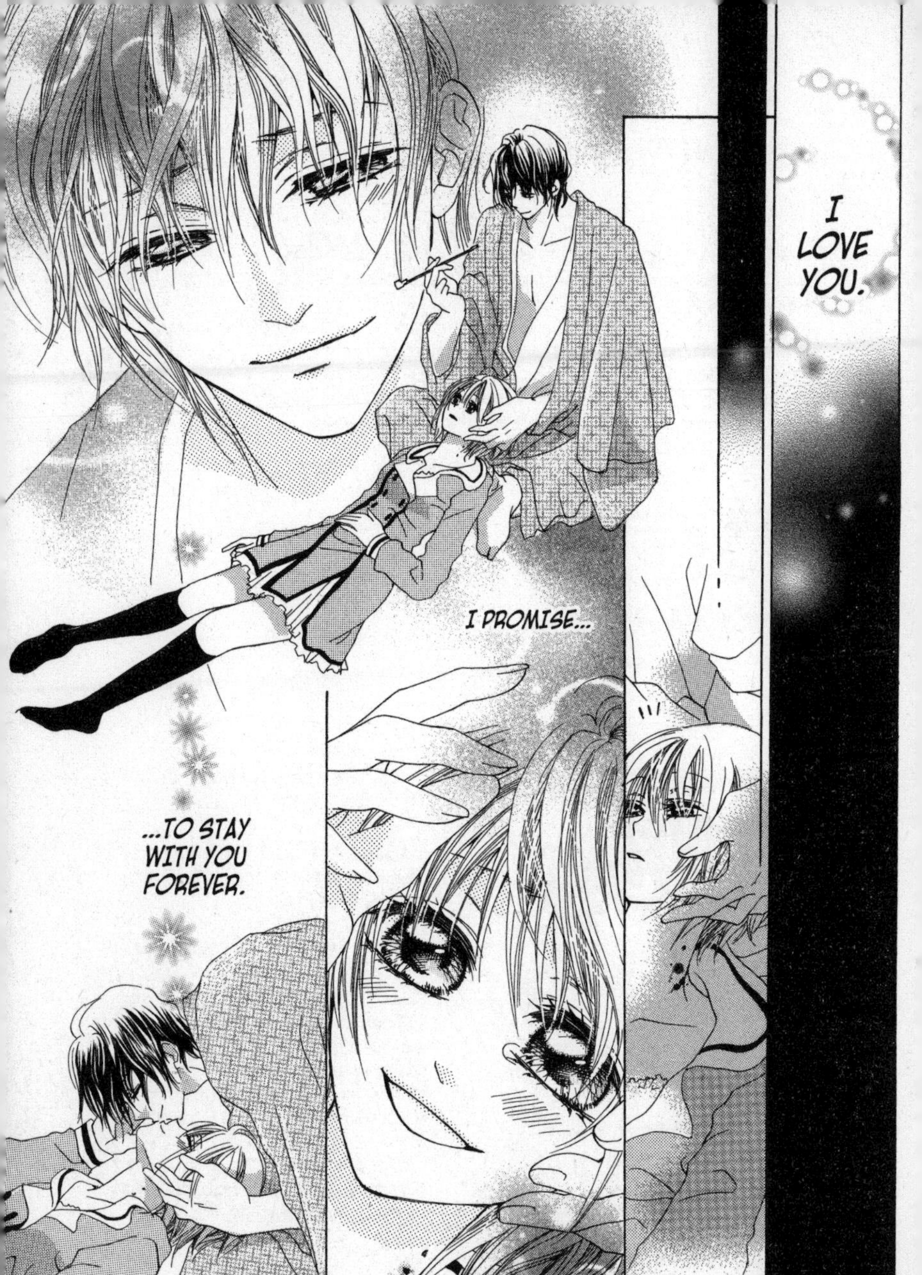
I LOVE YOU.
I PROMISE...
...TO STAY WITH YOU FOREVER.

Honey Blood: My Boyfriend is a...?! * The End *

Published in *Sho-Comi* Extra Edition Magazine (February 14, 2008)

✿ Greetings! ✿

I'm Miko Mitsuki, and the book you're holding is the original version of the *Honey Blood* series. Thank you for checking it out!

This collection of short stories includes three *Honey Blood* one-shots as well as two other standalone stories. Including my old and new work in one book is a bit embarrassing, but I hope you'll enjoy reading it anyway!

✿ "My Boyfriend ✿
is a...?!"

I guess I should celebrate (?) the very first incarnation of this series.

Wow, the art is really old...

I'd wanted to write a vampire story since long before I made my debut as a manga artist, so this was really in the works for a long time.

I loved writing it, and I'm so grateful to the editor who helped me develop it!

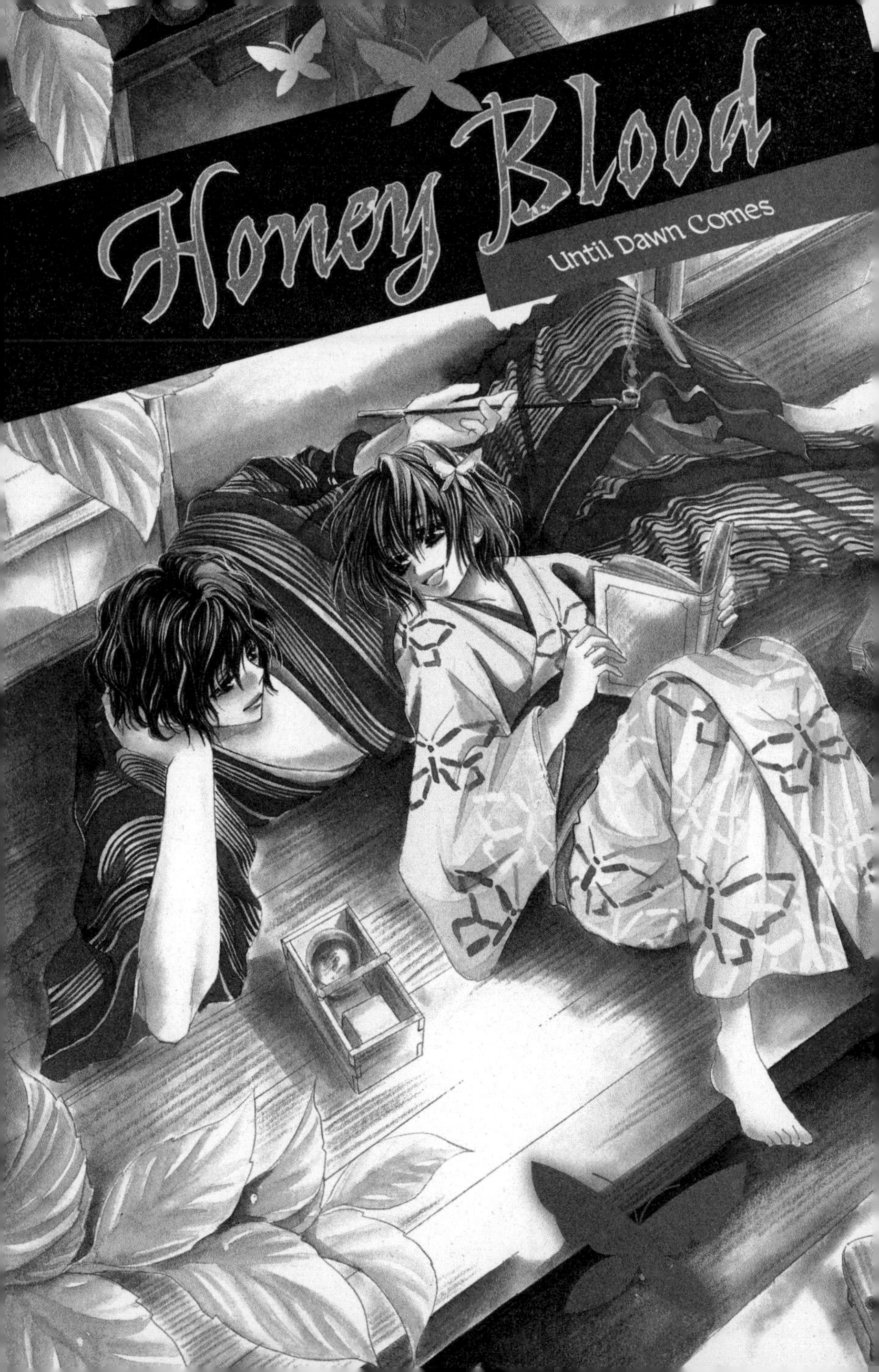
Honey Blood
Until Dawn Comes

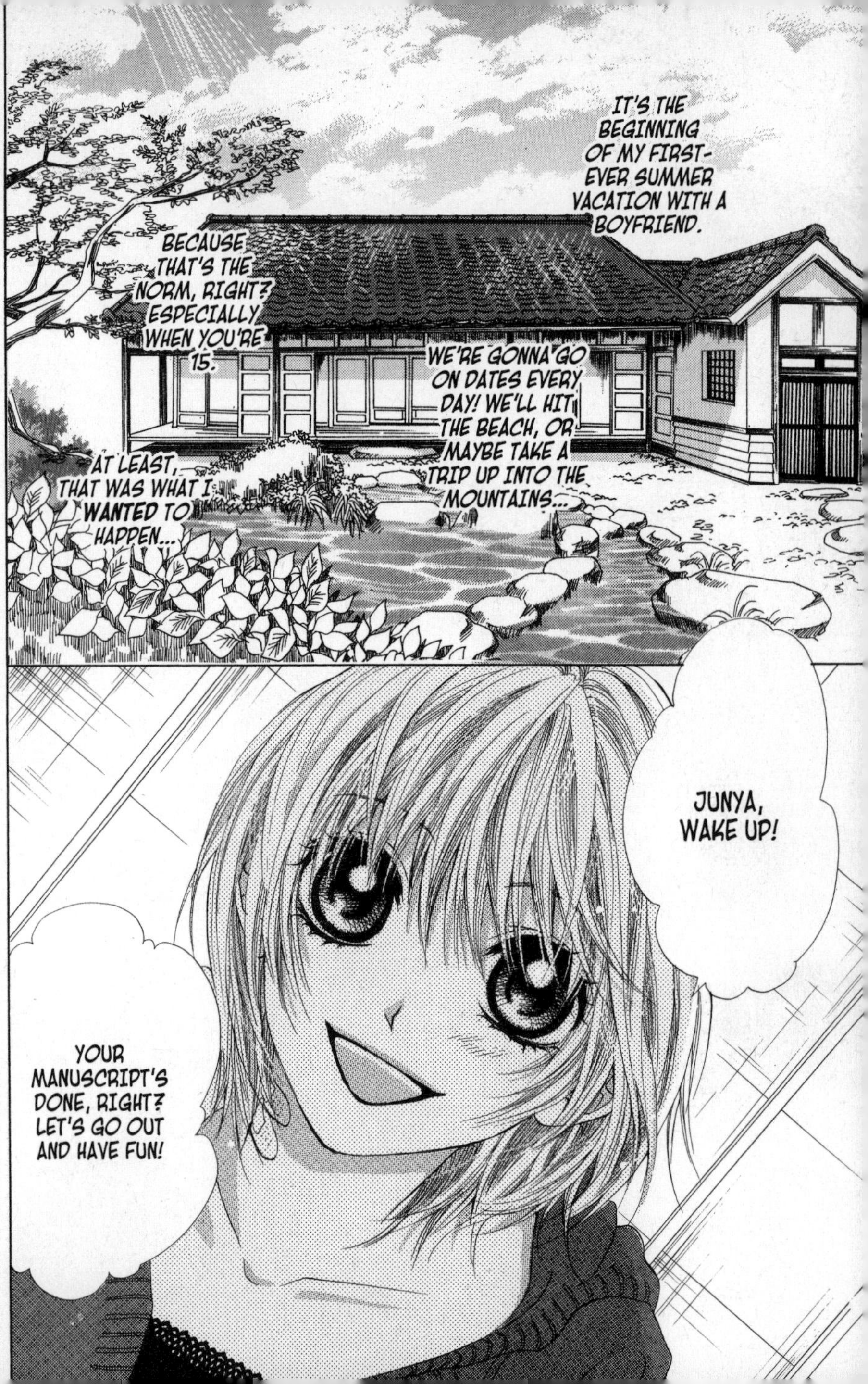
IT'S THE BEGINNING OF MY FIRST-EVER SUMMER VACATION WITH A BOYFRIEND.
BECAUSE THAT'S THE NORM, RIGHT? ESPECIALLY WHEN YOU'RE 15.
WE'RE GONNA GO ON DATES EVERY DAY! WE'LL HIT THE BEACH, OR MAYBE TAKE A TRIP UP INTO THE MOUNTAINS...
AT LEAST, THAT WAS WHAT I **WANTED** TO HAPPEN...
JUNYA, WAKE UP!
YOUR MANUSCRIPT'S DONE, RIGHT? LET'S GO OUT AND HAVE FUN!

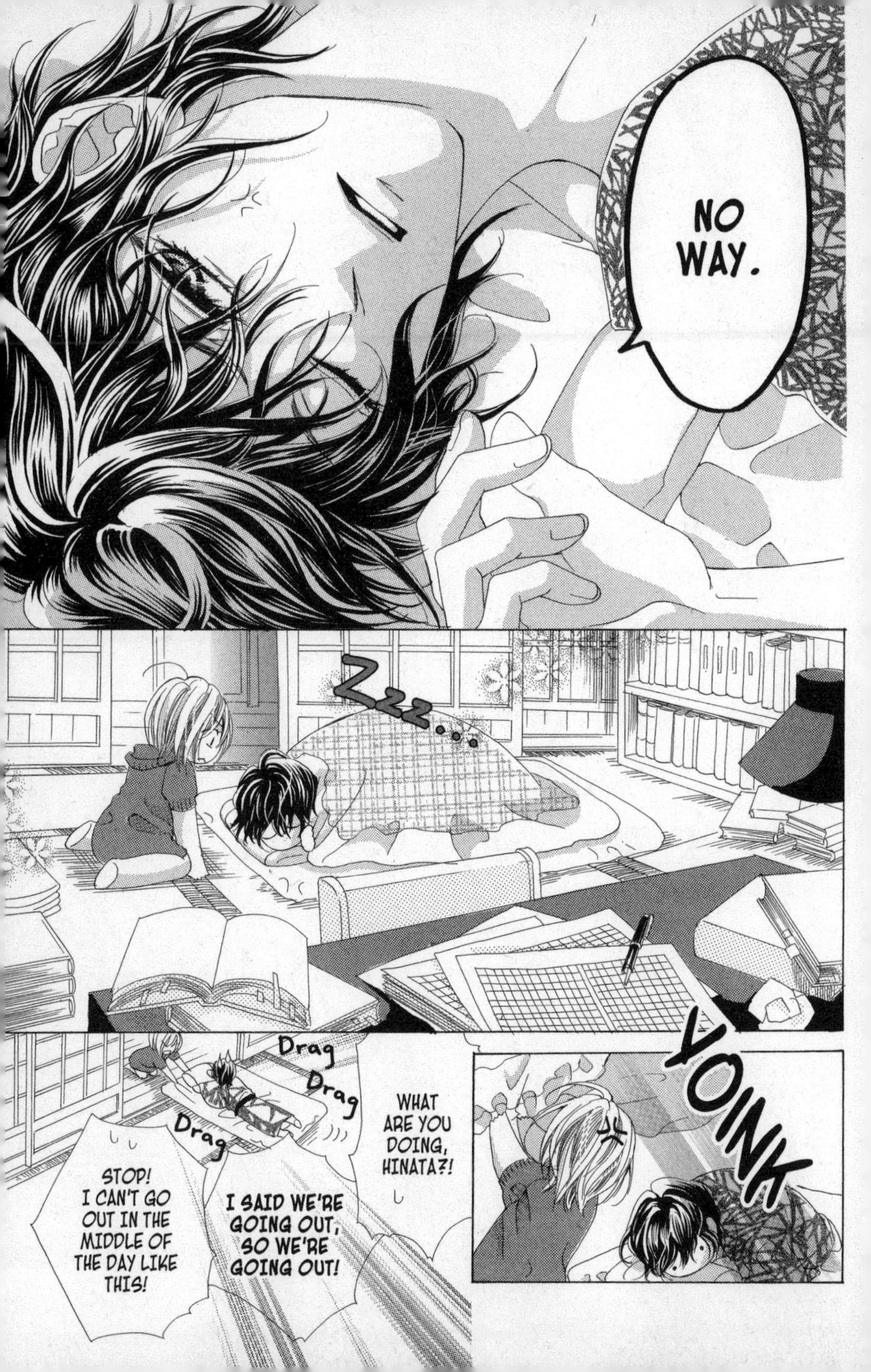
NO WAY.
Zzz...
YOINK
WHAT ARE YOU DOING, HINATA?!
Drag Drag Drag
I SAID WE'RE GOING OUT, SO WE'RE GOING OUT!
STOP! I CAN'T GO OUT IN THE MIDDLE OF THE DAY LIKE THIS!

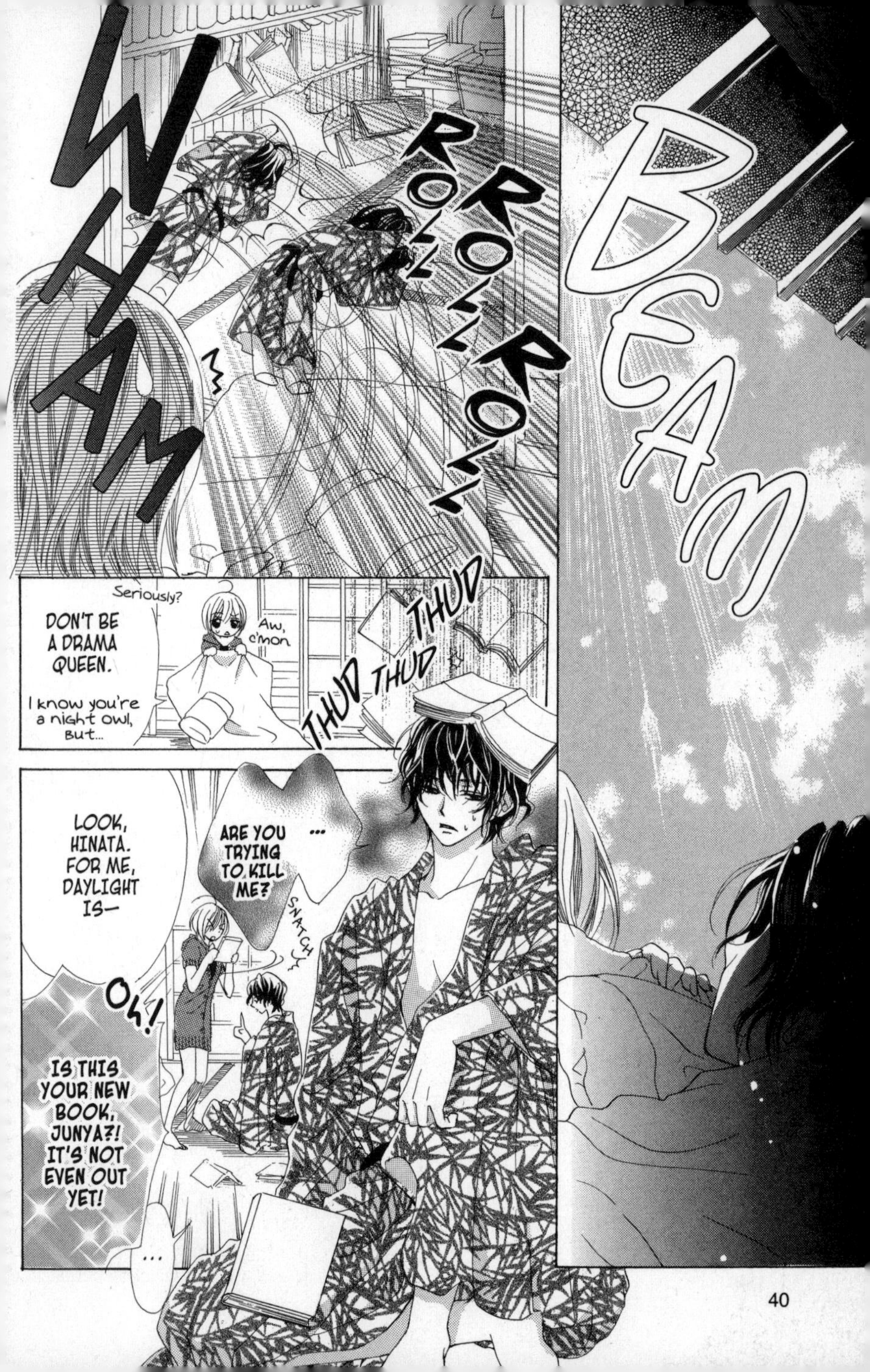
BEAM
ROLL ROLL
WHAM
THUD THUD THUD
Aw, c'mon.
Seriously?
DON'T BE A DRAMA QUEEN.
I know you're a night owl, but...
ARE YOU TRYING TO KILL ME?
...
LOOK, HINATA. FOR ME, DAYLIGHT IS—
SNATCH
Oh!
IS THIS YOUR NEW BOOK, JUNYA?! IT'S NOT EVEN OUT YET!
...

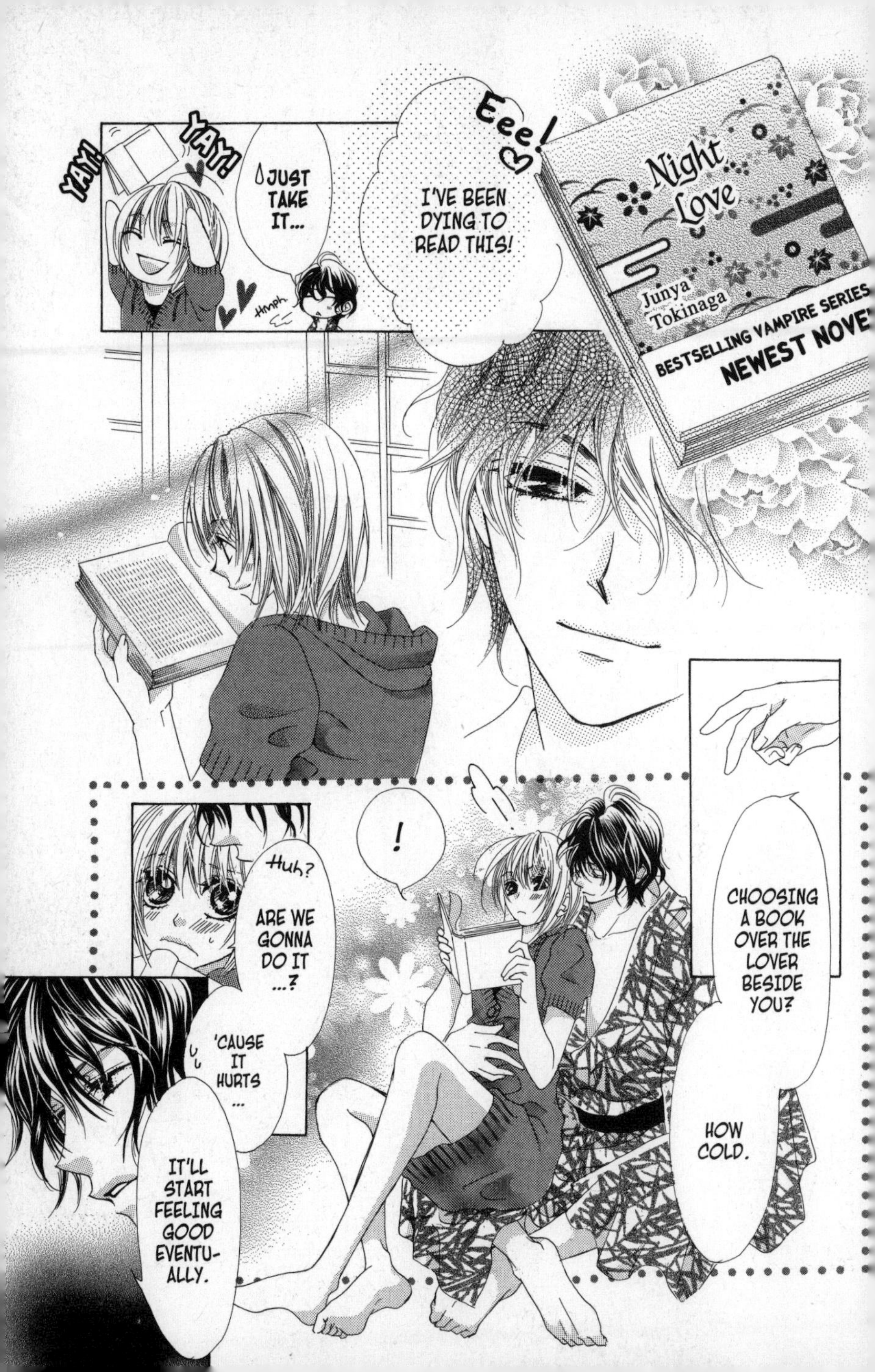
Eee!
I'VE BEEN DYING TO READ THIS!
Night Love
Junya Tokinaga
BESTSELLING VAMPIRE SERIES
NEWEST NOVE
YAY! YAY!
JUST TAKE IT...
Hmph.
CHOOSING A BOOK OVER THE LOVER BESIDE YOU?
HOW COLD.
!
Huh?
ARE WE GONNA DO IT ...?
'CAUSE IT HURTS ...
IT'LL START FEELING GOOD EVENTU-ALLY.

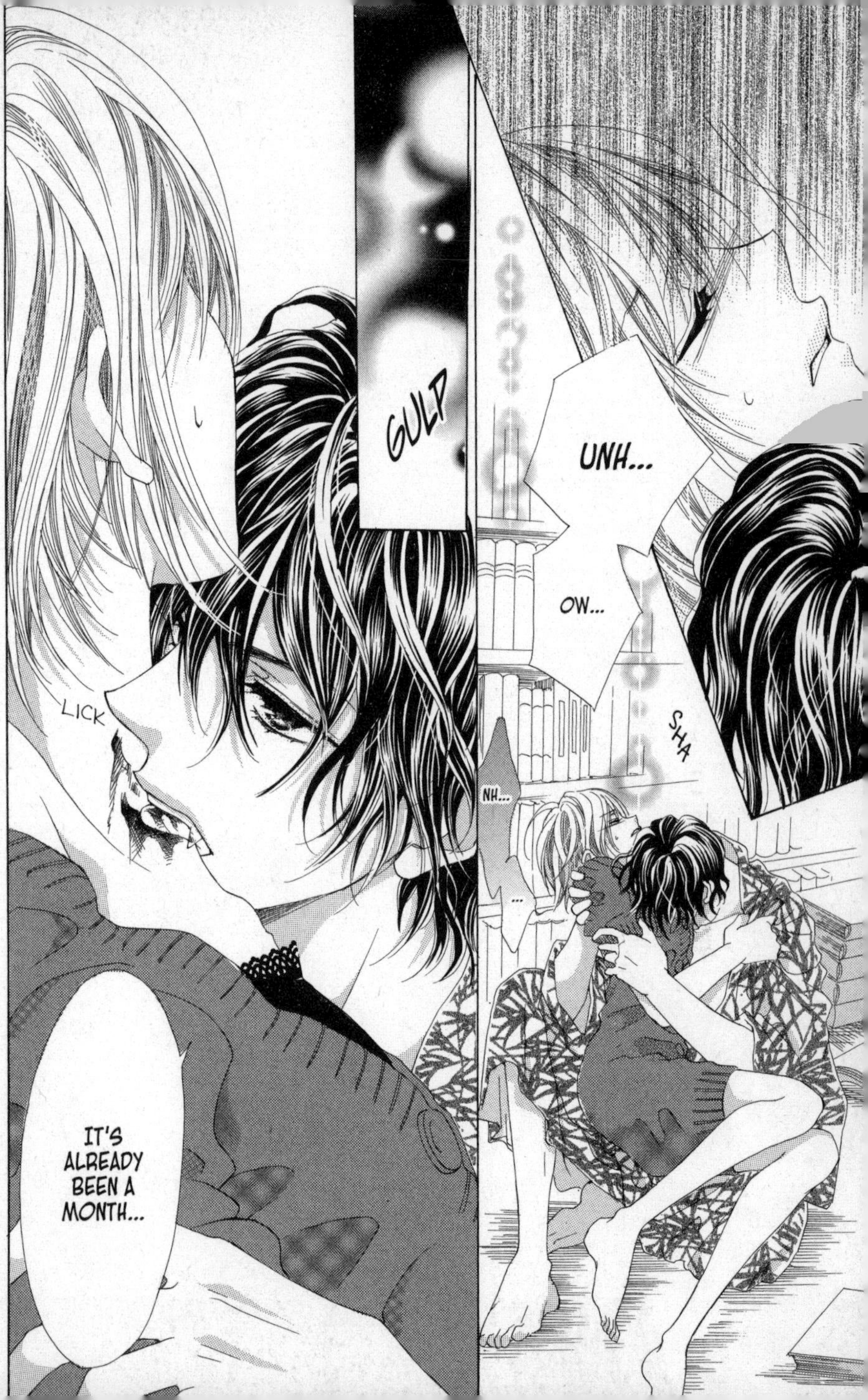
UNH...
OW...
SHA
NH...
...
GULP
LICK
IT'S ALREADY BEEN A MONTH...

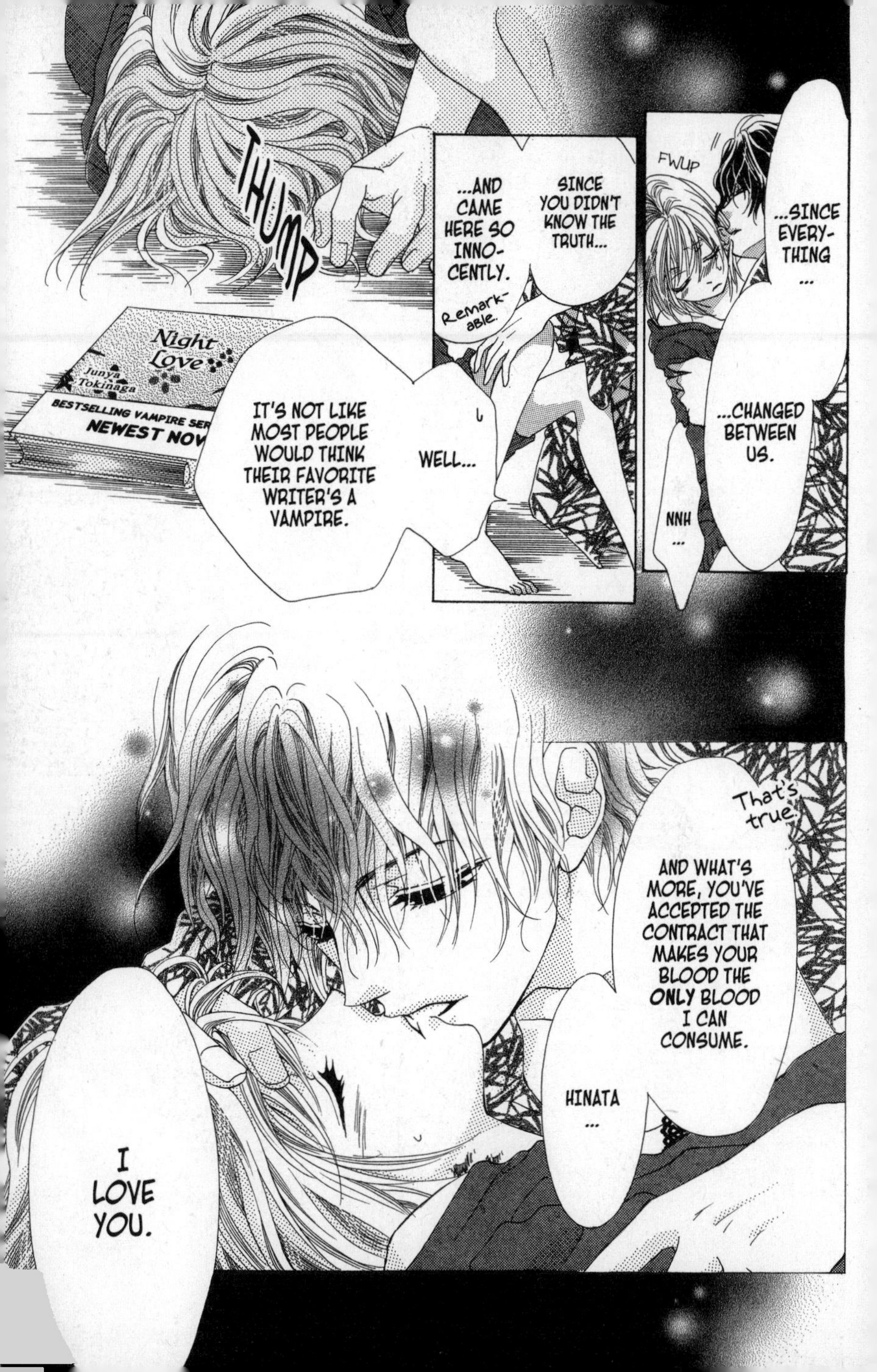
FWUP
...SINCE EVERYTHING...
...CHANGED BETWEEN US.
NNH...
SINCE YOU DIDN'T KNOW THE TRUTH...
...AND CAME HERE SO INNO-CENTLY.
Remark-able.
WELL...
IT'S NOT LIKE MOST PEOPLE WOULD THINK THEIR FAVORITE WRITER'S A VAMPIRE.
THUMP
Night Love
Junya Tokinaga
BESTSELLING VAMPIRE SER
NEWEST NOV
That's true.
AND WHAT'S MORE, YOU'VE ACCEPTED THE CONTRACT THAT MAKES YOUR BLOOD THE **ONLY** BLOOD I CAN CONSUME.
HINATA...
I LOVE YOU.

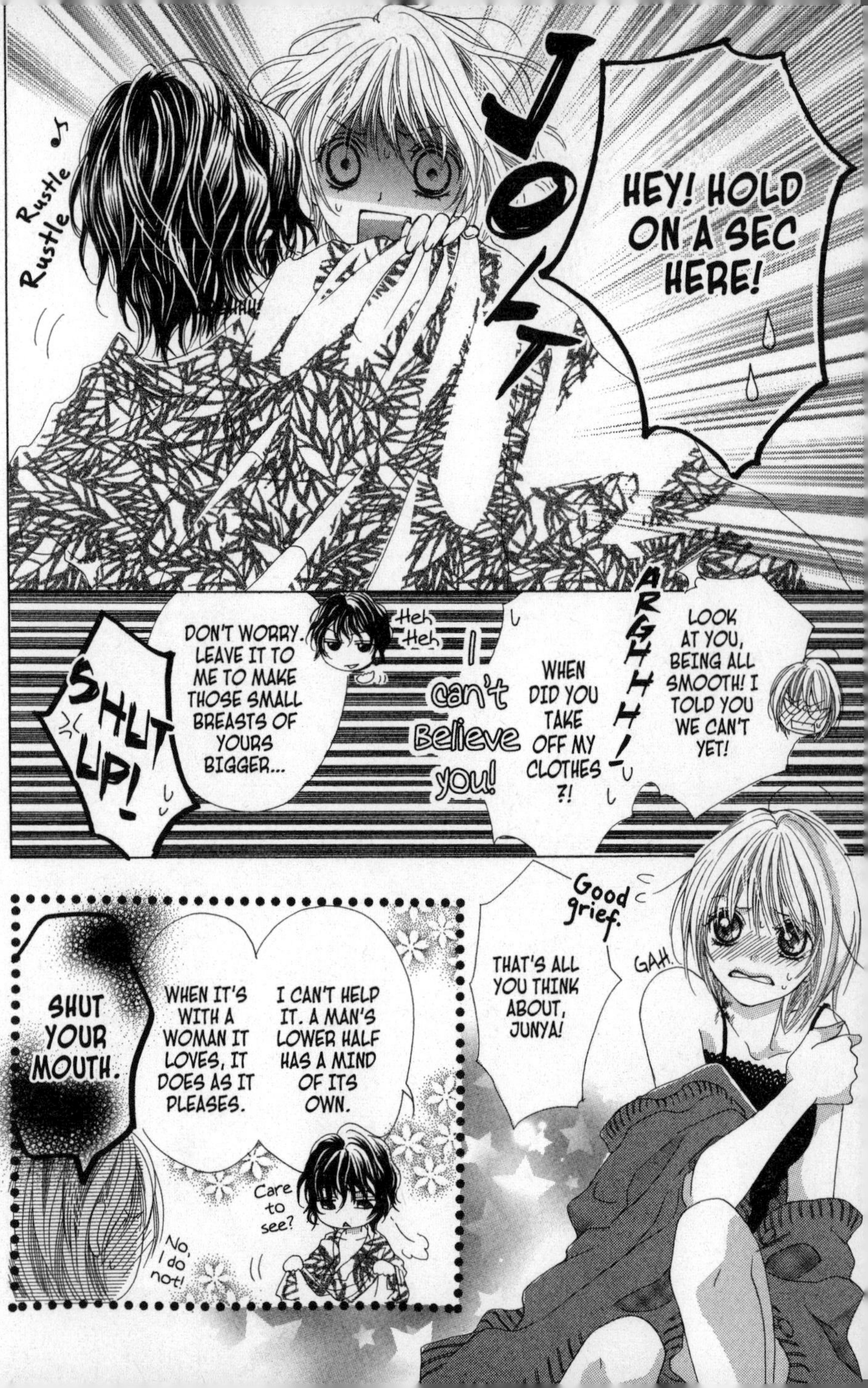
JOLT
HEY! HOLD ON A SEC HERE!
Rustle Rustle
LOOK AT YOU, BEING ALL SMOOTH! I TOLD YOU WE CAN'T YET!
ARGHHH!
WHEN DID YOU TAKE OFF MY CLOTHES ?!
I can't Believe you!
Heh Heh
DON'T WORRY. LEAVE IT TO ME TO MAKE THOSE SMALL BREASTS OF YOURS BIGGER...
SHUT UP!
Good grief.
GAH
THAT'S ALL YOU THINK ABOUT, JUNYA!
I CAN'T HELP IT. A MAN'S LOWER HALF HAS A MIND OF ITS OWN.
WHEN IT'S WITH A WOMAN IT LOVES, IT DOES AS IT PLEASES.
Care to see?
SHUT YOUR MOUTH.
No, I do not!

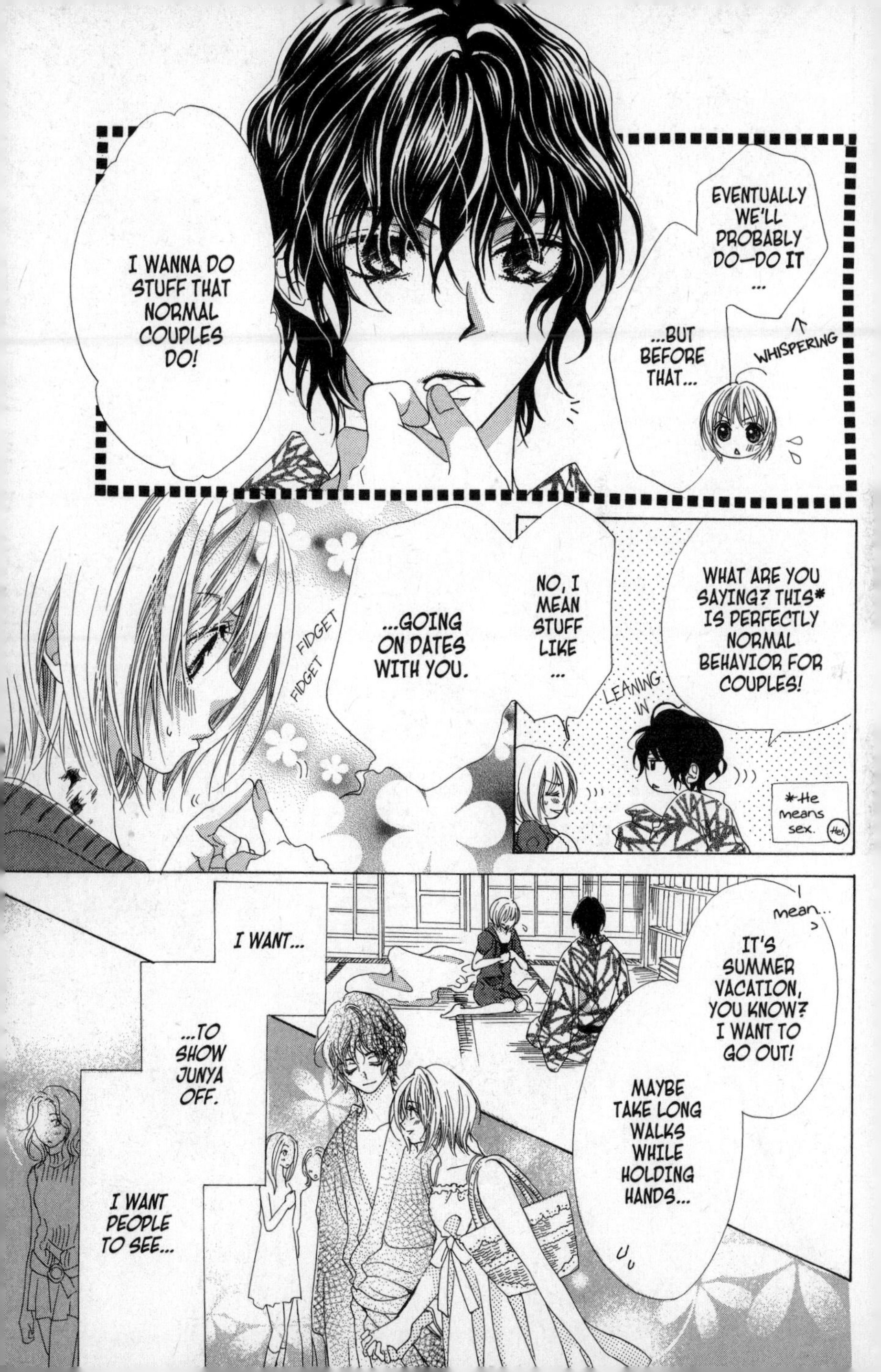
EVENTUALLY WE'LL PROBABLY DO—DO IT ...
WHISPERING
...BUT BEFORE THAT...
I WANNA DO STUFF THAT NORMAL COUPLES DO!
WHAT ARE YOU SAYING? THIS* IS PERFECTLY NORMAL BEHAVIOR FOR COUPLES!
LEANING IN
*He means sex. Heh
NO, I MEAN STUFF LIKE ...
...GOING ON DATES WITH YOU.
FIDGET FIDGET
I mean...
IT'S SUMMER VACATION, YOU KNOW? I WANT TO GO OUT!
MAYBE TAKE LONG WALKS WHILE HOLDING HANDS...
I WANT...
...TO SHOW JUNYA OFF.
I WANT PEOPLE TO SEE...

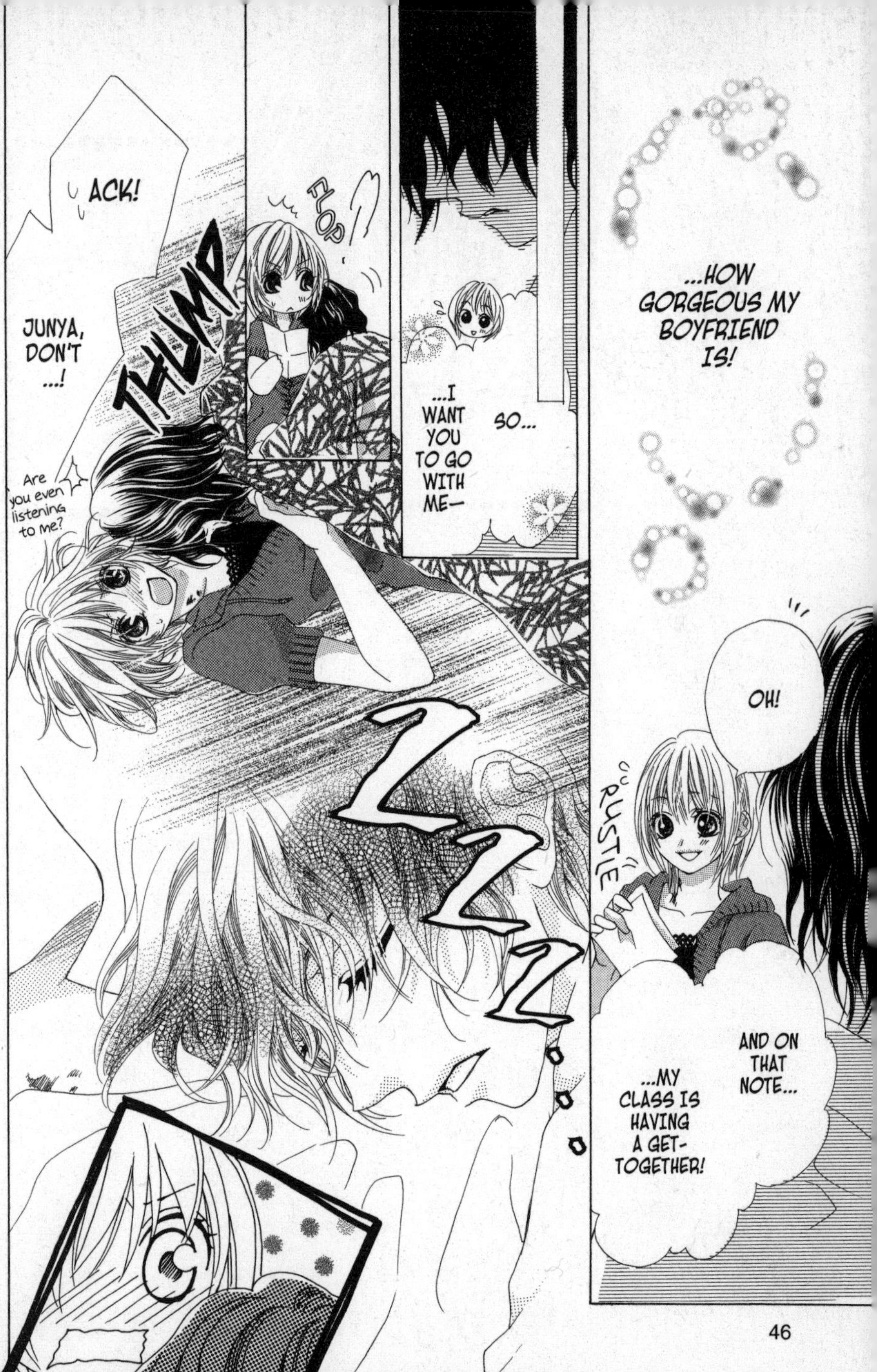
...HOW GORGEOUS MY BOYFRIEND IS!
OH!
RUSTLE
AND ON THAT NOTE...
...MY CLASS IS HAVING A GET-TOGETHER!
SO...
...I WANT YOU TO GO WITH ME—
FLOP
ACK!
THUMP
JUNYA, DON'T ...!
Are you even listening to me?
ZZZZ

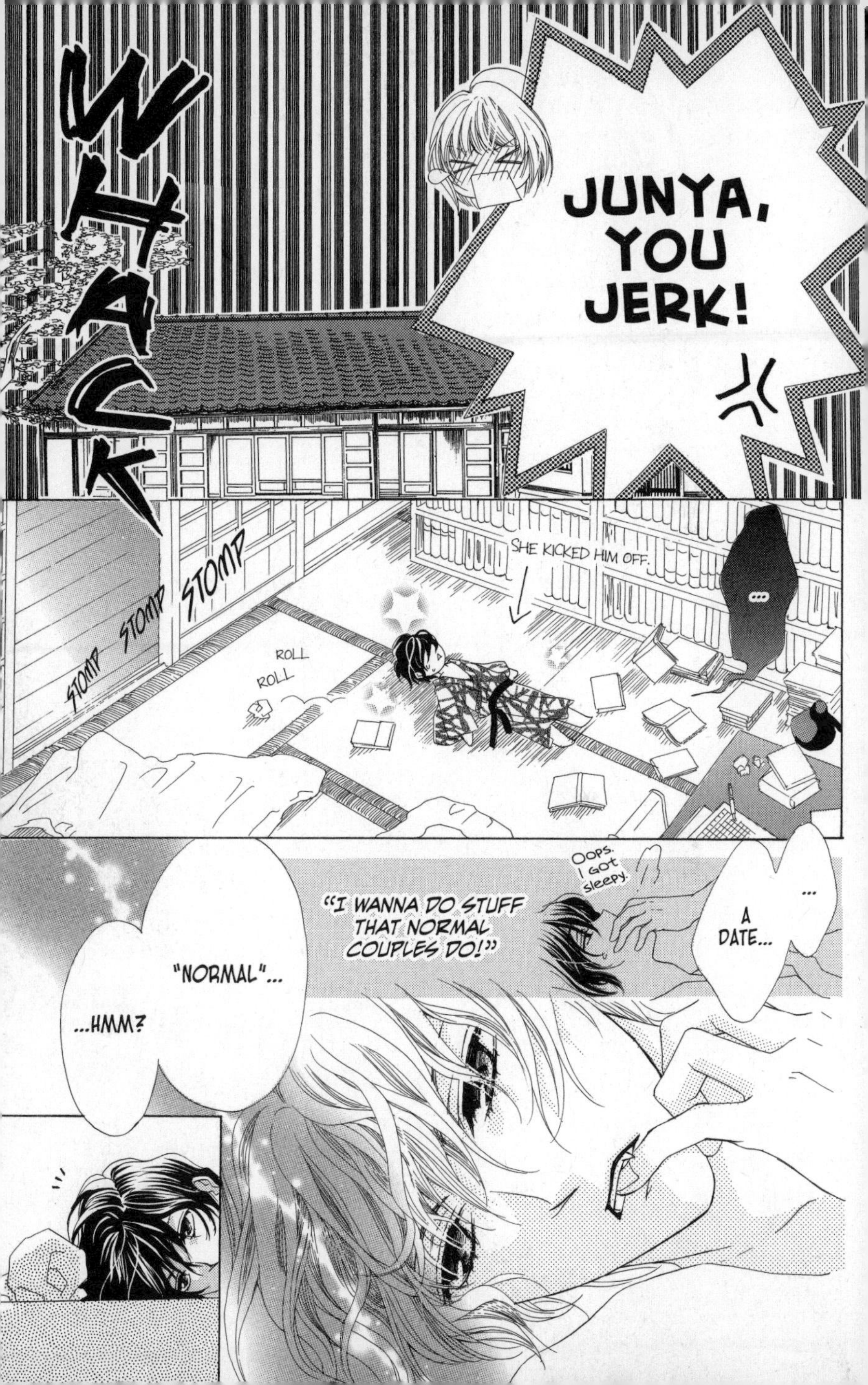
JUNYA, YOU JERK!
WHACK
...
SHE KICKED HIM OFF.
ROLL ROLL
STOMP STOMP STOMP
... A DATE...
Oops. I got sleepy.
"I WANNA DO STUFF THAT NORMAL COUPLES DO!"
"NORMAL"...
...HMM?

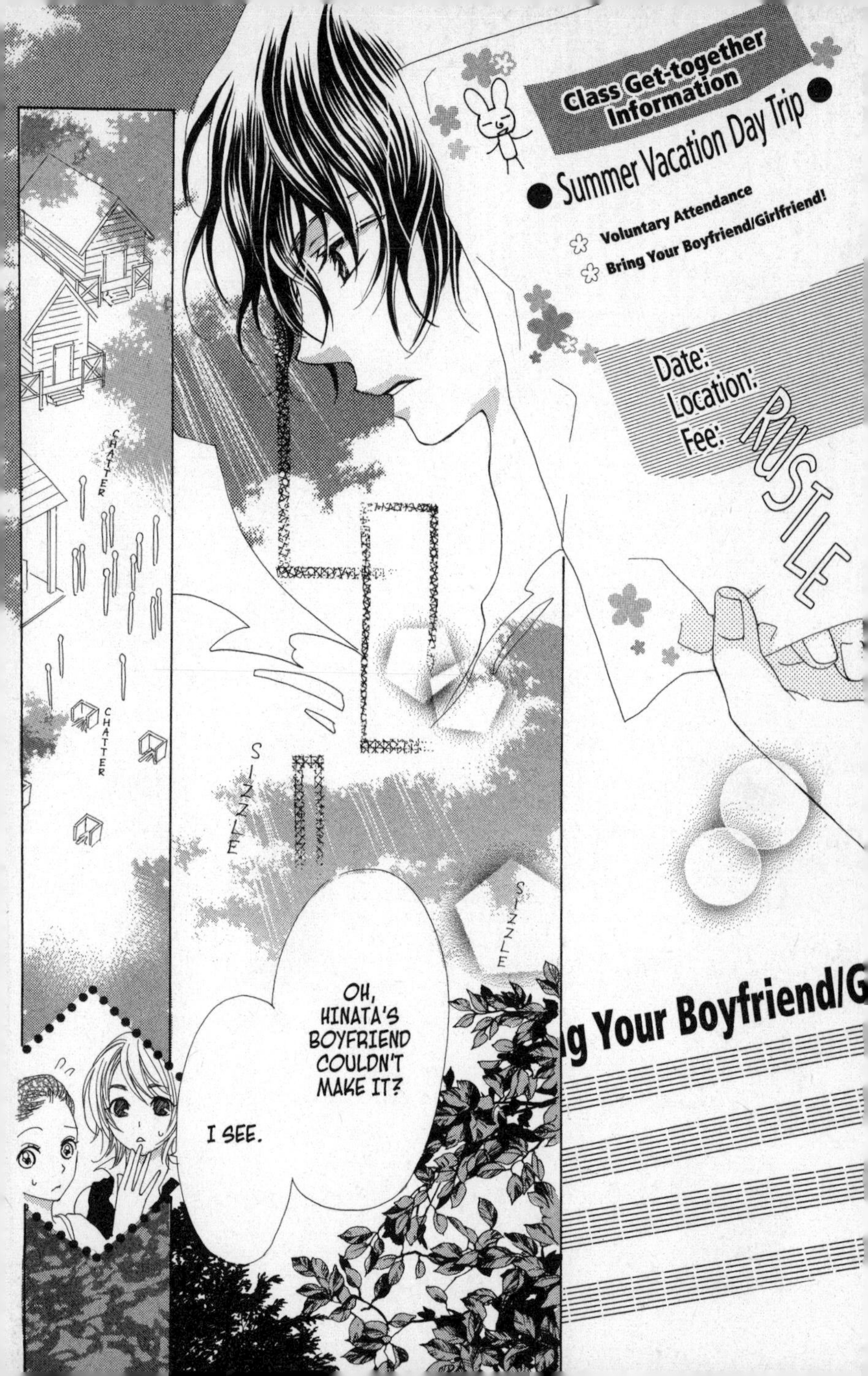
Class Get-together Information
Summer Vacation Day Trip
Voluntary Attendance
Bring Your Boyfriend/Girlfriend!
Date:
Location:
Fee:
RUSTLE
CHATTER
CHATTER
SIZZLE
SIZZLE
g Your Boyfriend/G
OH, HINATA'S BOYFRIEND COULDN'T MAKE IT?
I SEE.

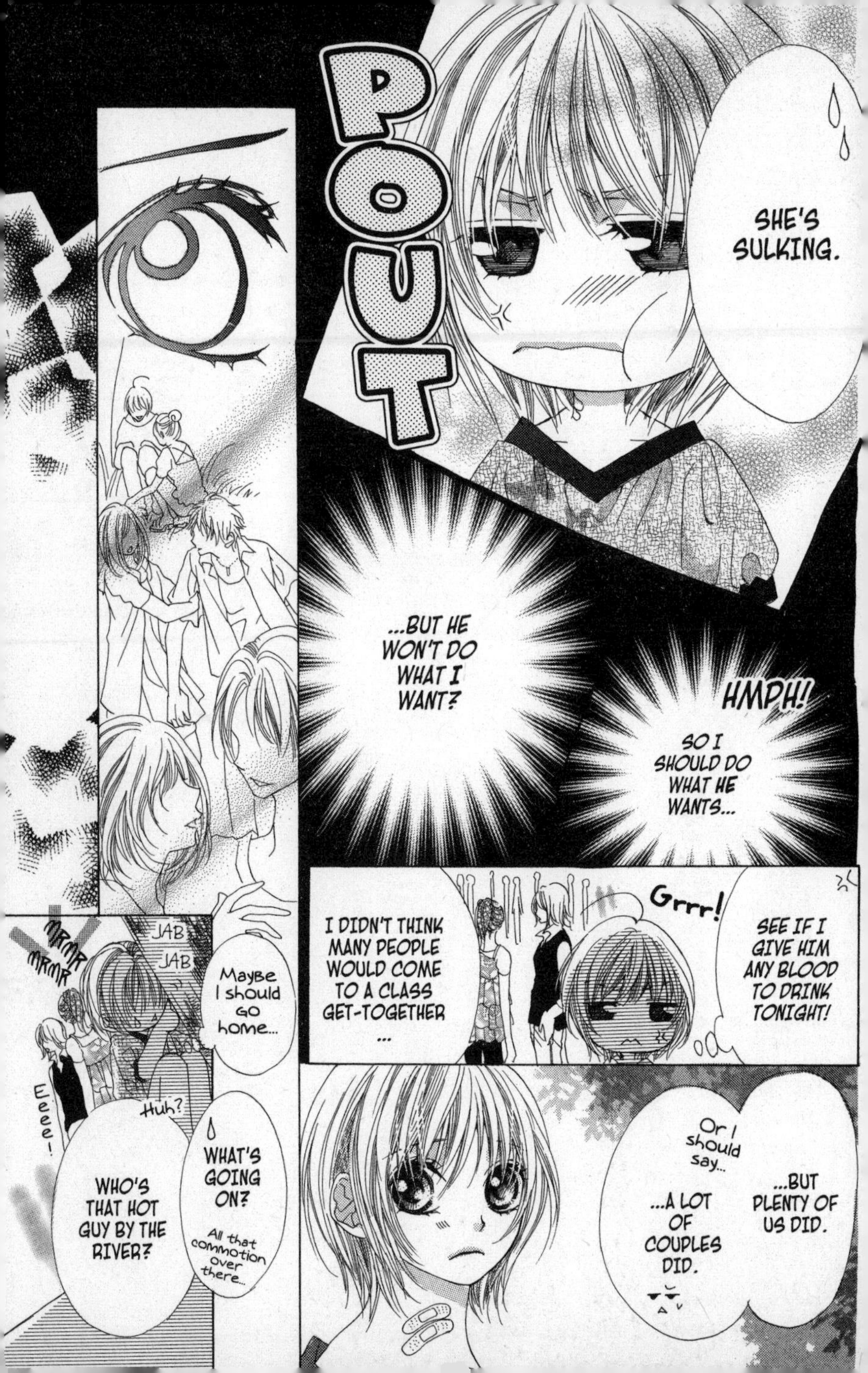
POUT
SHE'S SULKING.
HMPH!
SO I SHOULD DO WHAT HE WANTS...
...BUT HE WON'T DO WHAT I WANT?
Grrr!
SEE IF I GIVE HIM ANY BLOOD TO DRINK TONIGHT!
I DIDN'T THINK MANY PEOPLE WOULD COME TO A CLASS GET-TOGETHER...
...BUT PLENTY OF US DID.
Or I should say...
...A LOT OF COUPLES DID.
JAB JAB
MRMR MRMR
Maybe I should go home...
Huh?
WHAT'S GOING ON?
All that commotion over there...
Eeee!
WHO'S THAT HOT GUY BY THE RIVER?

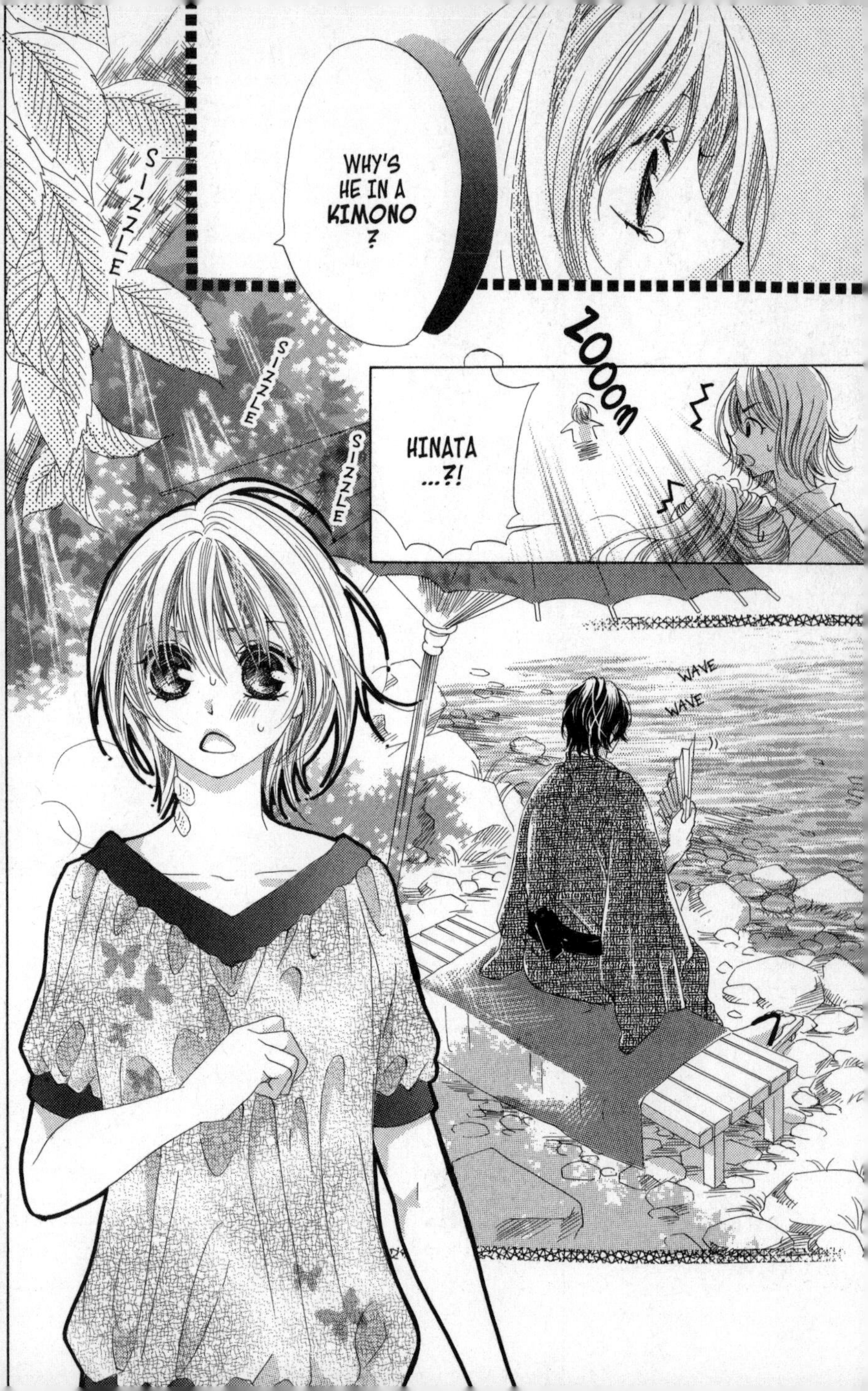
WHY'S HE IN A KIMONO?
ZOOOM
HINATA ...?!
SIZZLE
SIZZLE
SIZZLE
WAVE
WAVE

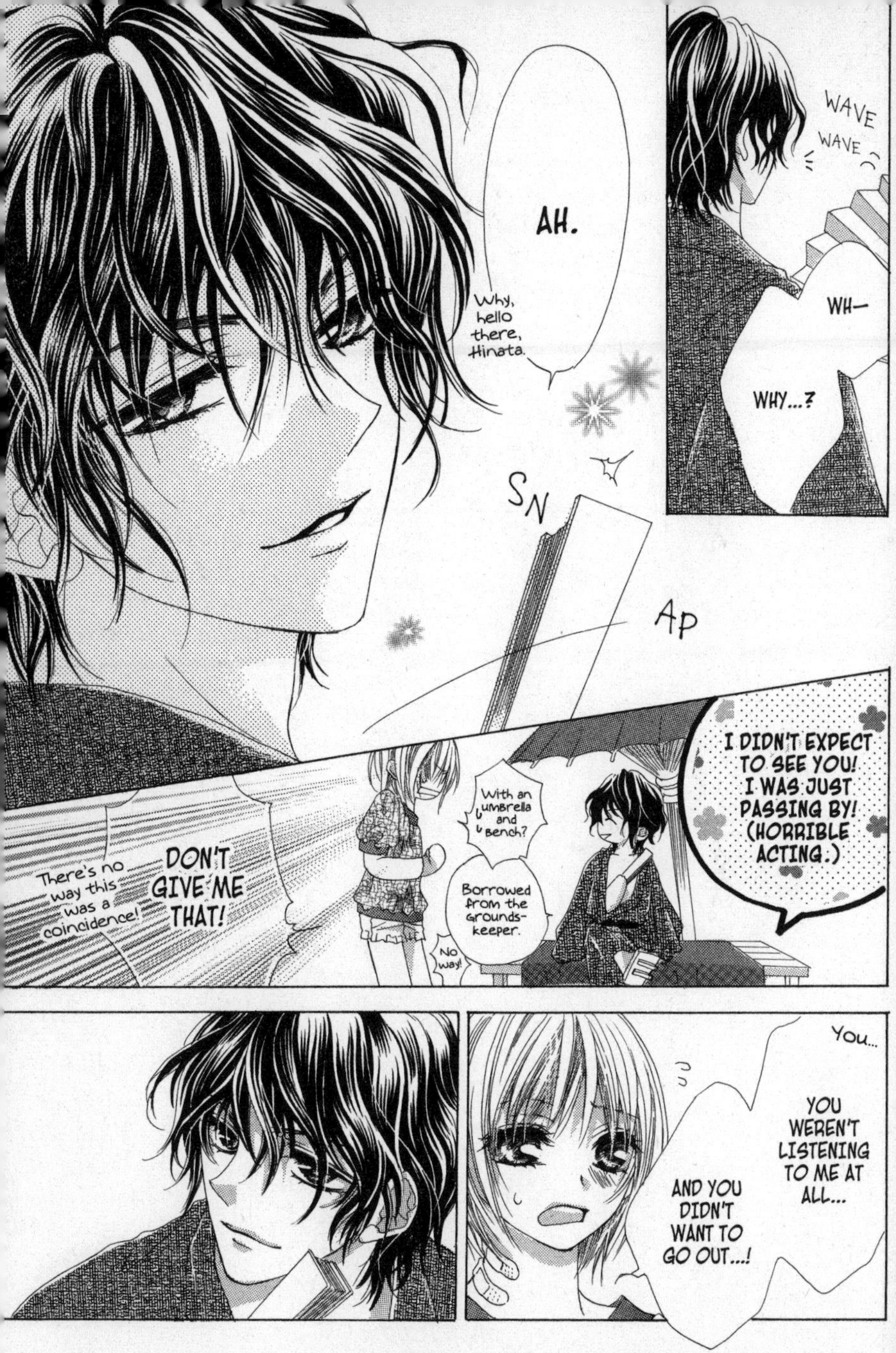
WAVE
WAVE
WH—
WHY...?
AH.
Why, hello there, Hinata.
SN
AP
I DIDN'T EXPECT TO SEE YOU! I WAS JUST PASSING BY! (HORRIBLE ACTING.)
With an umbrella and bench?
Borrowed from the grounds-keeper.
No way!
DON'T GIVE ME THAT!
There's no way this was a coincidence!
You...
YOU WEREN'T LISTENING TO ME AT ALL...
AND YOU DIDN'T WANT TO GO OUT...!

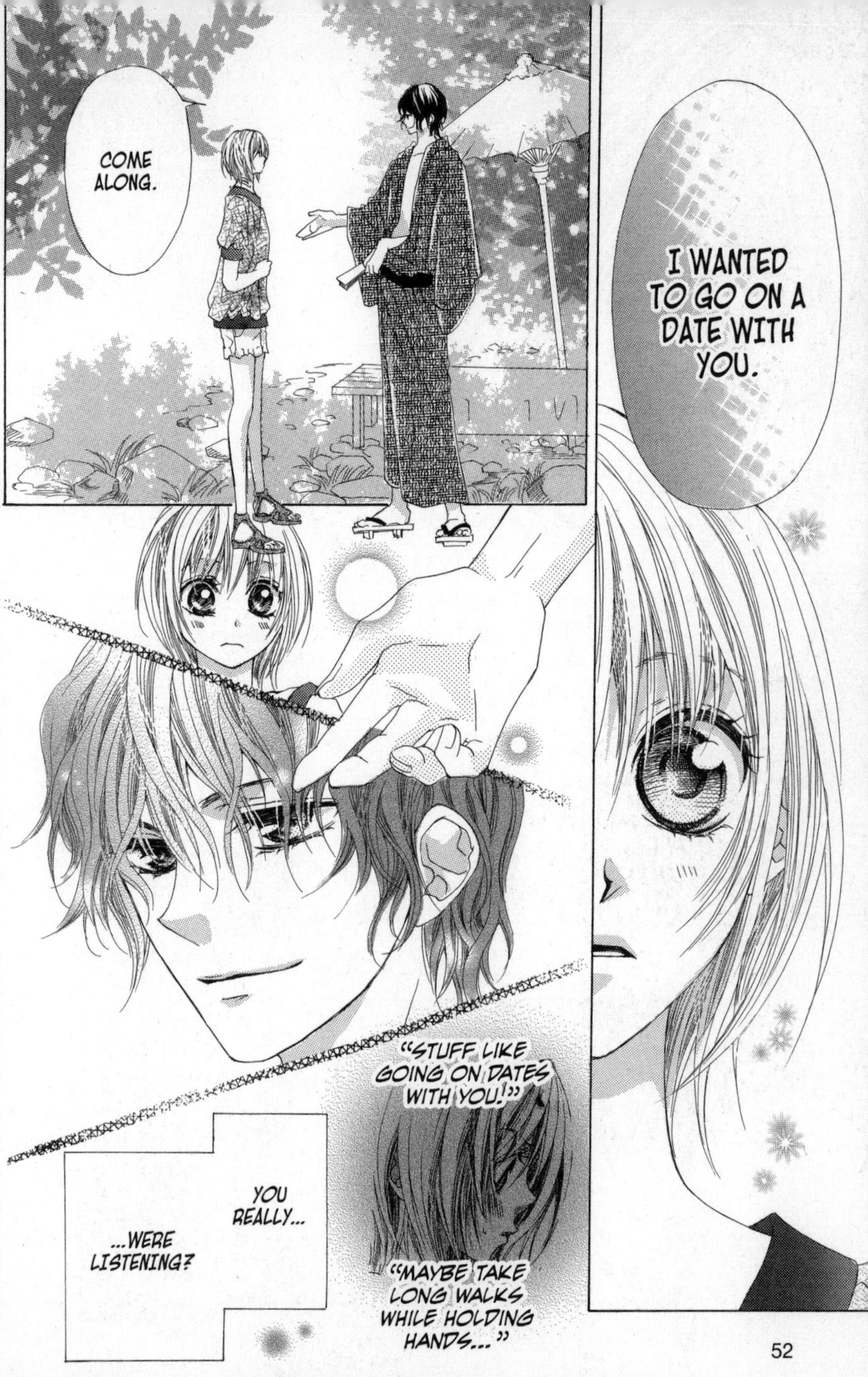
I WANTED TO GO ON A DATE WITH YOU.
COME ALONG.
"STUFF LIKE GOING ON DATES WITH YOU."
YOU REALLY...
...WERE LISTENING?
"MAYBE TAKE LONG WALKS WHILE HOLDING HANDS..."

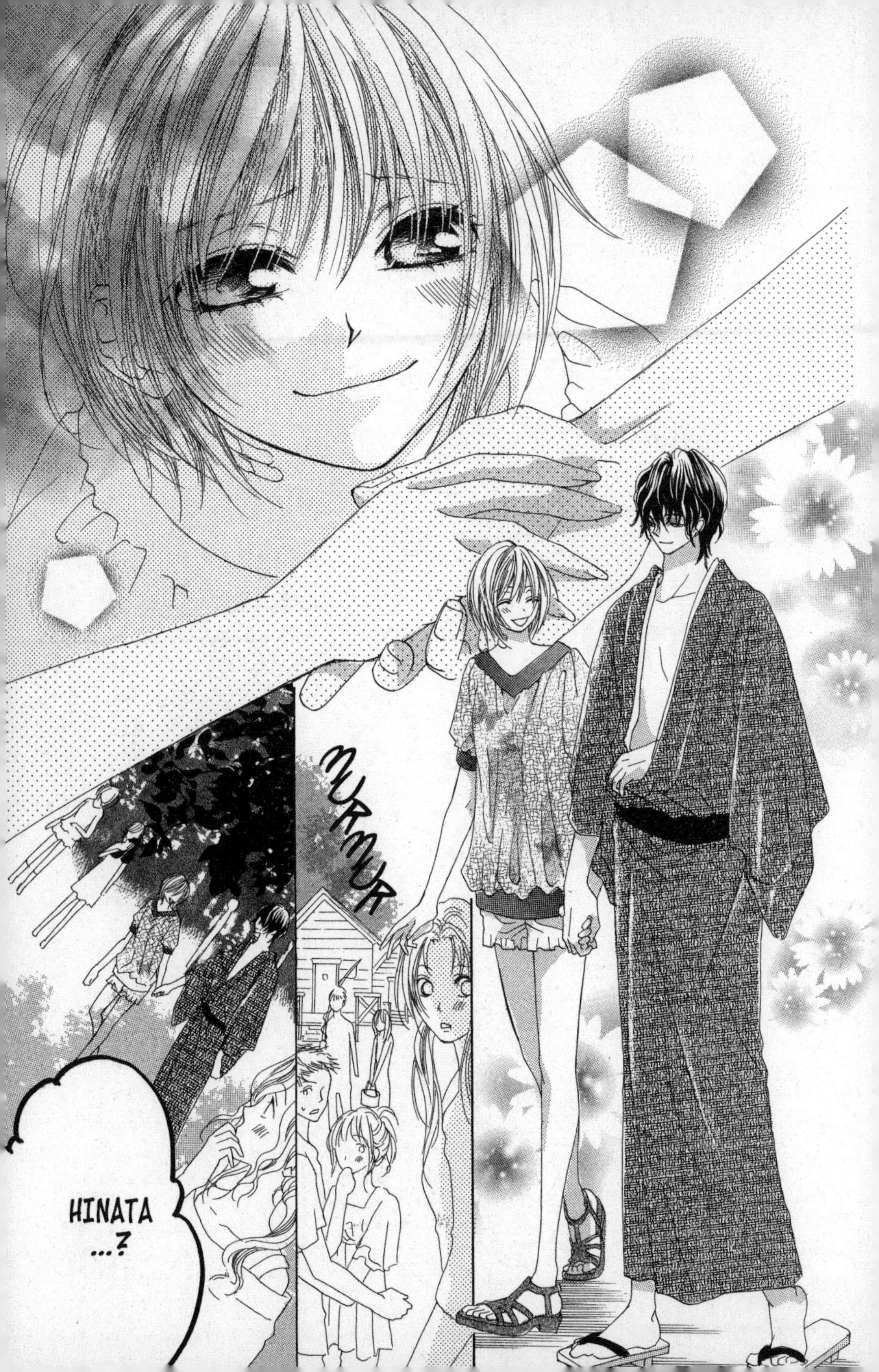
MURMUR
HINATA ...?

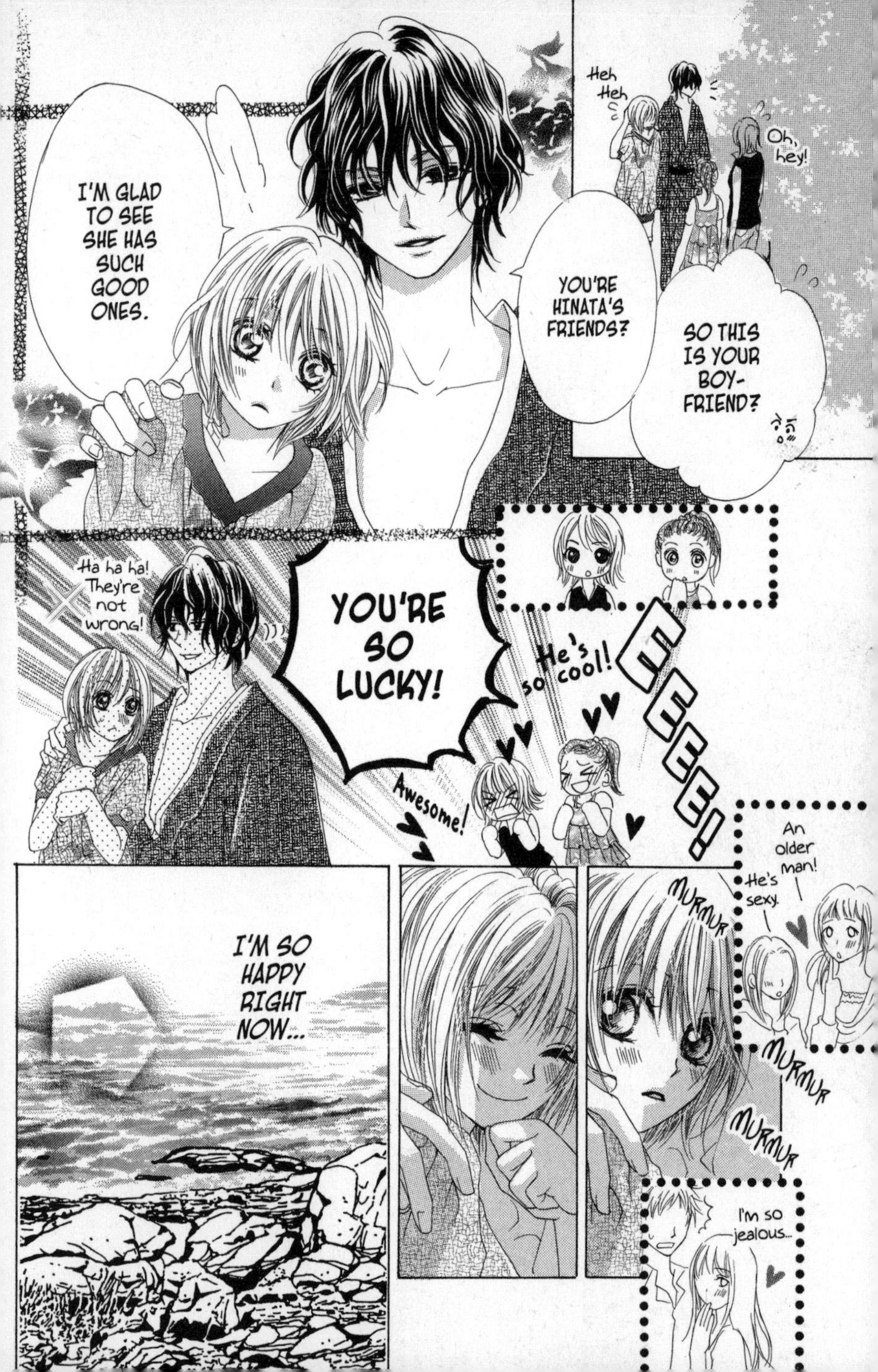
Oh, hey!
Heh Heh
So this is your boyfriend?
You're Hinata's friends?
I'm glad to see she has such good ones.
EEEEE!
He's so cool!
Awesome!
You're so lucky!
Ha ha ha! They're not wrong!
An older man!
He's sexy.
MURMUR
MURMUR
MURMUR
I'm so jealous...
I'm so happy right now...

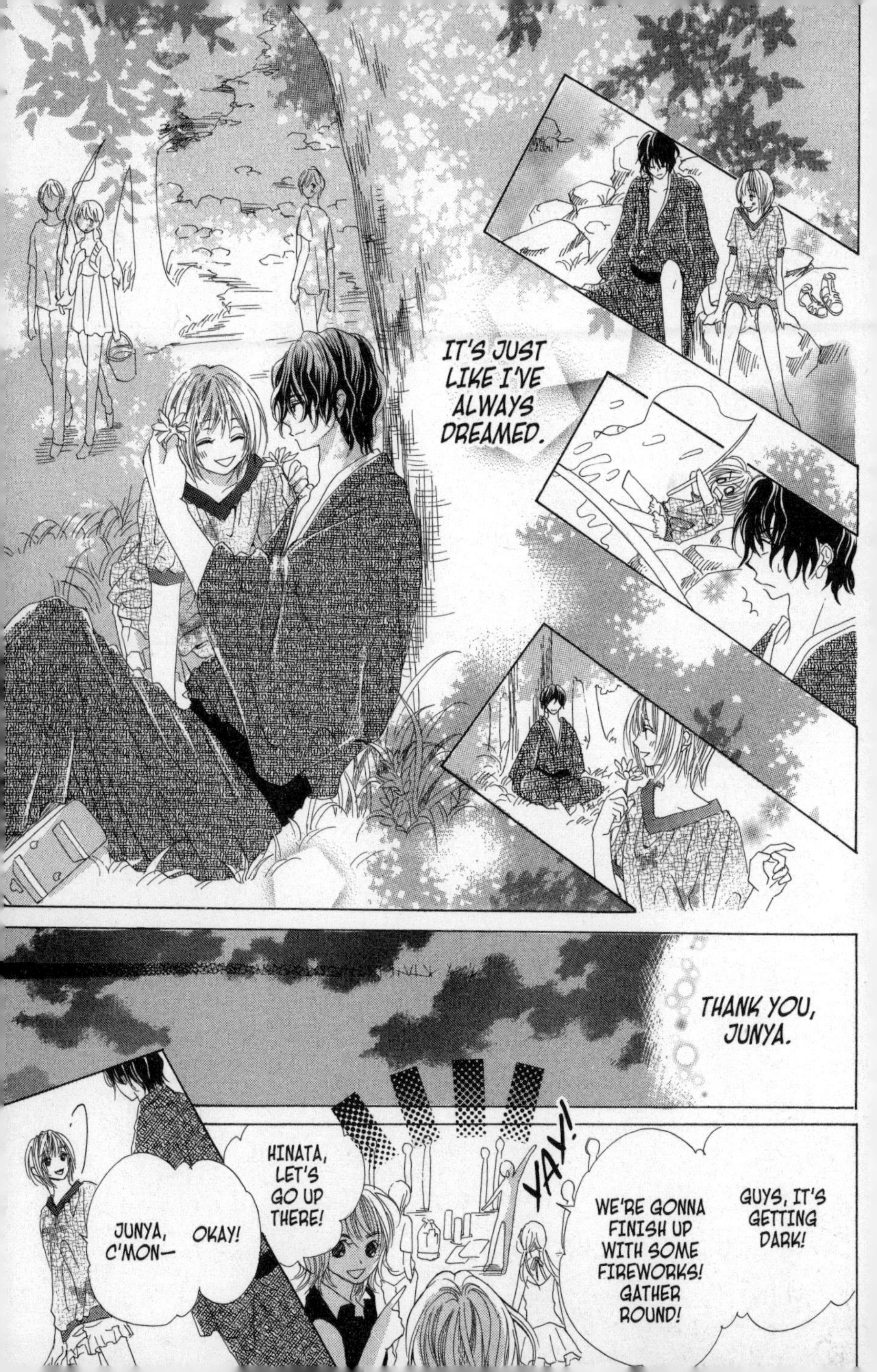
IT'S JUST LIKE I'VE ALWAYS DREAMED.
THANK YOU, JUNYA.
GUYS, IT'S GETTING DARK!
WE'RE GONNA FINISH UP WITH SOME FIREWORKS! GATHER ROUND!
YAY!
HINATA, LET'S GO UP THERE!
OKAY!
JUNYA, C'MON—

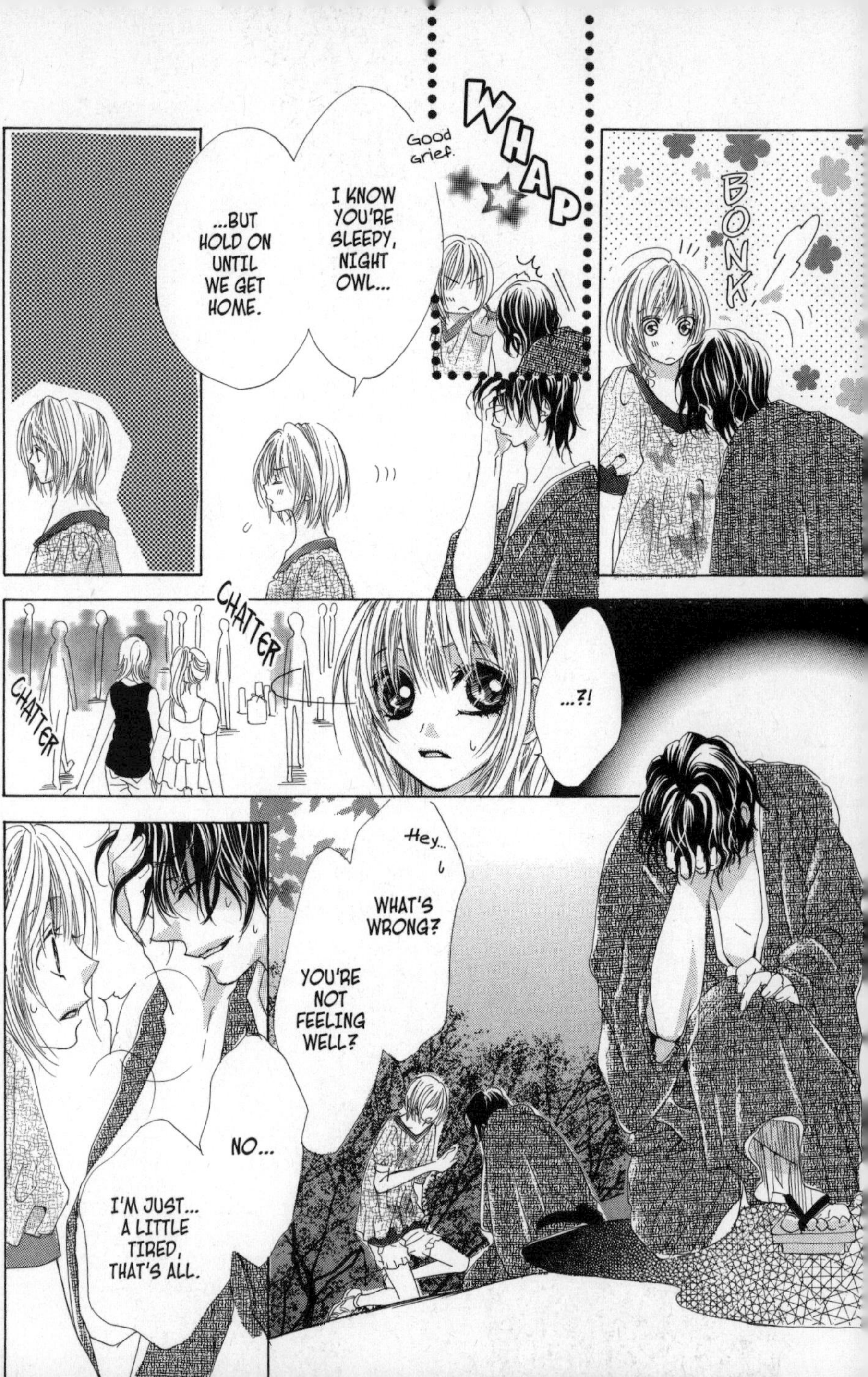
BONK
WHAP
Good grief.
I KNOW YOU'RE SLEEPY, NIGHT OWL...
...BUT HOLD ON UNTIL WE GET HOME.
...?!
CHATTER
CHATTER
Hey...
WHAT'S WRONG?
YOU'RE NOT FEELING WELL?
NO...
I'M JUST... A LITTLE TIRED, THAT'S ALL.

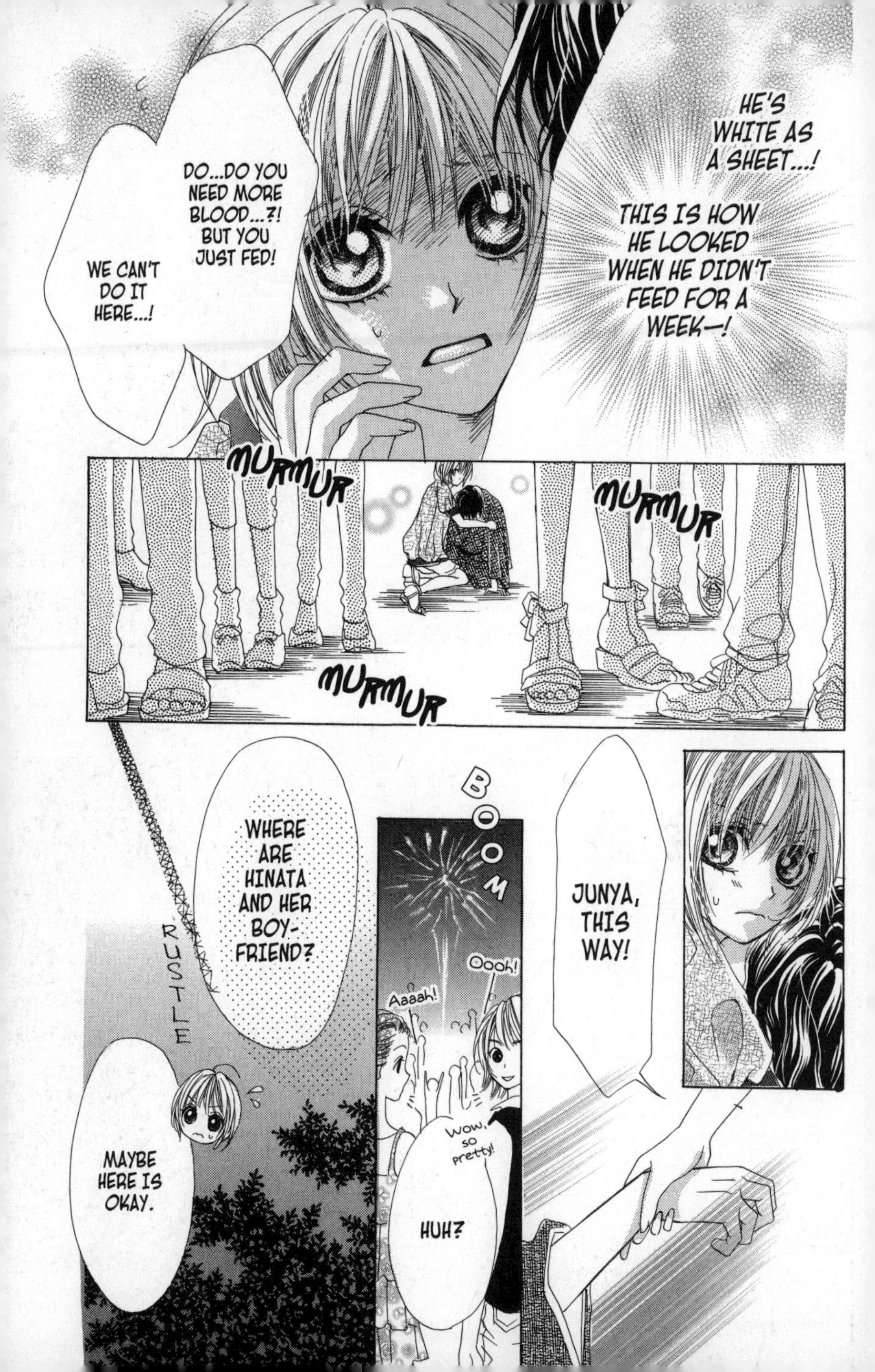
HE'S WHITE AS A SHEET...!
THIS IS HOW HE LOOKED WHEN HE DIDN'T FEED FOR A WEEK—!
DO...DO YOU NEED MORE BLOOD...?! BUT YOU JUST FED!
WE CAN'T DO IT HERE...!
MURMUR
MURMUR
MURMUR
JUNYA, THIS WAY!
BOOM
Oooh!
Aaaah!
Wow, so pretty!
HUH?
WHERE ARE HINATA AND HER BOY-FRIEND?
RUSTLE
MAYBE HERE IS OKAY.

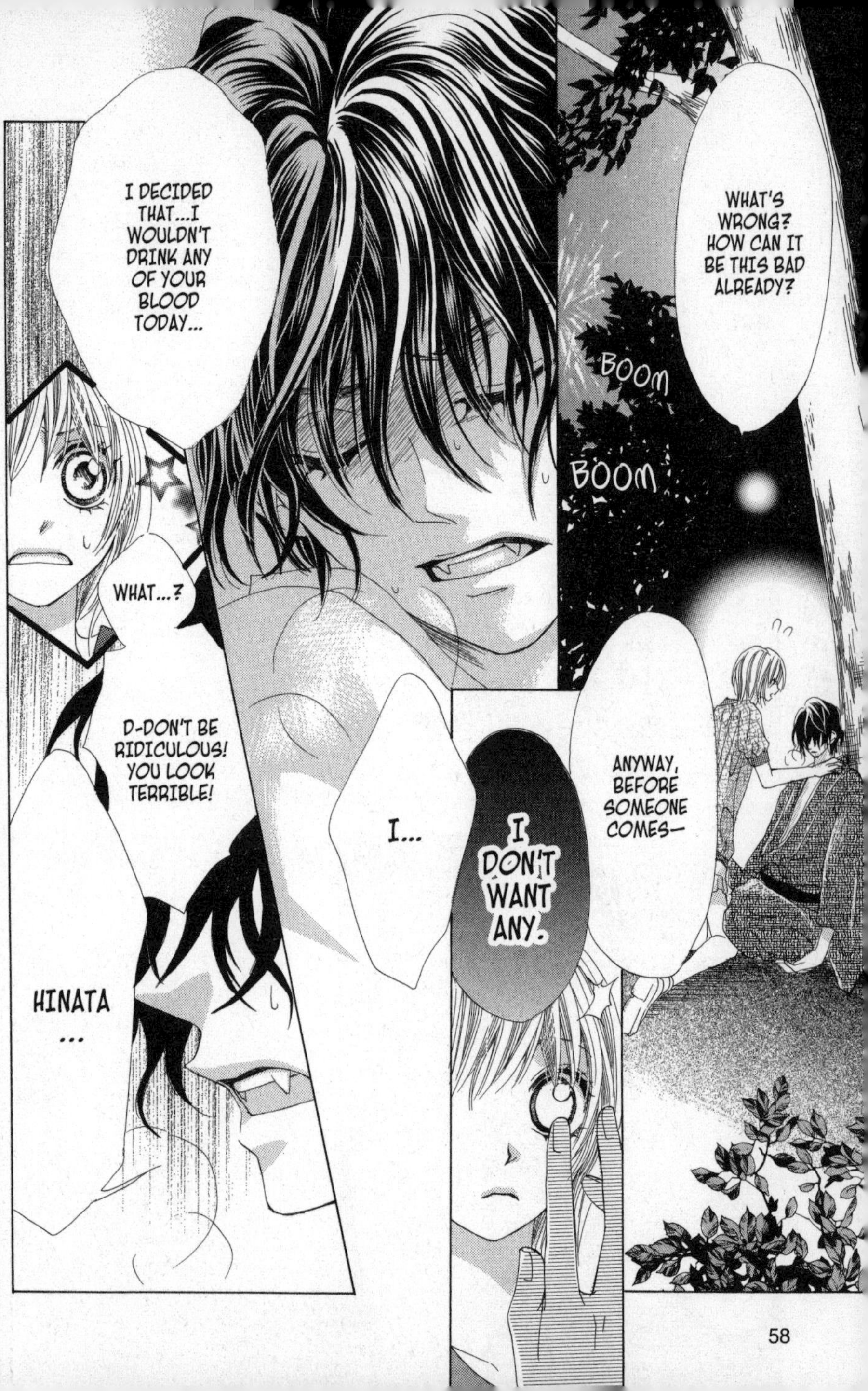
WHAT'S WRONG? HOW CAN IT BE THIS BAD ALREADY?
BOOM
BOOM
ANYWAY, BEFORE SOMEONE COMES—
I...
I DON'T WANT ANY.
HINATA ...
D-DON'T BE RIDICULOUS! YOU LOOK TERRIBLE!
I DECIDED THAT...I WOULDN'T DRINK ANY OF YOUR BLOOD TODAY...
WHAT...?

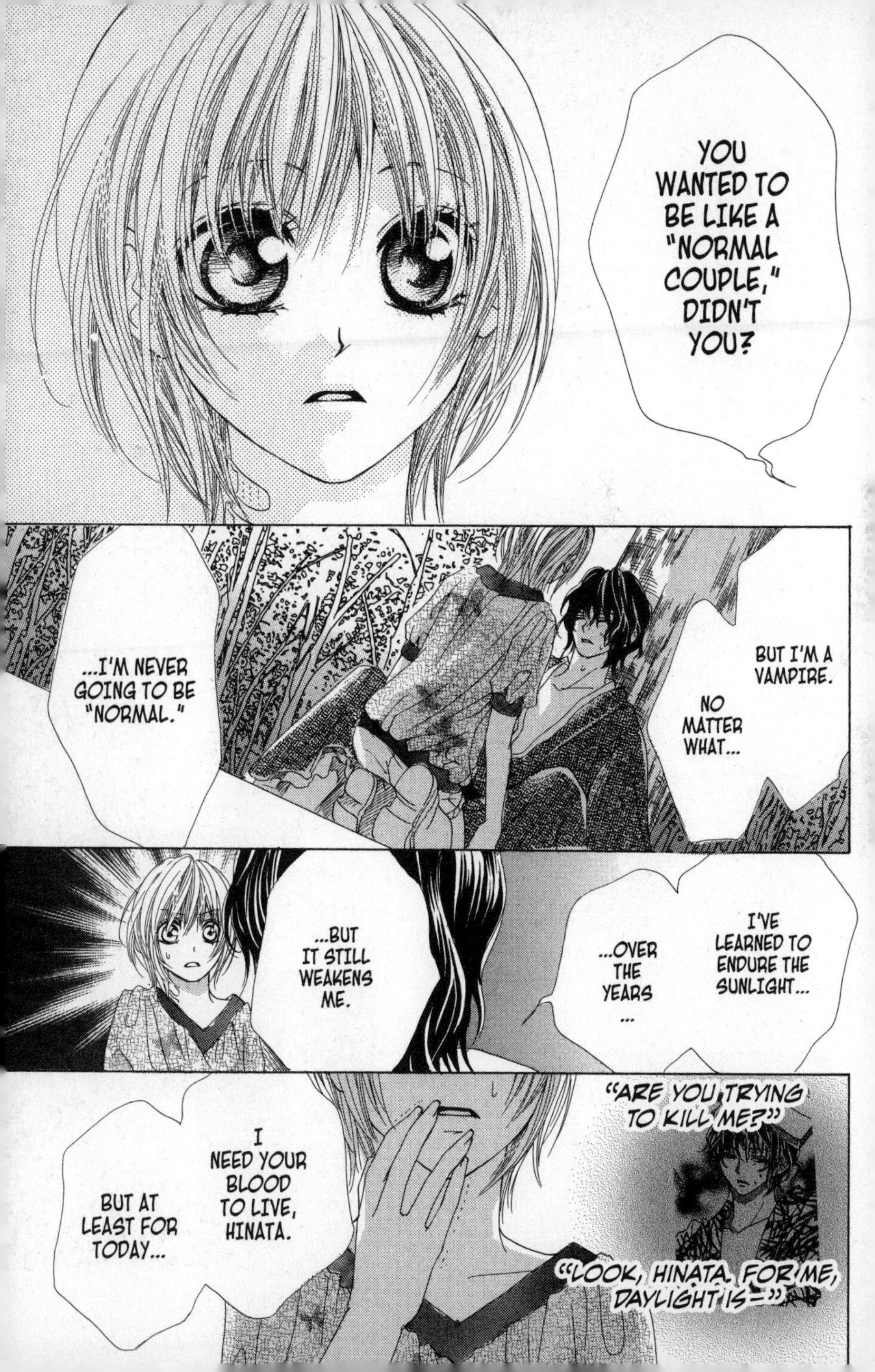
YOU WANTED TO BE LIKE A "NORMAL COUPLE," DIDN'T YOU?
BUT I'M A VAMPIRE.
NO MATTER WHAT...
...I'M NEVER GOING TO BE "NORMAL."
I'VE LEARNED TO ENDURE THE SUNLIGHT...
...OVER THE YEARS ...
...BUT IT STILL WEAKENS ME.
"ARE YOU TRYING TO KILL ME?"
"LOOK, HINATA. FOR ME, DAYLIGHT IS—"
I NEED YOUR BLOOD TO LIVE, HINATA.
BUT AT LEAST FOR TODAY...

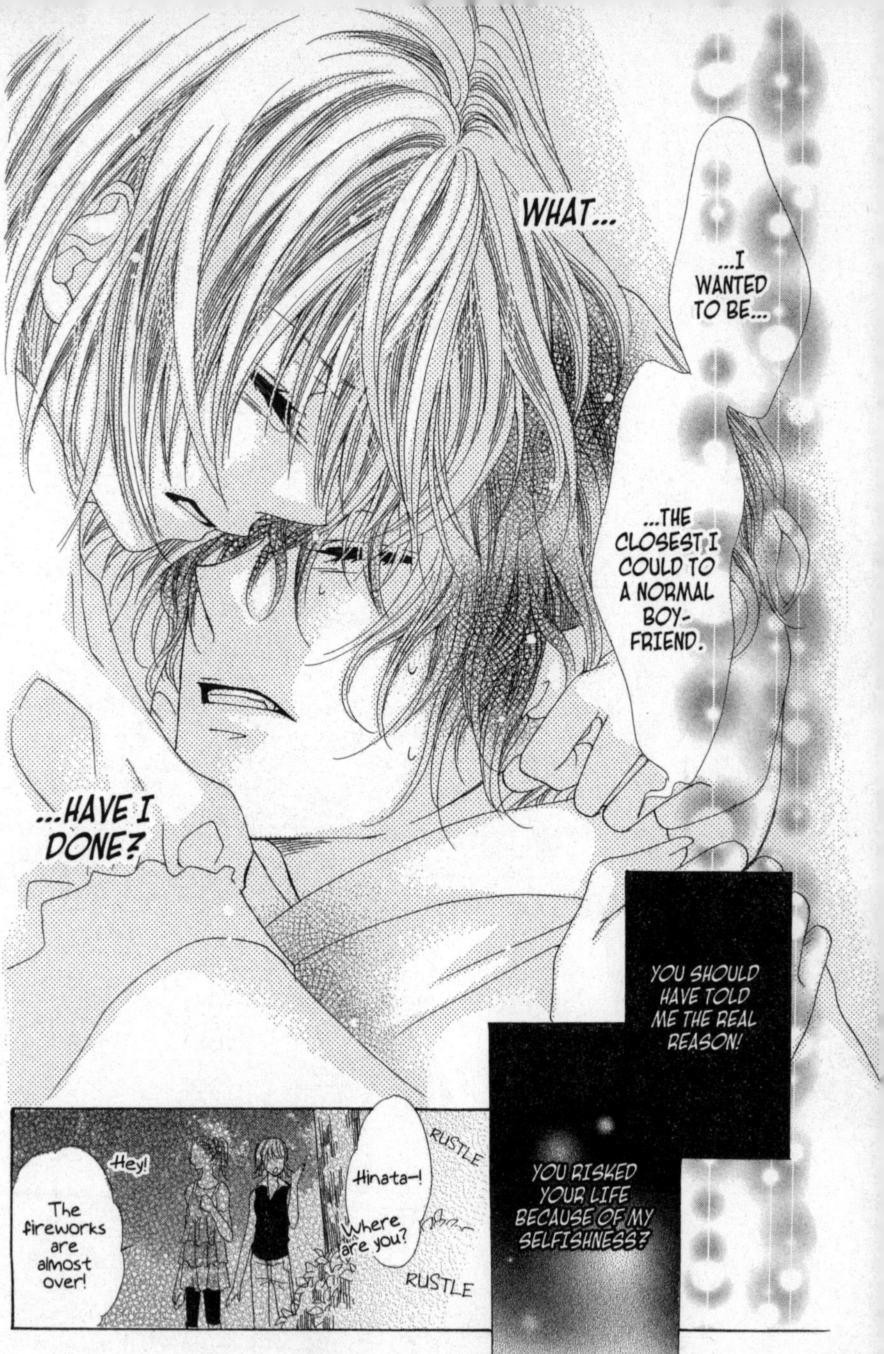
...I WANTED TO BE...
...THE CLOSEST I COULD TO A NORMAL BOY-FRIEND.
WHAT...
...HAVE I DONE?
YOU SHOULD HAVE TOLD ME THE REAL REASON!
YOU RISKED YOUR LIFE BECAUSE OF MY SELFISHNESS?
RUSTLE
Hinata-!
Where are you?
RUSTLE
Hey!
The fireworks are almost over!

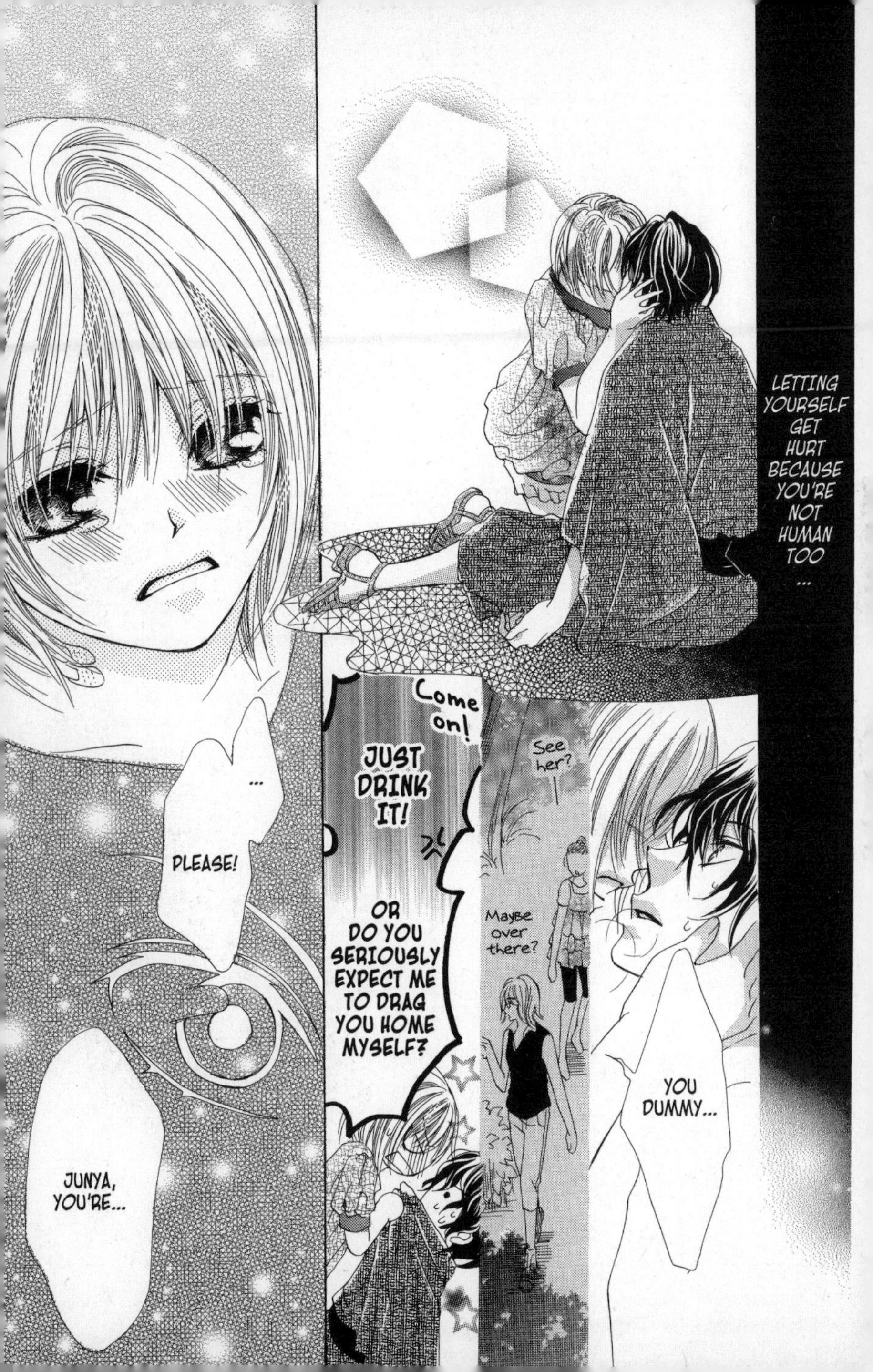

LETTING YOURSELF GET HURT BECAUSE YOU'RE NOT HUMAN TOO ...
YOU DUMMY...
See her?
Maybe over there?
Come on!
JUST DRINK IT!
OR DO YOU SERIOUSLY EXPECT ME TO DRAG YOU HOME MYSELF?
...
PLEASE!
JUNYA, YOU'RE...

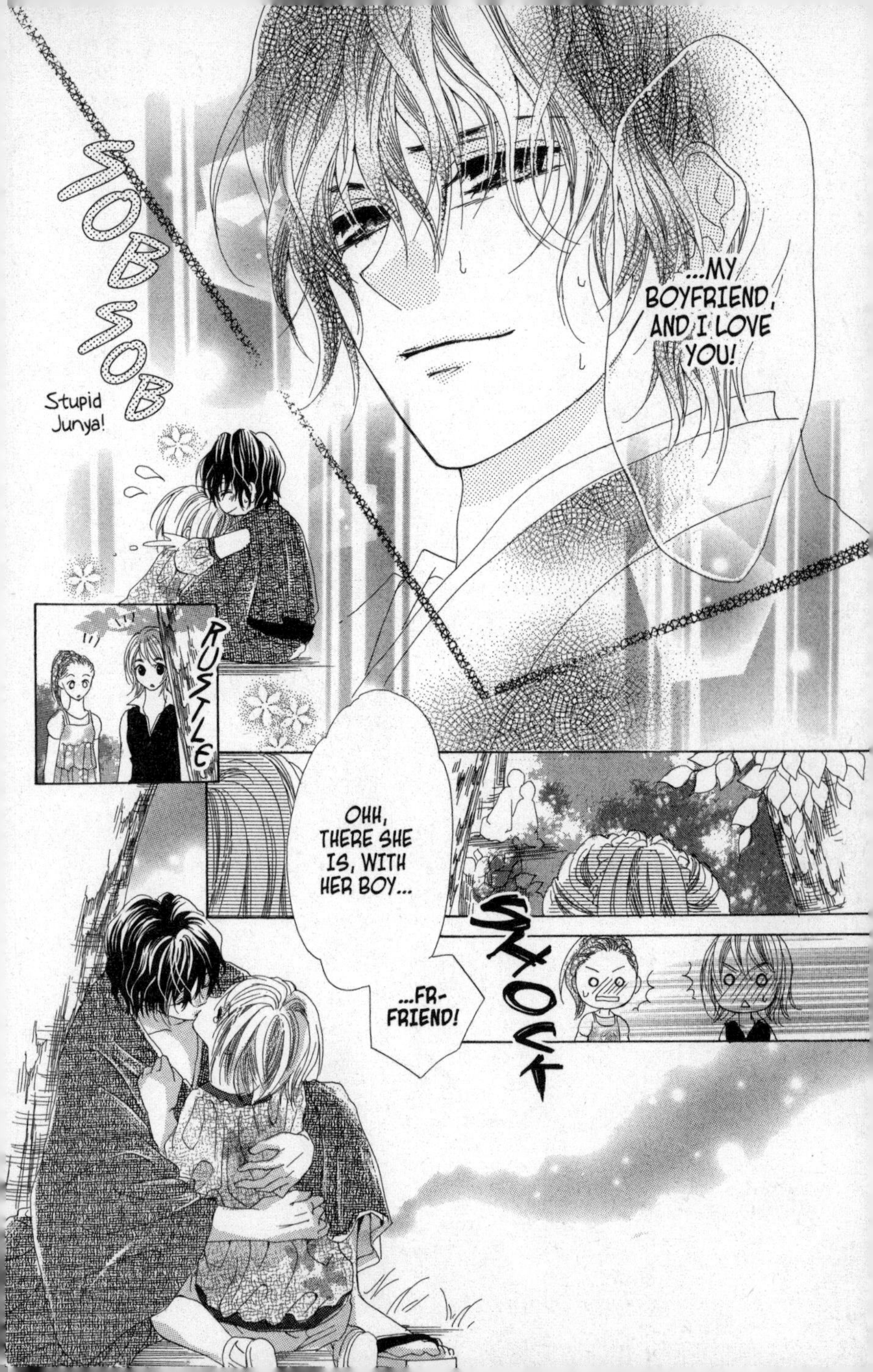
...MY BOYFRIEND, AND I LOVE YOU!
SOB SOB
Stupid Junya!
RUSTLE
OHH, THERE SHE IS, WITH HER BOY...
SHOCK
...FR-FRIEND!

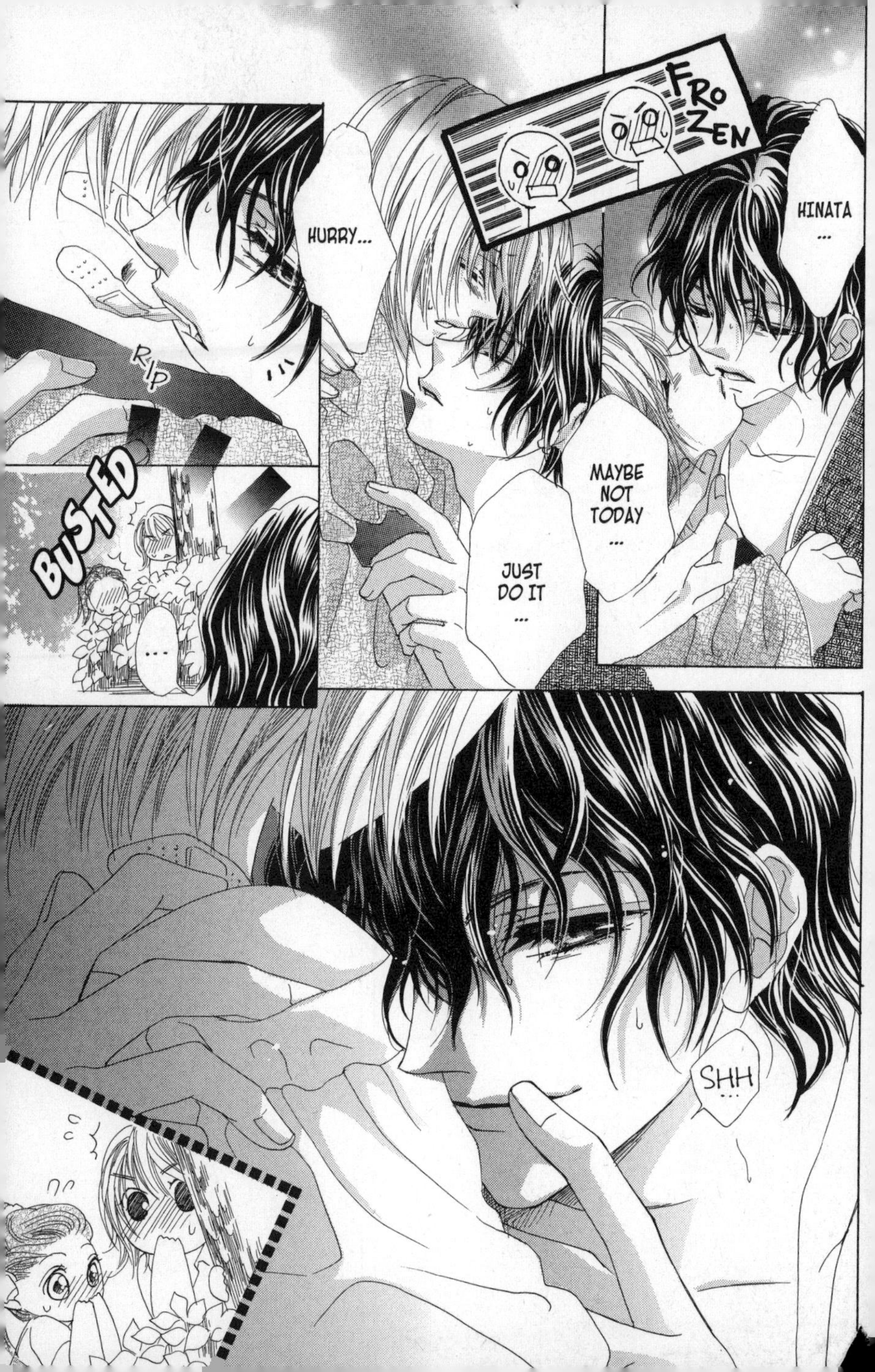
HINATA ...
MAYBE NOT TODAY ...
FROZEN
HURRY...
JUST DO IT ...
RIP
BUSTED
...
SHH ...

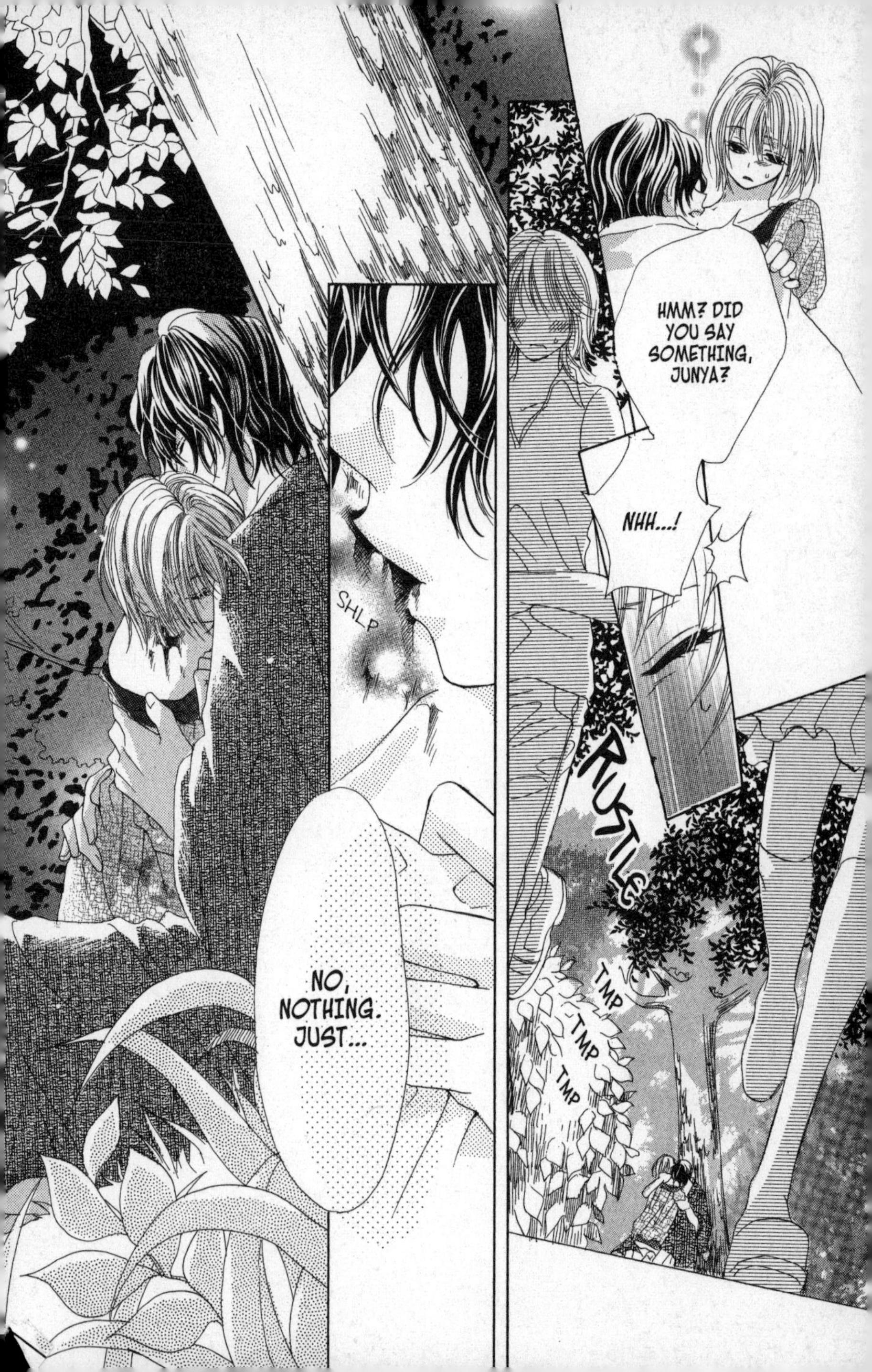
HMM? DID YOU SAY SOMETHING, JUNYA?
NHH...!
RUSTLE
TMP TMP TMP
SHLP
NO, NOTHING. JUST...

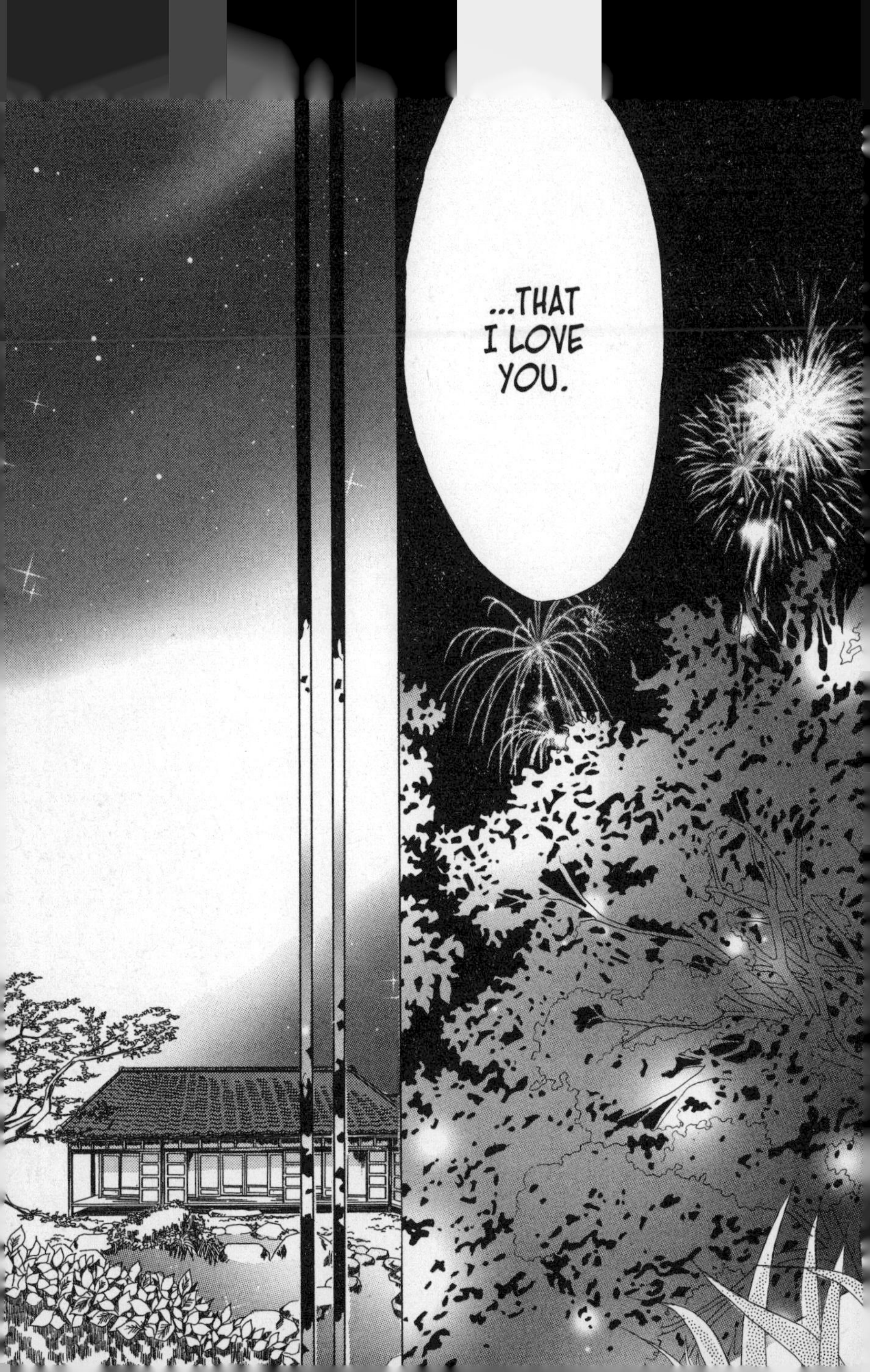
...THAT I LOVE YOU.

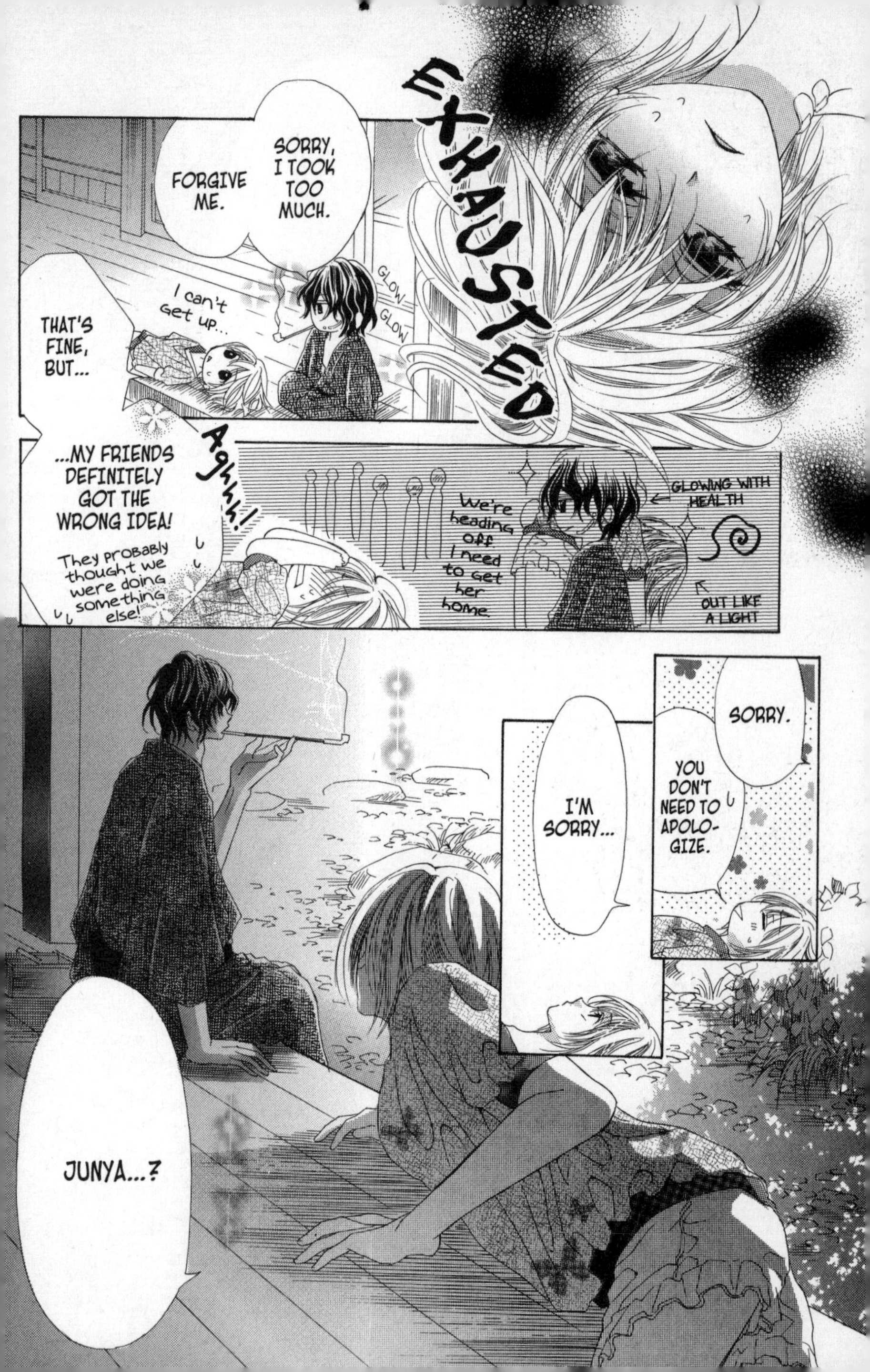
EXHAUSTED
SORRY, I TOOK TOO MUCH.
FORGIVE ME.
GLOW GLOW
I can't get up...
THAT'S FINE, BUT...
GLOWING WITH HEALTH
OUT LIKE A LIGHT
We're heading off. I need to get her home.
Aghhh!
...MY FRIENDS DEFINITELY GOT THE WRONG IDEA!
They probably thought we were doing something else!
SORRY.
YOU DON'T NEED TO APOLOGIZE.
I'M SORRY...
JUNYA...?

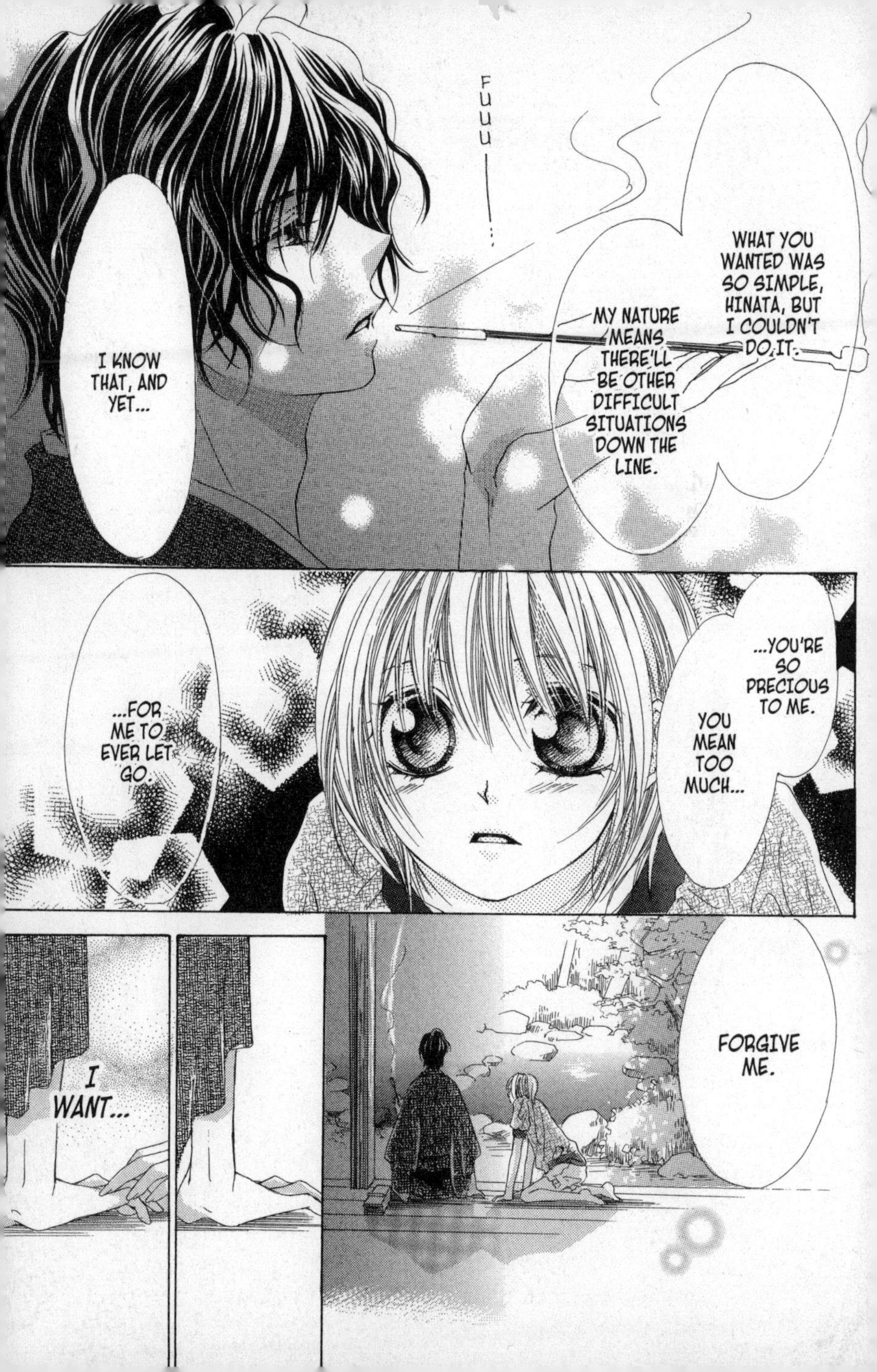

WHAT YOU WANTED WAS SO SIMPLE, HINATA, BUT I COULDN'T DO IT.
MY NATURE MEANS THERE'LL BE OTHER DIFFICULT SITUATIONS DOWN THE LINE.
FUUU—...
I KNOW THAT, AND YET...
...YOU'RE SO PRECIOUS TO ME.
YOU MEAN TOO MUCH...
...FOR ME TO EVER LET GO.
FORGIVE ME.
I WANT...

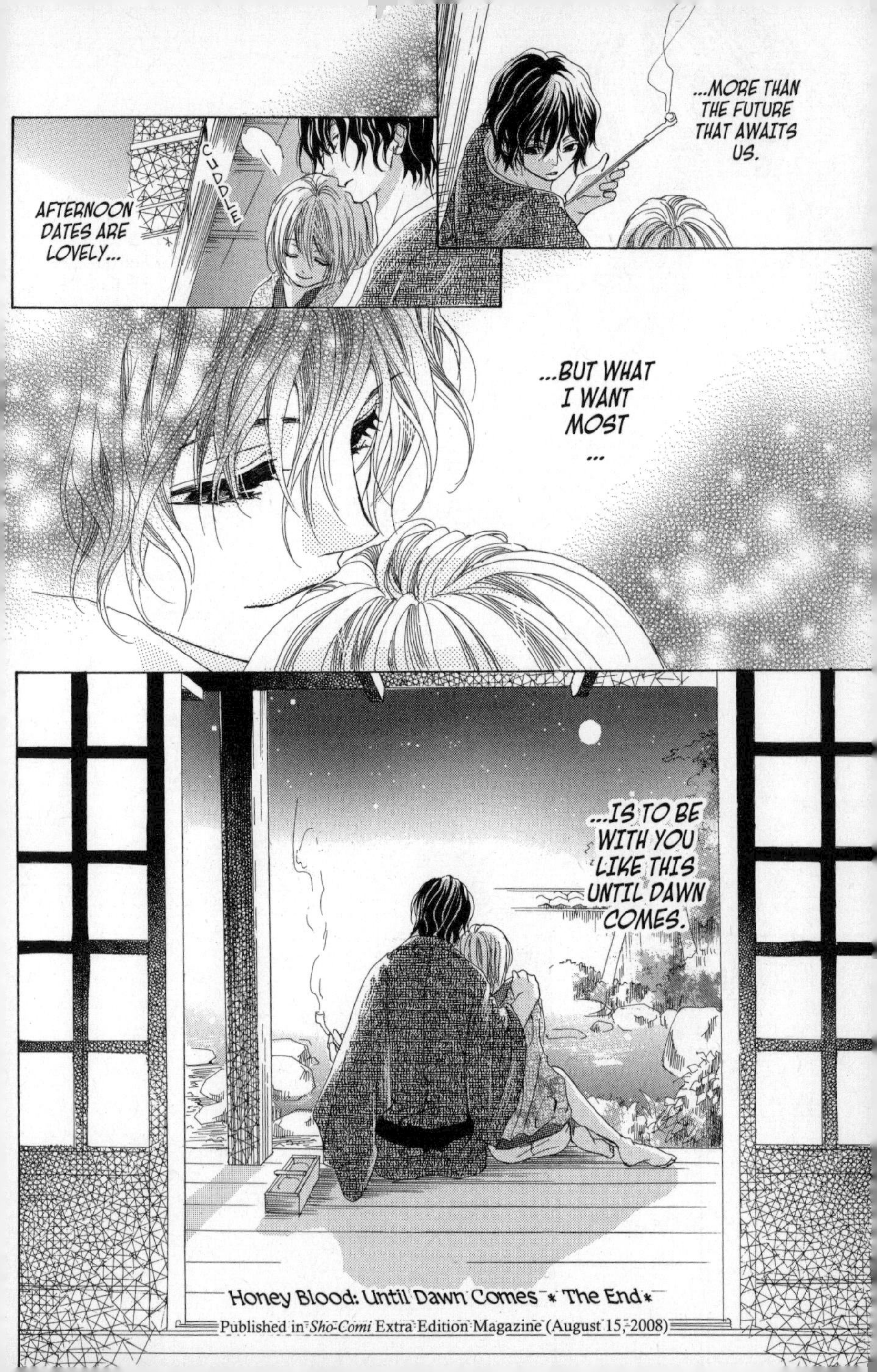
...MORE THAN THE FUTURE THAT AWAITS US.
AFTERNOON DATES ARE LOVELY...
CUDDLE
...BUT WHAT I WANT MOST ...
...IS TO BE WITH YOU LIKE THIS UNTIL DAWN COMES.
Honey Blood: Until Dawn Comes * The End*

Published in *Sho-Comi* Extra Edition Magazine (August 15, 2008)

✿ "Until Dawn Comes" ✿

The second short story! Thankfully, the first one went over well, so I had the opportunity to write this one. ⌣ ⸙
I was over the moon when I got to draw the front cover illustration and some color interior artwork for the magazine! ⸙ I love the cover I did. ⌣

Story-wise, I think I managed to successfully draw Hinata as an adorable teenager. ⸙ I also really like Junya's dialogue right at the end. ♪

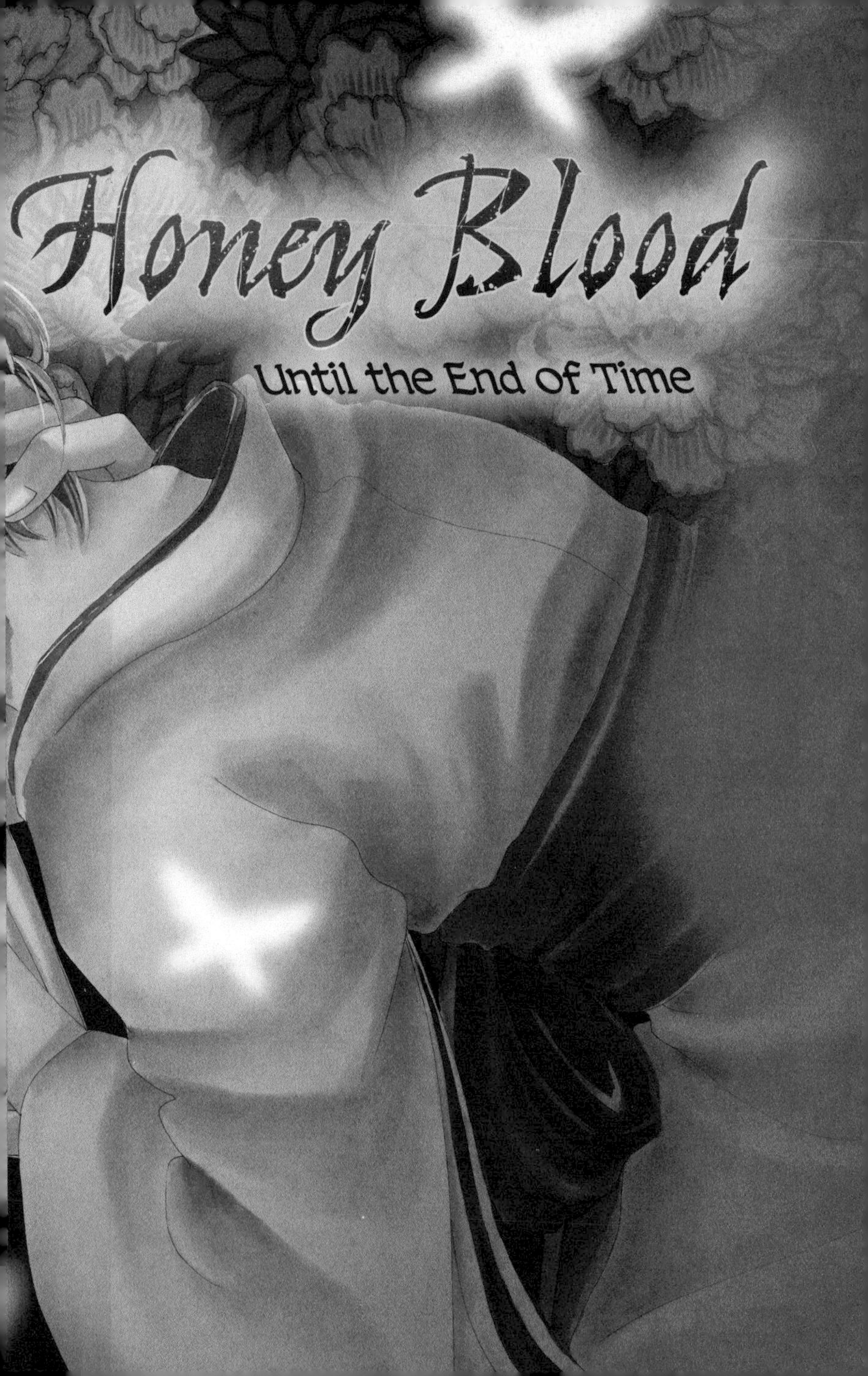
Honey Blood
Until the End of Time

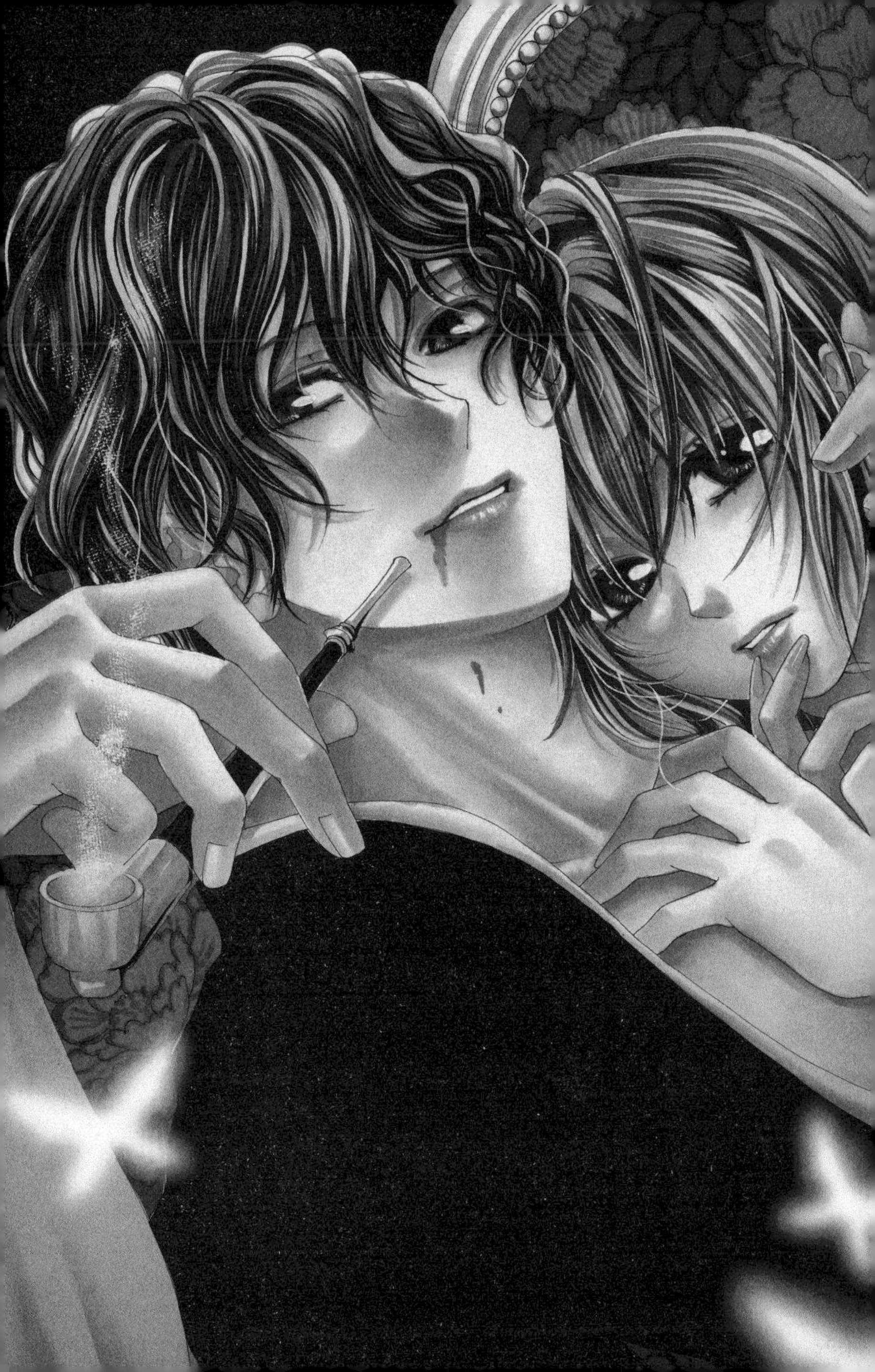

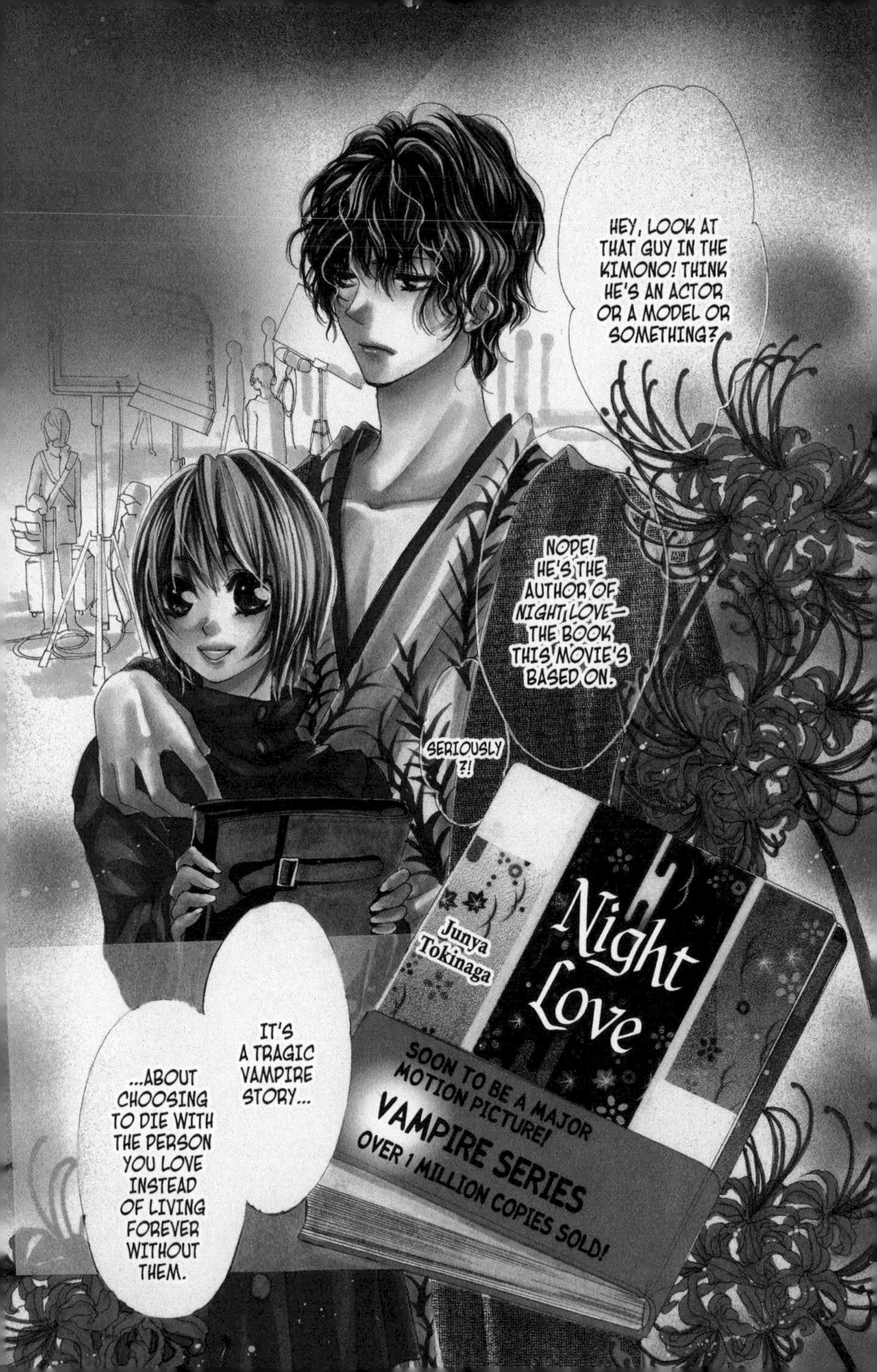
HEY, LOOK AT THAT GUY IN THE KIMONO! THINK HE'S AN ACTOR OR A MODEL OR SOMETHING?
NOPE! HE'S THE AUTHOR OF NIGHT LOVE— THE BOOK THIS MOVIE'S BASED ON.
SERIOUSLY?!
Night Love
Junya Tokinaga
SOON TO BE A MAJOR MOTION PICTURE!
VAMPIRE SERIES
OVER 1 MILLION COPIES SOLD!
IT'S A TRAGIC VAMPIRE STORY...
...ABOUT CHOOSING TO DIE WITH THE PERSON YOU LOVE INSTEAD OF LIVING FOREVER WITHOUT THEM.

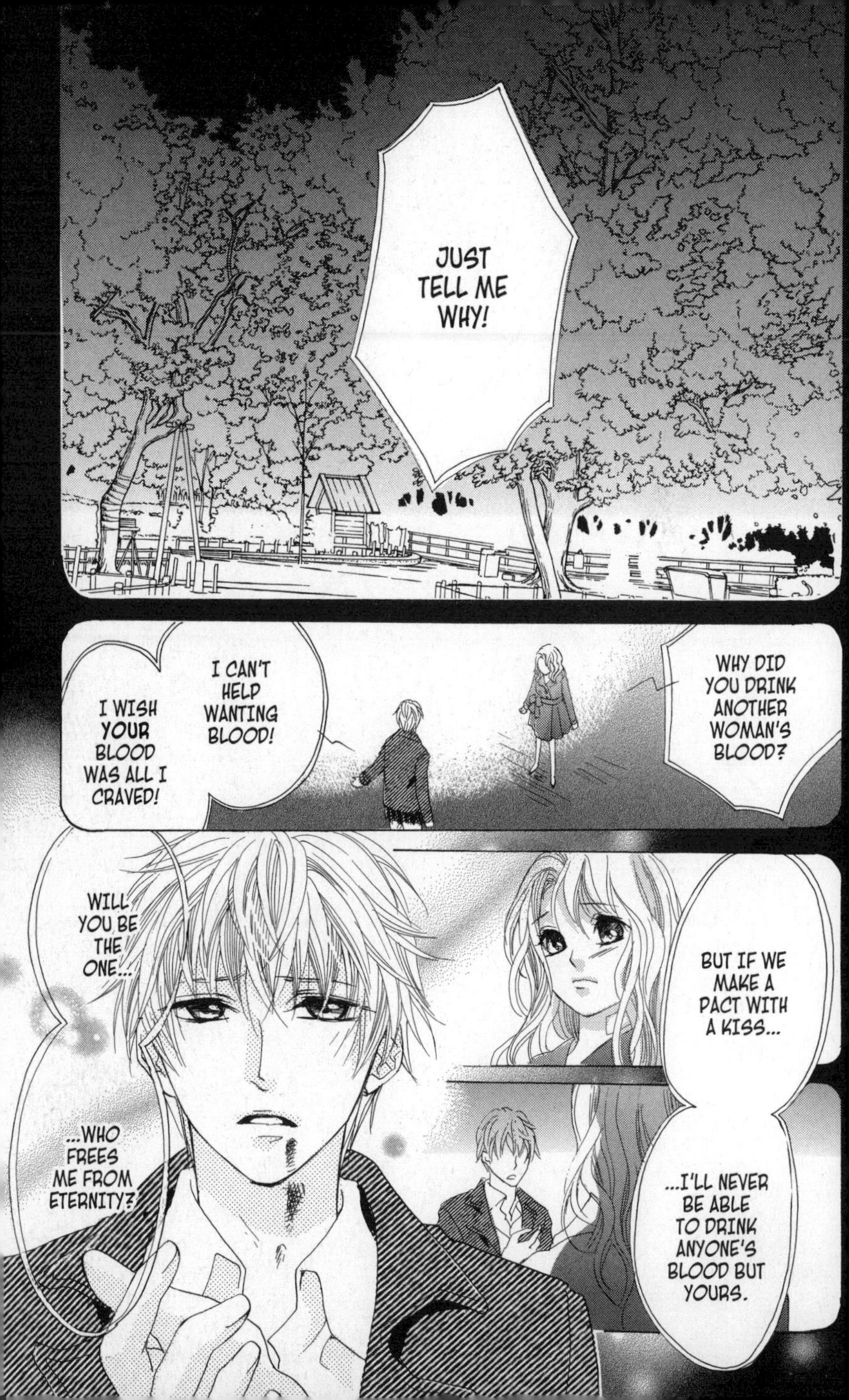
JUST TELL ME WHY!
WHY DID YOU DRINK ANOTHER WOMAN'S BLOOD?
I CAN'T HELP WANTING BLOOD!
I WISH YOUR BLOOD WAS ALL I CRAVED!
BUT IF WE MAKE A PACT WITH A KISS...
...I'LL NEVER BE ABLE TO DRINK ANYONE'S BLOOD BUT YOURS.
WILL YOU BE THE ONE...
...WHO FREES ME FROM ETERNITY?

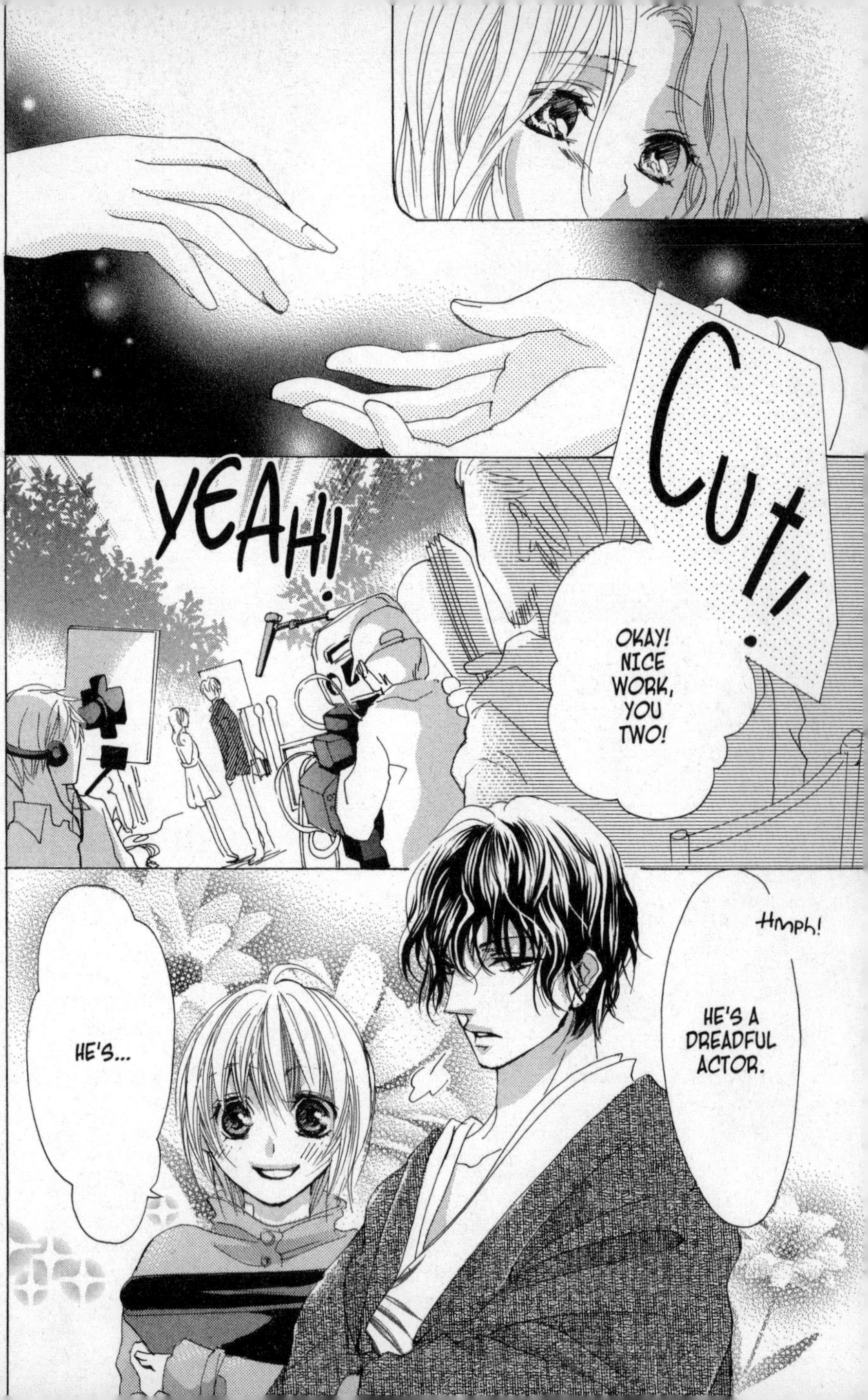
CUT!!
OKAY! NICE WORK, YOU TWO!
YEAH!
Hmph!
HE'S A DREADFUL ACTOR.
HE'S...

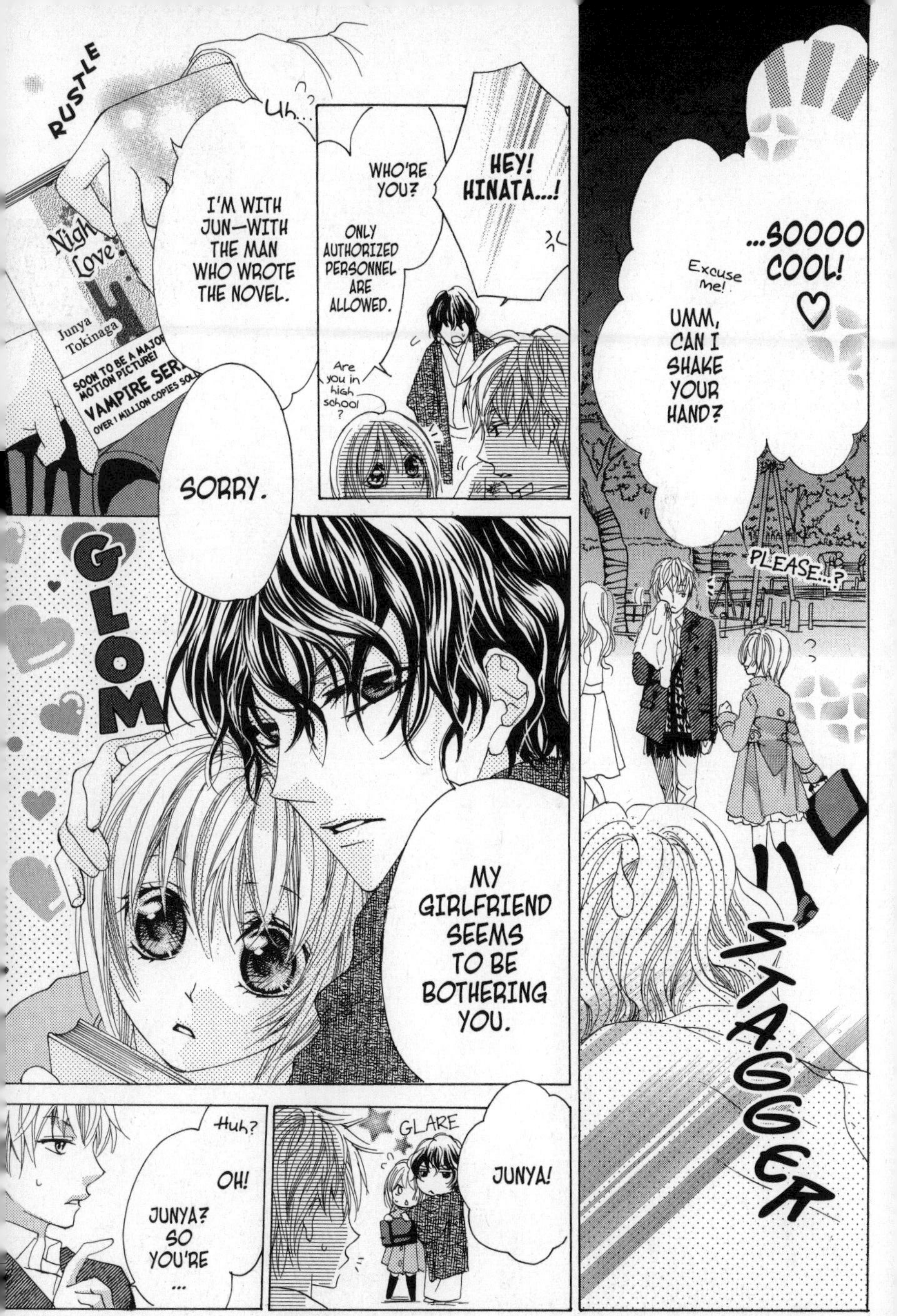
...SOOOO COOL! ♡
Excuse me!
UMM, CAN I SHAKE YOUR HAND?
PLEASE...?
STAGGER
HEY! HINATA...!
WHO'RE YOU?
ONLY AUTHORIZED PERSONNEL ARE ALLOWED.
Are you in high school?
RUSTLE
Uh...
Night Love
Junya Tokinaga
SOON TO BE A MAJOR MOTION PICTURE!
VAMPIRE SER
OVER 1 MILLION COPIES SOL
I'M WITH JUN—WITH THE MAN WHO WROTE THE NOVEL.
SORRY.
GLOM
MY GIRLFRIEND SEEMS TO BE BOTHERING YOU.
GLARE
JUNYA!
Huh?
OH!
JUNYA? SO YOU'RE ...

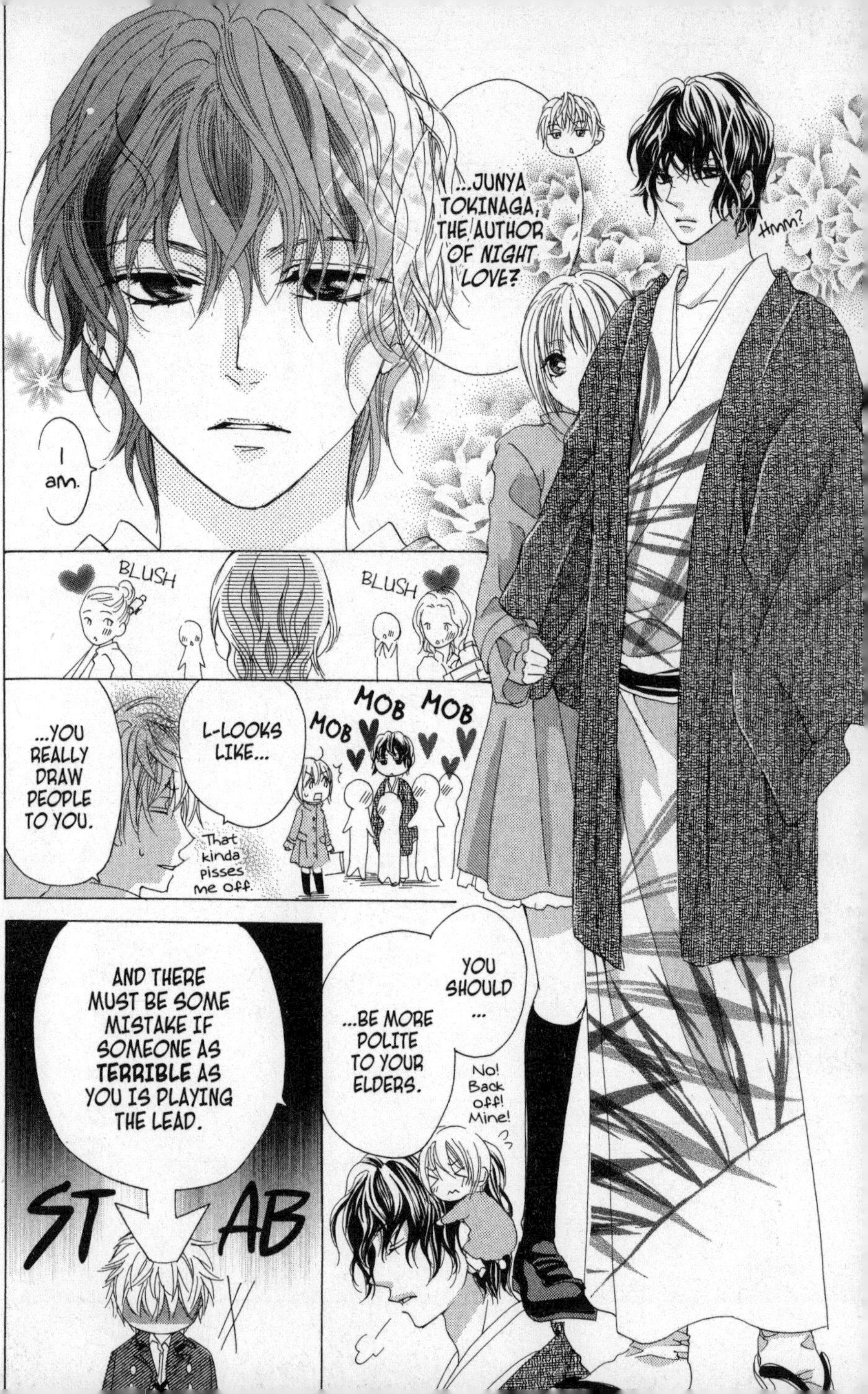
...JUNYA TOKINAGA, THE AUTHOR OF NIGHT LOVE?
Hmm?
I am.
BLUSH
BLUSH
L-LOOKS LIKE...
...YOU REALLY DRAW PEOPLE TO YOU.
MOB MOB
MOB
That kinda pisses me off.
YOU SHOULD ...
...BE MORE POLITE TO YOUR ELDERS.
No! Back off! Mine!
AND THERE MUST BE SOME MISTAKE IF SOMEONE AS TERRIBLE AS YOU IS PLAYING THE LEAD.
ST AB

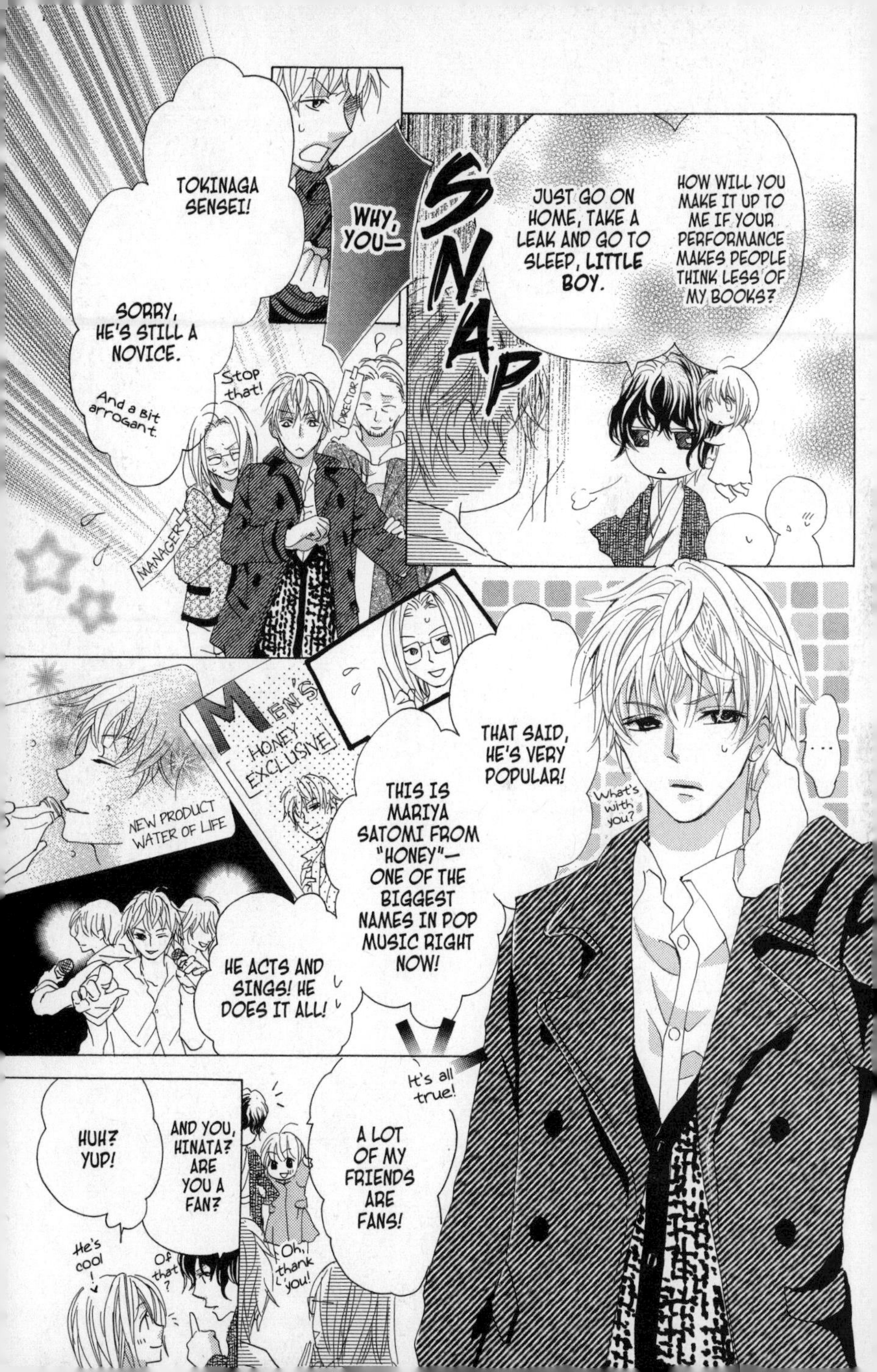
HOW WILL YOU MAKE IT UP TO ME IF YOUR PERFORMANCE MAKES PEOPLE THINK LESS OF MY BOOKS?
JUST GO ON HOME, TAKE A LEAK AND GO TO SLEEP, LITTLE BOY.
SNAP
WHY, YOU—
TOKINAGA SENSEI!
DIRECTOR
SORRY, HE'S STILL A NOVICE.
Stop that!
And a bit arrogant.
MANAGER
...
What's with you?
THAT SAID, HE'S VERY POPULAR!
THIS IS MARIYA SATOMI FROM "HONEY"—ONE OF THE BIGGEST NAMES IN POP MUSIC RIGHT NOW!
MEN'S
HONEY EXCLUSIVE
NEW PRODUCT WATER OF LIFE
HE ACTS AND SINGS! HE DOES IT ALL!
A LOT OF MY FRIENDS ARE FANS!
It's all true!
Oh, thank you!
AND YOU, HINATA? ARE YOU A FAN?
HUH? YUP!
Of that?
He's cool

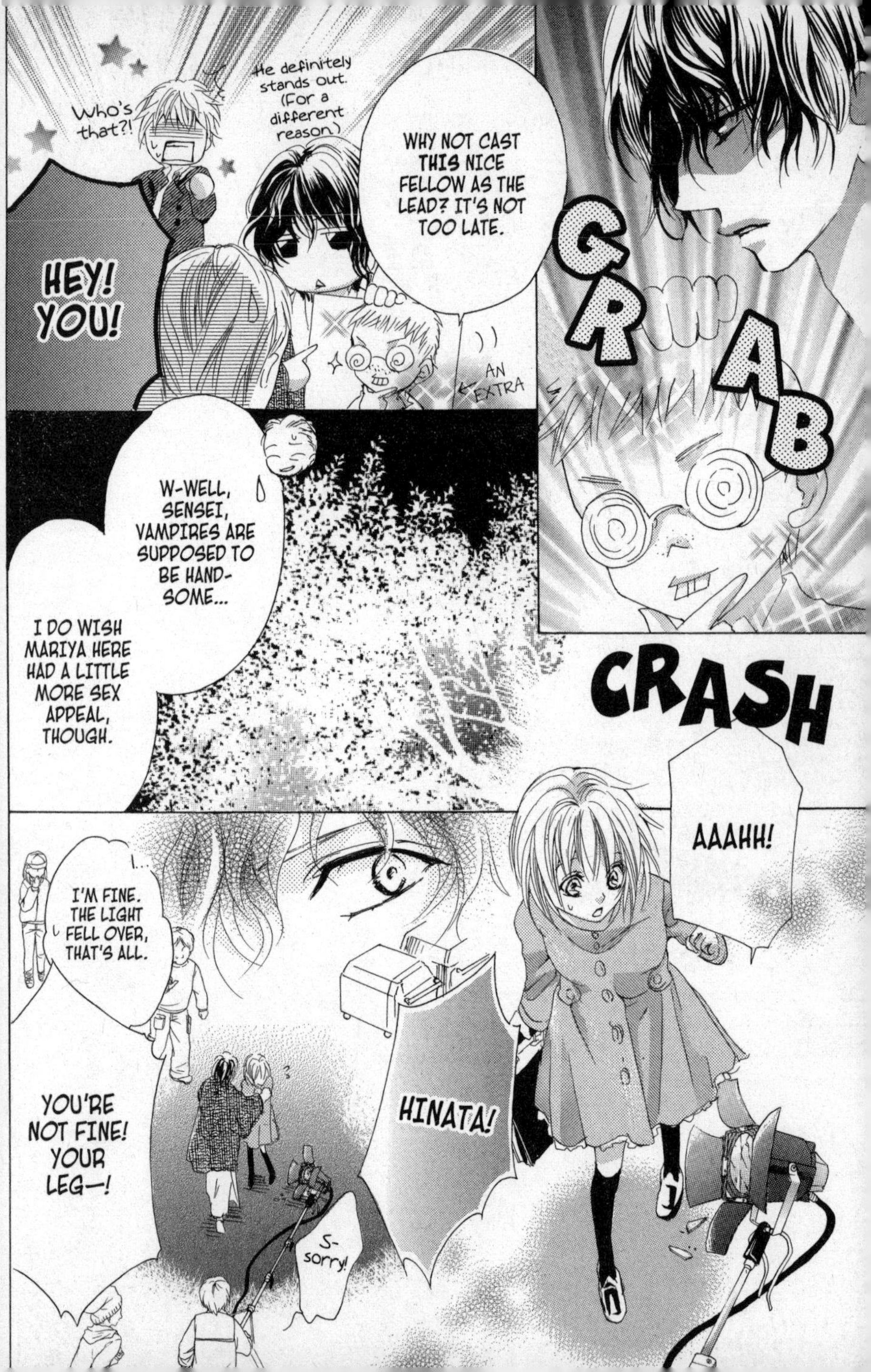
GRAB
WHY NOT CAST THIS NICE FELLOW AS THE LEAD? IT'S NOT TOO LATE.
He definitely stands out. (For a different reason.)
Who's that?!
HEY! YOU!
AN EXTRA
W-WELL, SENSEI, VAMPIRES ARE SUPPOSED TO BE HANDSOME...
I DO WISH MARIYA HERE HAD A LITTLE MORE SEX APPEAL, THOUGH.
CRASH
AAAHH!
HINATA!
I...
I'M FINE. THE LIGHT FELL OVER, THAT'S ALL.
YOU'RE NOT FINE! YOUR LEG—!
S-sorry!

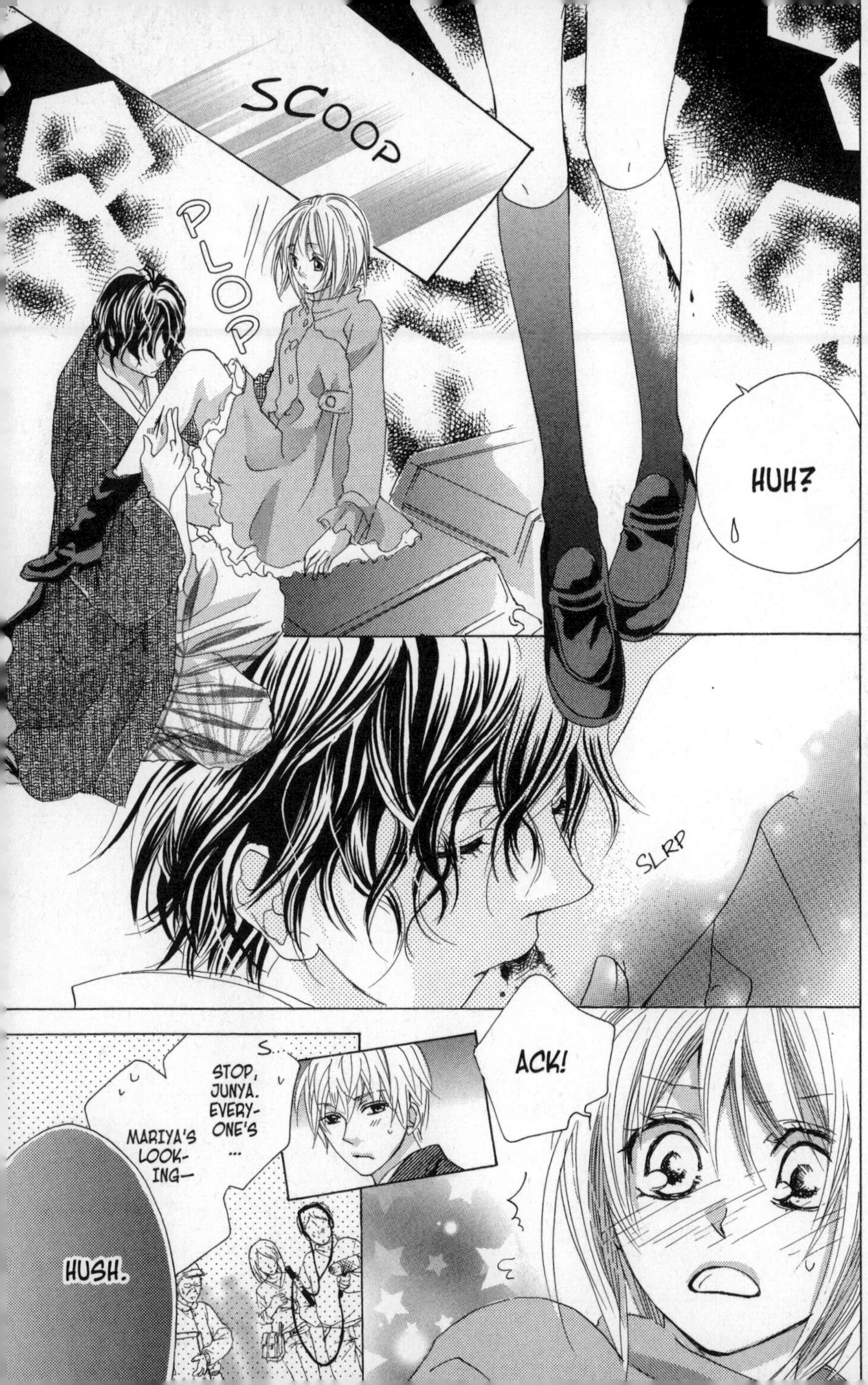
HUH?
SCOOP
PLOP
SLRP
ACK!
S...
STOP, JUNYA. EVERY-ONE'S ...
MARIYA'S LOOK-ING—
HUSH.

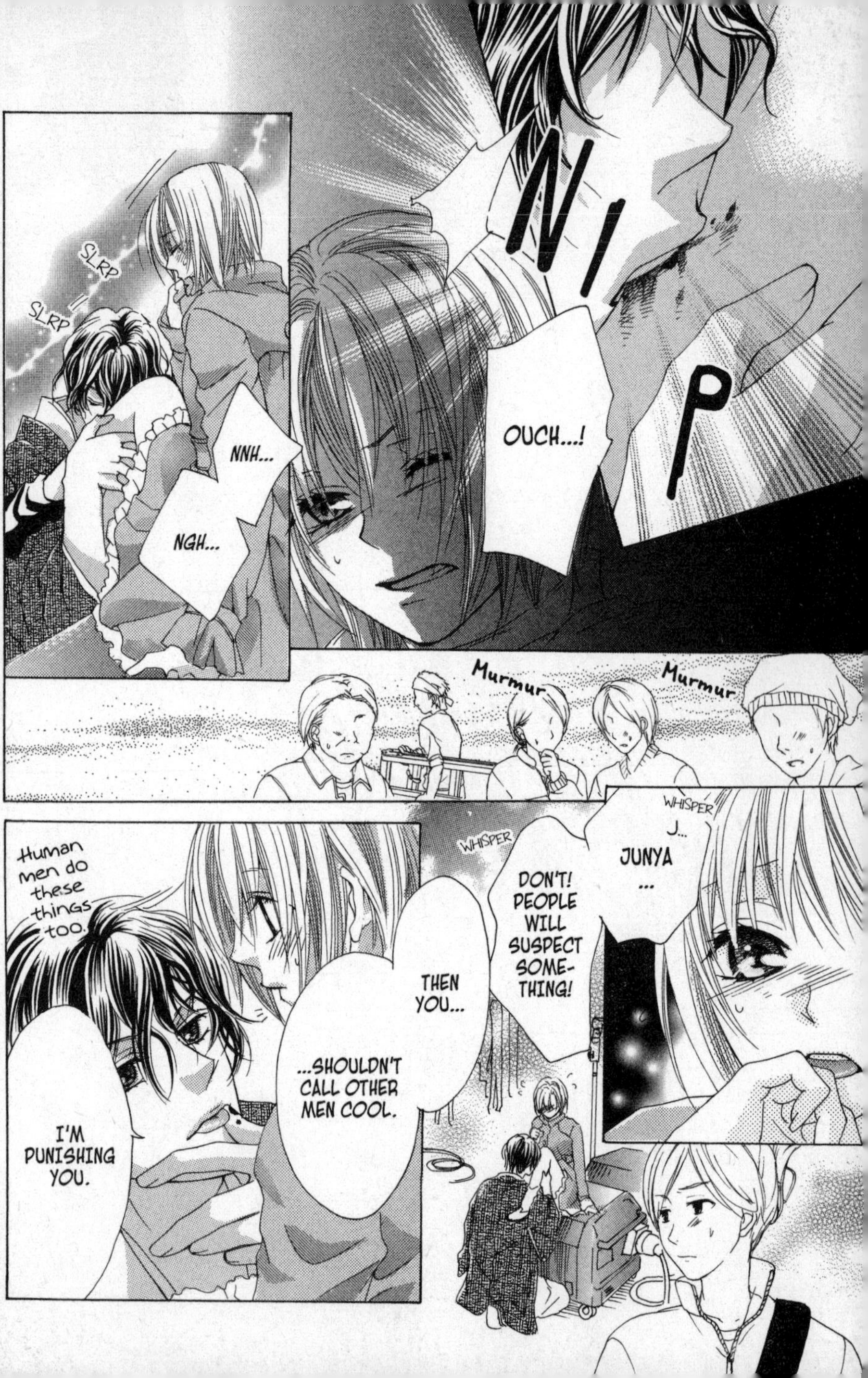
NIP
OUCH...!
SLRP
SLRP
NNH...
NGH...
Murmur
Murmur
WHISPER
J...
JUNYA
...
WHISPER
DON'T! PEOPLE WILL SUSPECT SOME-THING!
THEN YOU...
...SHOULDN'T CALL OTHER MEN COOL.
Human men do these things too.
I'M PUNISHING YOU.

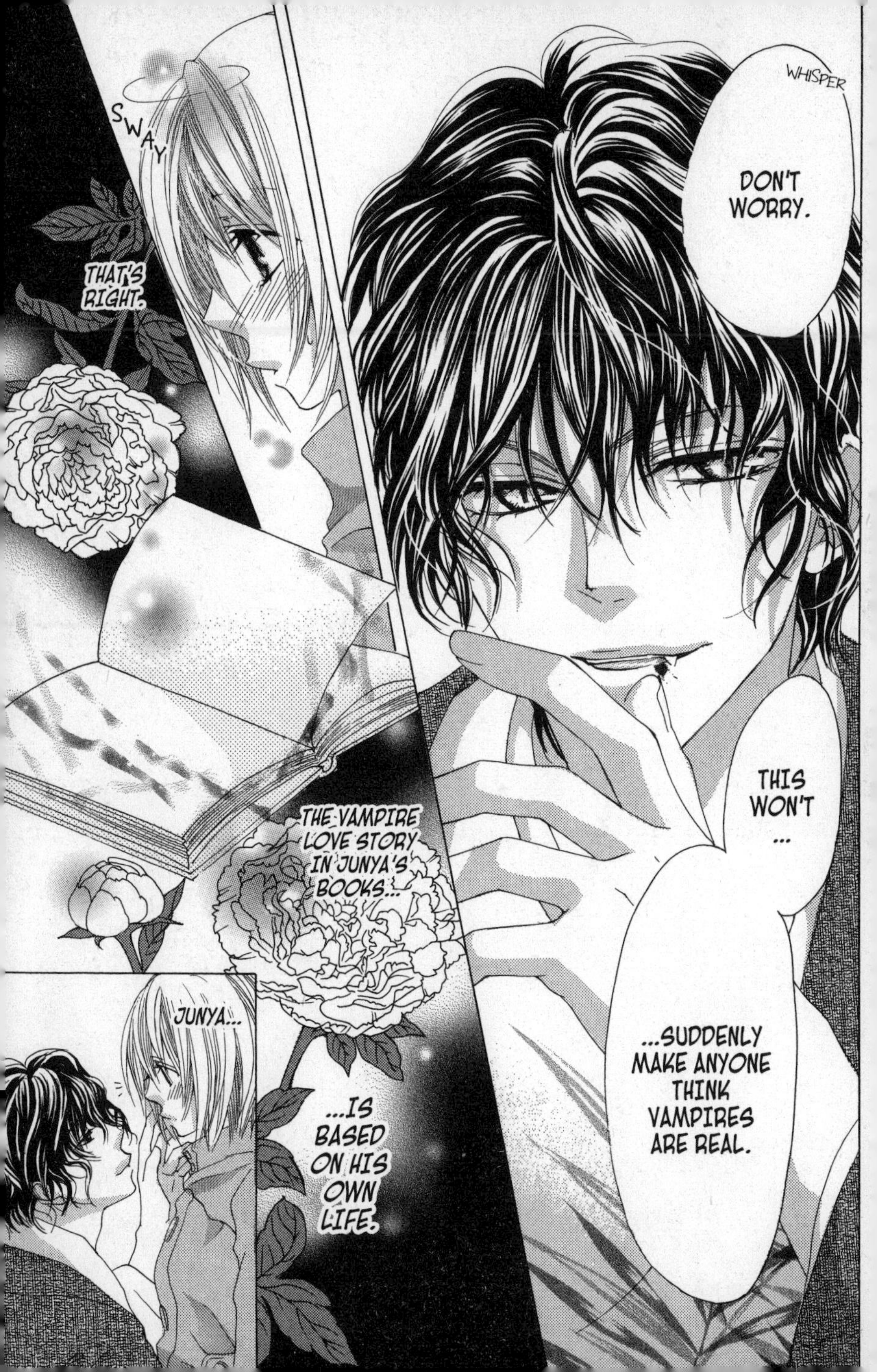
WHISPER
DON'T WORRY.
THIS WON'T ...
...SUDDENLY MAKE ANYONE THINK VAMPIRES ARE REAL.
SWAY
THAT'S RIGHT.
THE VAMPIRE LOVE STORY IN JUNYA'S BOOKS...
JUNYA...
...IS BASED ON HIS OWN LIFE.

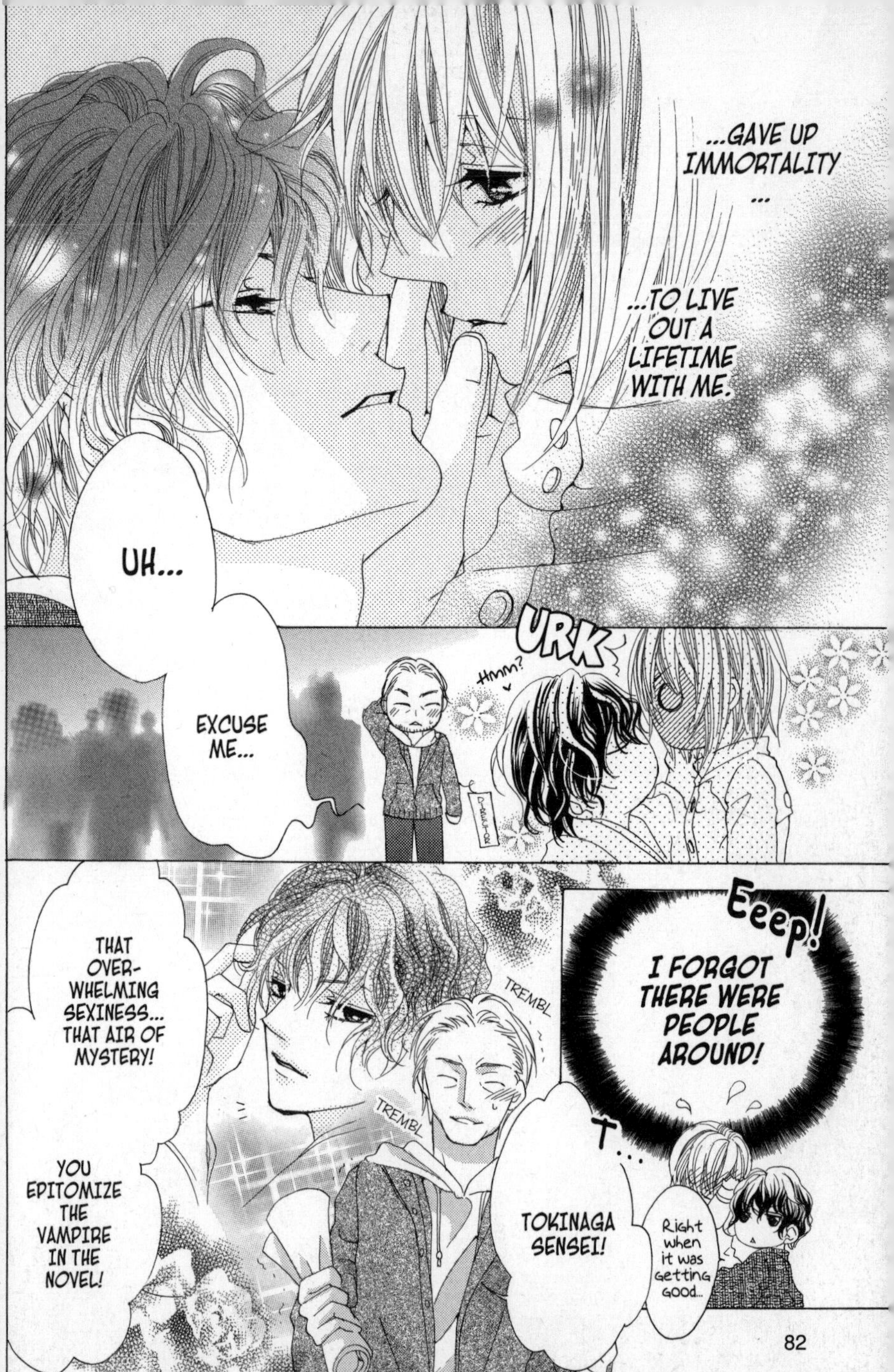
...GAVE UP IMMORTALITY ...
...TO LIVE OUT A LIFETIME WITH ME.
UH...
URK
Hmm?
EXCUSE ME...
DIRECTOR
Eeep!
I FORGOT THERE WERE PEOPLE AROUND!
Right when it was getting good...
T...
TOKINAGA SENSEI!
TREMBL
TREMBL
THAT OVER-WHELMING SEXINESS... THAT AIR OF MYSTERY!
YOU EPITOMIZE THE VAMPIRE IN THE NOVEL!

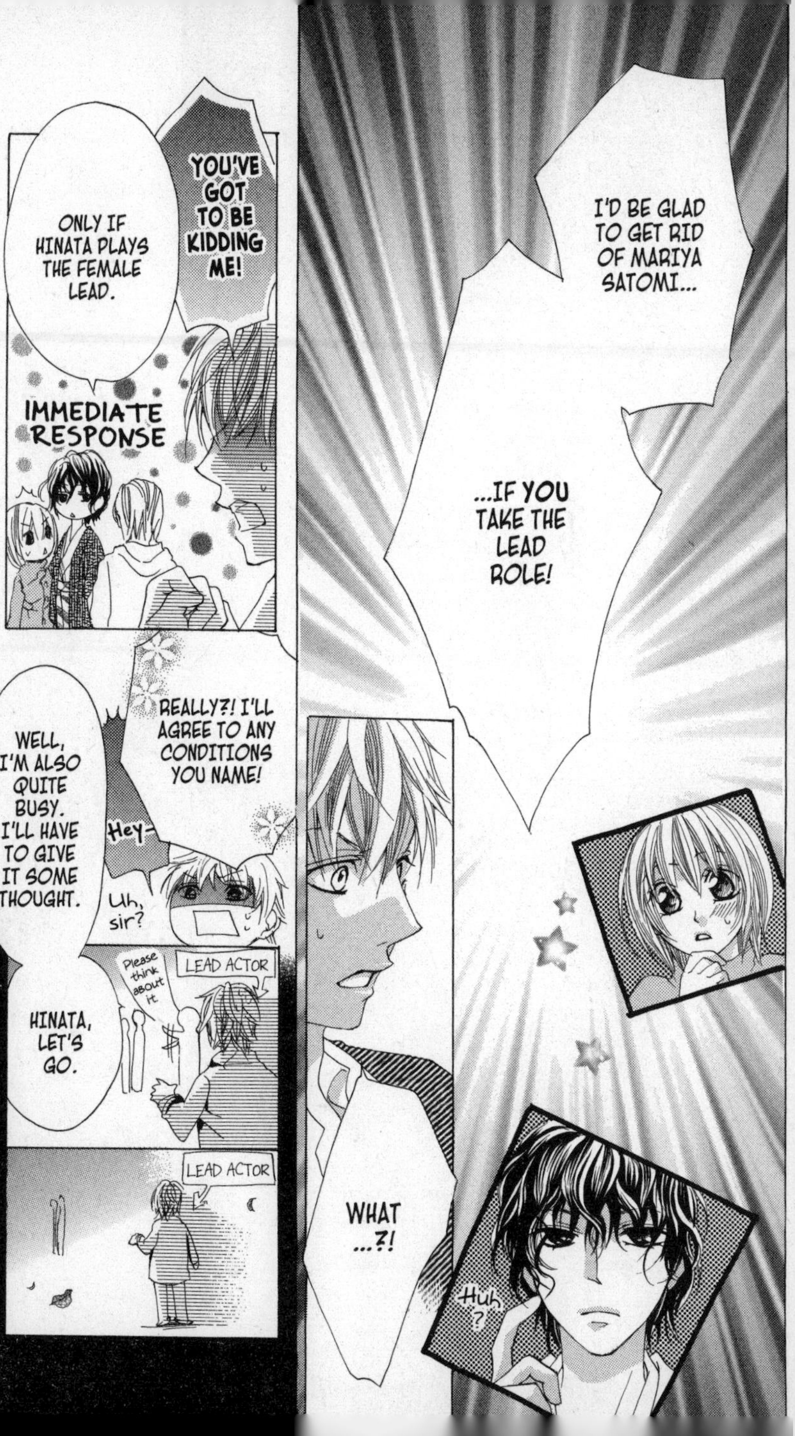
I'D BE GLAD TO GET RID OF MARIYA SATOMI...
...IF YOU TAKE THE LEAD ROLE!
WHAT ...?!
Huh ?
YOU'VE GOT TO BE KIDDING ME!
ONLY IF HINATA PLAYS THE FEMALE LEAD.
IMMEDIATE RESPONSE
REALLY?! I'LL AGREE TO ANY CONDITIONS YOU NAME!
Hey-
Uh, sir?
WELL, I'M ALSO QUITE BUSY. I'LL HAVE TO GIVE IT SOME THOUGHT.
LEAD ACTOR
Please think about it
HINATA, LET'S GO.
LEAD ACTOR

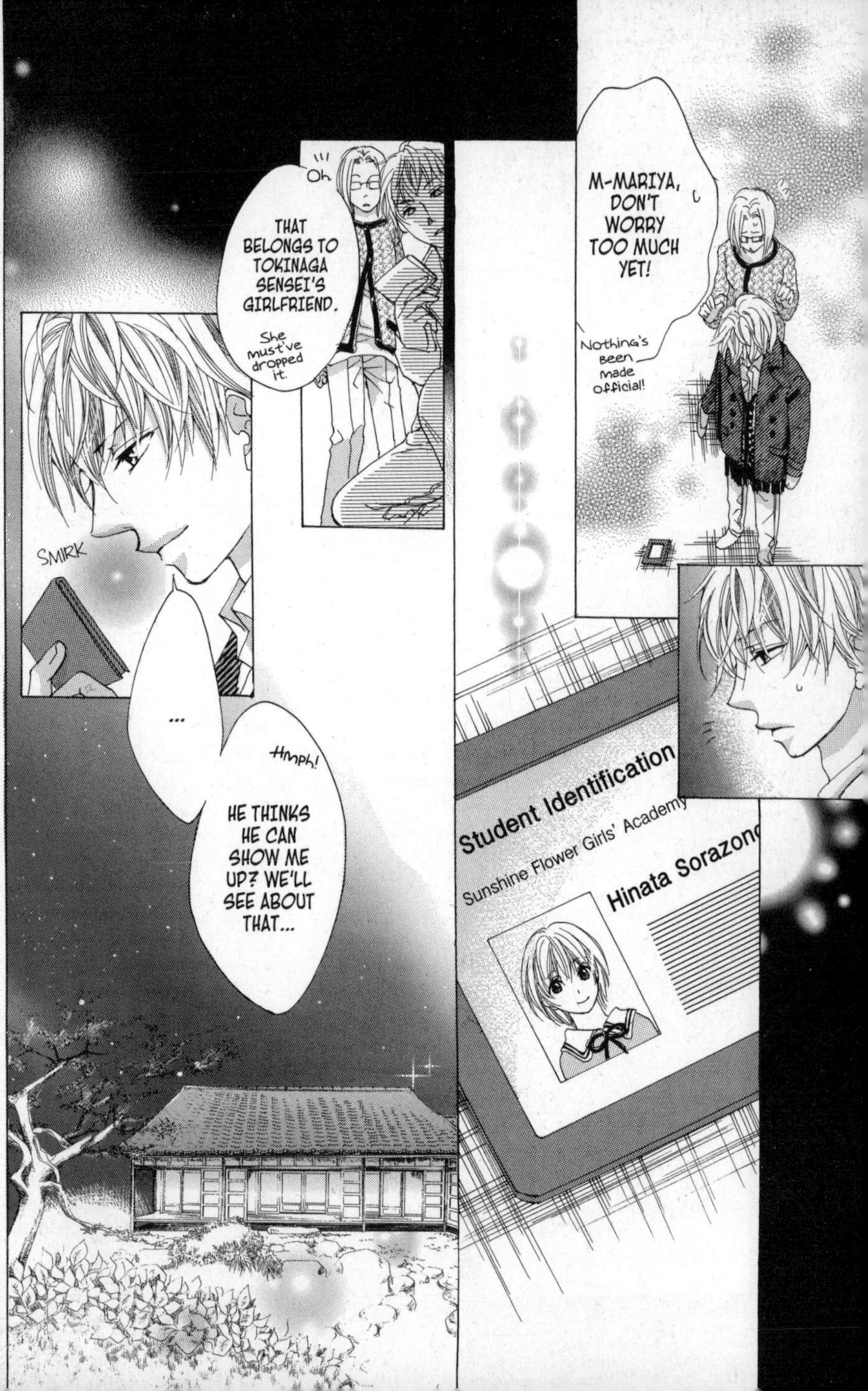
M-MARIYA, DON'T WORRY TOO MUCH YET!
Nothing's been made official!
Oh.
THAT BELONGS TO TOKINAGA SENSEI'S GIRLFRIEND.
She must've dropped it.
Student Identification
Sunshine Flower Girls' Academy
Hinata Sorazono
SMIRK
...
Hmph!
HE THINKS HE CAN SHOW ME UP? WE'LL SEE ABOUT THAT...

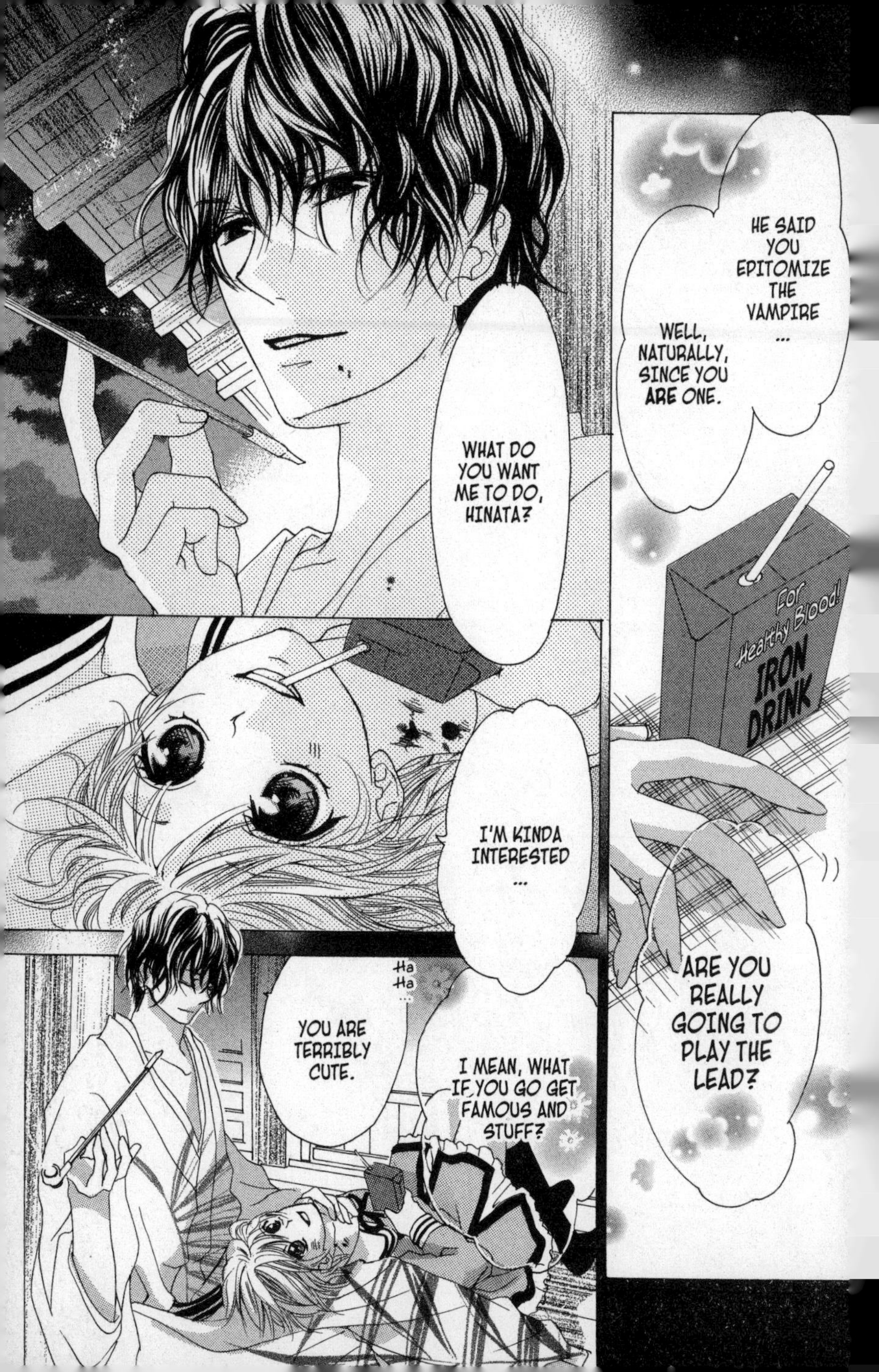
HE SAID YOU EPITOMIZE THE VAMPIRE ...
WELL, NATURALLY, SINCE YOU ARE ONE.
For Healthy Blood!
IRON DRINK
ARE YOU REALLY GOING TO PLAY THE LEAD?
WHAT DO YOU WANT ME TO DO, HINATA?
I'M KINDA INTERESTED ...
I MEAN, WHAT IF YOU GO GET FAMOUS AND STUFF?
Ha Ha ...
YOU ARE TERRIBLY CUTE.

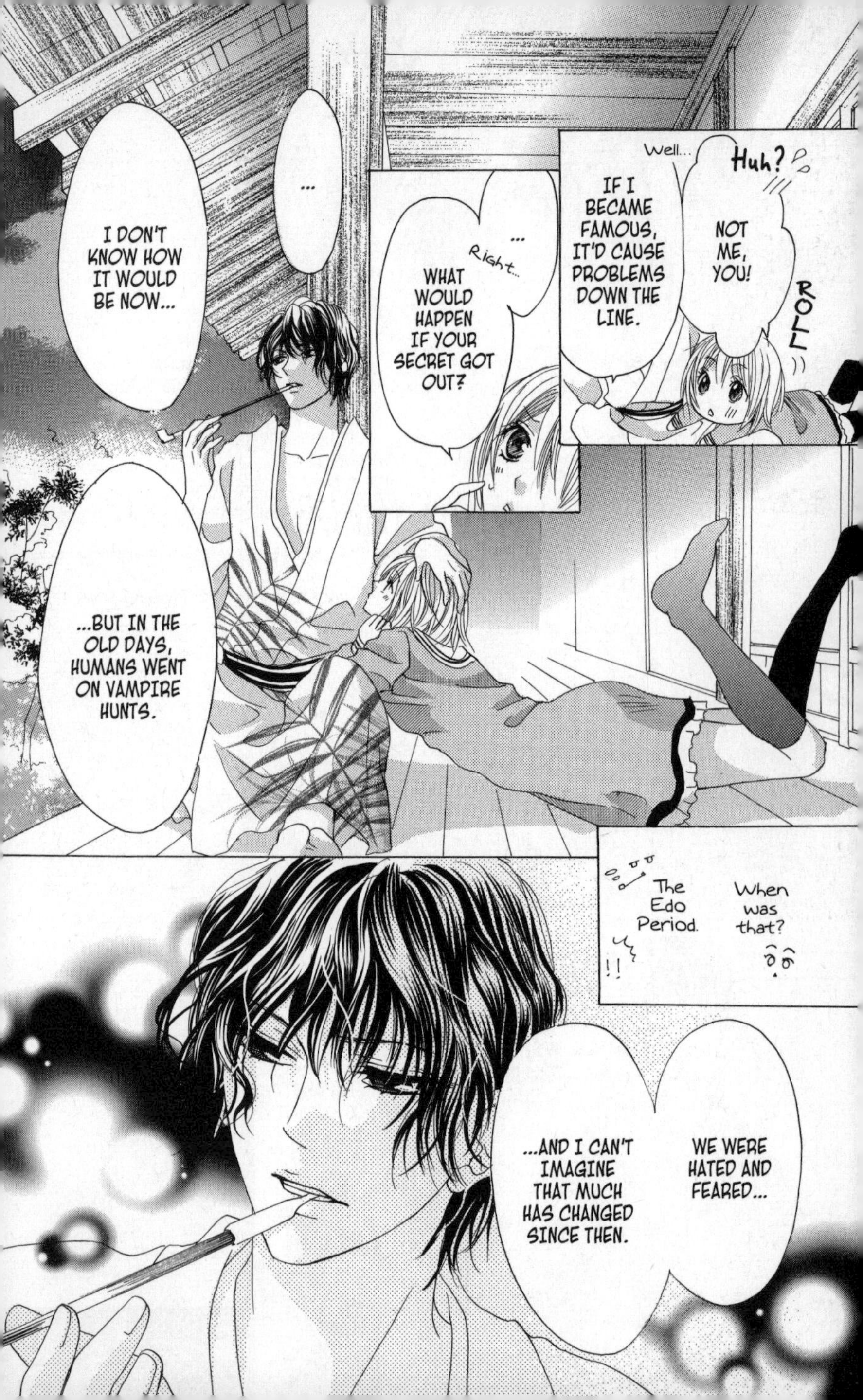
Huh?
NOT ME, YOU!
ROLL
Well...
IF I BECAME FAMOUS, IT'D CAUSE PROBLEMS DOWN THE LINE.
...
Right...
WHAT WOULD HAPPEN IF YOUR SECRET GOT OUT?
...
I DON'T KNOW HOW IT WOULD BE NOW...
...BUT IN THE OLD DAYS, HUMANS WENT ON VAMPIRE HUNTS.
When was that?
The Edo Period.
!!
WE WERE HATED AND FEARED...
...AND I CAN'T IMAGINE THAT MUCH HAS CHANGED SINCE THEN.

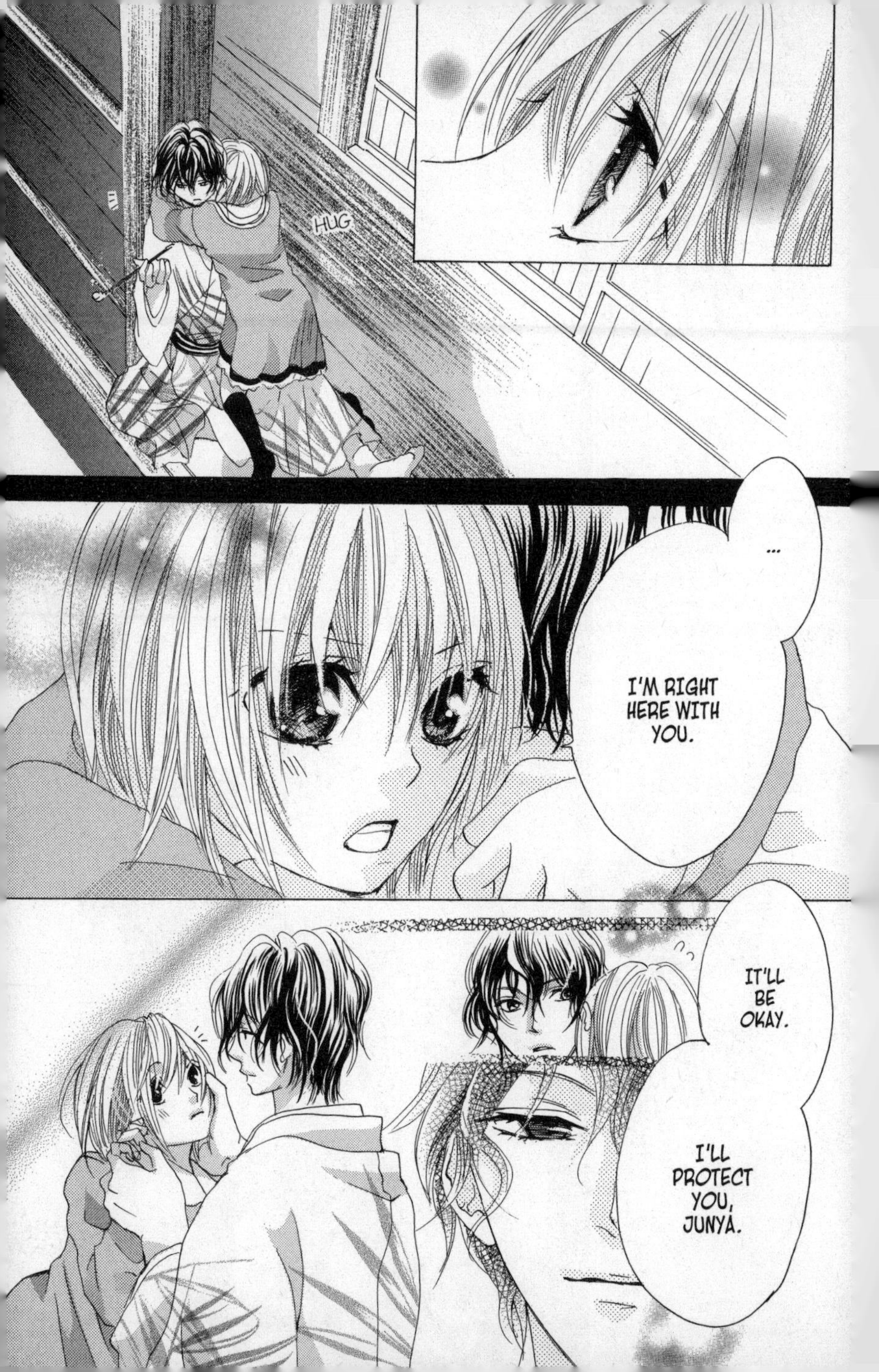
HUG
...
I'M RIGHT HERE WITH YOU.
IT'LL BE OKAY.
I'LL PROTECT YOU, JUNYA.

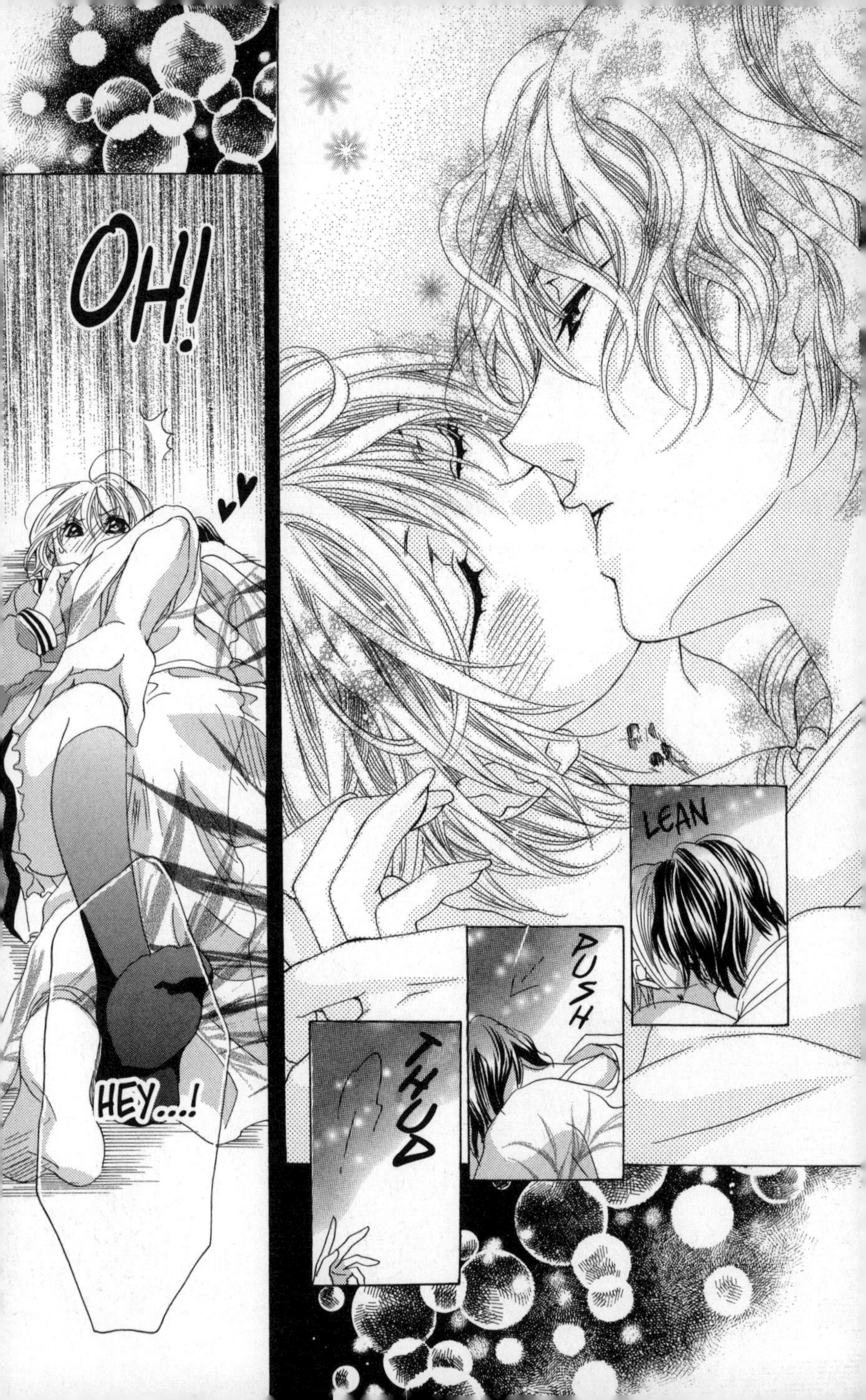
LEAN
PUSH
THUD
OH!
HEY...!

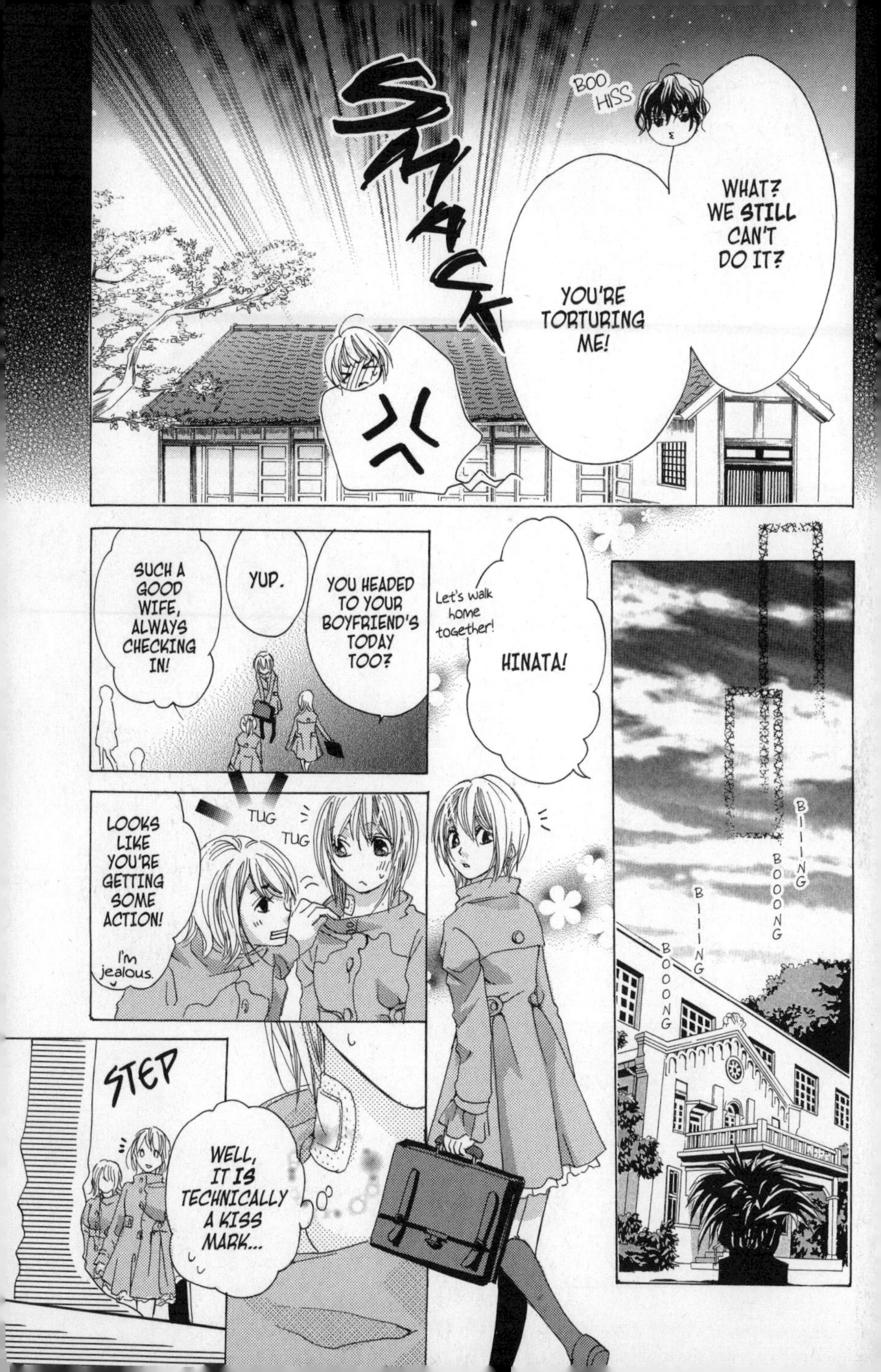

WHAT? WE STILL CAN'T DO IT?
BOO HISS
YOU'RE TORTURING ME!
SMACK
BIING
BOOONG
BIING
BOOONG
HINATA!
Let's walk home together!
YOU HEADED TO YOUR BOYFRIEND'S TODAY TOO?
YUP.
SUCH A GOOD WIFE, ALWAYS CHECKING IN!
TUG
TUG
LOOKS LIKE YOU'RE GETTING SOME ACTION!
I'm jealous.
WELL, IT IS TECHNICALLY A KISS MARK...
STEP

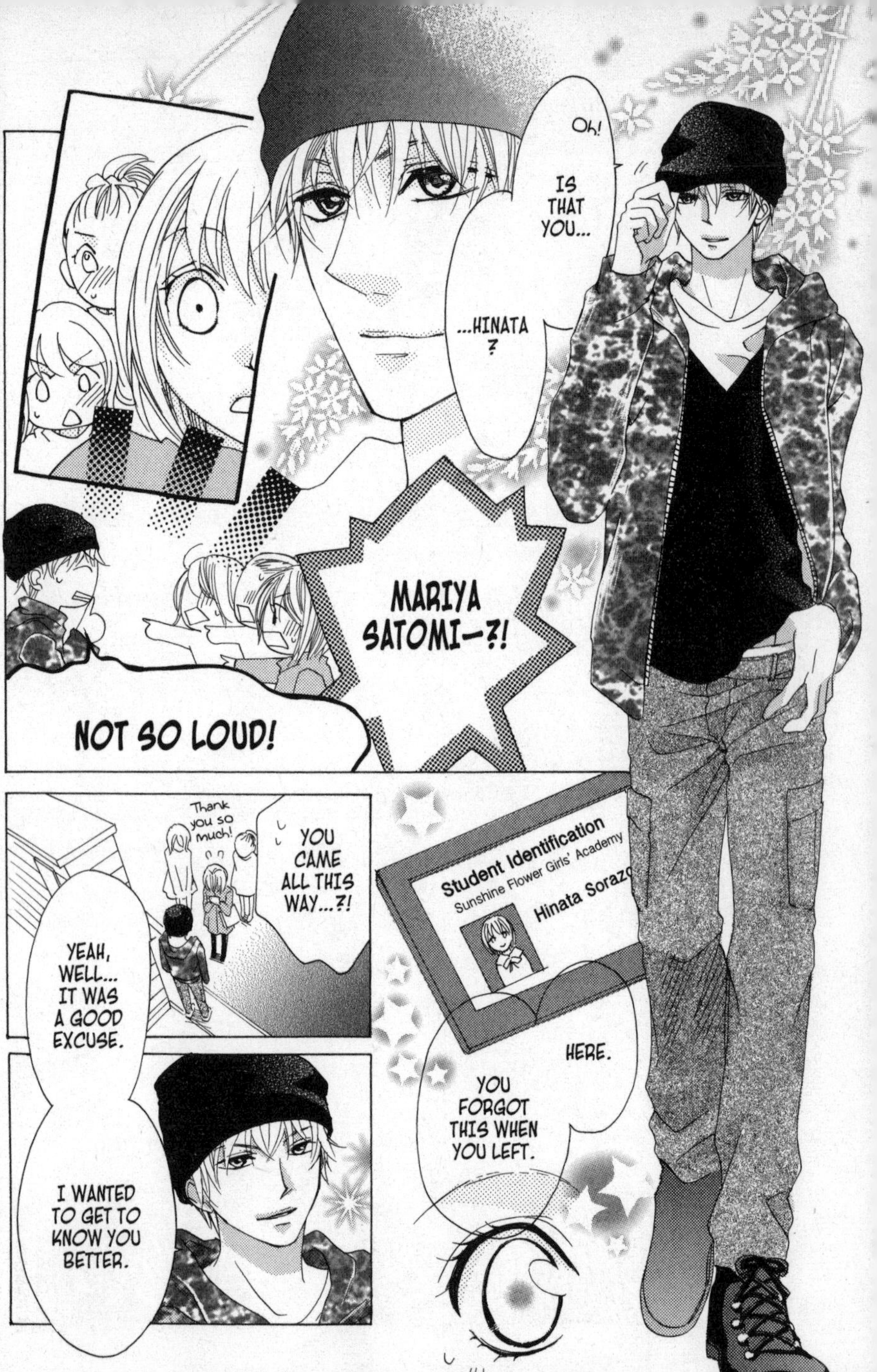
Oh!
IS THAT YOU...
...HINATA?
Student Identification
Sunshine Flower Girls' Academy
Hinata Sorazo
HERE.
YOU FORGOT THIS WHEN YOU LEFT.
MARIYA SATOMI—?!
NOT SO LOUD!
YOU CAME ALL THIS WAY...?!
Thank you so much!
YEAH, WELL... IT WAS A GOOD EXCUSE.
I WANTED TO GET TO KNOW YOU BETTER.

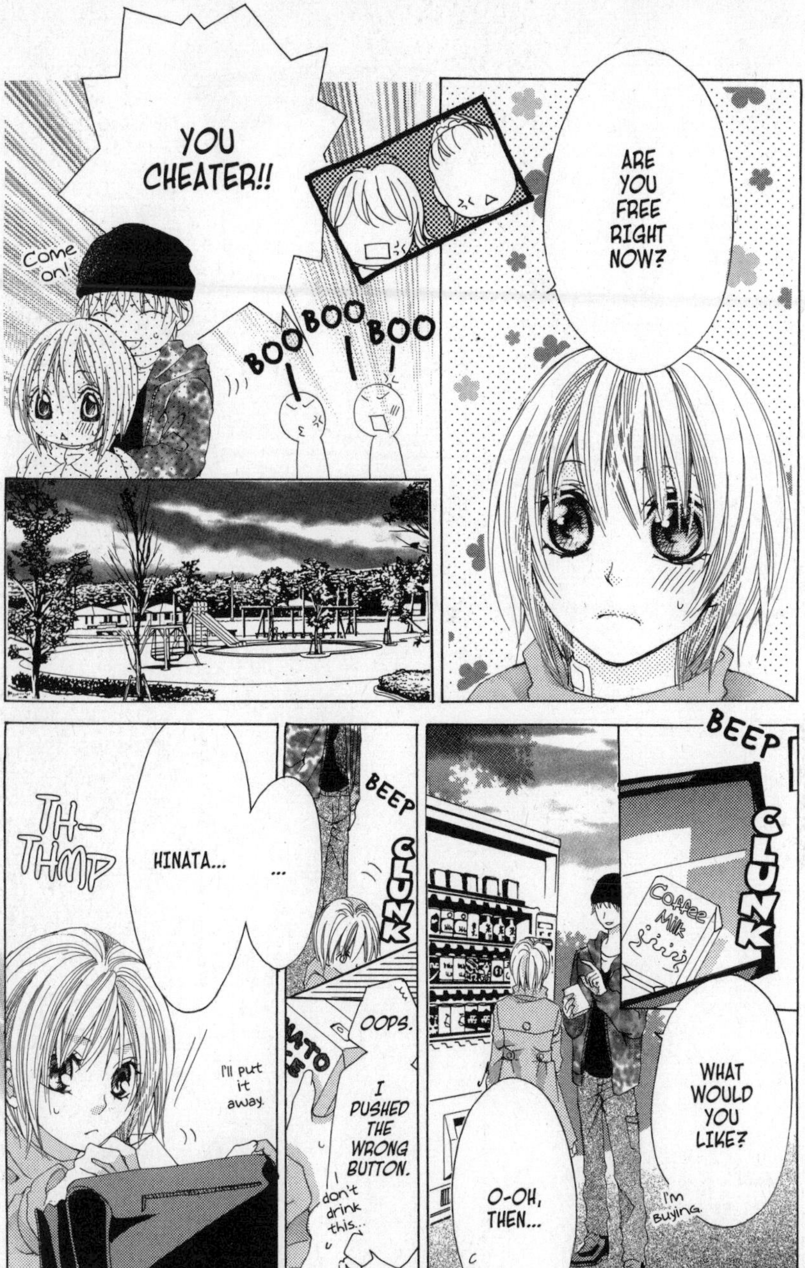
ARE YOU FREE RIGHT NOW?
YOU CHEATER!!
Come on!
BOO BOO BOO
BEEP
CLUNK
WHAT WOULD YOU LIKE?
I'm buying.
O-OH, THEN...
BEEP
CLUNK
OOPS.
I PUSHED THE WRONG BUTTON.
don't drink this...
TH-THMP
HINATA...
...
I'll put it away.

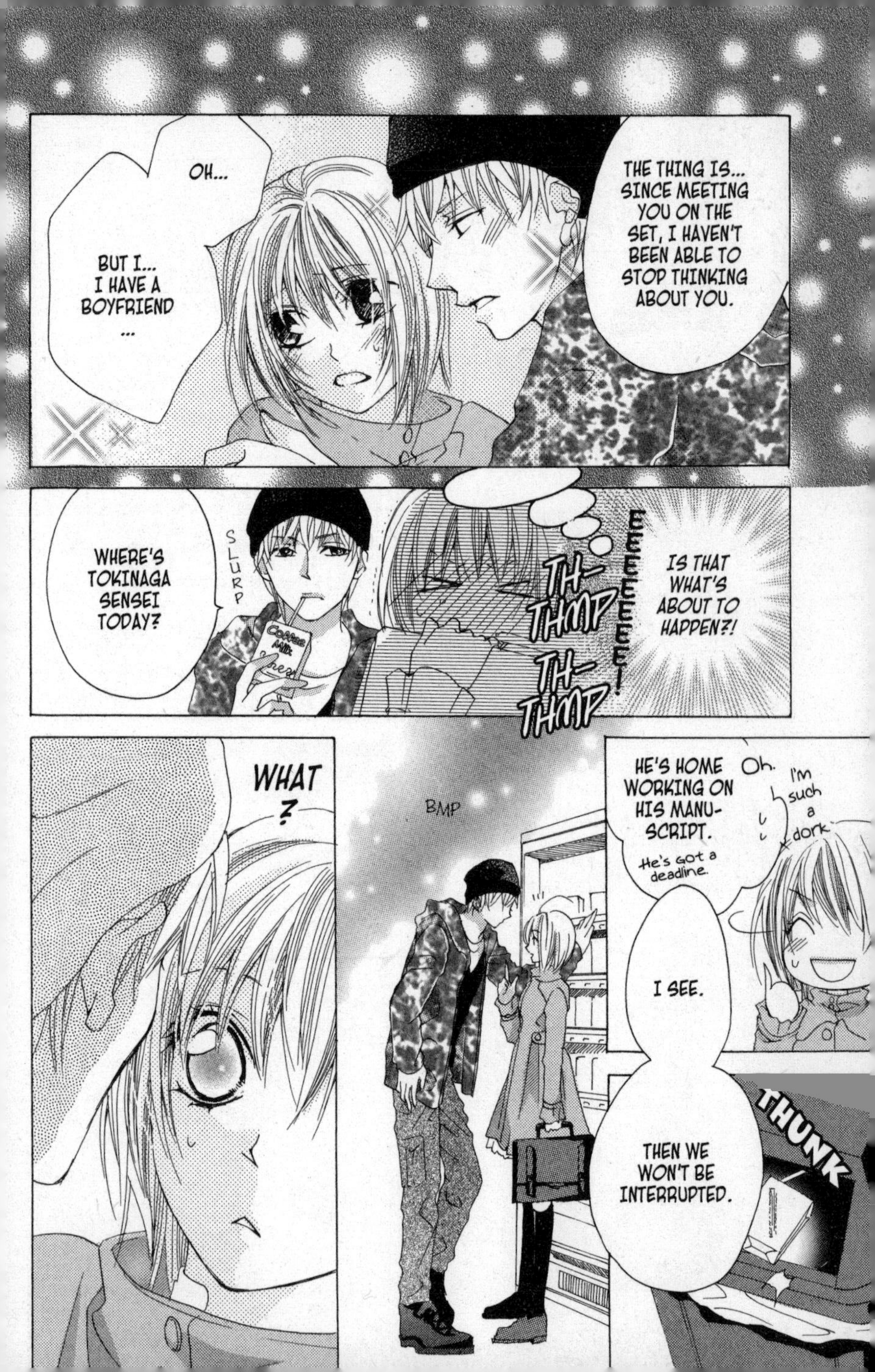
THE THING IS... SINCE MEETING YOU ON THE SET, I HAVEN'T BEEN ABLE TO STOP THINKING ABOUT YOU.
OH...
BUT I... I HAVE A BOYFRIEND ...
IS THAT WHAT'S ABOUT TO HAPPEN?!
EEEEEEEE!
TH-THMP TH-THMP
SLURP
WHERE'S TOKINAGA SENSEI TODAY?
HE'S HOME WORKING ON HIS MANU-SCRIPT.
He's got a deadline.
Oh.
I'm such a dork
I SEE.
BMP
THEN WE WON'T BE INTERRUPTED.
THUNK
WHAT?

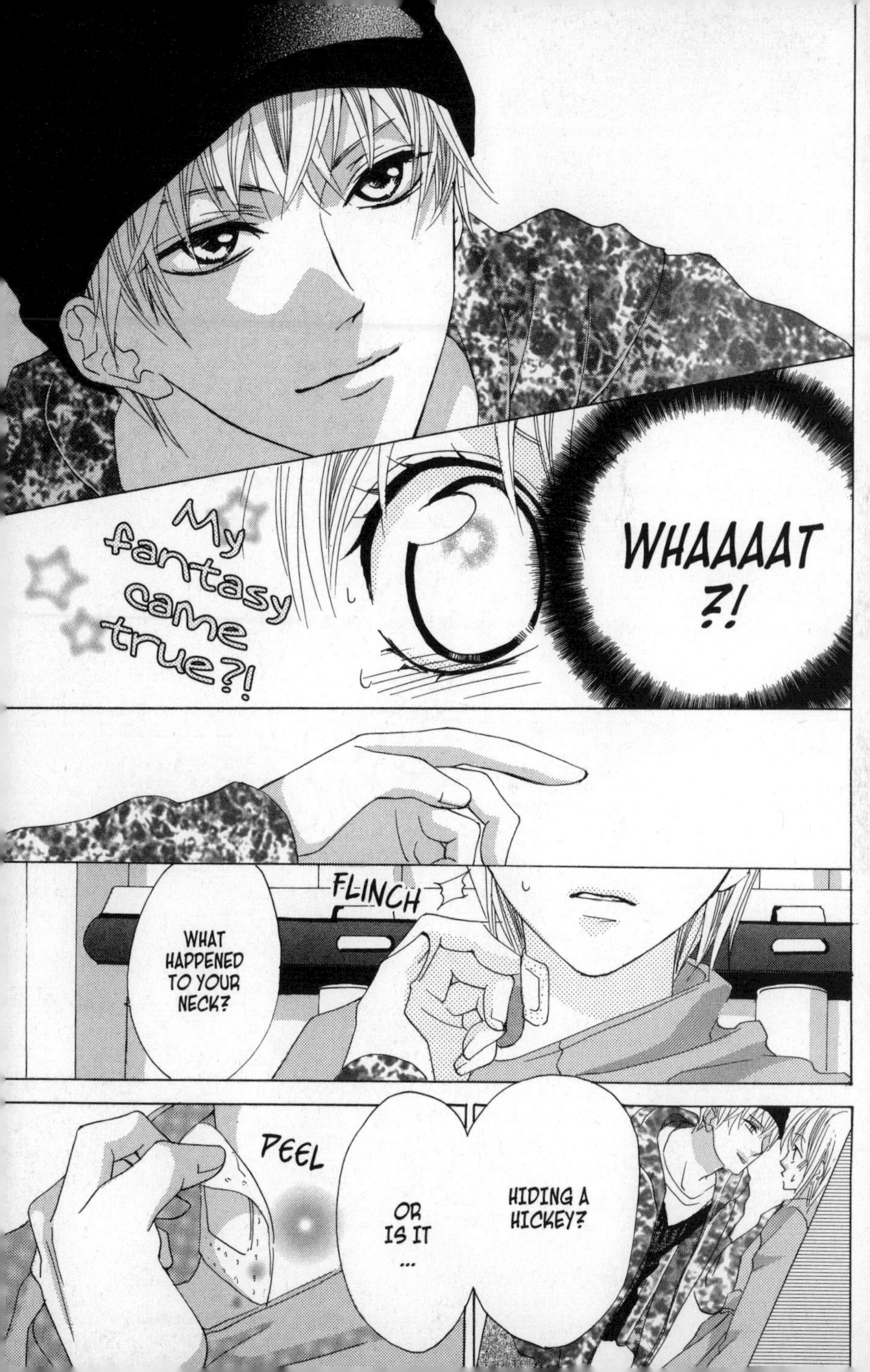
WHAAAAT ?!
My fantasy came true?!
FLINCH
WHAT HAPPENED TO YOUR NECK?
OR IS IT ...
HIDING A HICKEY?
PEEL

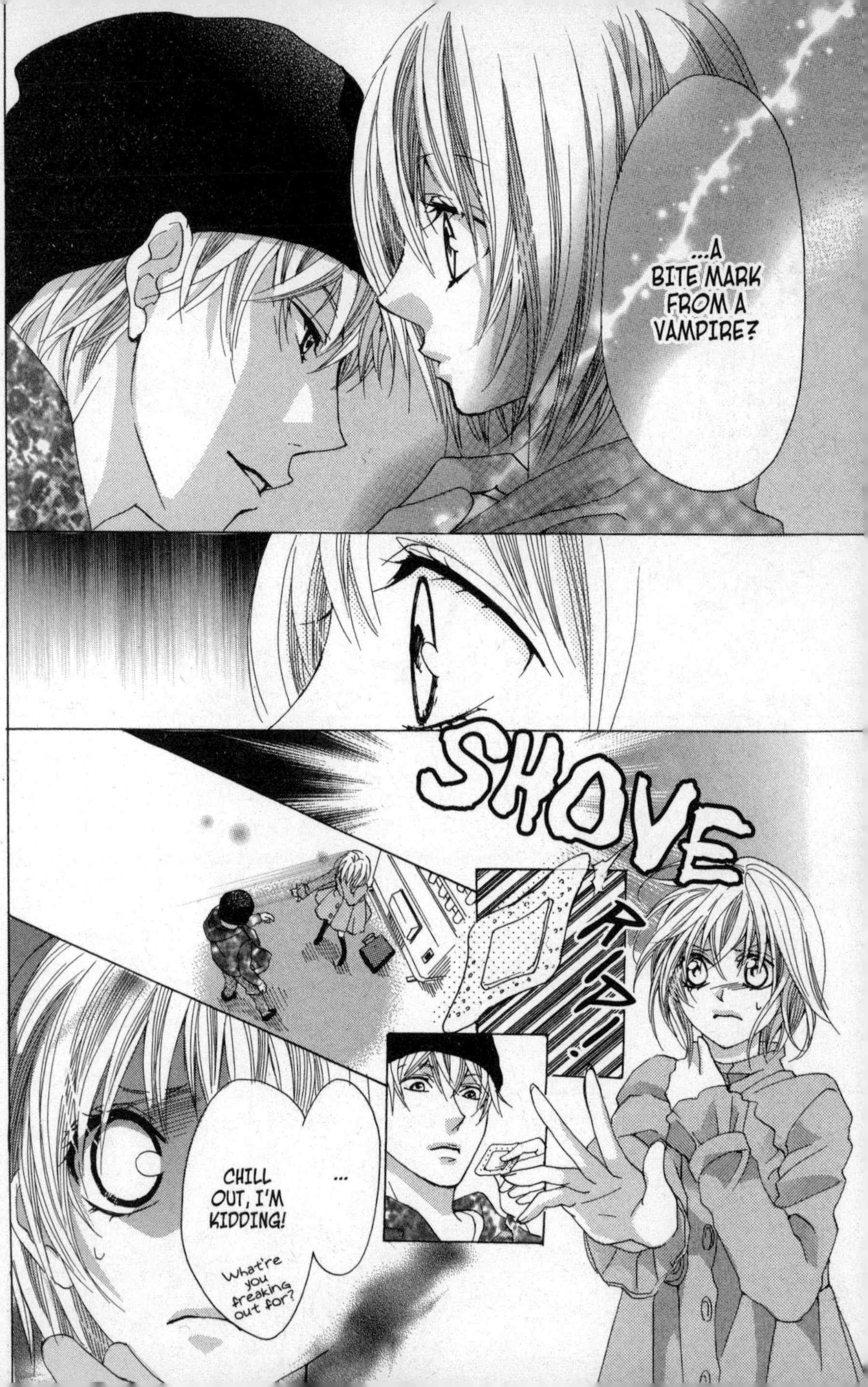
...A BITE MARK FROM A VAMPIRE?
SHOVE
RIP!!
...
CHILL OUT, I'M KIDDING!
What're you freaking out for?

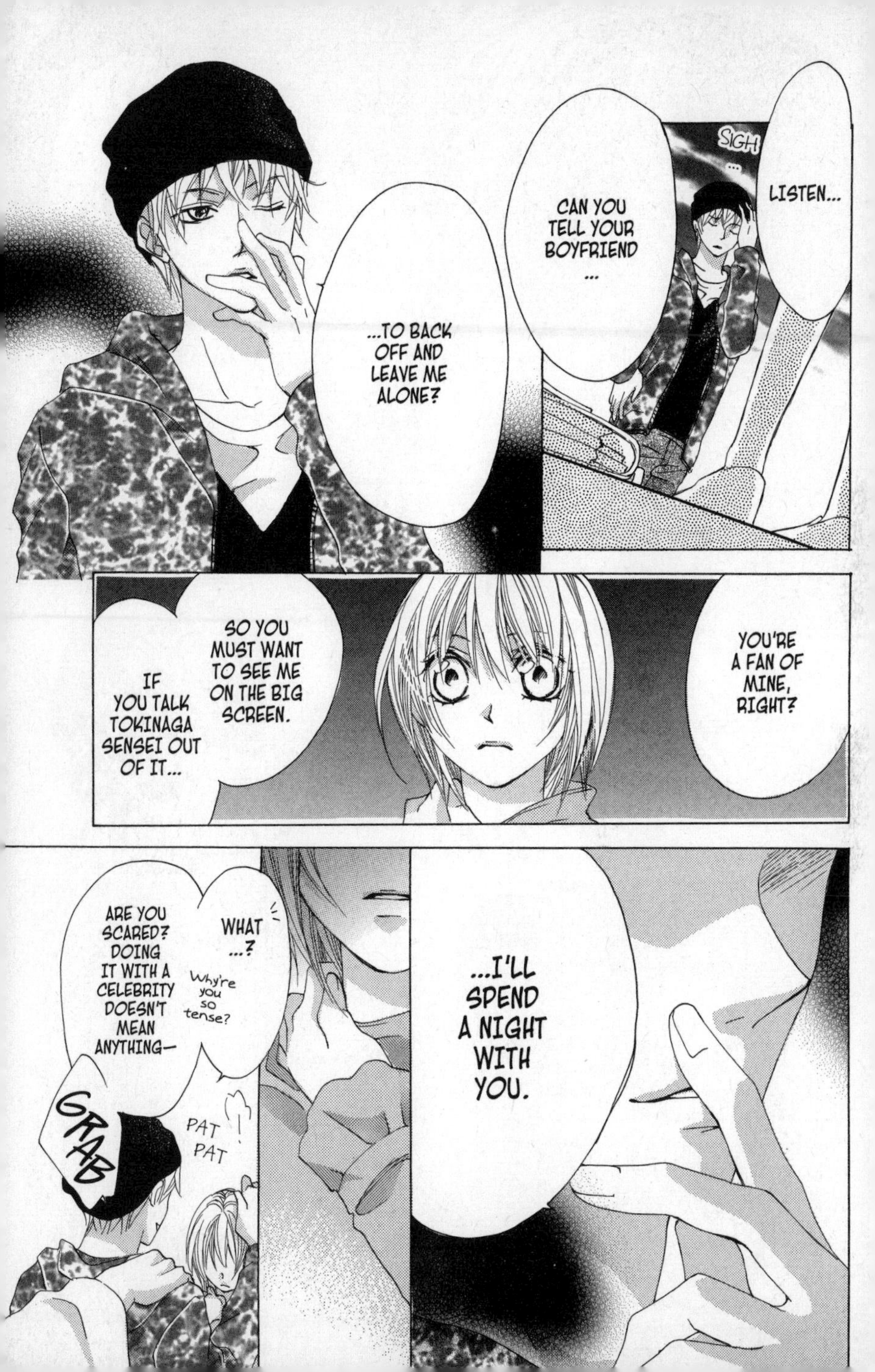
SIGH...
LISTEN...
CAN YOU TELL YOUR BOYFRIEND...
...TO BACK OFF AND LEAVE ME ALONE?
YOU'RE A FAN OF MINE, RIGHT?
SO YOU MUST WANT TO SEE ME ON THE BIG SCREEN.
IF YOU TALK TOKINAGA SENSEI OUT OF IT...
...I'LL SPEND A NIGHT WITH YOU.
WHAT...?
ARE YOU SCARED? DOING IT WITH A CELEBRITY DOESN'T MEAN ANYTHING—
Why're you so tense?
GRAB
PAT PAT

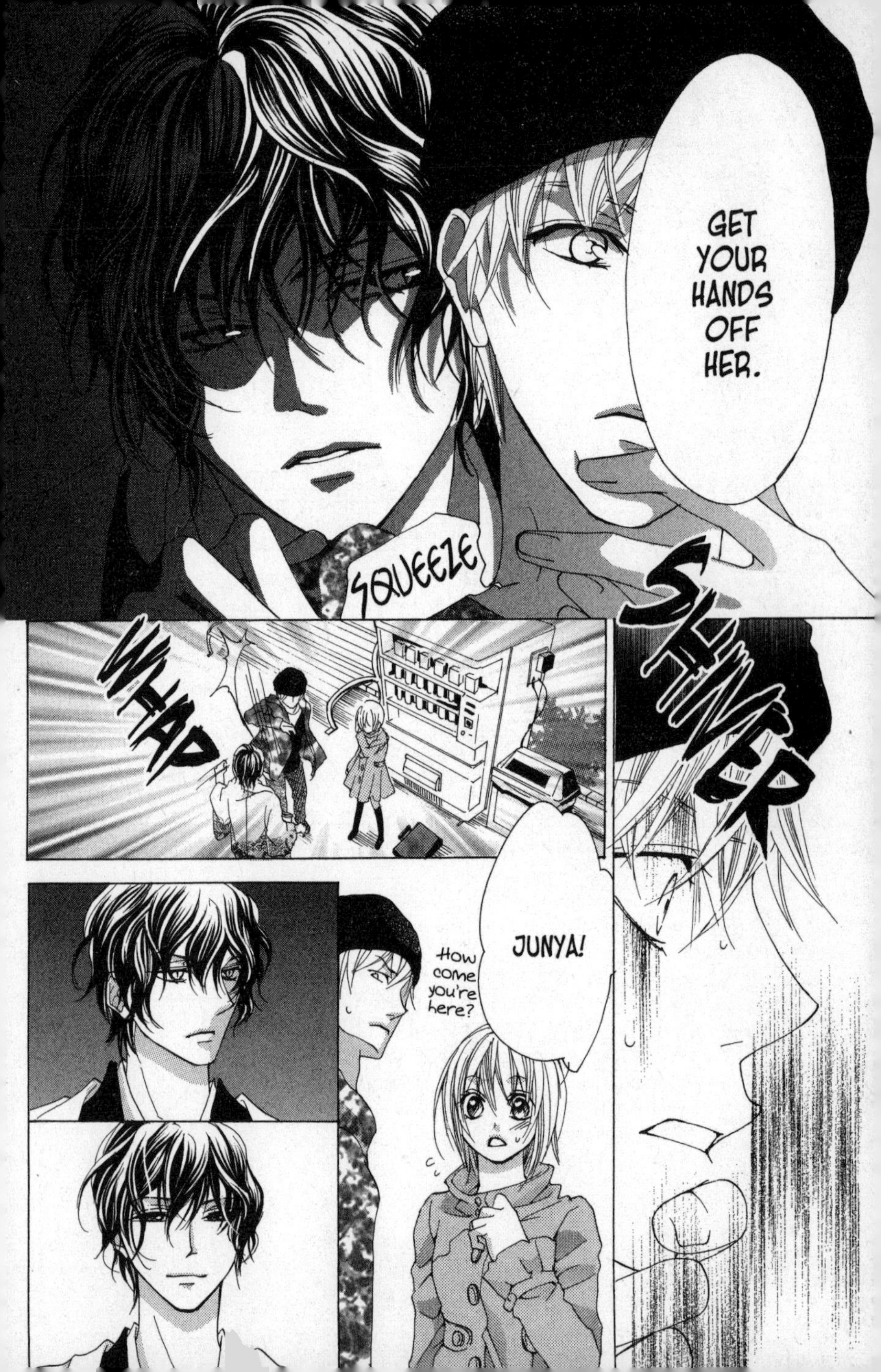
GET YOUR HANDS OFF HER.
SQUEEZE
SHIVER
WHAP
JUNYA!
How come you're here?

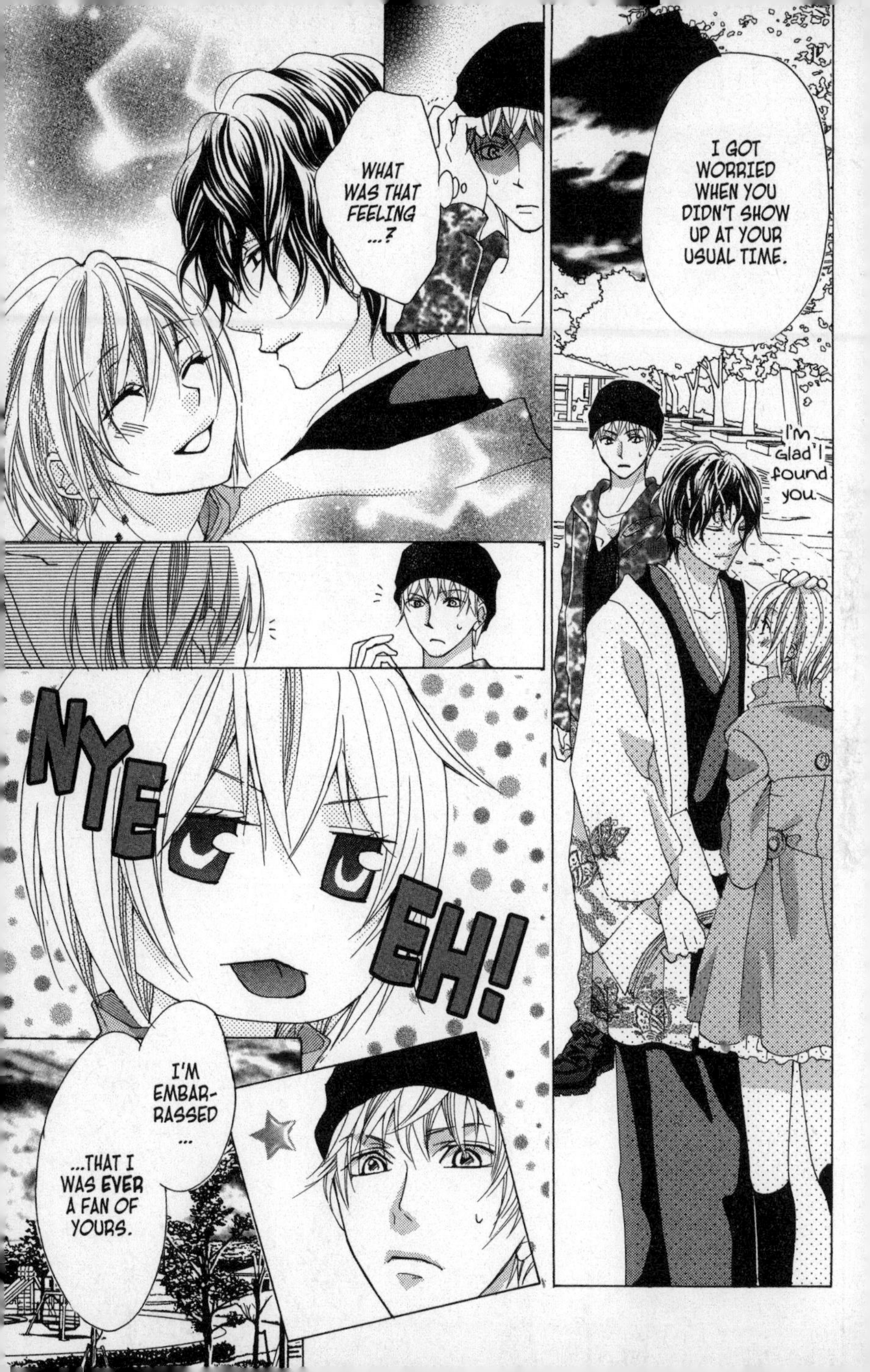
I GOT WORRIED WHEN YOU DIDN'T SHOW UP AT YOUR USUAL TIME.
I'm Glad I found you.
WHAT WAS THAT FEELING ...?
NYEEH!
I'M EMBAR-RASSED ...
...THAT I WAS EVER A FAN OF YOURS.

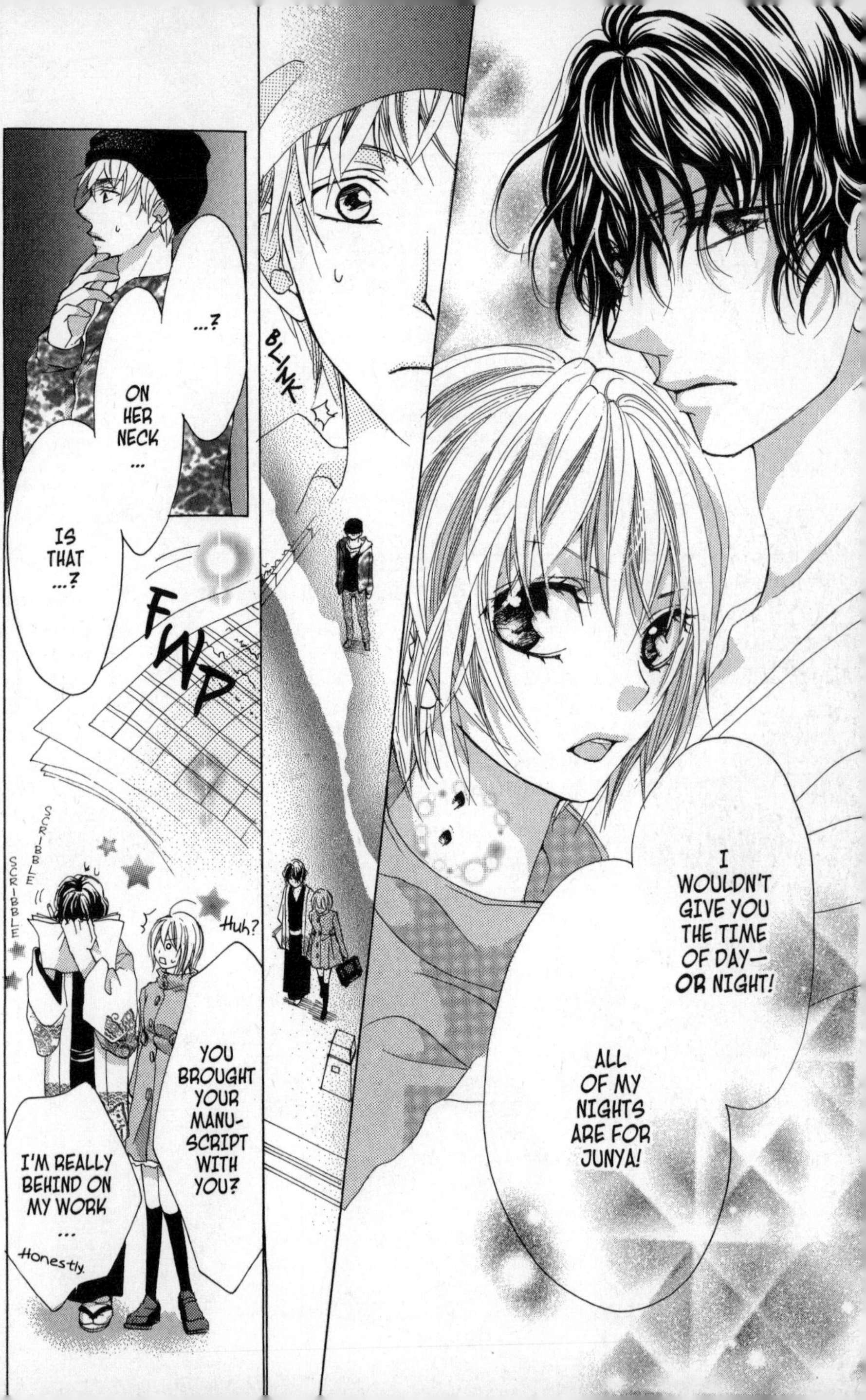
I WOULDN'T GIVE YOU THE TIME OF DAY— OR NIGHT!
ALL OF MY NIGHTS ARE FOR JUNYA!
BLINK
...?
ON HER NECK...
IS THAT...?
FWP
SCRIBBLE SCRIBBLE
Huh?
YOU BROUGHT YOUR MANUSCRIPT WITH YOU?
I'M REALLY BEHIND ON MY WORK...
Honestly.

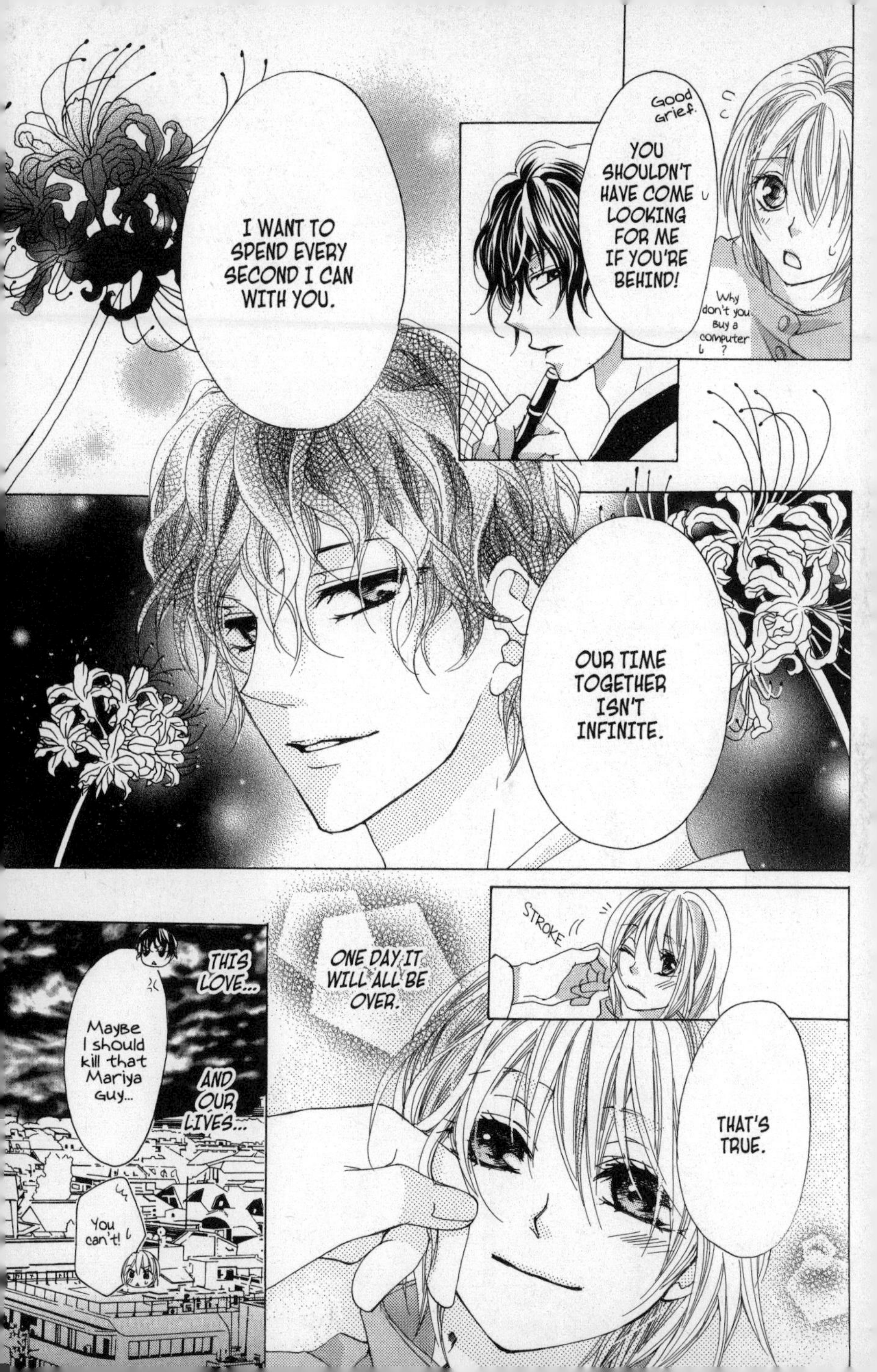
Good Grief.
YOU SHOULDN'T HAVE COME LOOKING FOR ME IF YOU'RE BEHIND!
Why don't you buy a computer?
I WANT TO SPEND EVERY SECOND I CAN WITH YOU.
OUR TIME TOGETHER ISN'T INFINITE.
STROKE
THAT'S TRUE.
ONE DAY IT WILL ALL BE OVER.
THIS LOVE...
AND OUR LIVES...
Maybe I should kill that Mariya guy...
You can't!

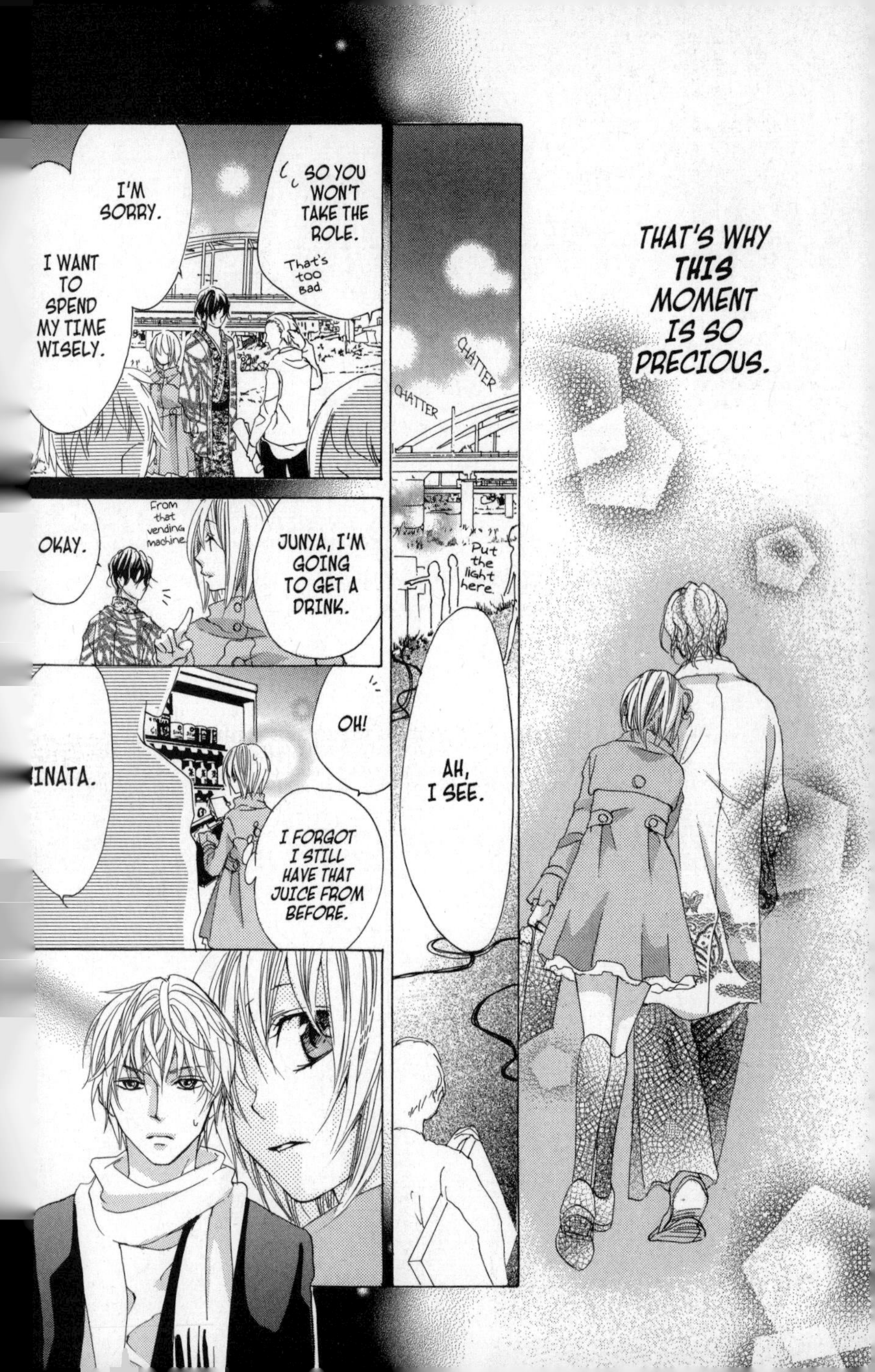
THAT'S WHY THIS MOMENT IS SO PRECIOUS.
CHATTER
CHATTER
Put the light here.
AH, I SEE.
SO YOU WON'T TAKE THE ROLE.
That's too bad.
I'M SORRY.
I WANT TO SPEND MY TIME WISELY.
JUNYA, I'M GOING TO GET A DRINK.
From that vending machine.
OKAY.
OH!
I FORGOT I STILL HAVE THAT JUICE FROM BEFORE.
INATA.

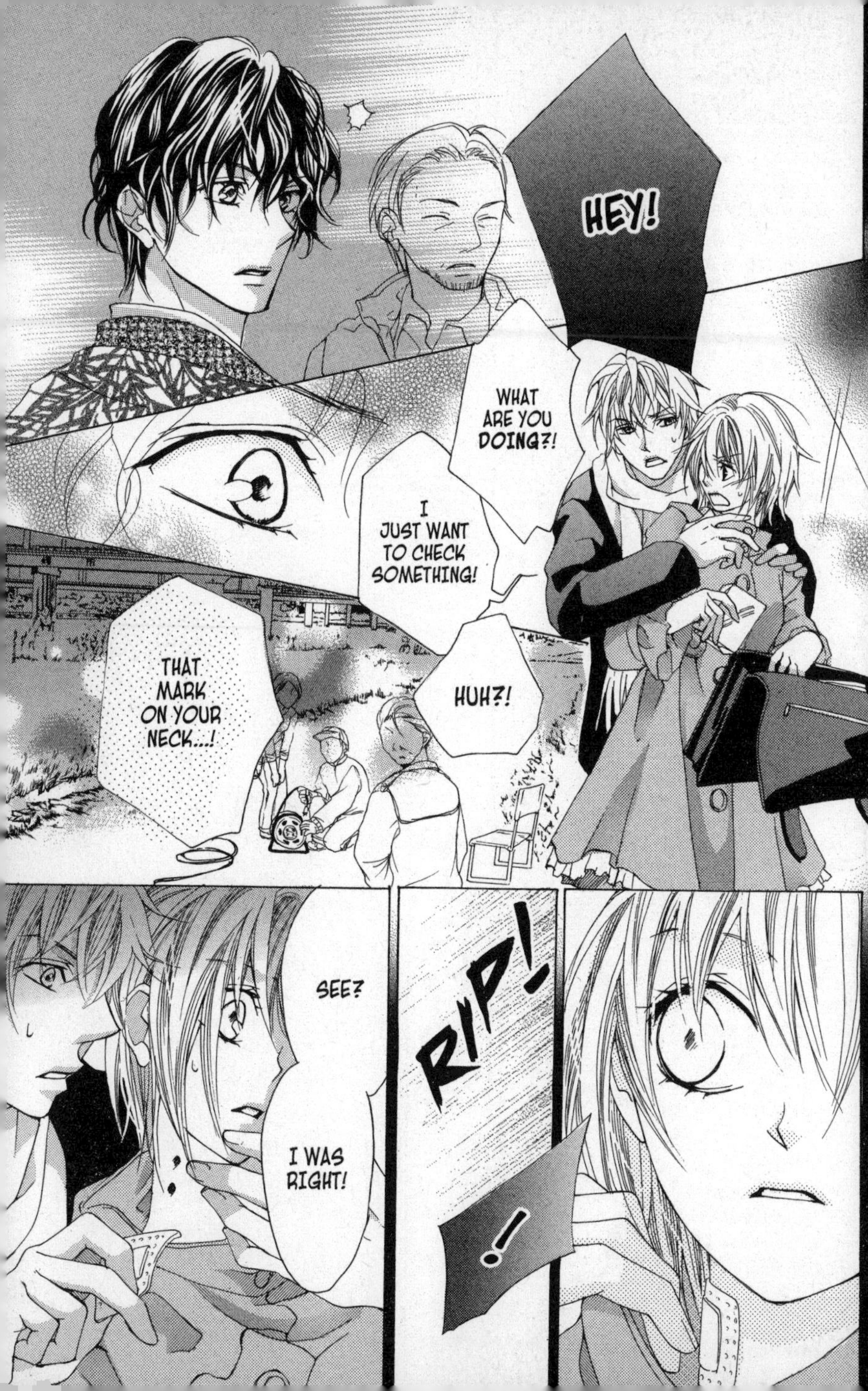
HEY!
WHAT ARE YOU DOING?!
I JUST WANT TO CHECK SOMETHING!
HUH?!
THAT MARK ON YOUR NECK...!
!
RIP!
SEE?
I WAS RIGHT!

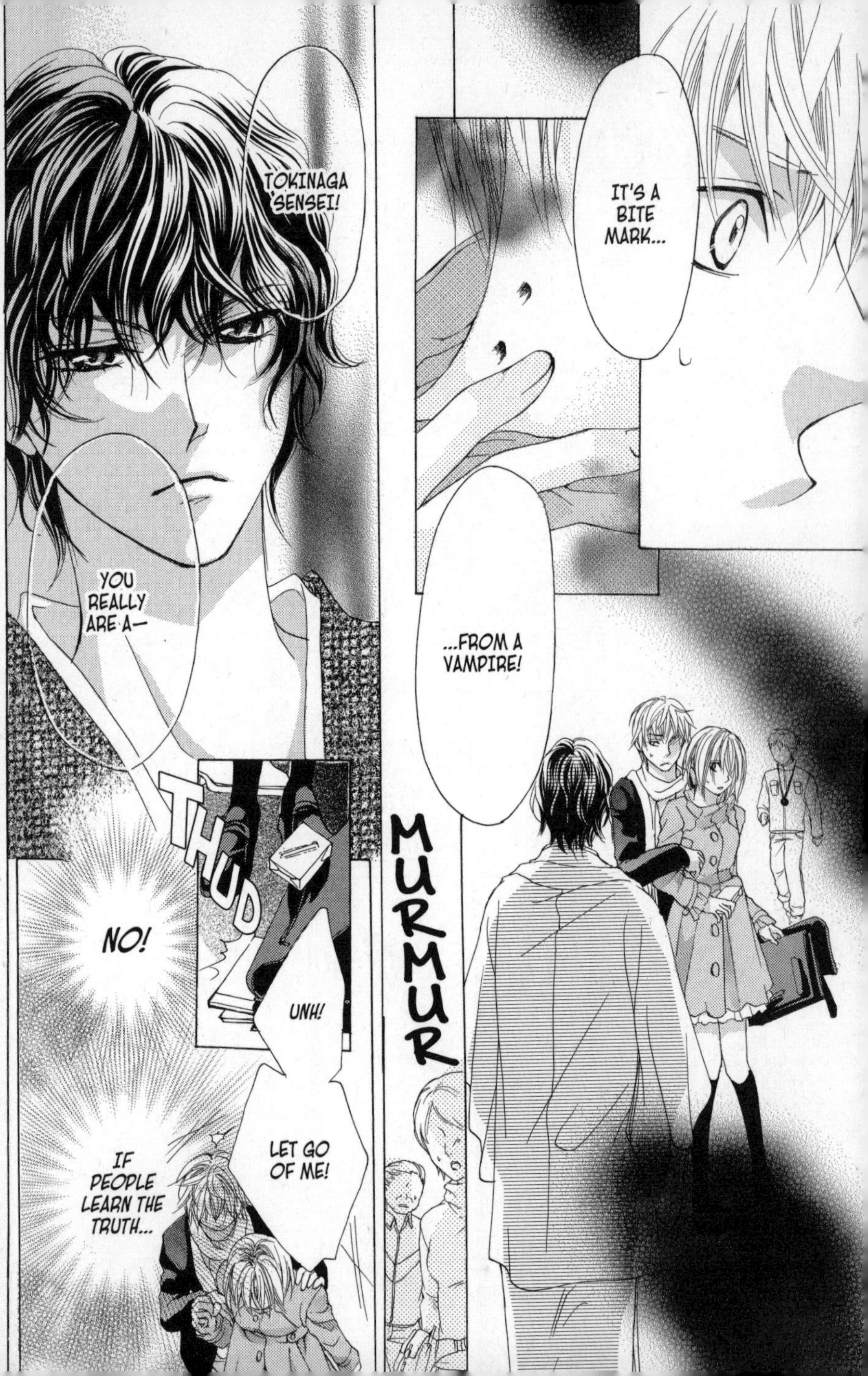
IT'S A BITE MARK...
...FROM A VAMPIRE!
MURMUR
TOKINAGA SENSEI!
YOU REALLY ARE A—
THUD
UNH!
NO!
LET GO OF ME!
IF PEOPLE LEARN THE TRUTH...

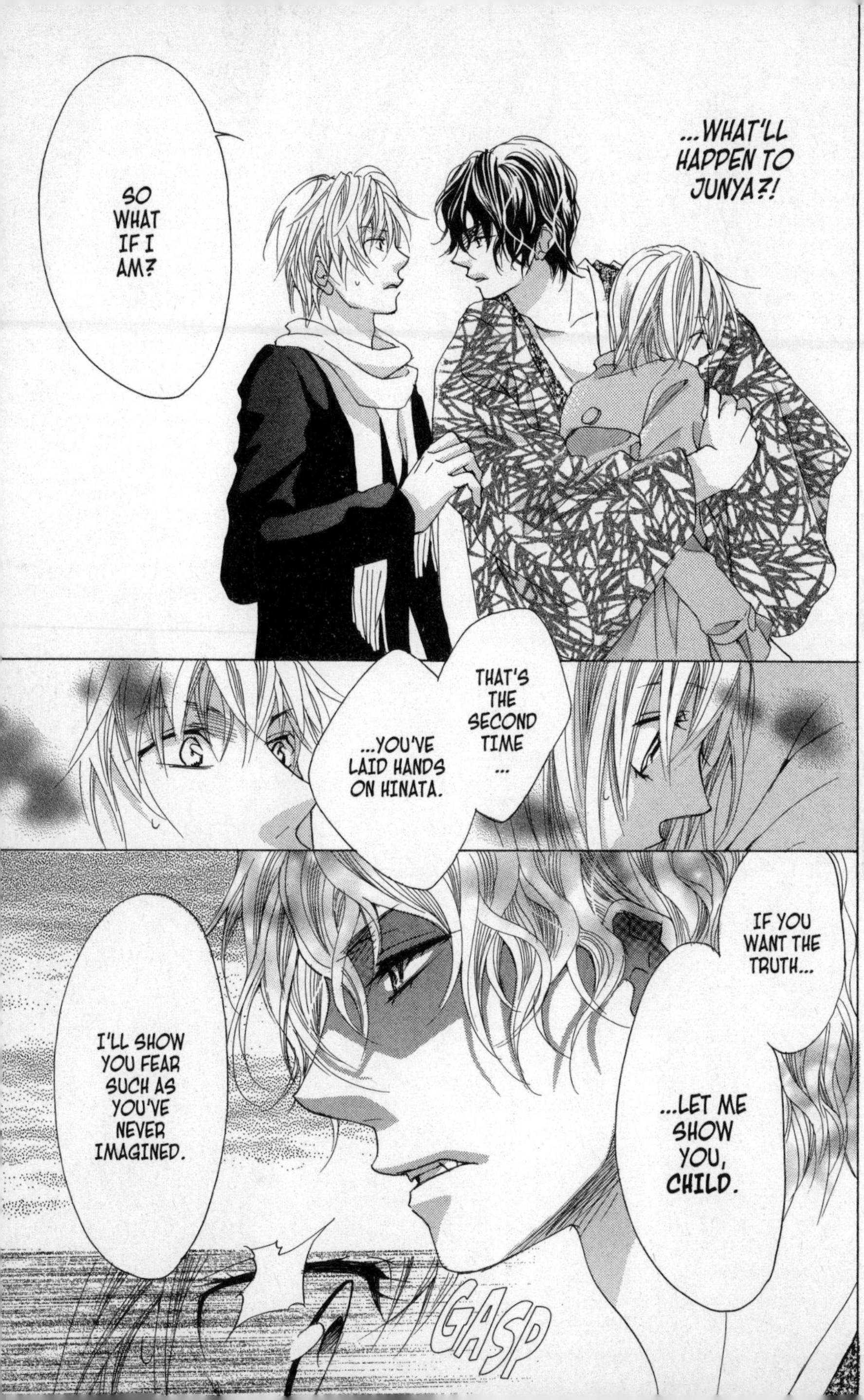
...WHAT'LL HAPPEN TO JUNYA?!
SO WHAT IF I AM?
THAT'S THE SECOND TIME ...
...YOU'VE LAID HANDS ON HINATA.
IF YOU WANT THE TRUTH...
...LET ME SHOW YOU, CHILD.
I'LL SHOW YOU FEAR SUCH AS YOU'VE NEVER IMAGINED.
GASP

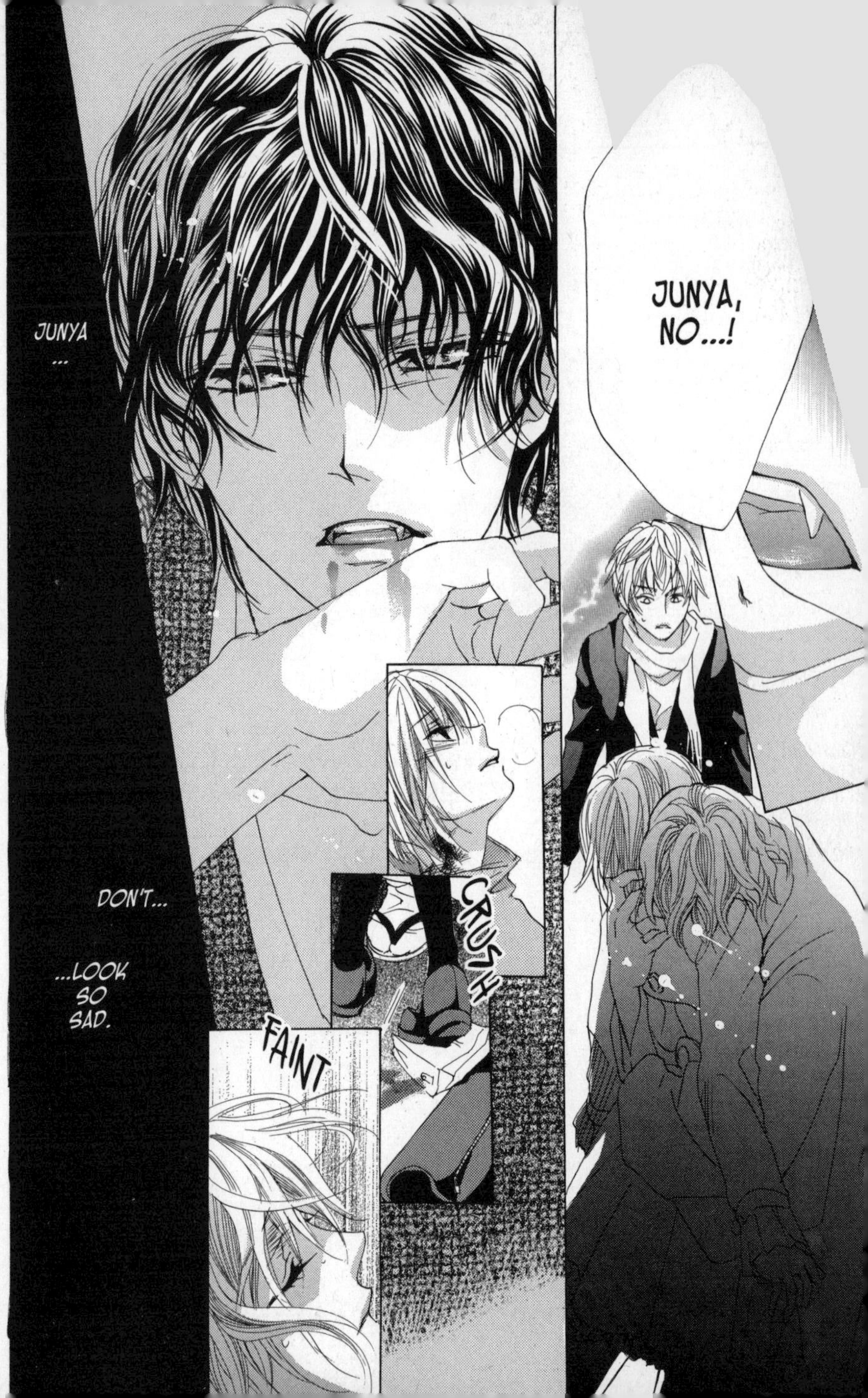
JUNYA, NO...!
JUNYA ...
CRUSH
DON'T...
...LOOK SO SAD.
FAINT

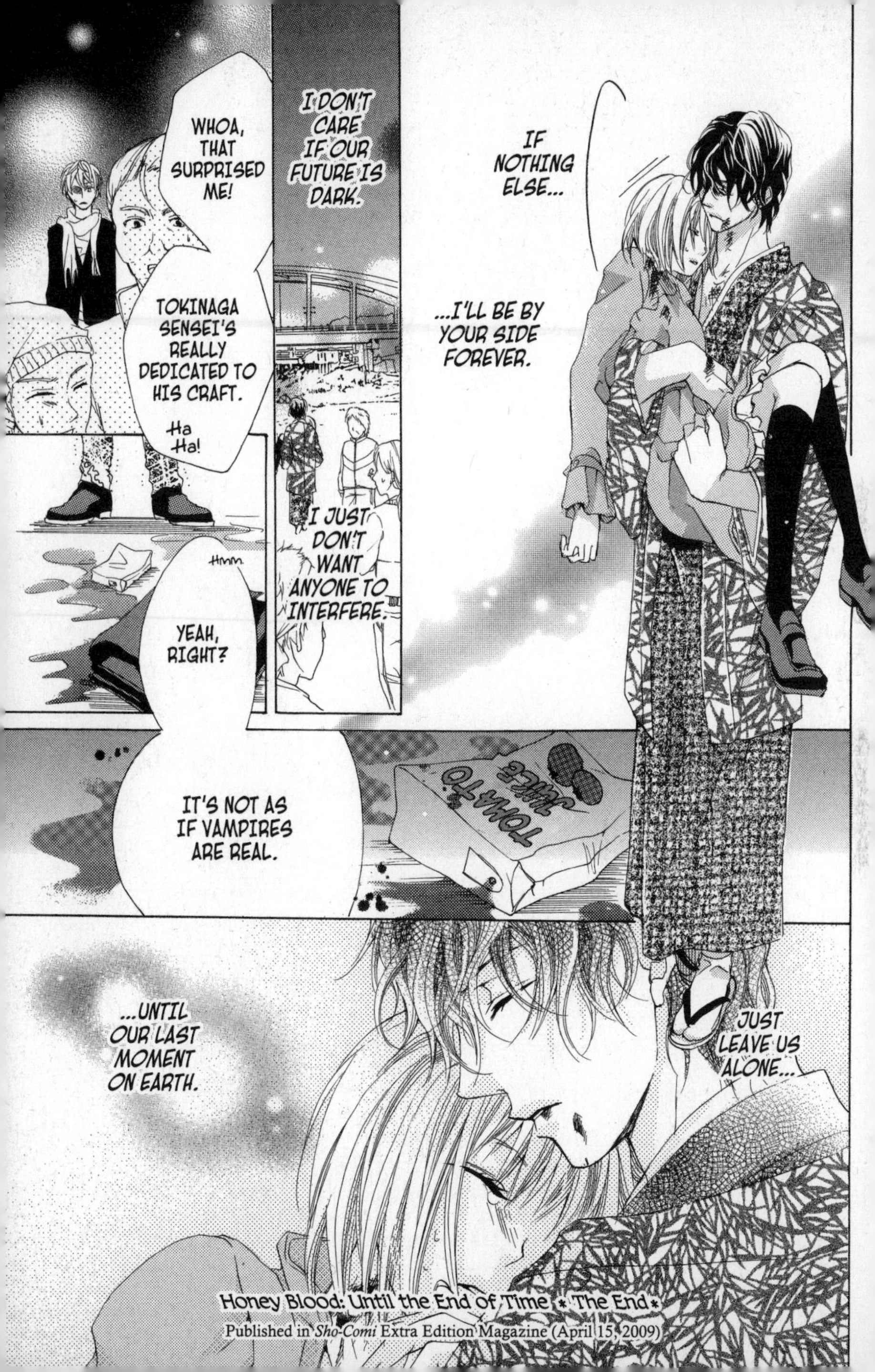
IF NOTHING ELSE...
...I'LL BE BY YOUR SIDE FOREVER.
I DON'T CARE IF OUR FUTURE IS DARK.
I JUST DON'T WANT ANYONE TO INTERFERE.
WHOA, THAT SURPRISED ME!
TOKINAGA SENSEI'S REALLY DEDICATED TO HIS CRAFT.
Ha Ha!
Hmm.
YEAH, RIGHT?
IT'S NOT AS IF VAMPIRES ARE REAL.
TOMATO JUICE
JUST LEAVE US ALONE...
...UNTIL OUR LAST MOMENT ON EARTH.

Honey Blood: Until the End of Time * The End *

Published in *Sho-Comi* Extra Edition Magazine (April 15, 2009)

❀ "Until the End of Time" ❀

This is the third story in the series. Sorry about the artwork and the plot... >‿< ♭

The work schedule for the regular series in the main magazine + 36 pages for the Extra Edition magazine + a big fight with my editor = me crying non-stop from beginning to end while drawing this. It was exhausting. ⌣̈ ♭

To all of my readers, I'm so sorry! ♪ But even though I wish I'd done things differently, I love this story as much as the other two.

While I was writing, I was thinking about what the future would hold for a romance between a vampire and a human.

I really wanted to use the word "eternal" in a better way. ♪

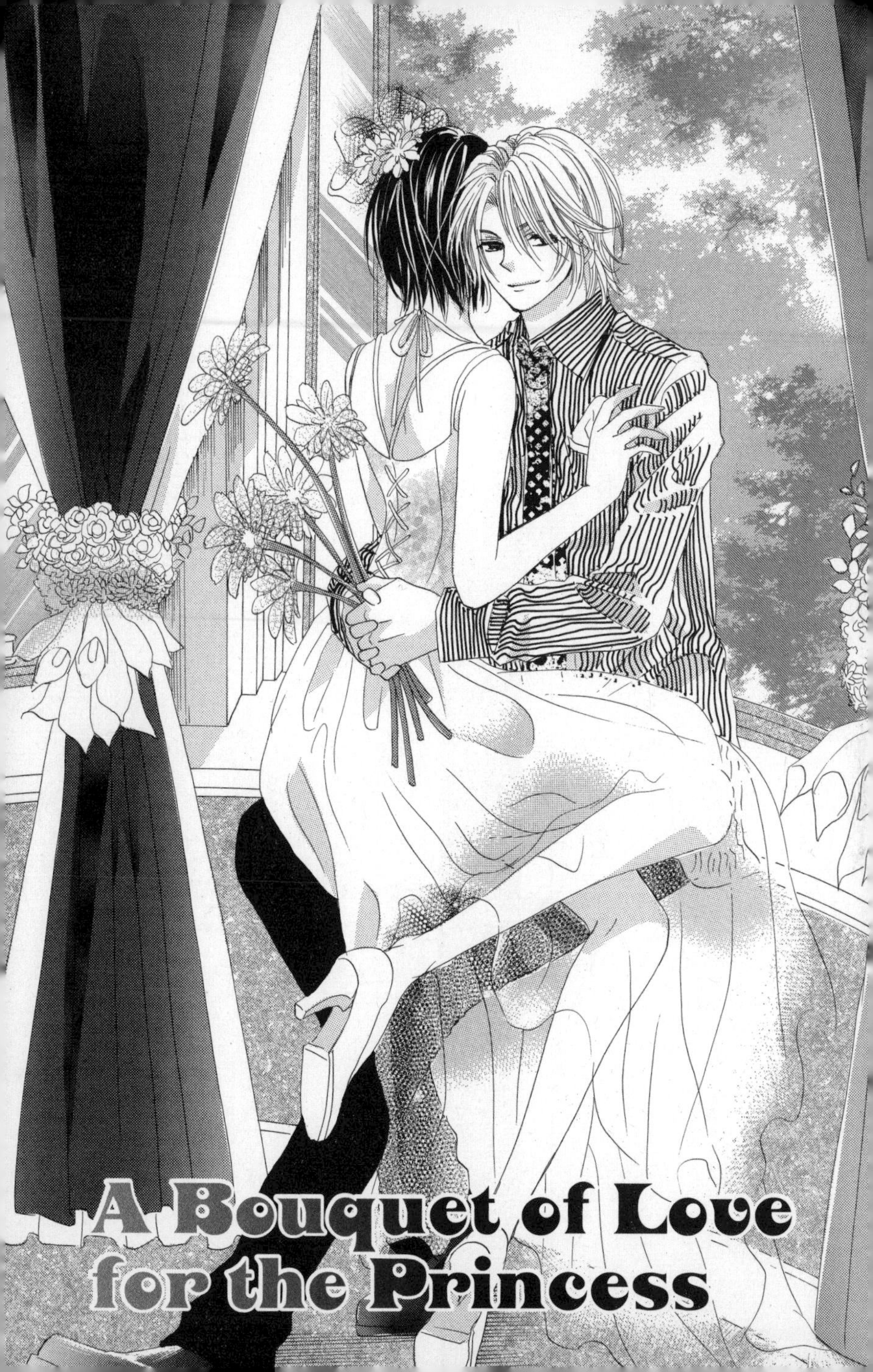
A Bouquet of Love
for the Princess

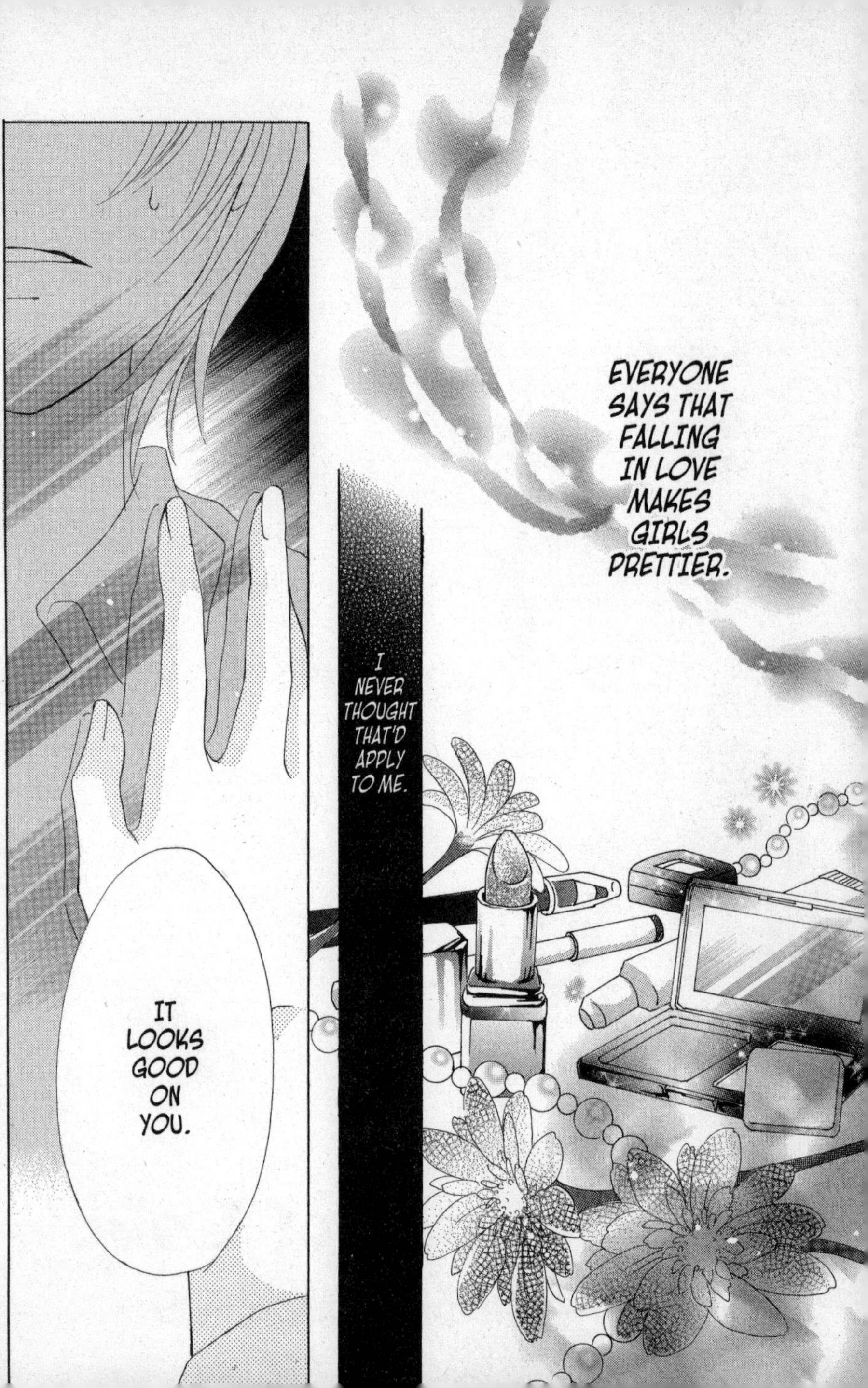
EVERYONE SAYS THAT FALLING IN LOVE MAKES GIRLS PRETTIER.
I NEVER THOUGHT THAT'D APPLY TO ME.
IT LOOKS GOOD ON YOU.

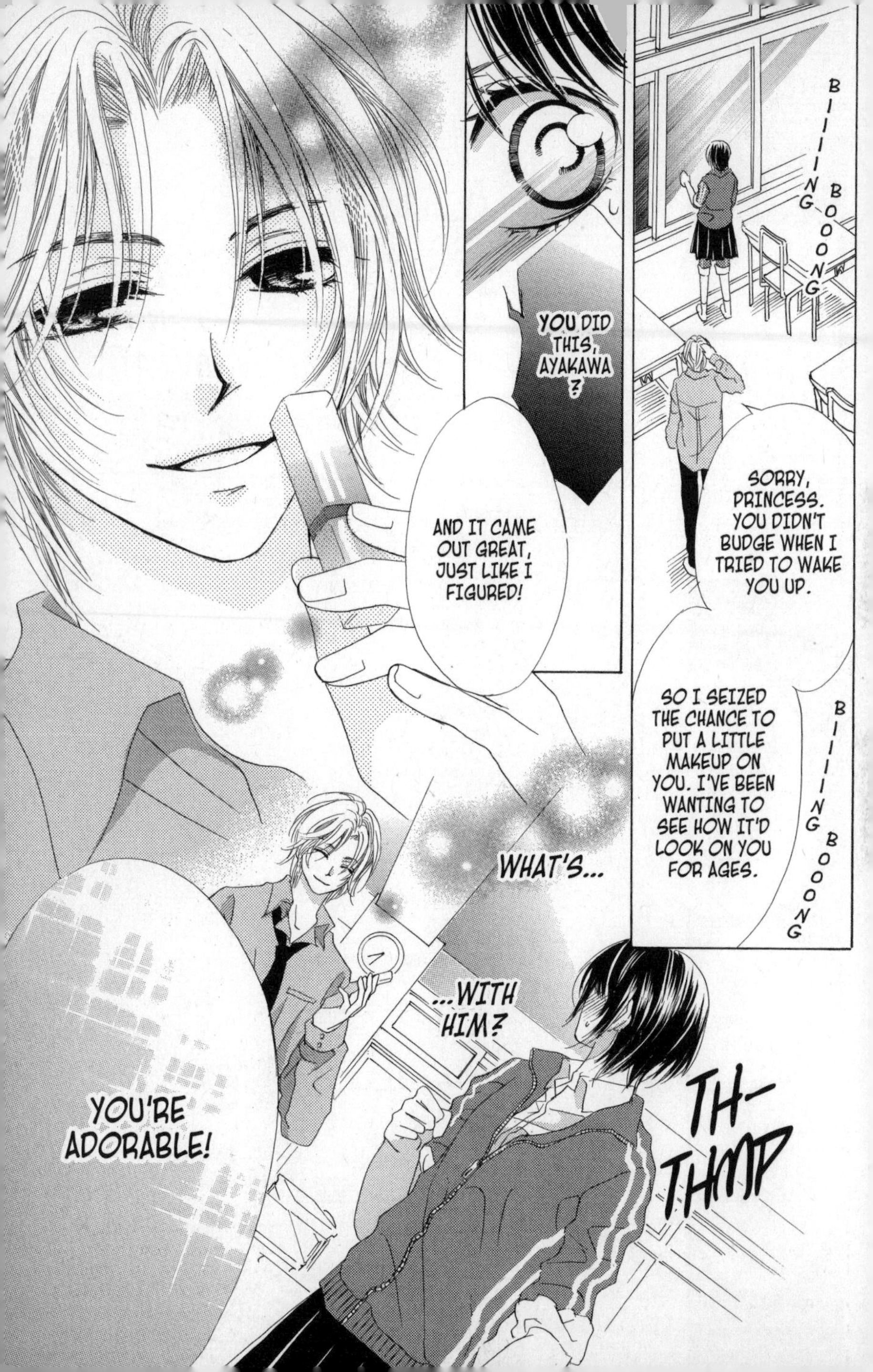
BIIING BOOONG
SORRY, PRINCESS. YOU DIDN'T BUDGE WHEN I TRIED TO WAKE YOU UP.
SO I SEIZED THE CHANCE TO PUT A LITTLE MAKEUP ON YOU. I'VE BEEN WANTING TO SEE HOW IT'D LOOK ON YOU FOR AGES.
BIIING BOOONG
YOU DID THIS, AYAKAWA?
AND IT CAME OUT GREAT, JUST LIKE I FIGURED!
WHAT'S...
...WITH HIM?
TH-THMP
YOU'RE ADORABLE!

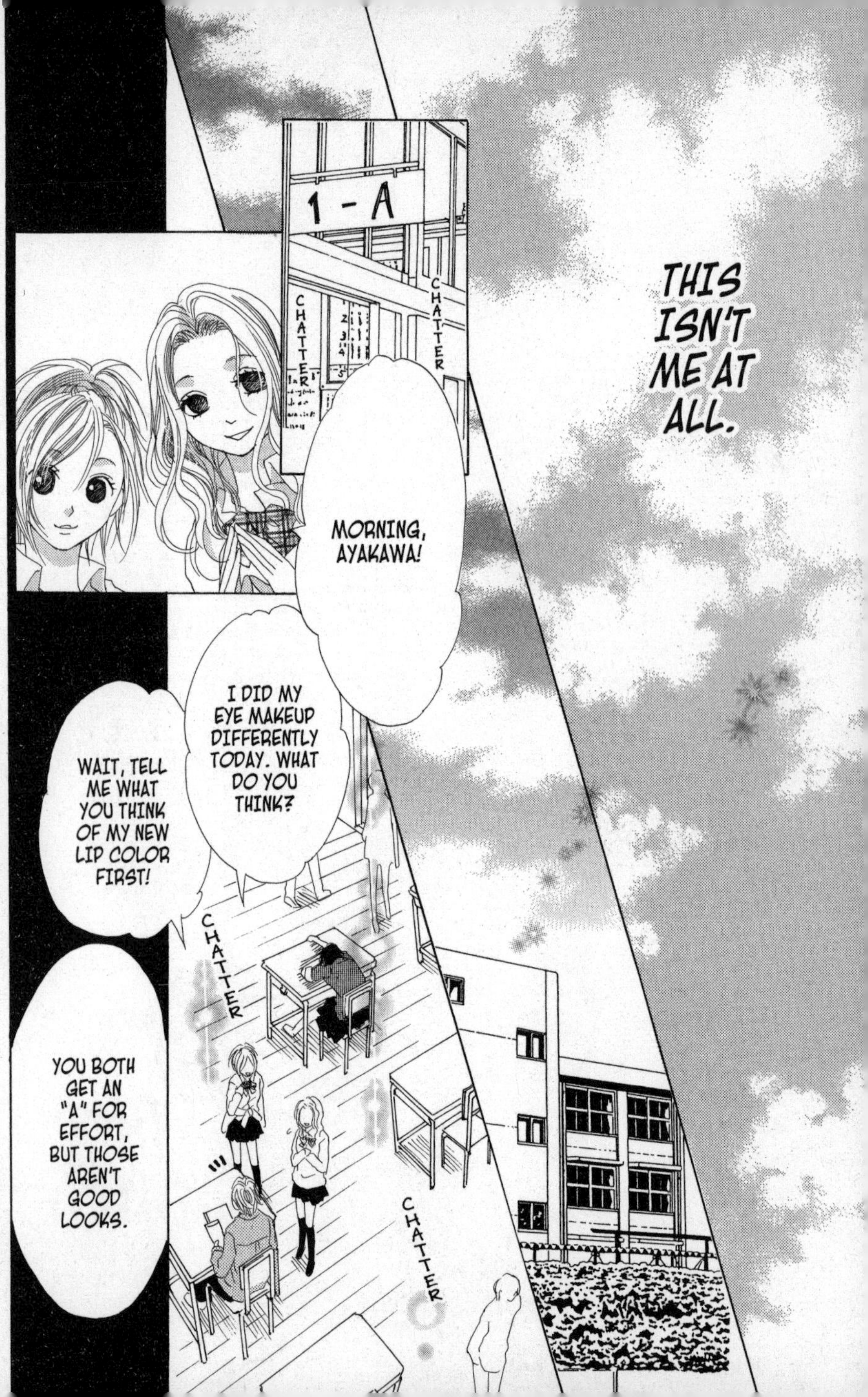
THIS ISN'T ME AT ALL.
1-A
CHATTER
CHATTER
MORNING, AYAKAWA!
I DID MY EYE MAKEUP DIFFERENTLY TODAY. WHAT DO YOU THINK?
WAIT, TELL ME WHAT YOU THINK OF MY NEW LIP COLOR FIRST!
CHATTER
YOU BOTH GET AN "A" FOR EFFORT, BUT THOSE AREN'T GOOD LOOKS.
CHATTER

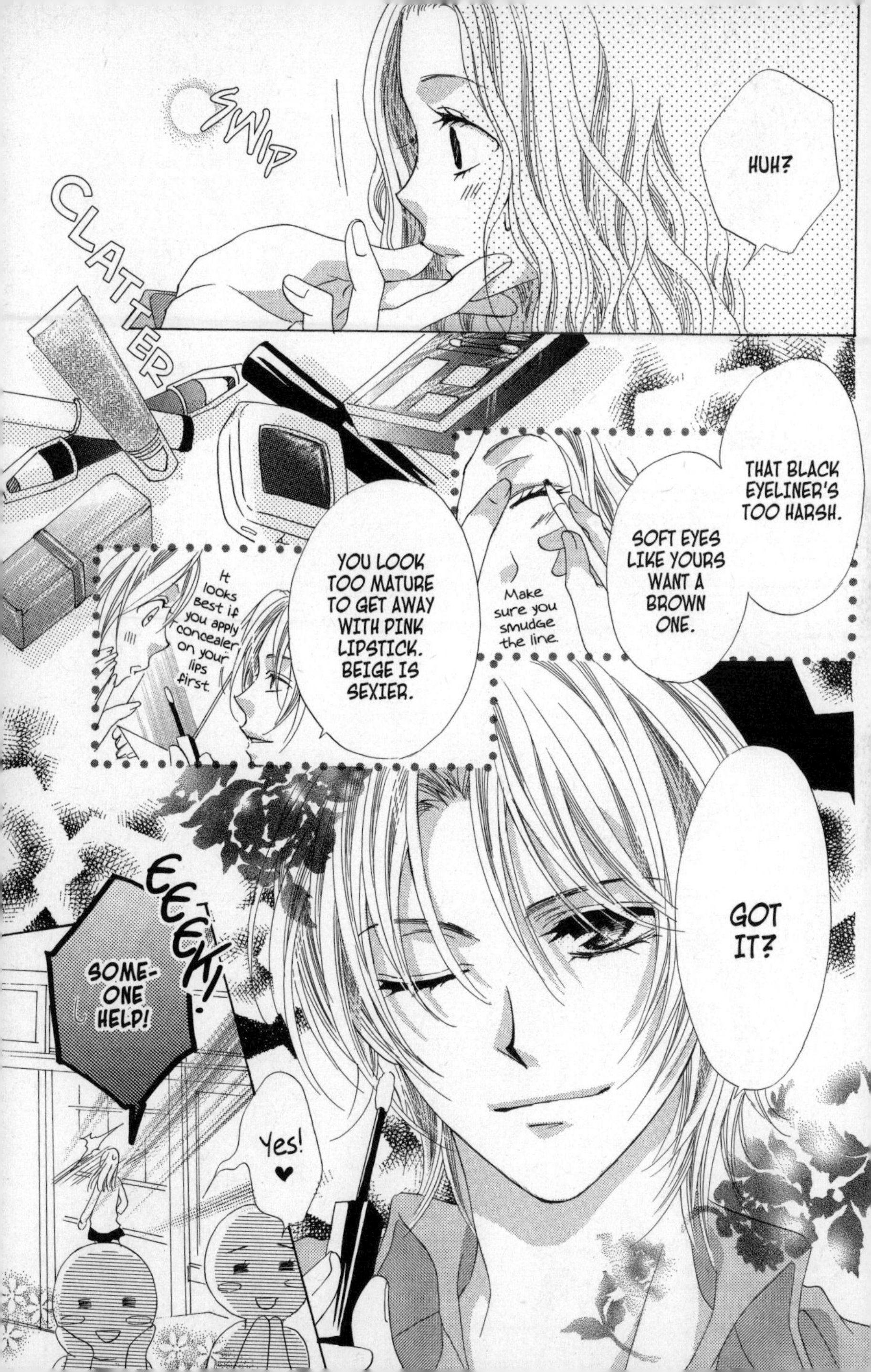
HUH?
SWIP
CLATTER
THAT BLACK EYELINER'S TOO HARSH.
SOFT EYES LIKE YOURS WANT A BROWN ONE.
Make sure you smudge the line.
YOU LOOK TOO MATURE TO GET AWAY WITH PINK LIPSTICK. BEIGE IS SEXIER.
It looks best if you apply concealer on your lips first.
GOT IT?
EEEEK!
SOME-ONE HELP!
Yes! ♥

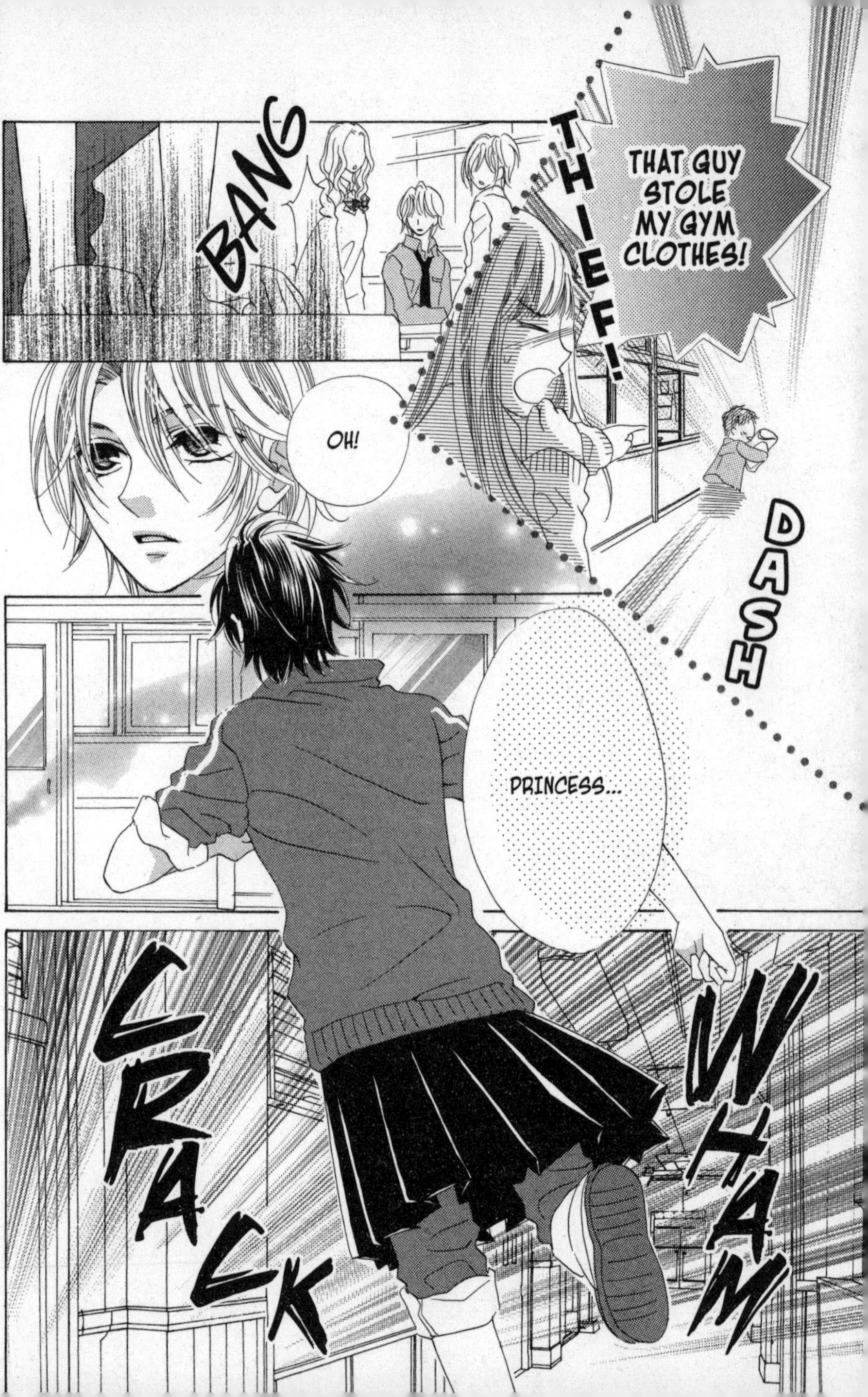
THIEF!
THAT GUY STOLE MY GYM CLOTHES!
BANG
DASH
OH!
PRINCESS...
WHAM
CRACK

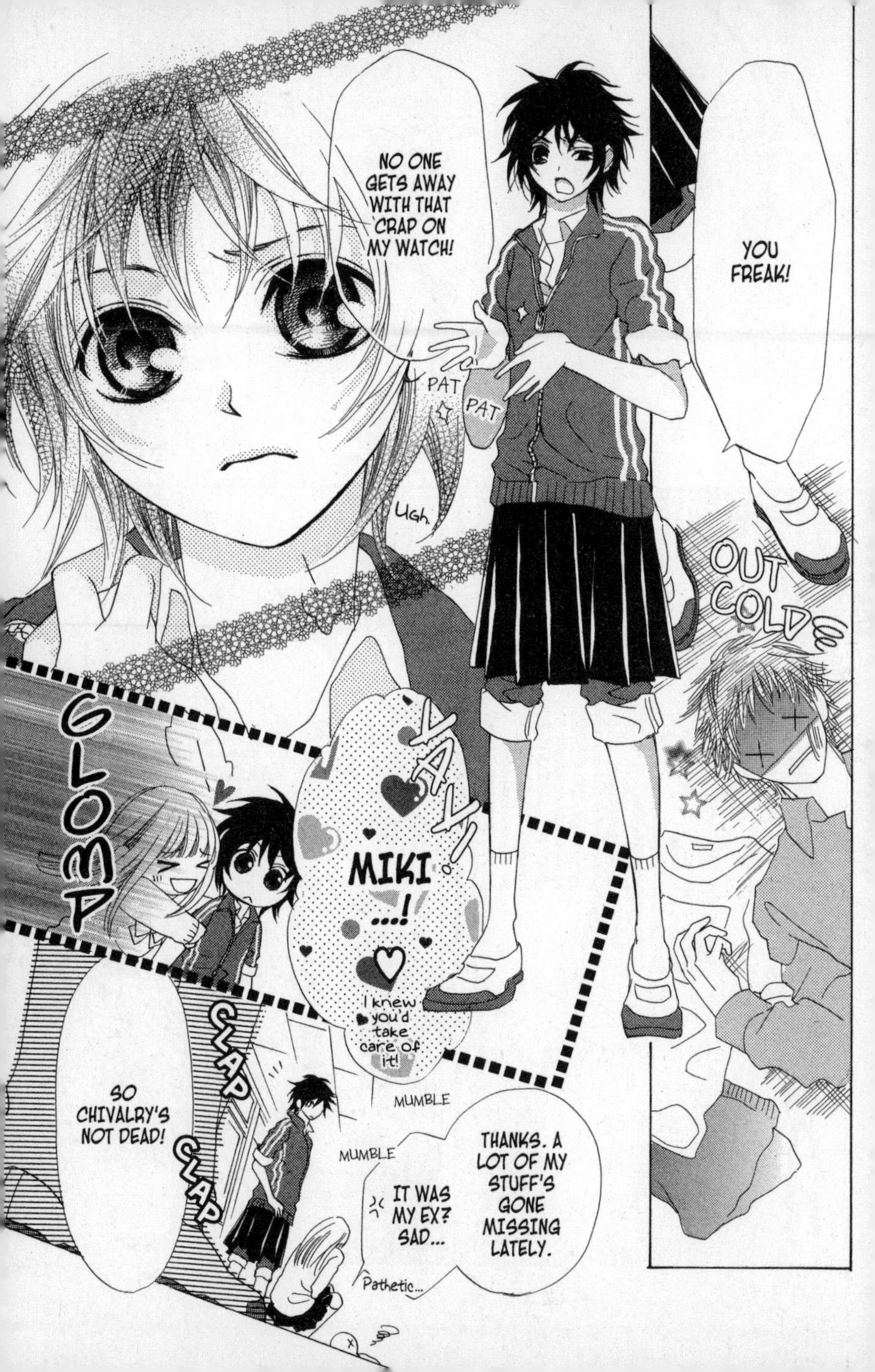
YOU FREAK!
OUT COLD
NO ONE GETS AWAY WITH THAT CRAP ON MY WATCH!
PAT PAT
Ugh.
YAY! MIKI ...!
I knew you'd take care of it!
GLOMP
THANKS. A LOT OF MY STUFF'S GONE MISSING LATELY.
IT WAS MY EX? SAD...
MUMBLE
MUMBLE
Pathetic...
SO CHIVALRY'S NOT DEAD!
CLAP CLAP

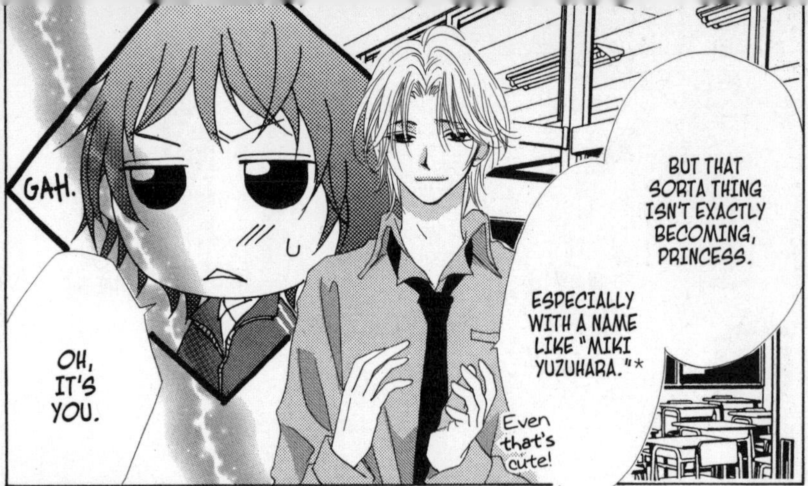
BUT THAT SORTA THING ISN'T EXACTLY BECOMING, PRINCESS.
ESPECIALLY WITH A NAME LIKE "MIKI YUZUHARA."*
Even that's cute!
GAH.
OH, IT'S YOU.

*Ayakawa calls her "Princess" because the kanji for "Miki" means "beautiful princess."

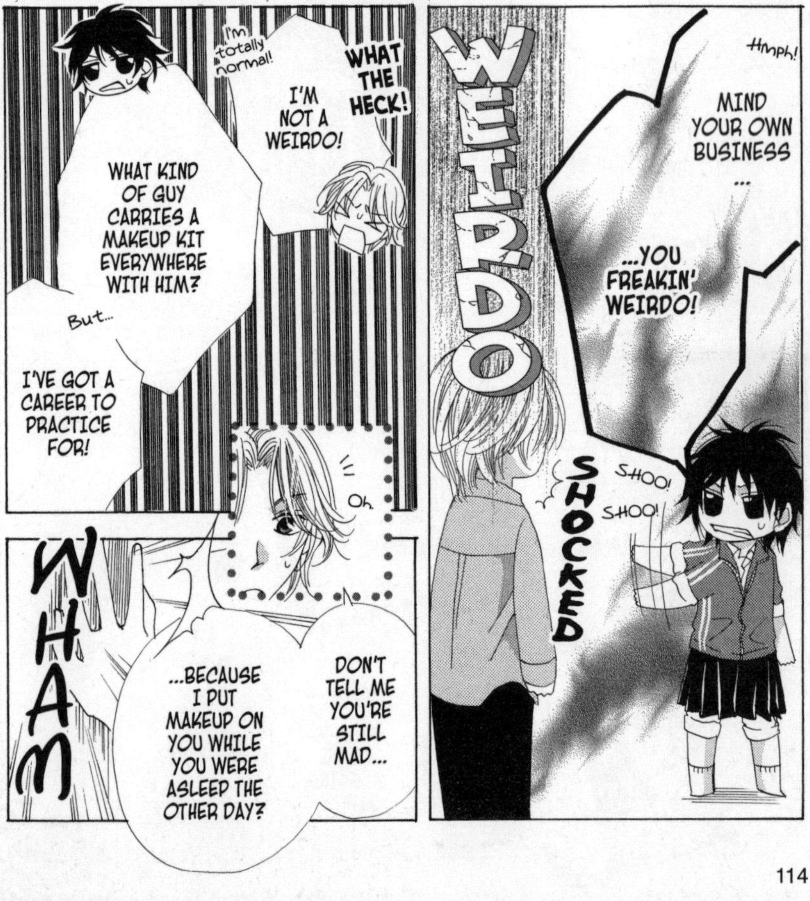
Hmph!
MIND YOUR OWN BUSINESS...
...YOU FREAKIN' WEIRDO!
WEIRDO
SHOO!
SHOO!
SHOCKED
WHAT THE HECK!
I'M NOT A WEIRDO!
I'm totally normal!
WHAT KIND OF GUY CARRIES A MAKEUP KIT EVERYWHERE WITH HIM?
But...
I'VE GOT A CAREER TO PRACTICE FOR!
Oh.
DON'T TELL ME YOU'RE STILL MAD...
...BECAUSE I PUT MAKEUP ON YOU WHILE YOU WERE ASLEEP THE OTHER DAY?
WHAM

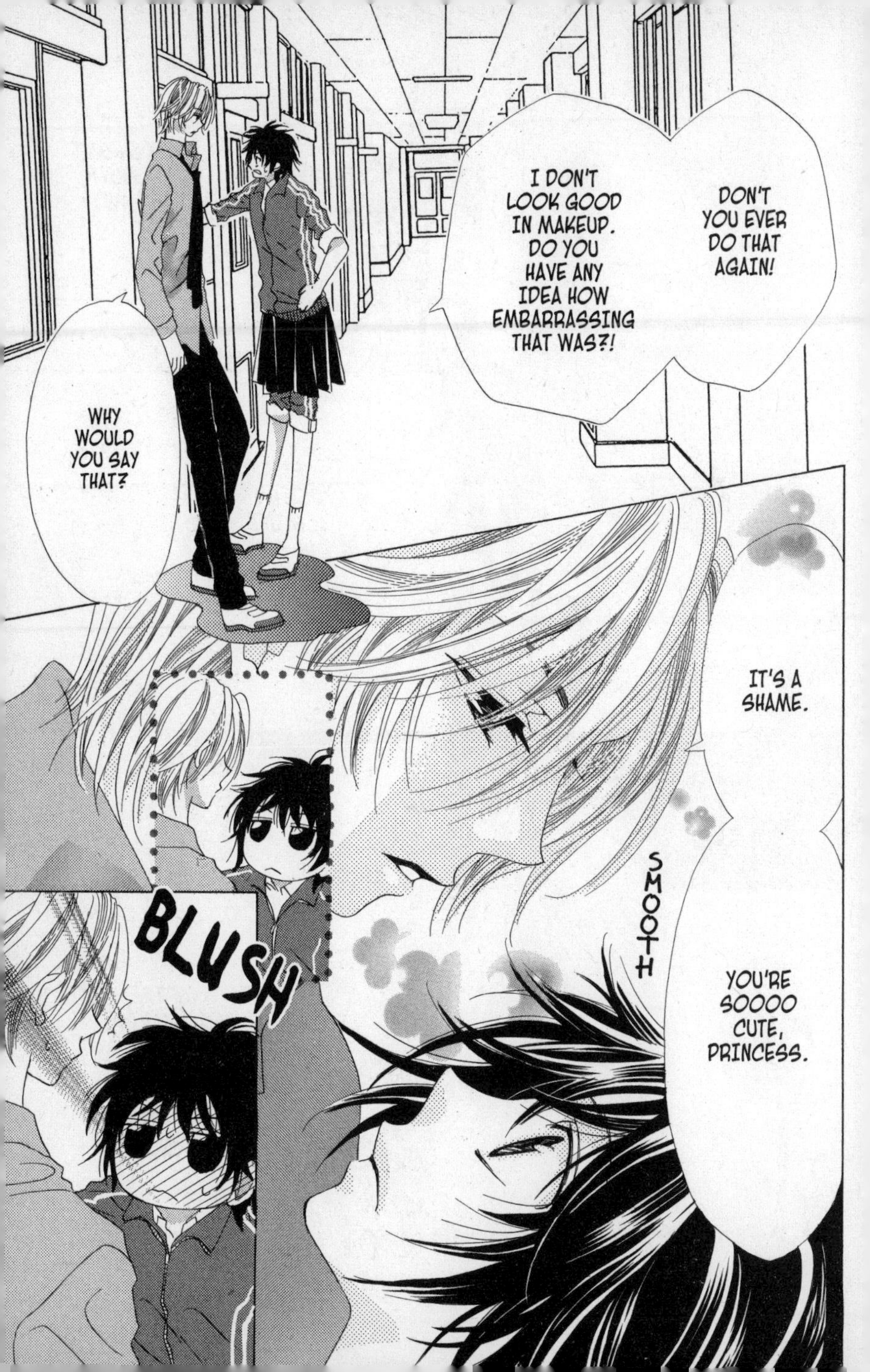
DON'T YOU EVER DO THAT AGAIN!
I DON'T LOOK GOOD IN MAKEUP. DO YOU HAVE ANY IDEA HOW EMBARRASSING THAT WAS?!
WHY WOULD YOU SAY THAT?
IT'S A SHAME.
YOU'RE SOOOO CUTE, PRINCESS.
SMOOTH
BLUSH

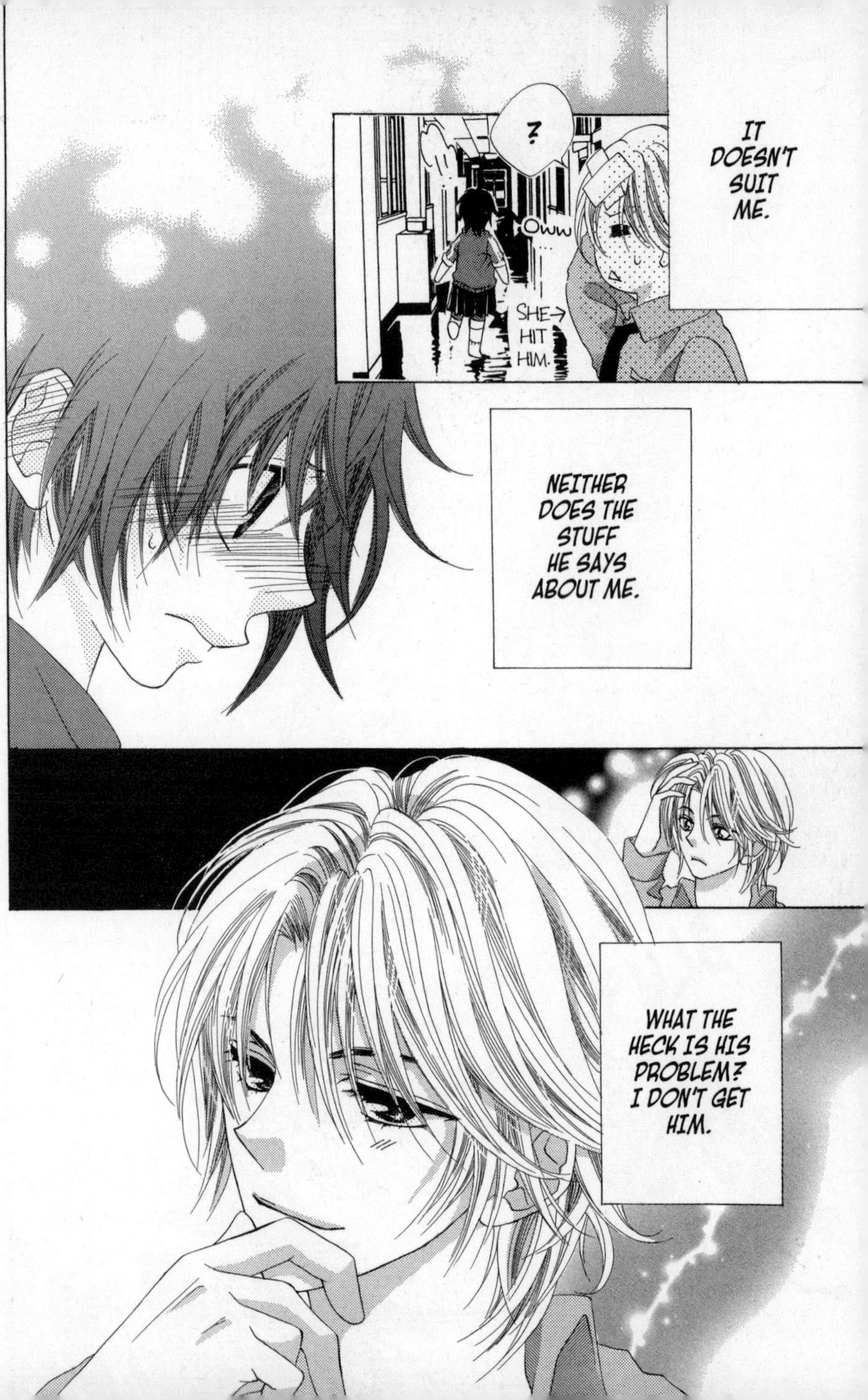
IT DOESN'T SUIT ME.
?
Oww...
SHE→ HIT HIM.
NEITHER DOES THE STUFF HE SAYS ABOUT ME.
WHAT THE HECK IS HIS PROBLEM? I DON'T GET HIM.

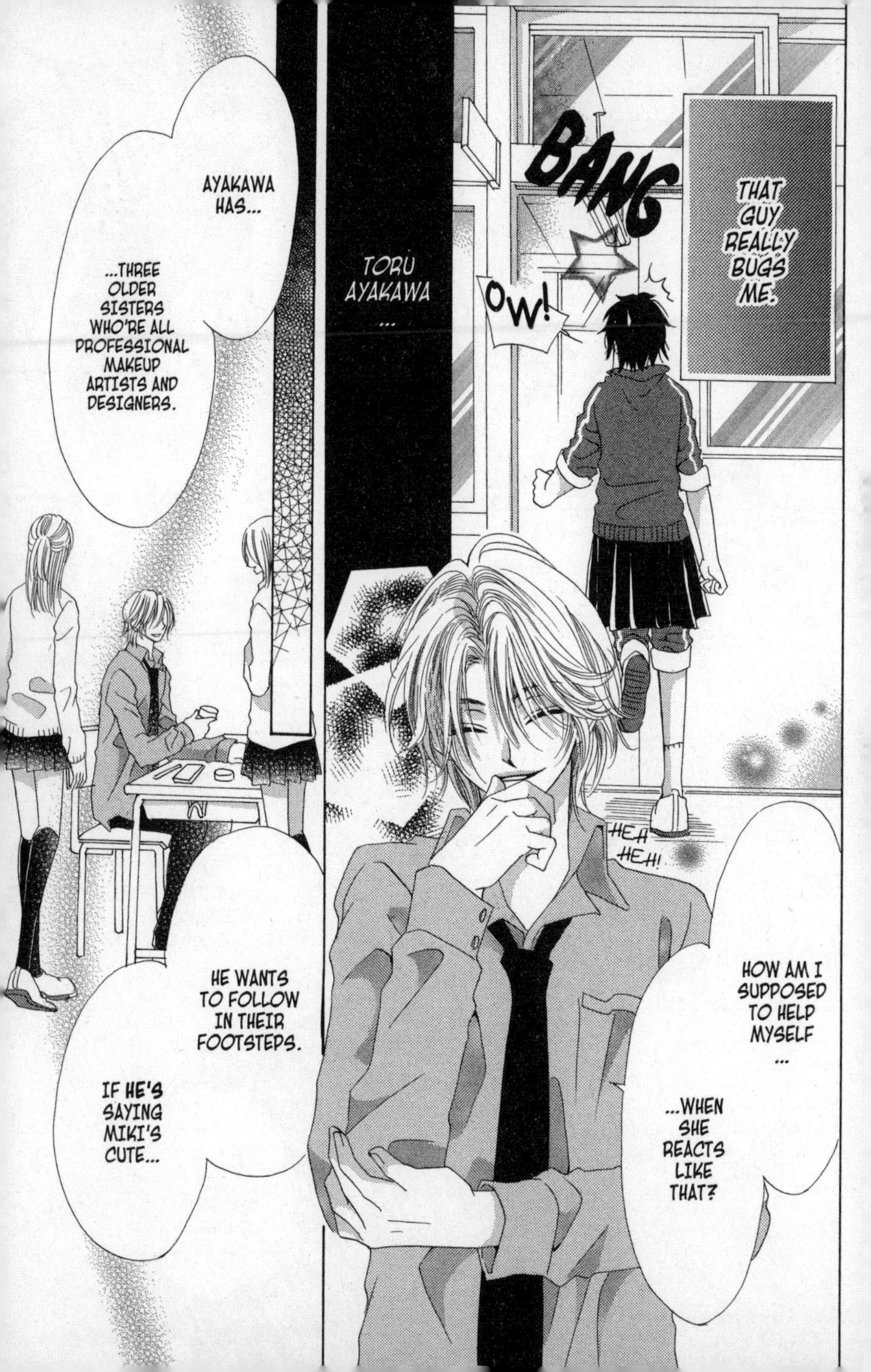
THAT GUY REALLY BUGS ME.
BANG
OW!
TORU AYAKAWA ...
HEH HEH!
HOW AM I SUPPOSED TO HELP MYSELF ...
...WHEN SHE REACTS LIKE THAT?
AYAKAWA HAS...
...THREE OLDER SISTERS WHO'RE ALL PROFESSIONAL MAKEUP ARTISTS AND DESIGNERS.
HE WANTS TO FOLLOW IN THEIR FOOTSTEPS.
IF HE'S SAYING MIKI'S CUTE...

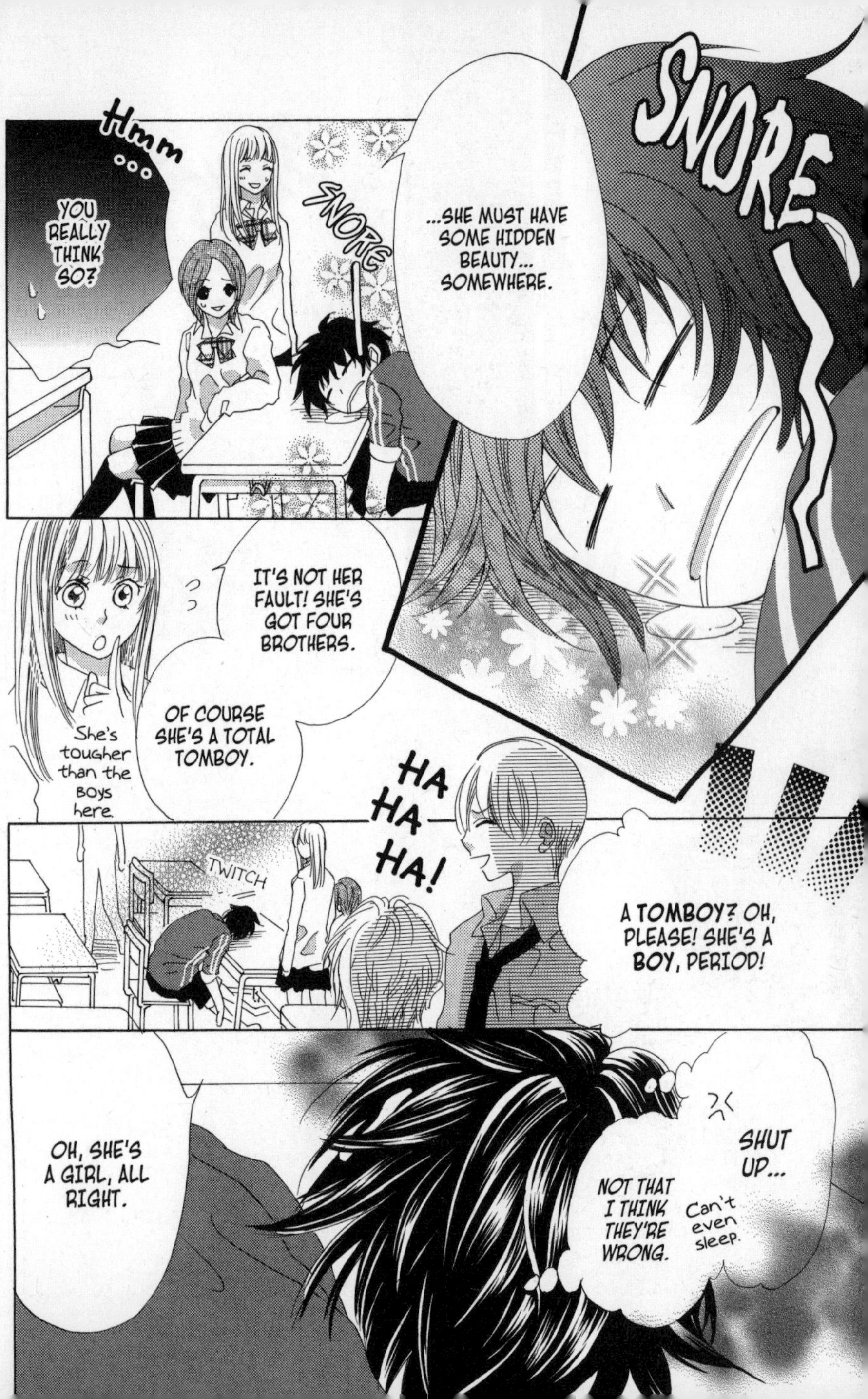
SNORE
...SHE MUST HAVE SOME HIDDEN BEAUTY... SOMEWHERE.
Hmm...
YOU REALLY THINK SO?
SNORE
IT'S NOT HER FAULT! SHE'S GOT FOUR BROTHERS.
OF COURSE SHE'S A TOTAL TOMBOY.
She's tougher than the boys here.
HA HA HA!
A TOMBOY? OH, PLEASE! SHE'S A BOY, PERIOD!
TWITCH
SHUT UP...
Can't even sleep.
NOT THAT I THINK THEY'RE WRONG.
OH, SHE'S A GIRL, ALL RIGHT.

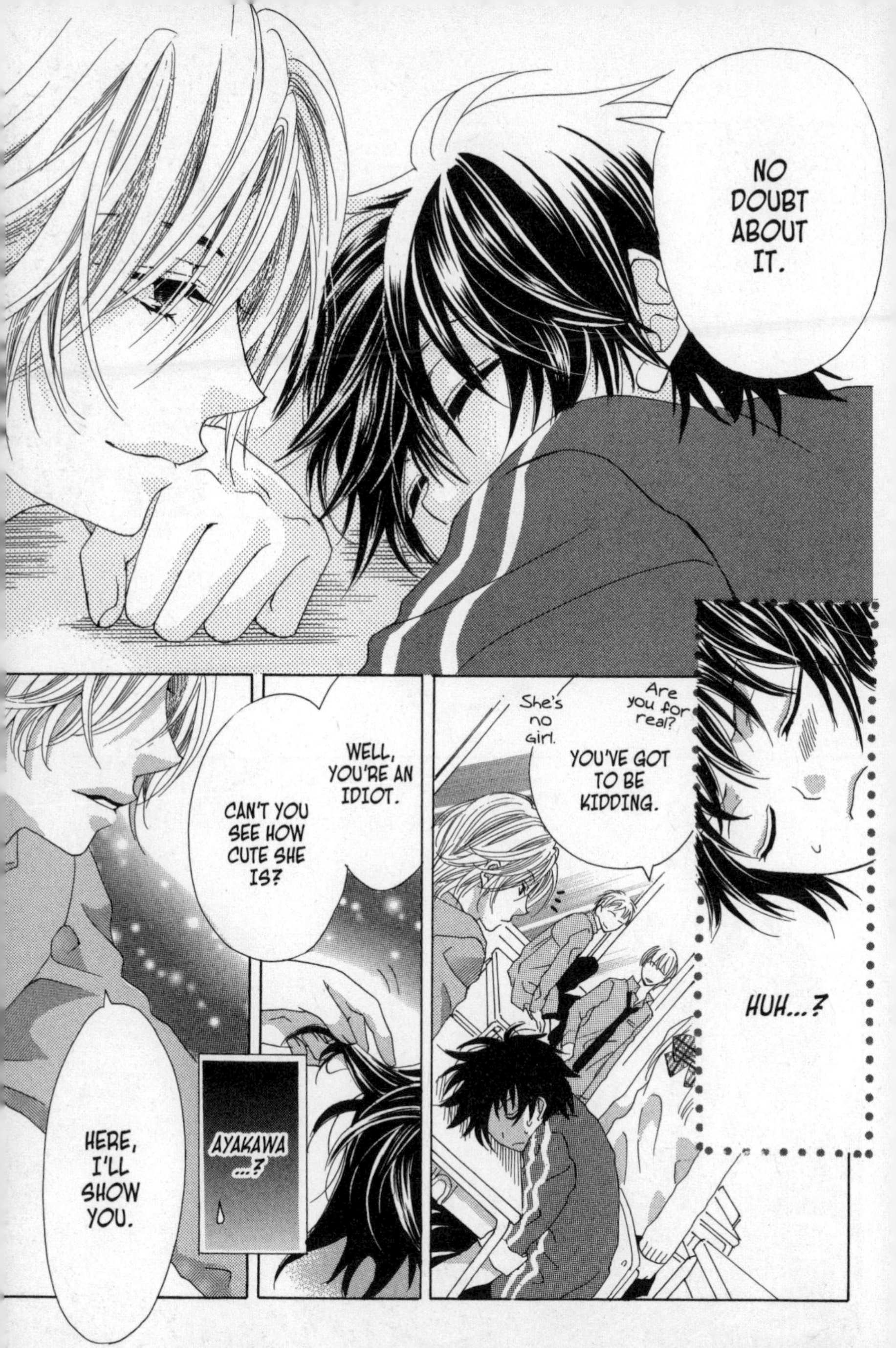
NO DOUBT ABOUT IT.
HUH...?
Are you for real?
She's no girl.
YOU'VE GOT TO BE KIDDING.
WELL, YOU'RE AN IDIOT.
CAN'T YOU SEE HOW CUTE SHE IS?
AYAKAWA ...?
HERE, I'LL SHOW YOU.

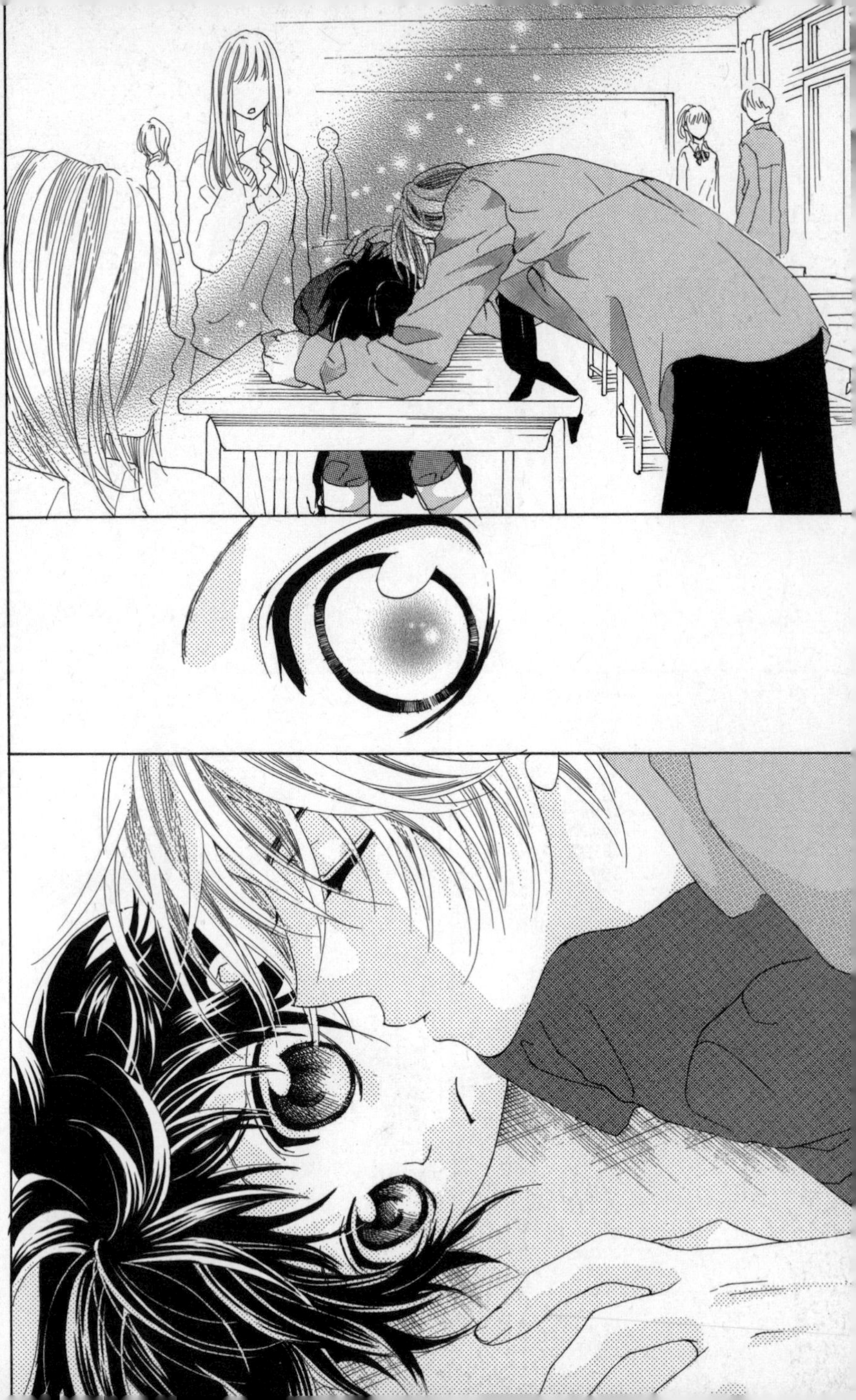

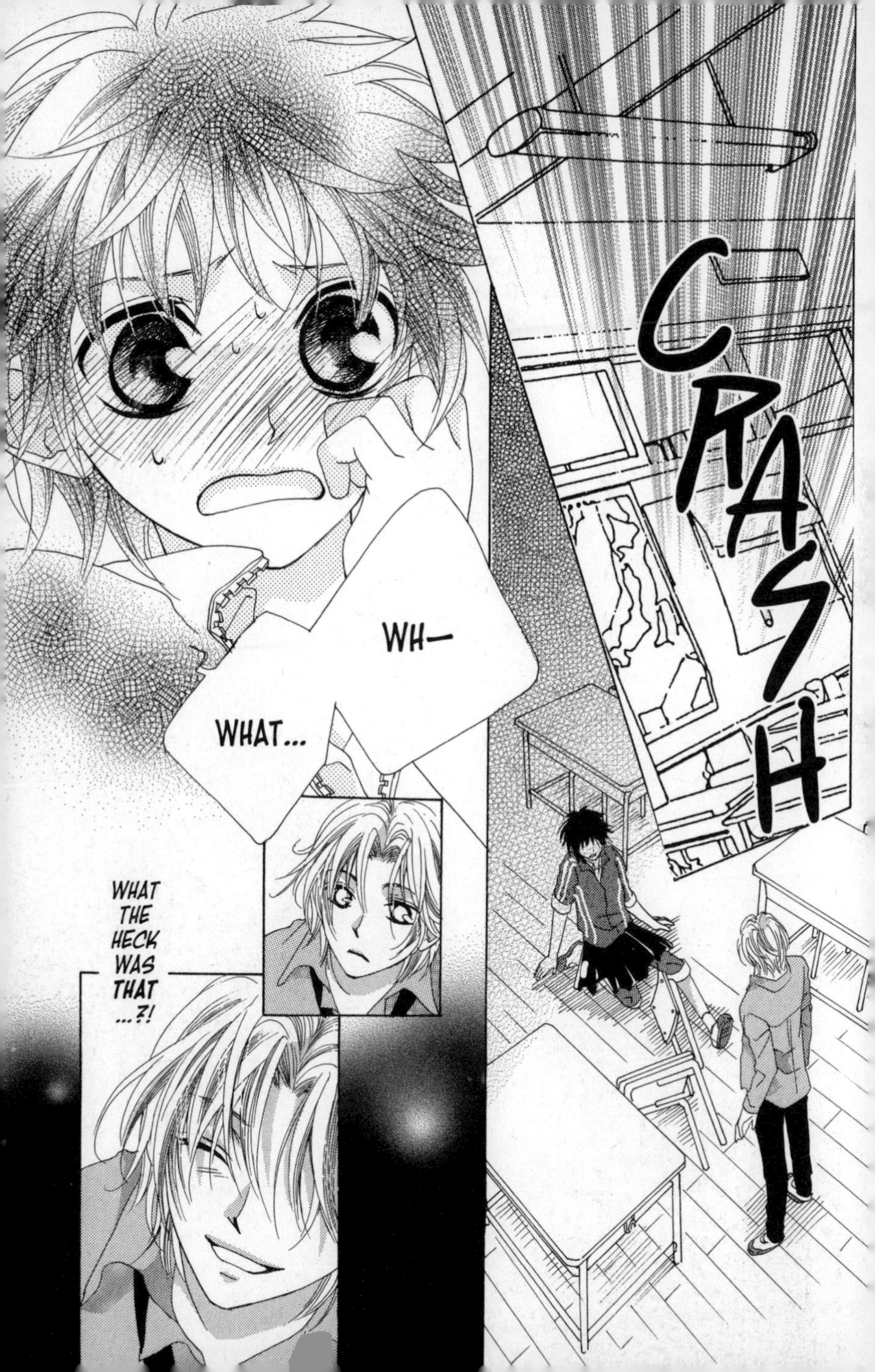
CRASH
WH—
WHAT...
WHAT THE HECK WAS THAT ...?!

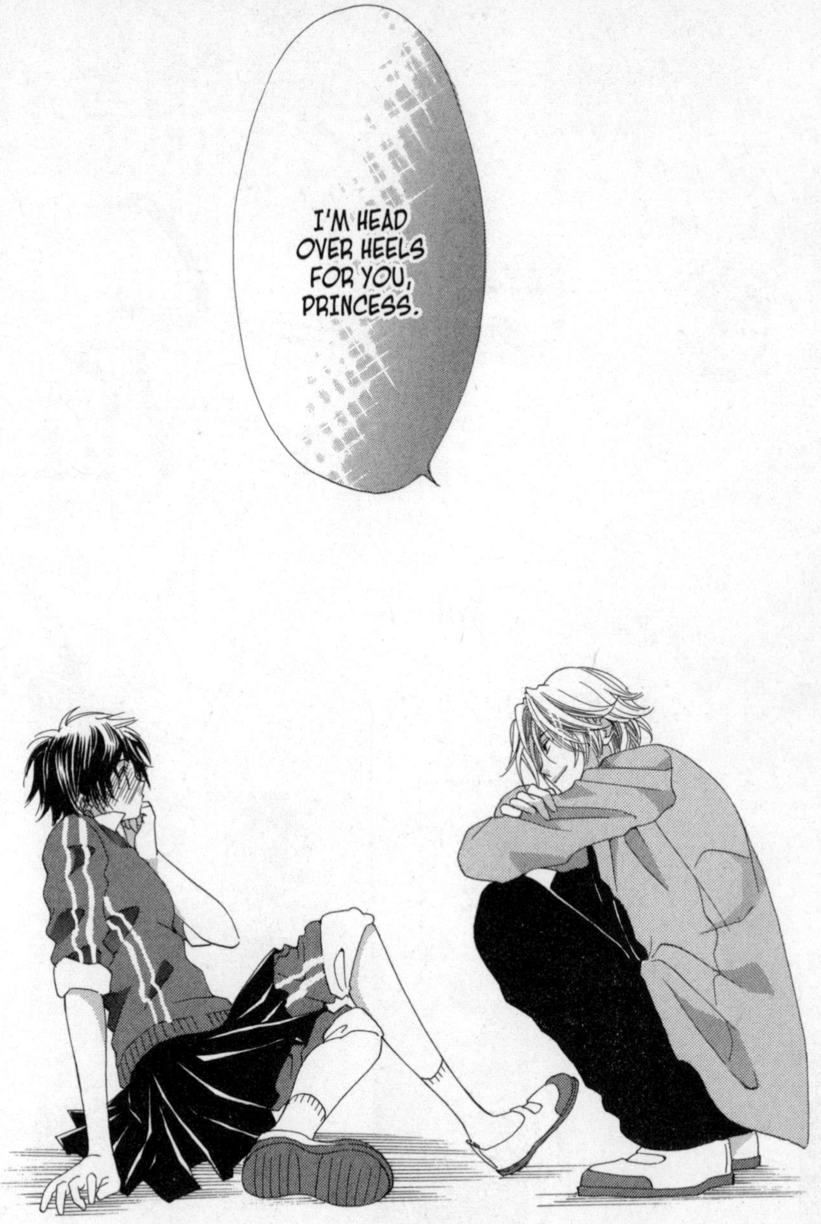
I'M HEAD OVER HEELS FOR YOU, PRINCESS.

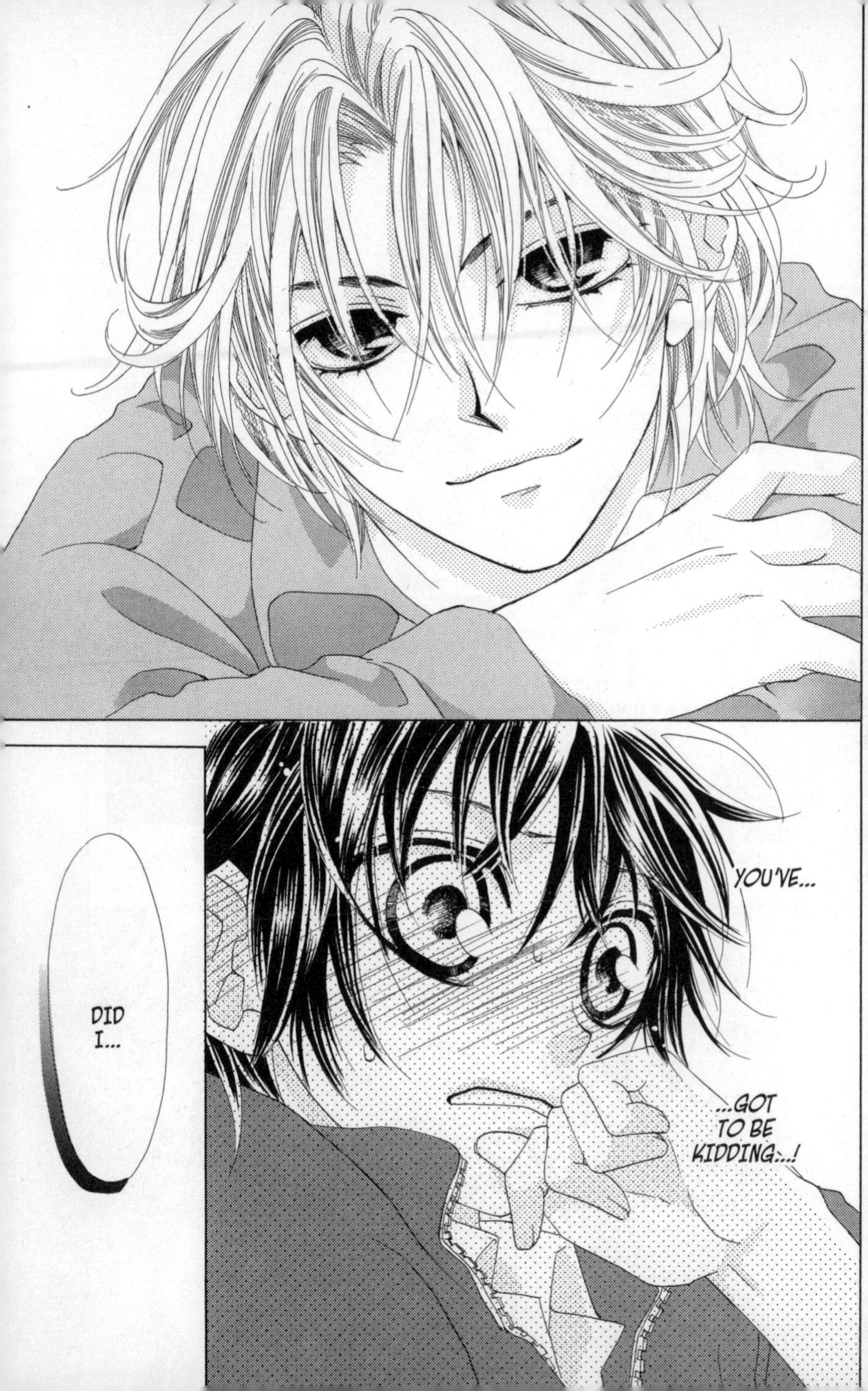
YOU'VE...
...GOT TO BE KIDDING...!
DID I...

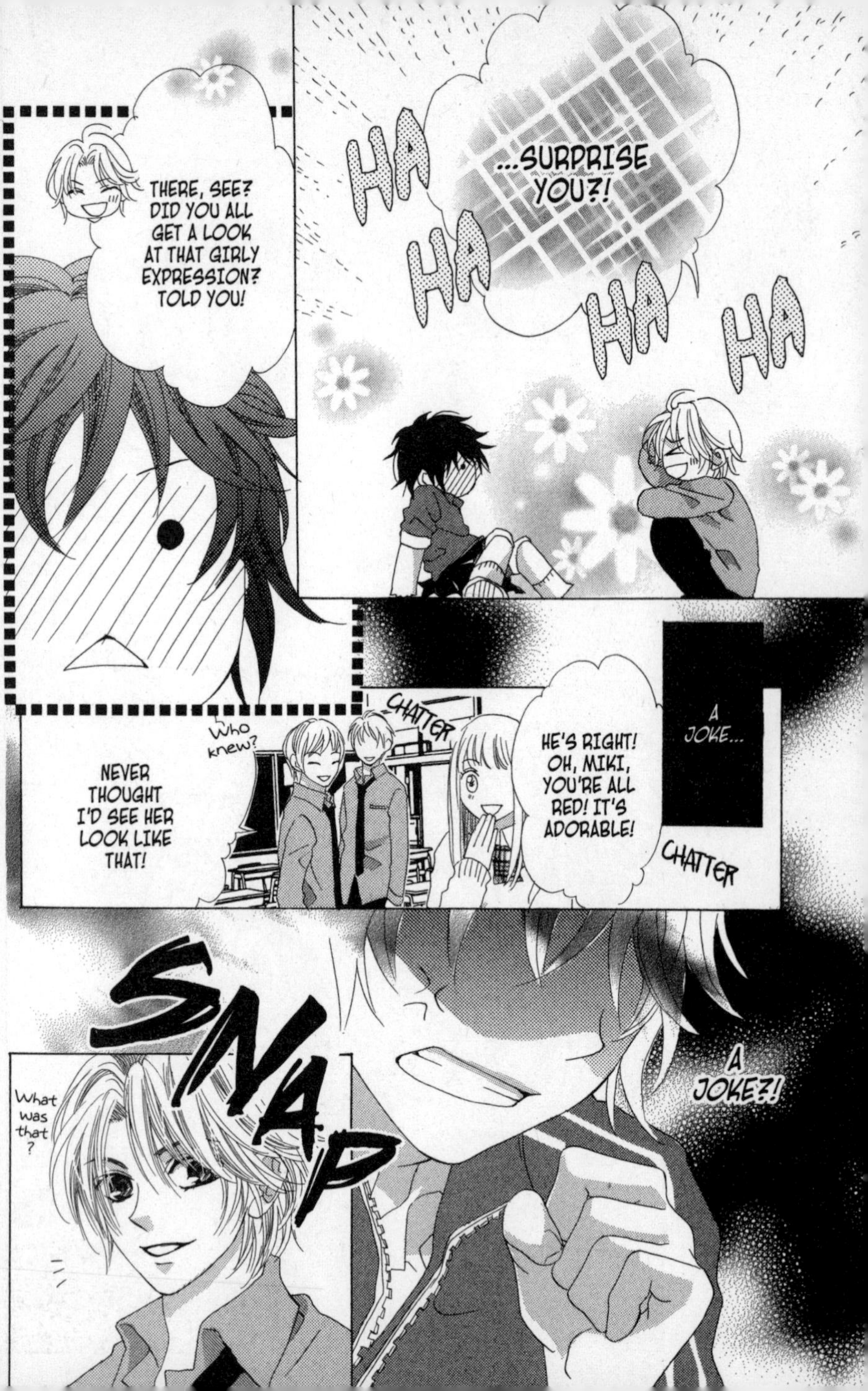
...SURPRISE YOU?!
HA HA HA HA
THERE, SEE? DID YOU ALL GET A LOOK AT THAT GIRLY EXPRESSION? TOLD YOU!
A JOKE...
CHATTER
HE'S RIGHT! OH, MIKI, YOU'RE ALL RED! IT'S ADORABLE!
CHATTER
Who knew?
NEVER THOUGHT I'D SEE HER LOOK LIKE THAT!
A JOKE?!
SNAP
What was that?

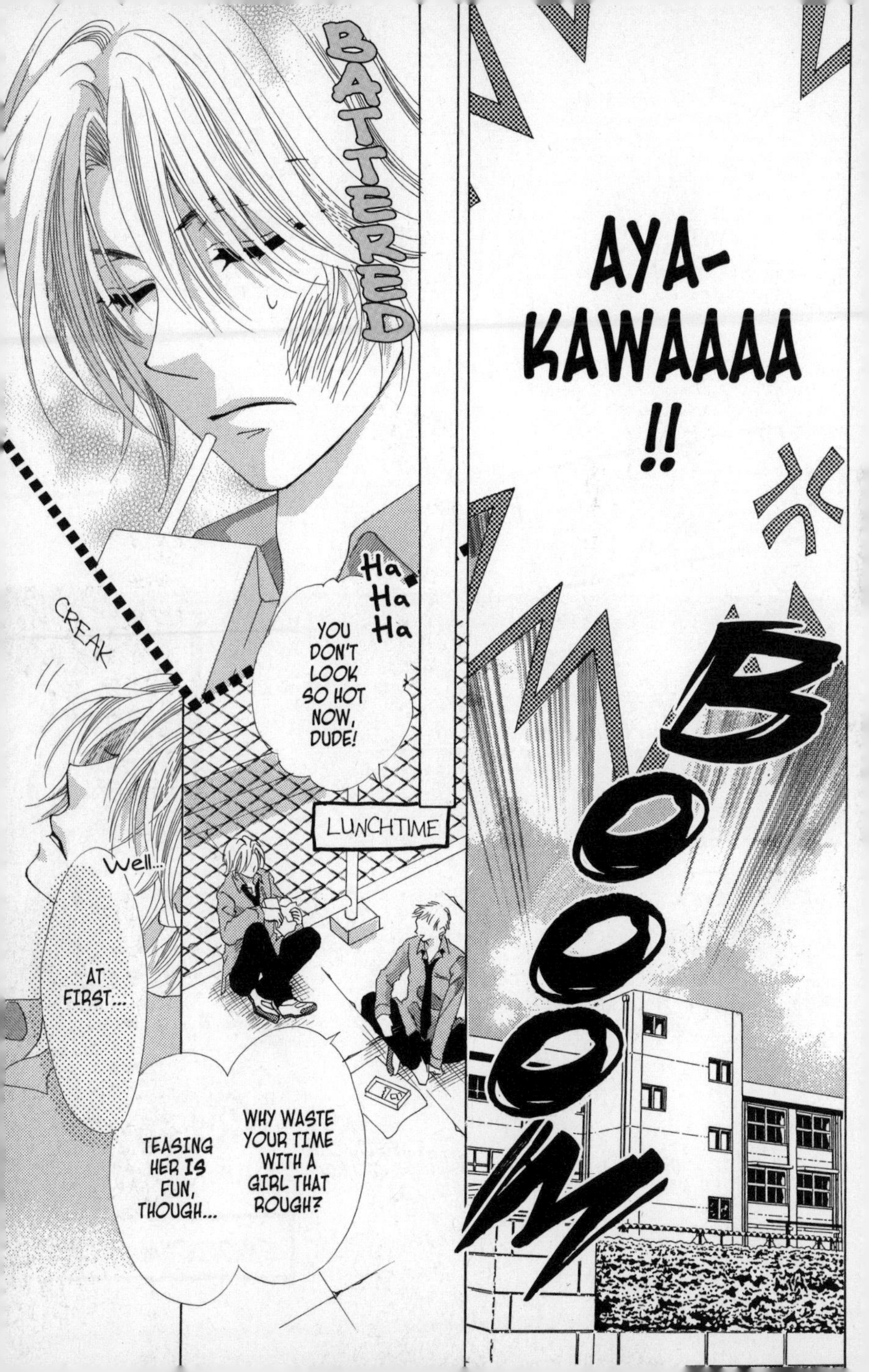

AYA-KAWAAAA!!
BOOOOM
BATTERED
Ha Ha Ha
YOU DON'T LOOK SO HOT NOW, DUDE!
LUNCHTIME
CREAK
WHY WASTE YOUR TIME WITH A GIRL THAT ROUGH?
Well...
AT FIRST...
TEASING HER IS FUN, THOUGH...

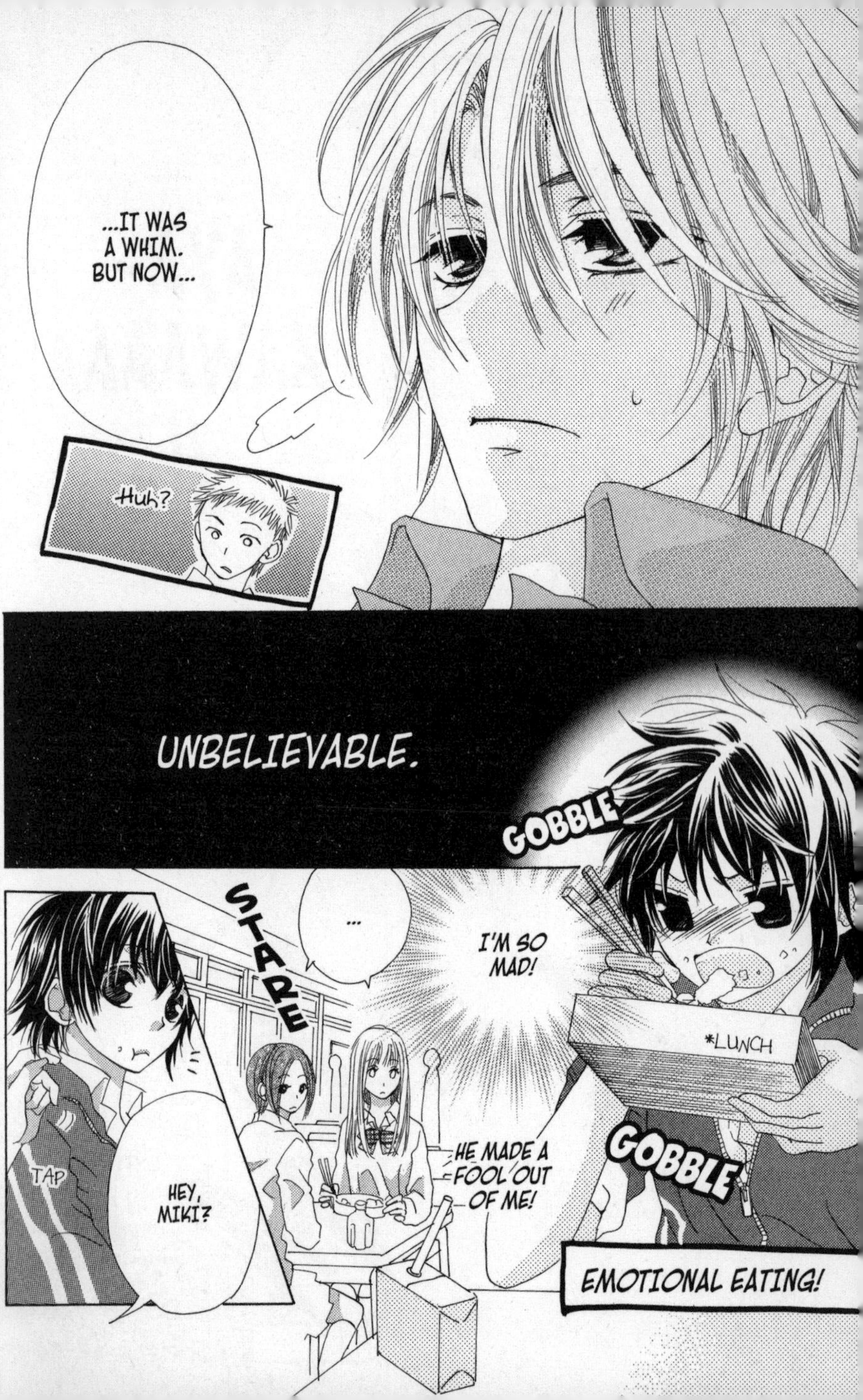
...IT WAS A WHIM. BUT NOW...
Huh?
GOBBLE
UNBELIEVABLE.
I'M SO MAD!
*LUNCH
GOBBLE
HE MADE A FOOL OUT OF ME!
EMOTIONAL EATING!
STARE
...
TAP
HEY, MIKI?

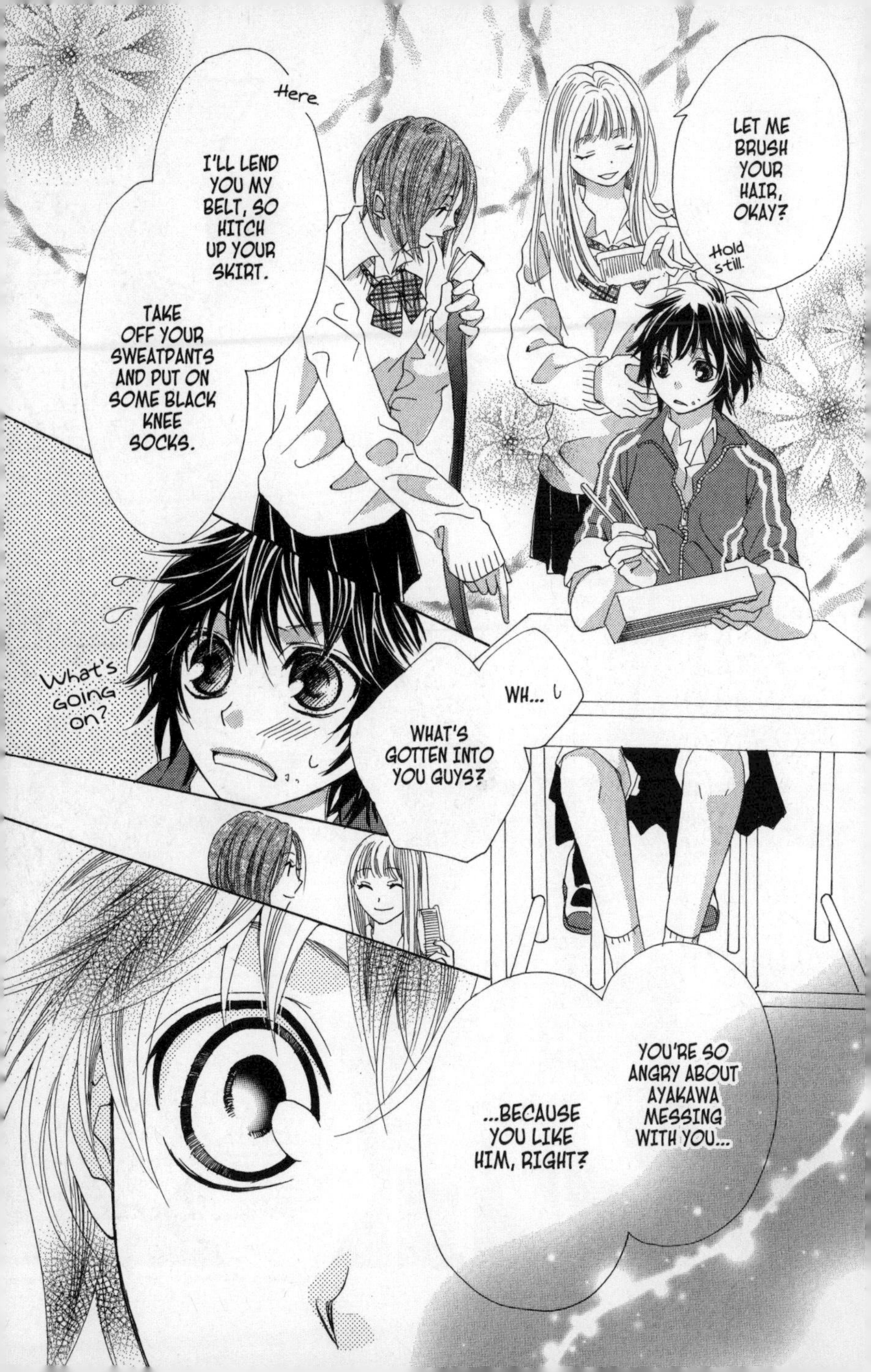
LET ME BRUSH YOUR HAIR, OKAY?
Hold still.
Here.
I'LL LEND YOU MY BELT, SO HITCH UP YOUR SKIRT.
TAKE OFF YOUR SWEATPANTS AND PUT ON SOME BLACK KNEE SOCKS.
WH...
WHAT'S GOTTEN INTO YOU GUYS?
What's going on?
YOU'RE SO ANGRY ABOUT AYAKAWA MESSING WITH YOU...
...BECAUSE YOU LIKE HIM, RIGHT?

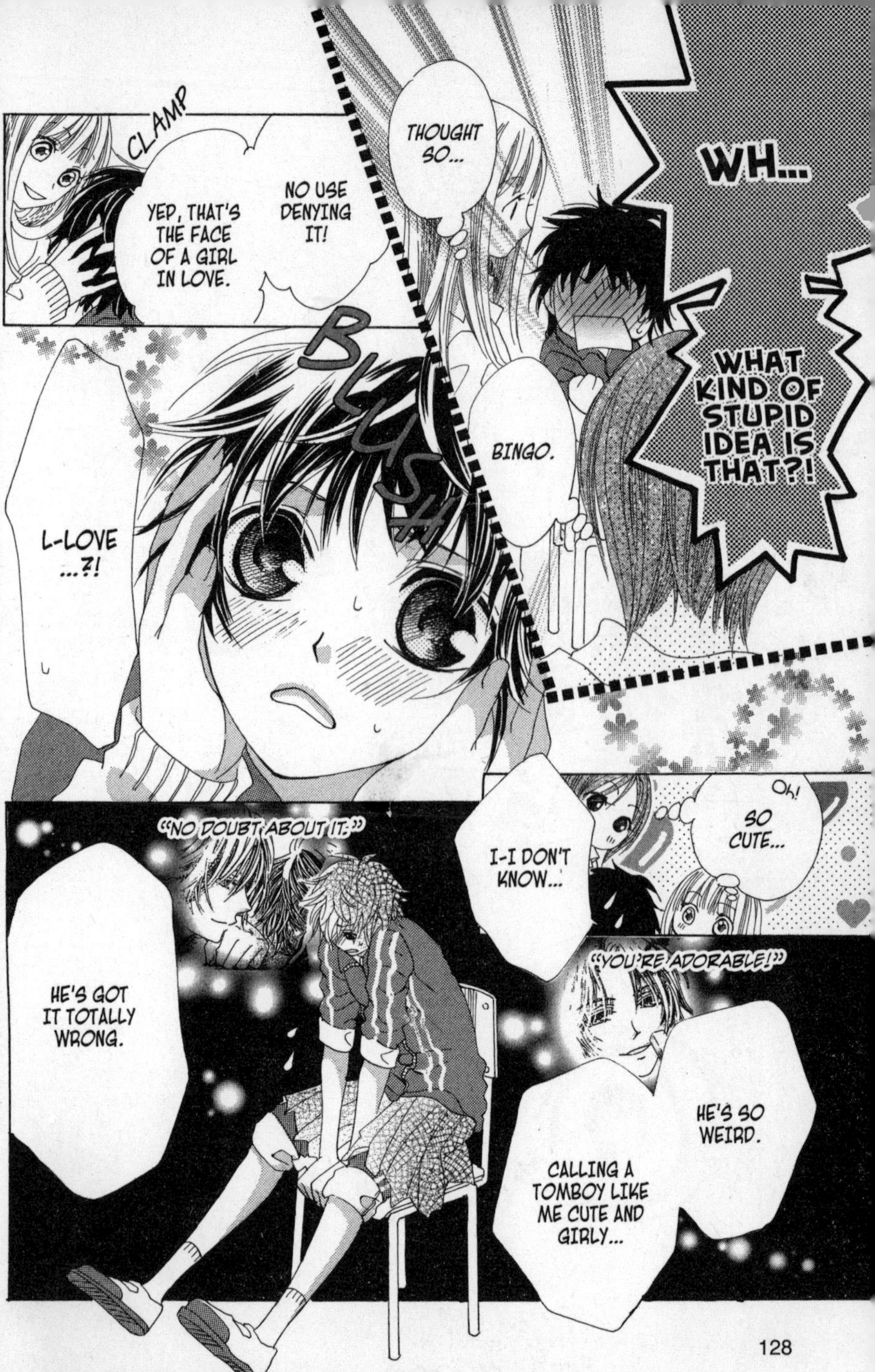
WH...
WHAT KIND OF STUPID IDEA IS THAT?!
THOUGHT SO...
BINGO.
CLAMP
NO USE DENYING IT!
YEP, THAT'S THE FACE OF A GIRL IN LOVE.
BLUSH
L-LOVE ...?!
I-I DON'T KNOW...
Oh!
SO CUTE...
"YOU'RE ADORABLE!"
HE'S SO WEIRD.
CALLING A TOMBOY LIKE ME CUTE AND GIRLY...
"NO DOUBT ABOUT IT."
HE'S GOT IT TOTALLY WRONG.

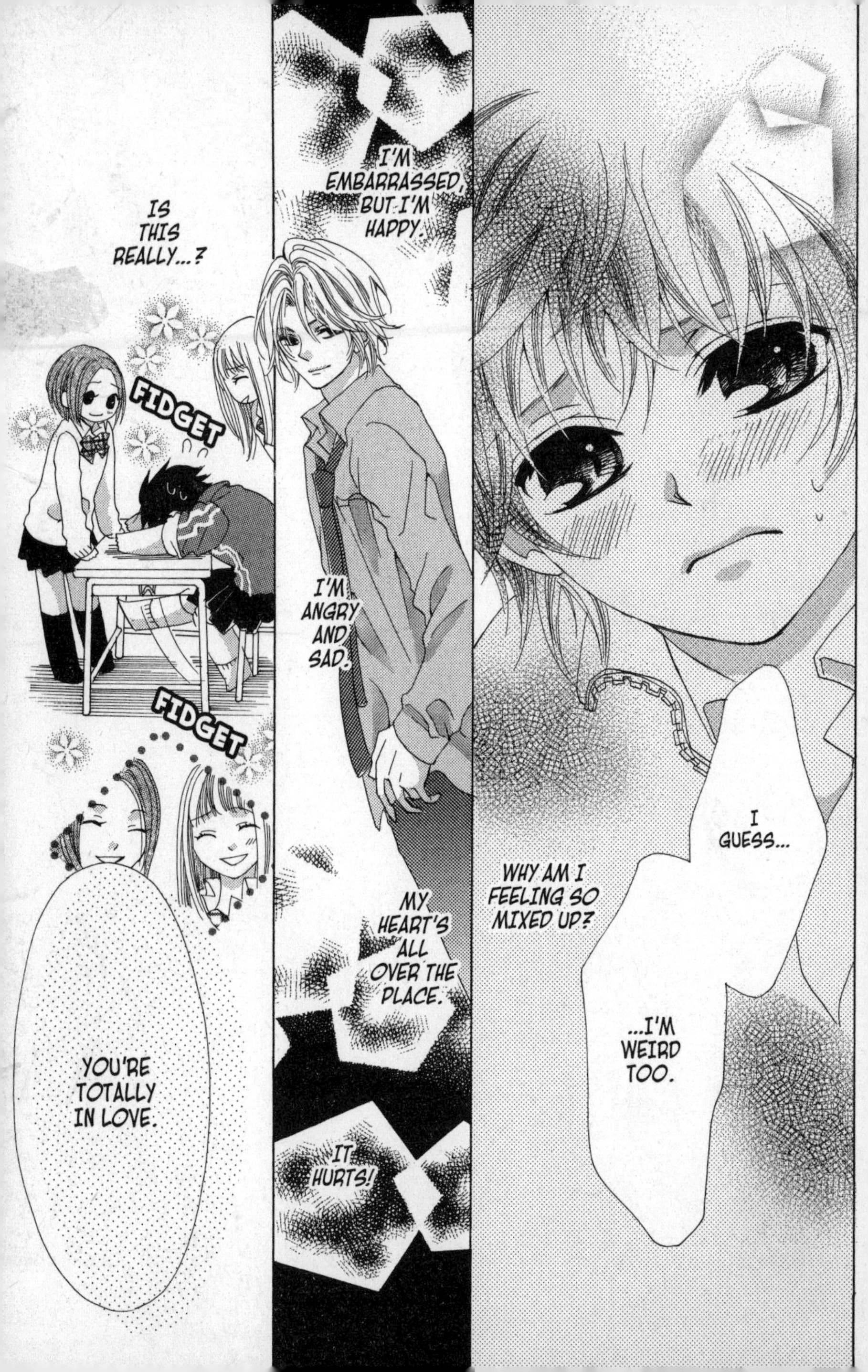
I GUESS...
WHY AM I FEELING SO MIXED UP?
...I'M WEIRD TOO.
I'M EMBARRASSED, BUT I'M HAPPY.
I'M ANGRY AND SAD.
MY HEART'S ALL OVER THE PLACE.
IT HURTS!
IS THIS REALLY...?
FIDGET
FIDGET
YOU'RE TOTALLY IN LOVE.

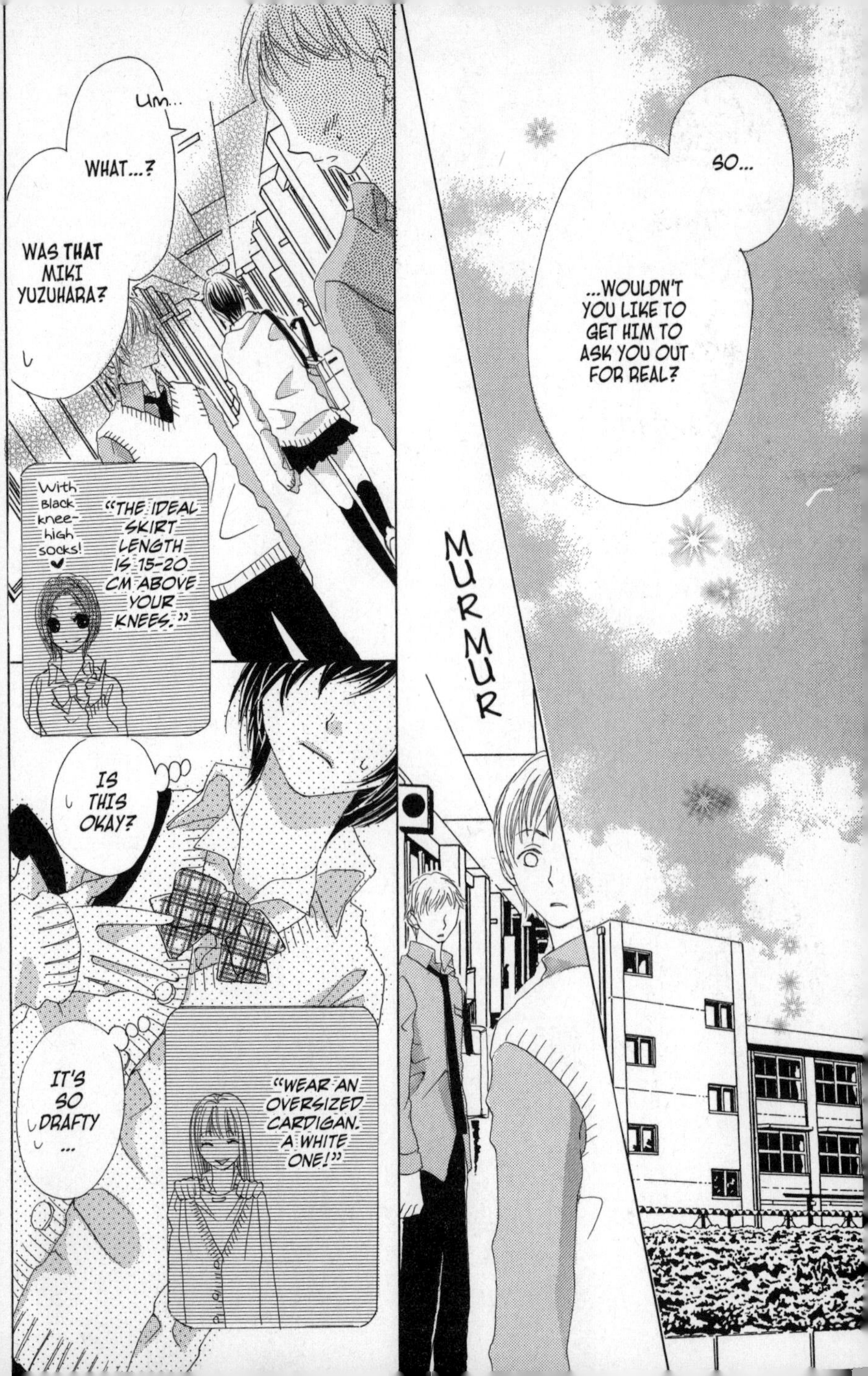
SO...
...WOULDN'T YOU LIKE TO GET HIM TO ASK YOU OUT FOR REAL?
MURMUR
Um...
WHAT...?
WAS THAT MIKI YUZUHARA?
"THE IDEAL SKIRT LENGTH IS 15-20 CM ABOVE YOUR KNEES."
With black knee-high socks!
IS THIS OKAY?
"WEAR AN OVERSIZED CARDIGAN. A WHITE ONE!"
IT'S SO DRAFTY...

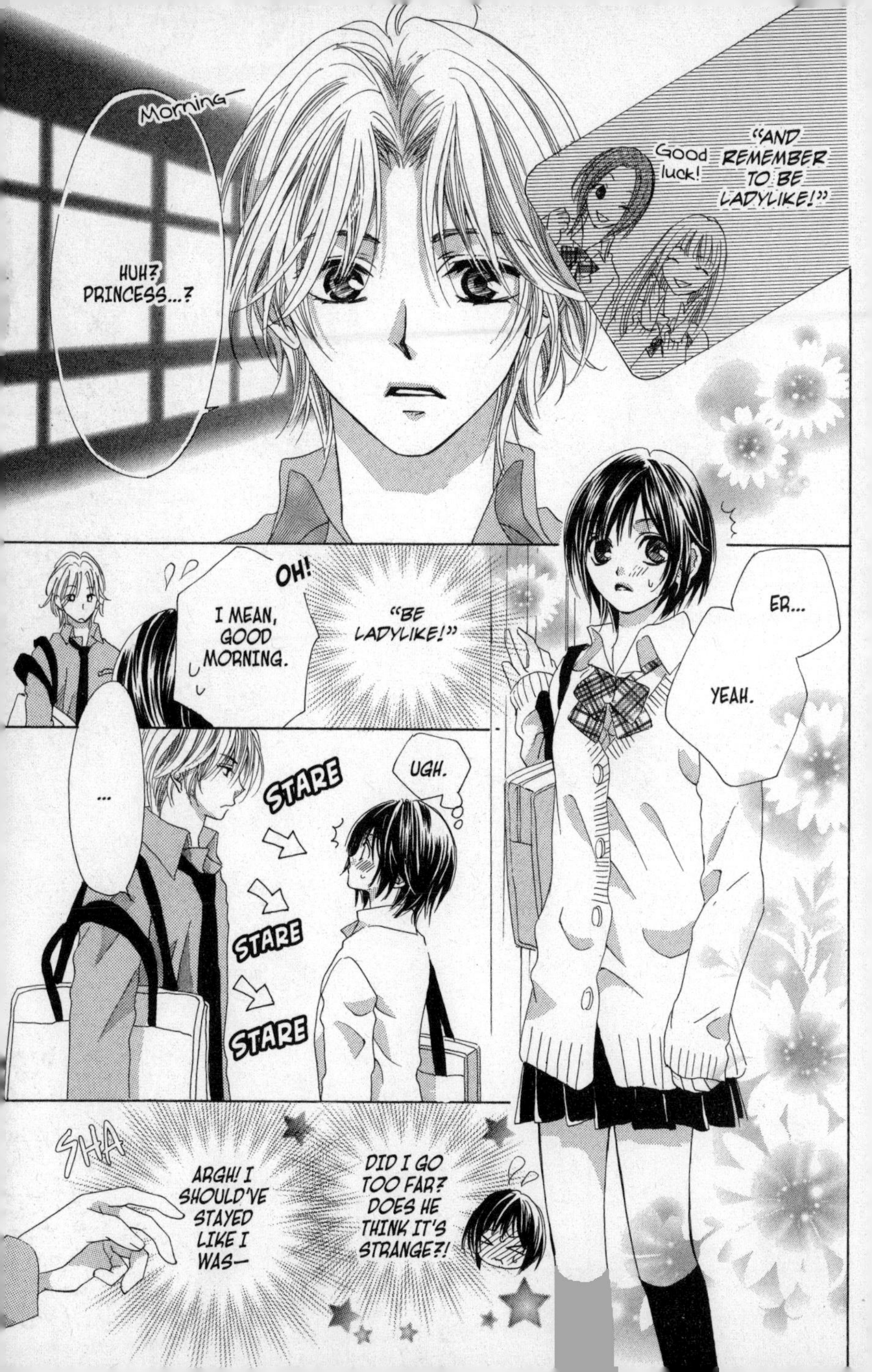
"AND REMEMBER TO BE LADYLIKE!"
Good luck!
Morning—
HUH? PRINCESS...?
ER...
YEAH.
OH!
"BE LADYLIKE!"
I MEAN, GOOD MORNING.
UGH.
STARE
STARE
STARE
...
DID I GO TOO FAR? DOES HE THINK IT'S STRANGE?!
ARGH! I SHOULD'VE STAYED LIKE I WAS—
SHA

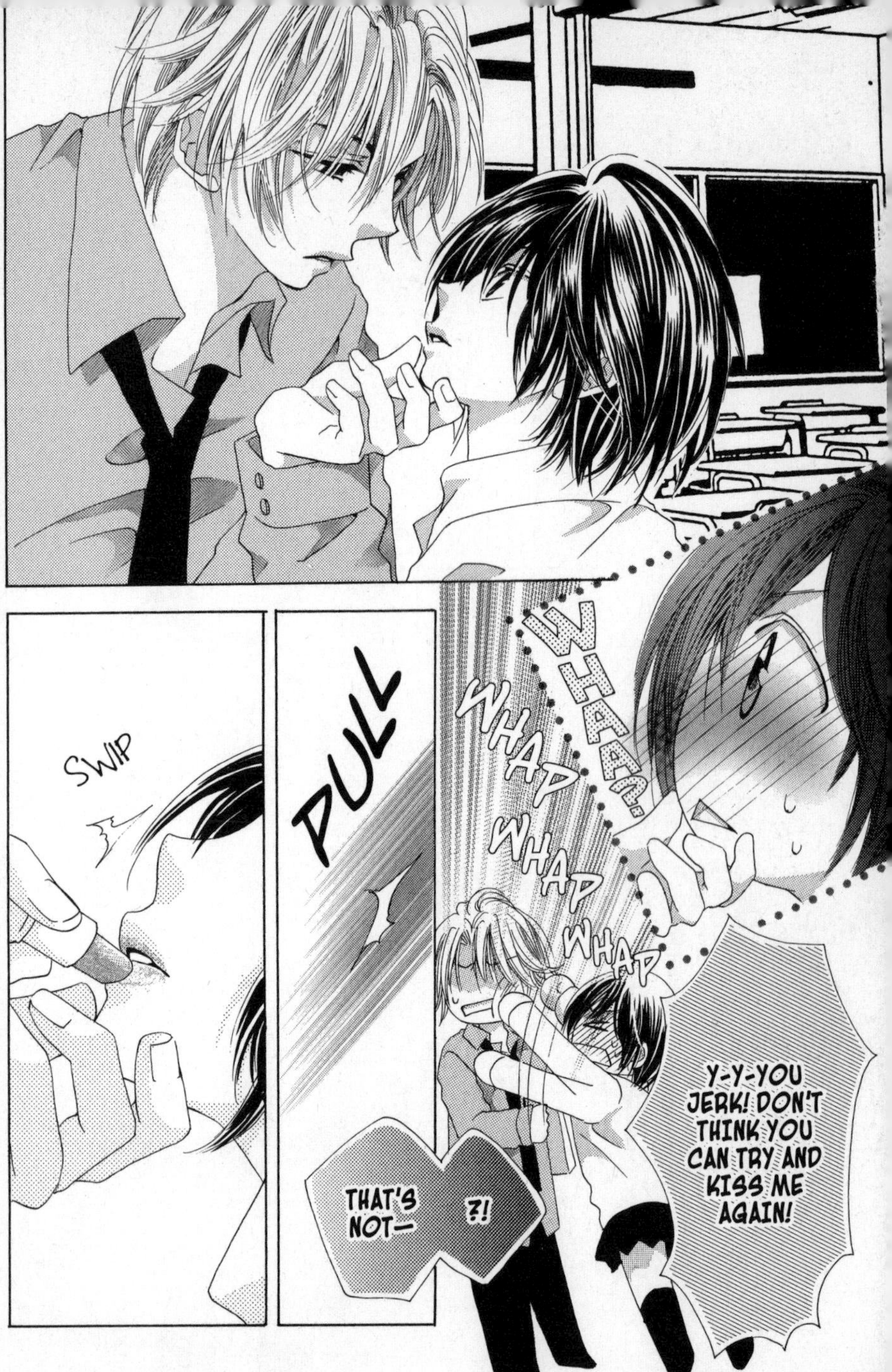
WHAAA?!
WHAP WHAP WHAP WHAP
Y-Y-YOU JERK! DON'T THINK YOU CAN TRY AND KISS ME AGAIN!
THAT'S NOT—
?!
PULL
SWIP

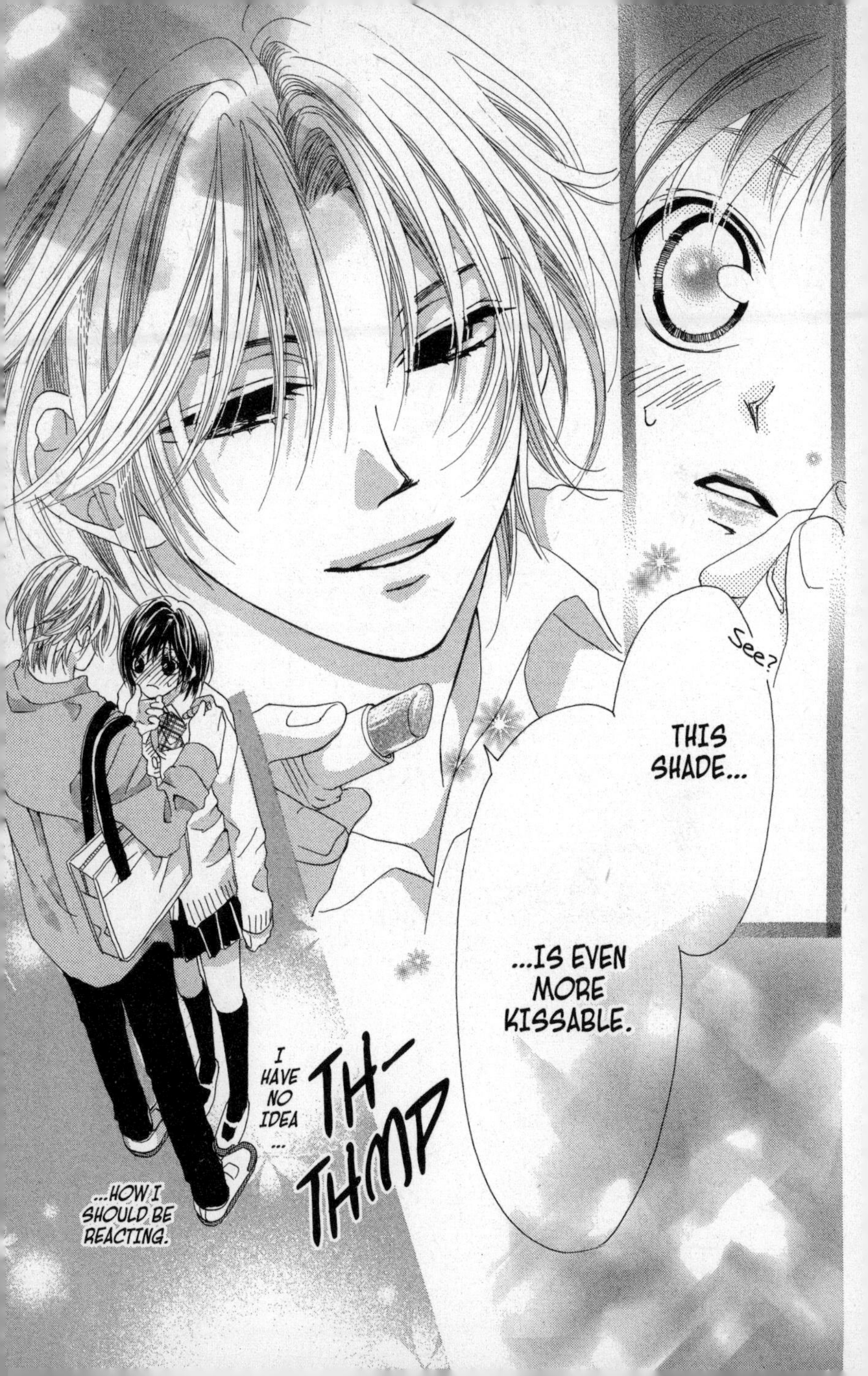
See?
THIS SHADE...
...IS EVEN MORE KISSABLE.
I HAVE NO IDEA...
TH-THMP
...HOW I SHOULD BE REACTING.

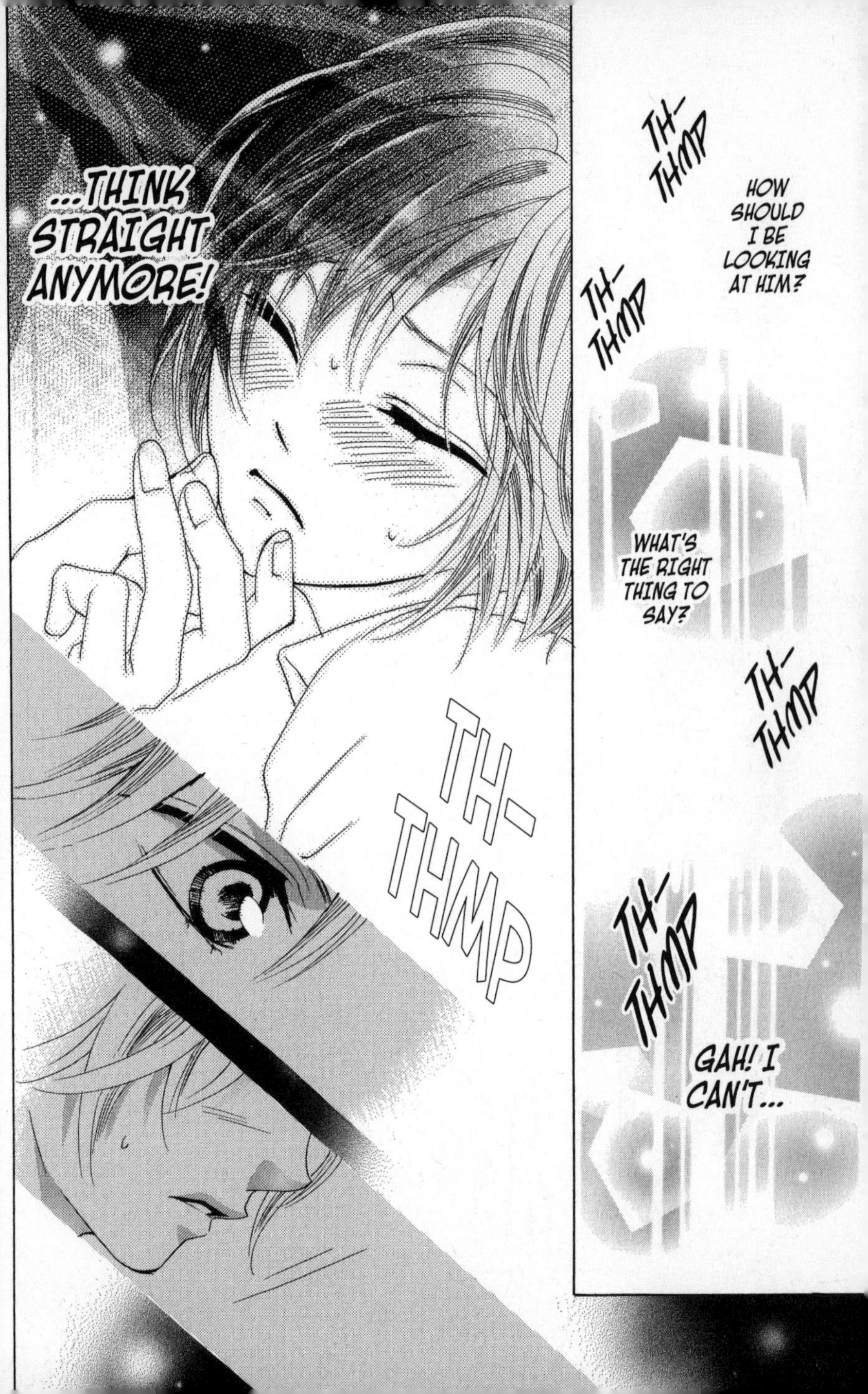
TH-THMP
HOW SHOULD I BE LOOKING AT HIM?
TH-THMP
WHAT'S THE RIGHT THING TO SAY?
TH-THMP
TH-THMP
GAH! I CAN'T...
...THINK STRAIGHT ANYMORE!
TH-THMP

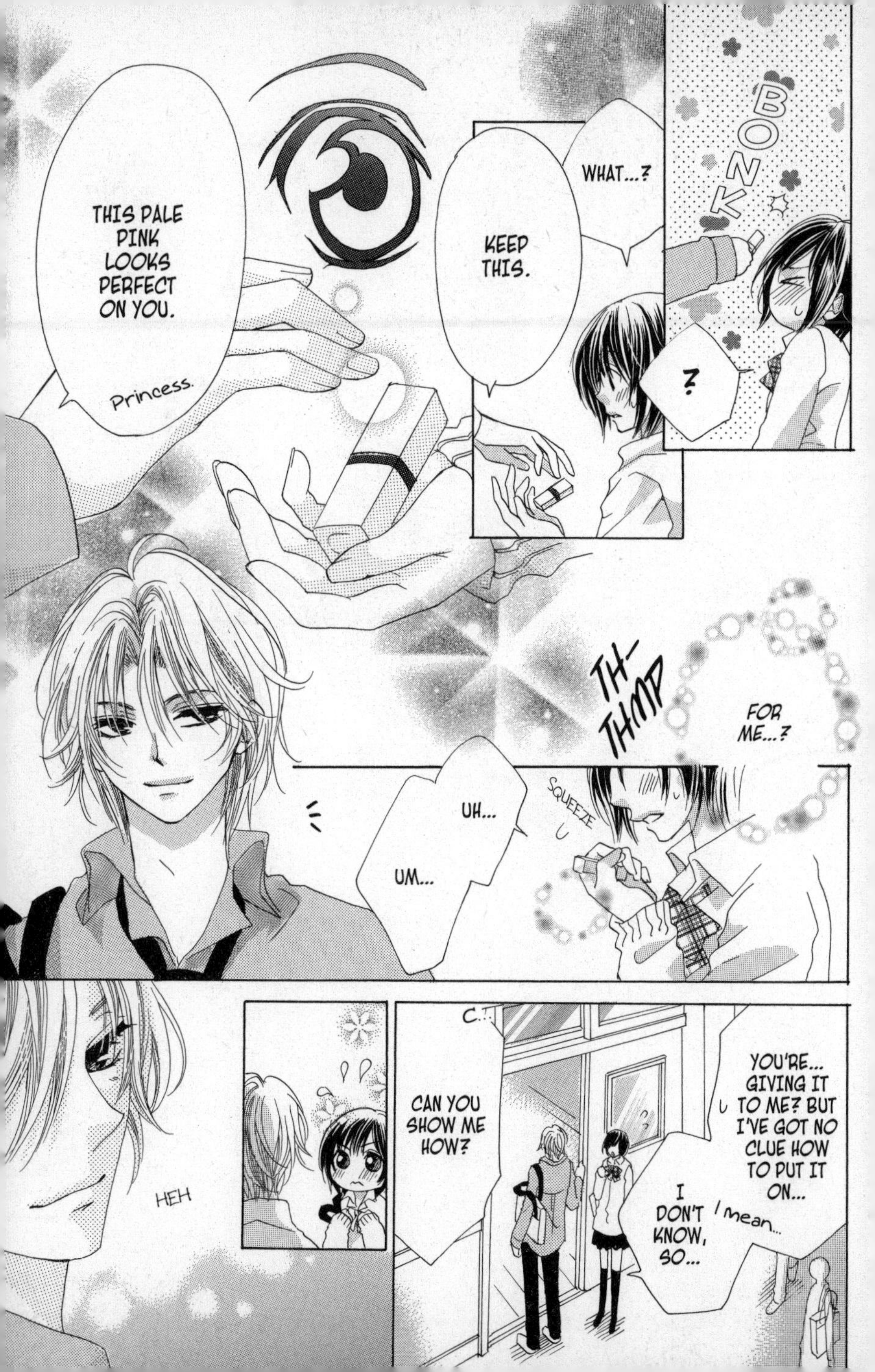
BONK!
?
WHAT...?
KEEP THIS.
THIS PALE PINK LOOKS PERFECT ON YOU.
Princess.
TH-THMP
FOR ME...?
SQUEEZE
UH...
UM...
YOU'RE... GIVING IT TO ME? BUT I'VE GOT NO CLUE HOW TO PUT IT ON...
I mean...
I DON'T KNOW, SO...
C...
CAN YOU SHOW ME HOW?
HEH

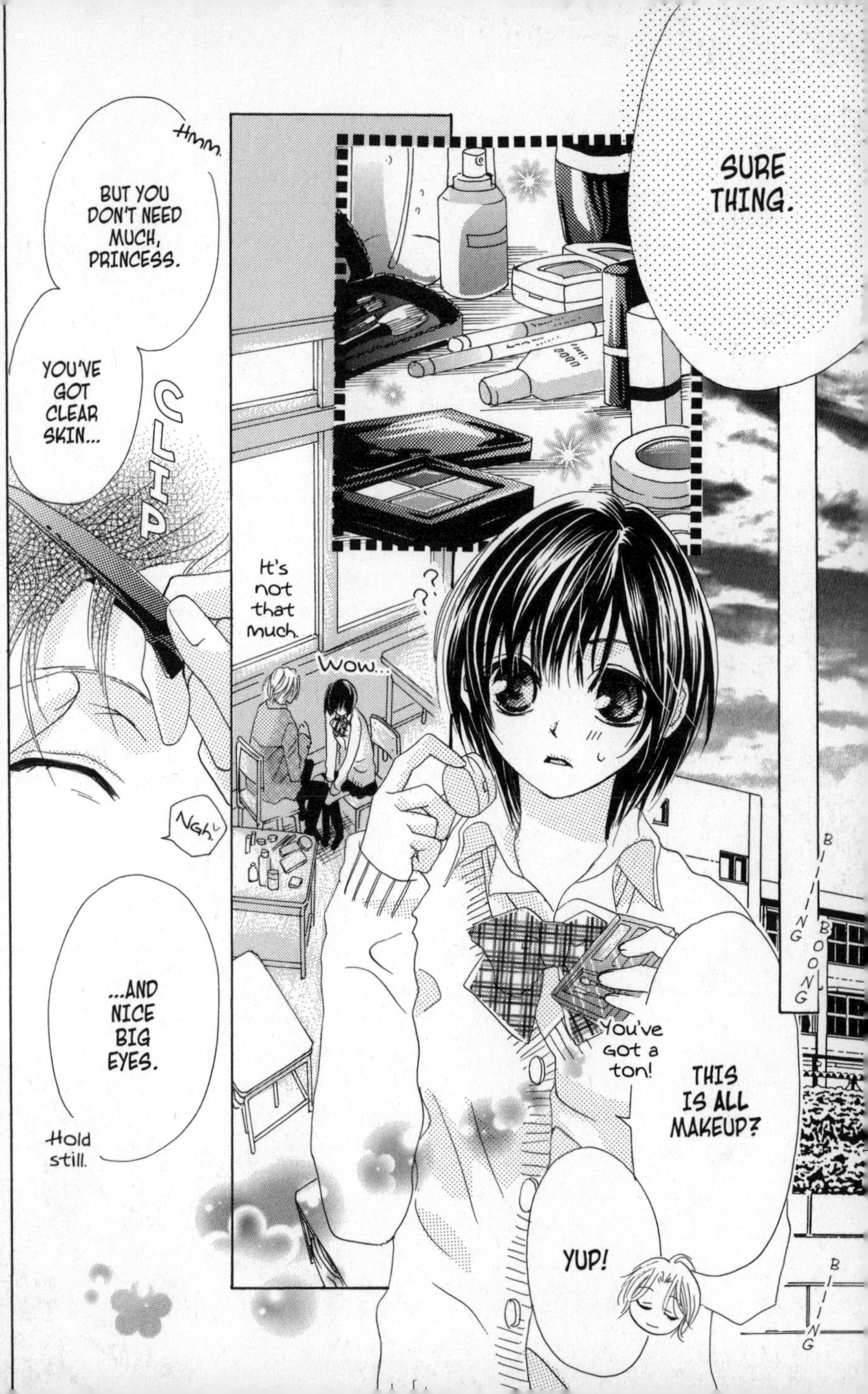
SURE THING.
BIIING BOONG
THIS IS ALL MAKEUP?
You've got a ton!
YUP!
It's not that much.
Wow...
BIIING
Hmm.
BUT YOU DON'T NEED MUCH, PRINCESS.
YOU'VE GOT CLEAR SKIN...
CLIP
Ngh.
...AND NICE BIG EYES.
Hold still.

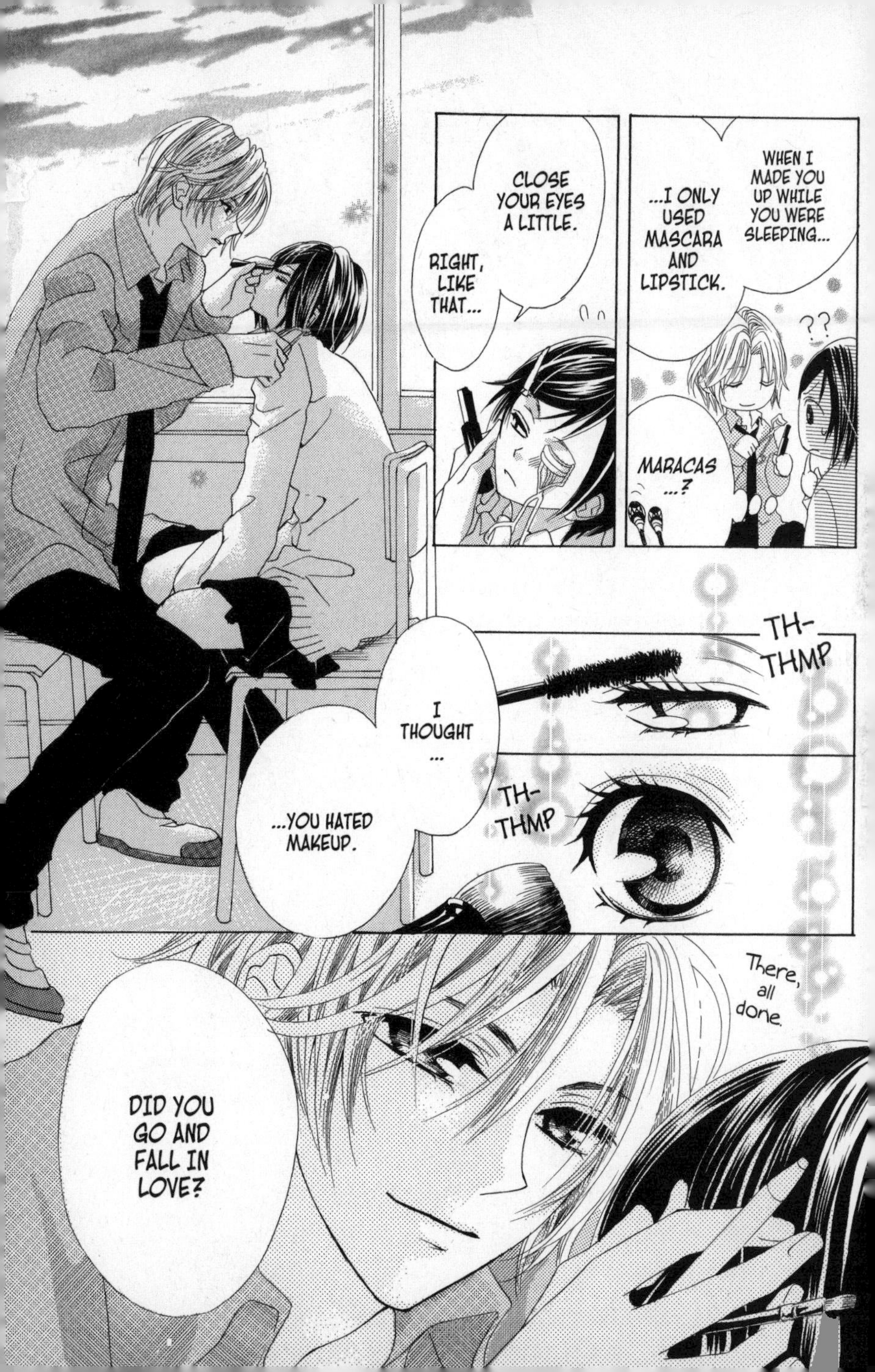
WHEN I MADE YOU UP WHILE YOU WERE SLEEPING...
...I ONLY USED MASCARA AND LIPSTICK.
MARACAS ...?
CLOSE YOUR EYES A LITTLE.
RIGHT, LIKE THAT...
TH-THMP
I THOUGHT ...
TH-THMP
...YOU HATED MAKEUP.
There, all done.
DID YOU GO AND FALL IN LOVE?

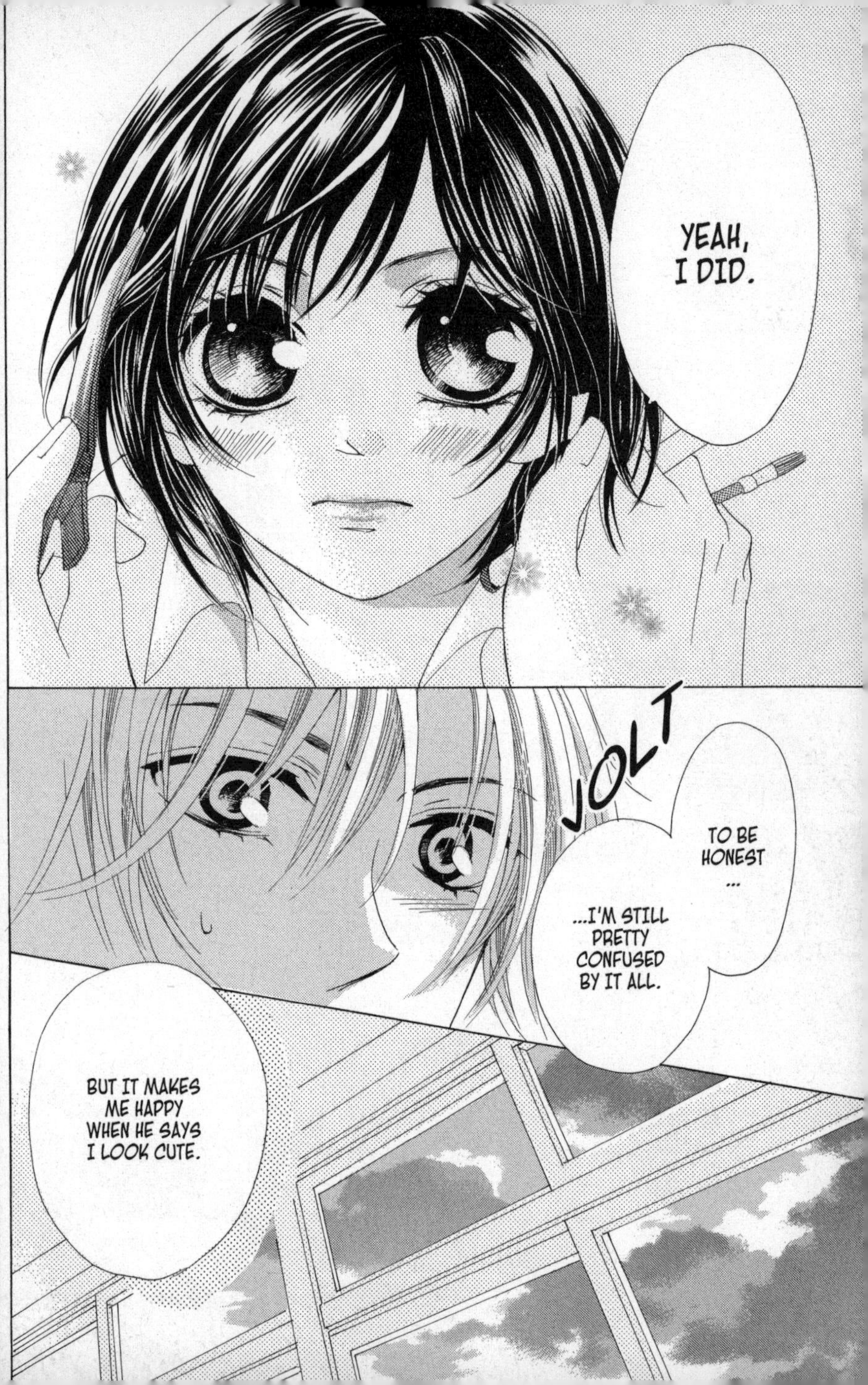
YEAH, I DID.
JOLT
TO BE HONEST ...
...I'M STILL PRETTY CONFUSED BY IT ALL.
BUT IT MAKES ME HAPPY WHEN HE SAYS I LOOK CUTE.

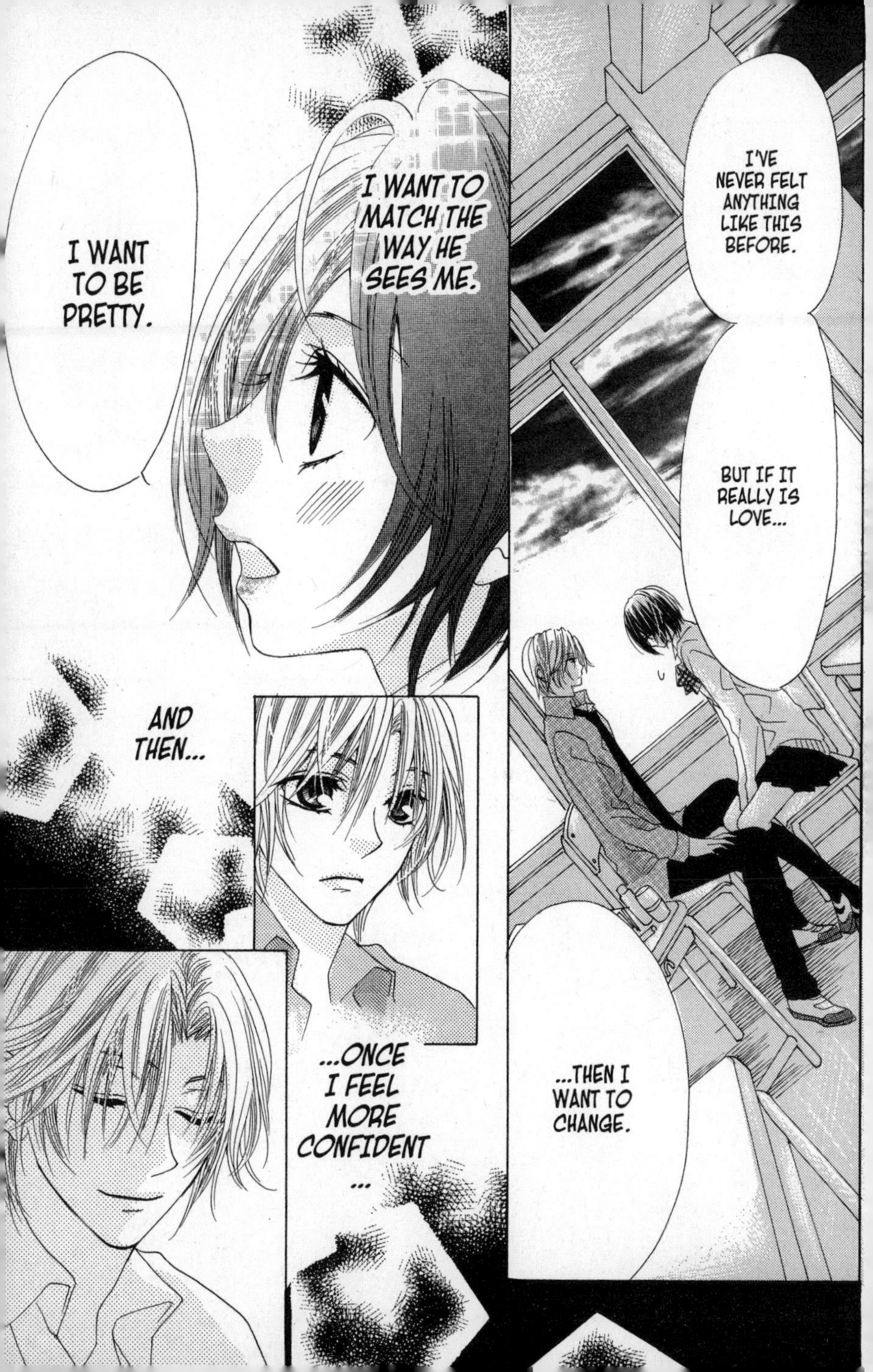

I'VE NEVER FELT ANYTHING LIKE THIS BEFORE.
BUT IF IT REALLY IS LOVE...
...THEN I WANT TO CHANGE.
I WANT TO MATCH THE WAY HE SEES ME.
I WANT TO BE PRETTY.
AND THEN...
...ONCE I FEEL MORE CONFIDENT...

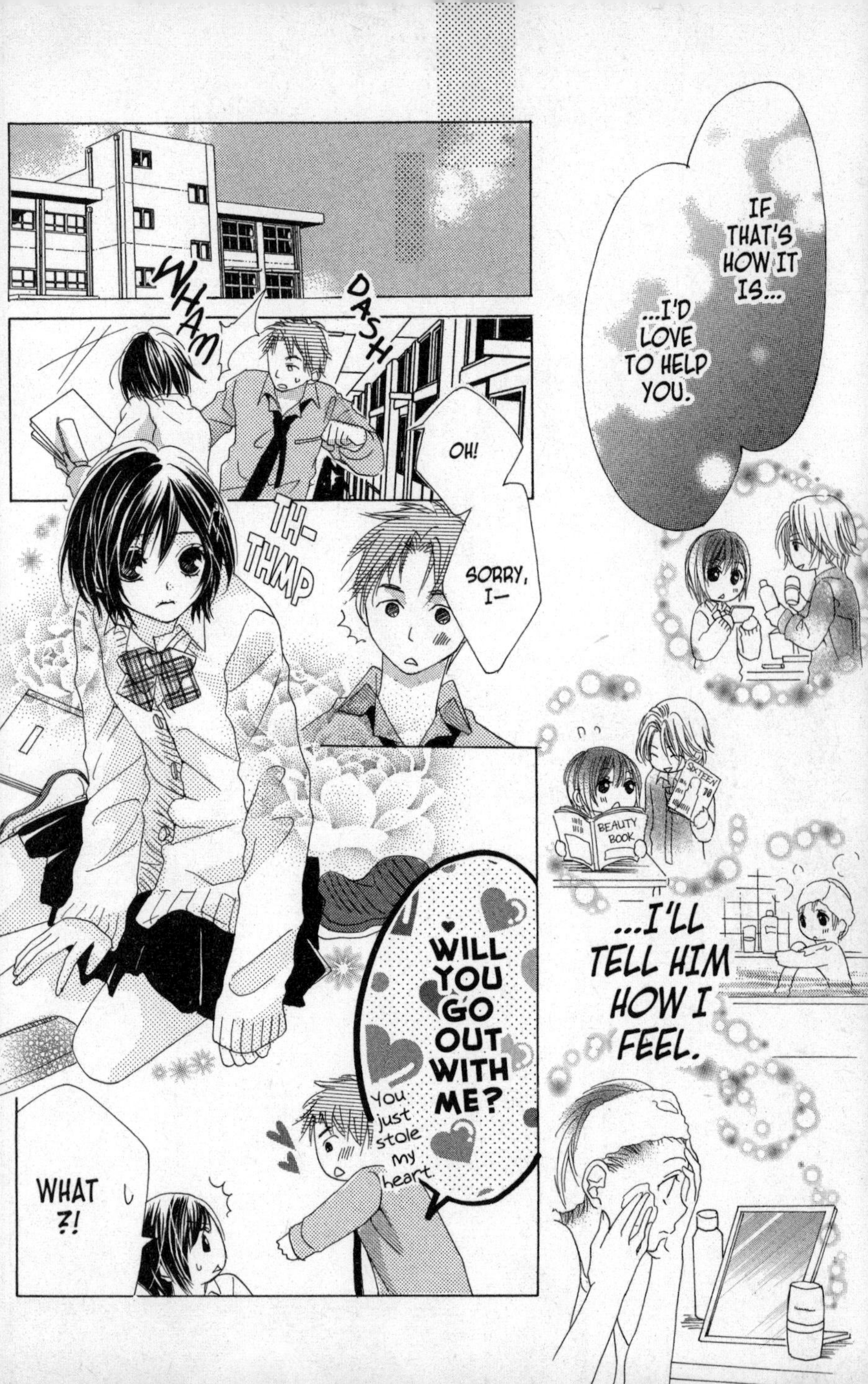
IF THAT'S HOW IT IS...
...I'D LOVE TO HELP YOU.
BEAUTY BOOK
SIXTEEN
...I'LL TELL HIM HOW I FEEL.
WHAM
DASH
OH!
TH-THMP
SORRY, I—
WILL YOU GO OUT WITH ME?
You just stole my heart.
WHAT?!

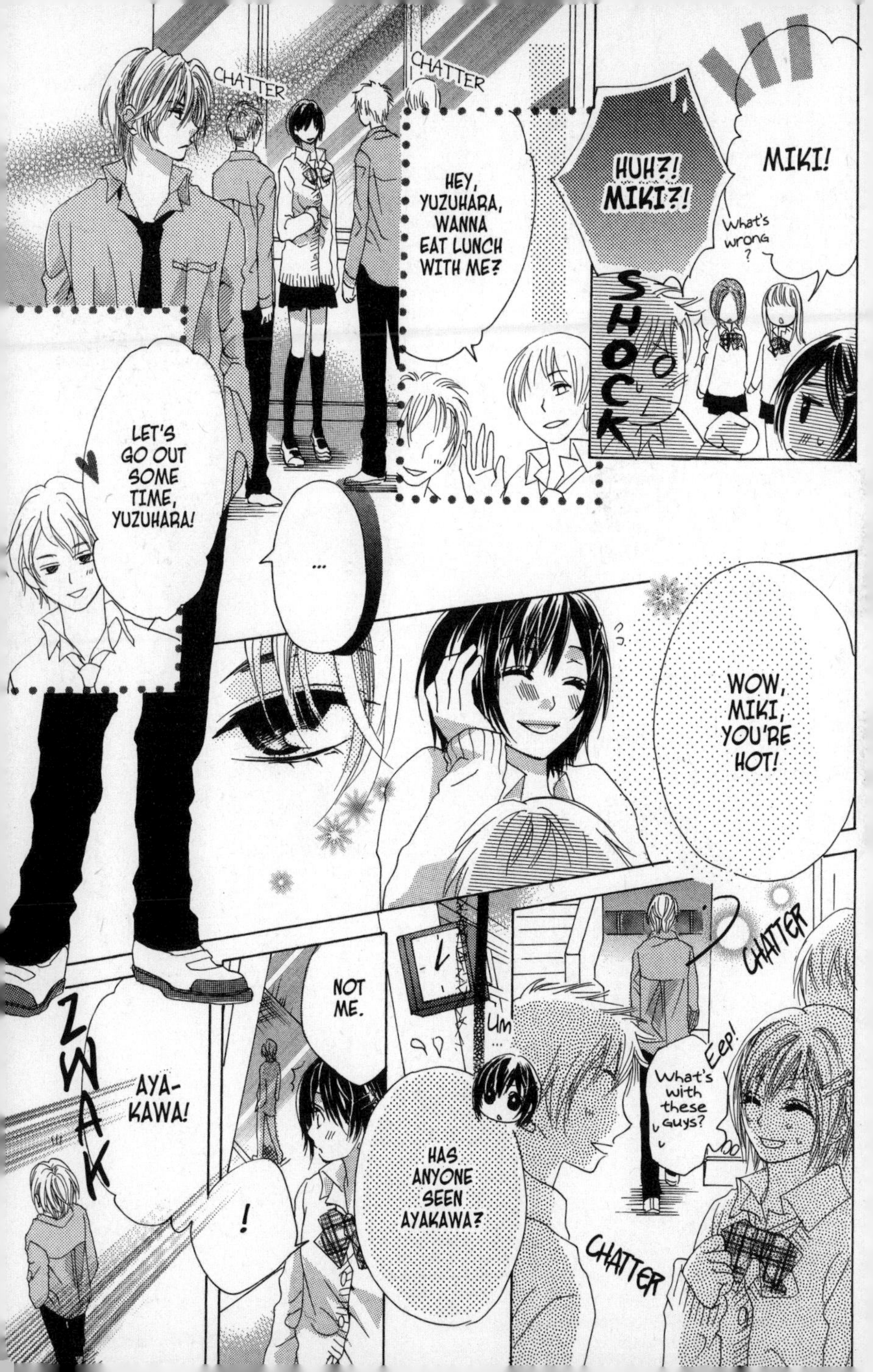
MIKI!
What's wrong?
HUH?! MIKI?!
SHOCK
HEY, YUZUHARA, WANNA EAT LUNCH WITH ME?
CHATTER
CHATTER
LET'S GO OUT SOME TIME, YUZUHARA!
WOW, MIKI, YOU'RE HOT!
...
CHATTER
Eep!
What's with these guys?
Um...
HAS ANYONE SEEN AYAKAWA?
CHATTER
NOT ME.
!
AYA-KAWA!
ZWAK

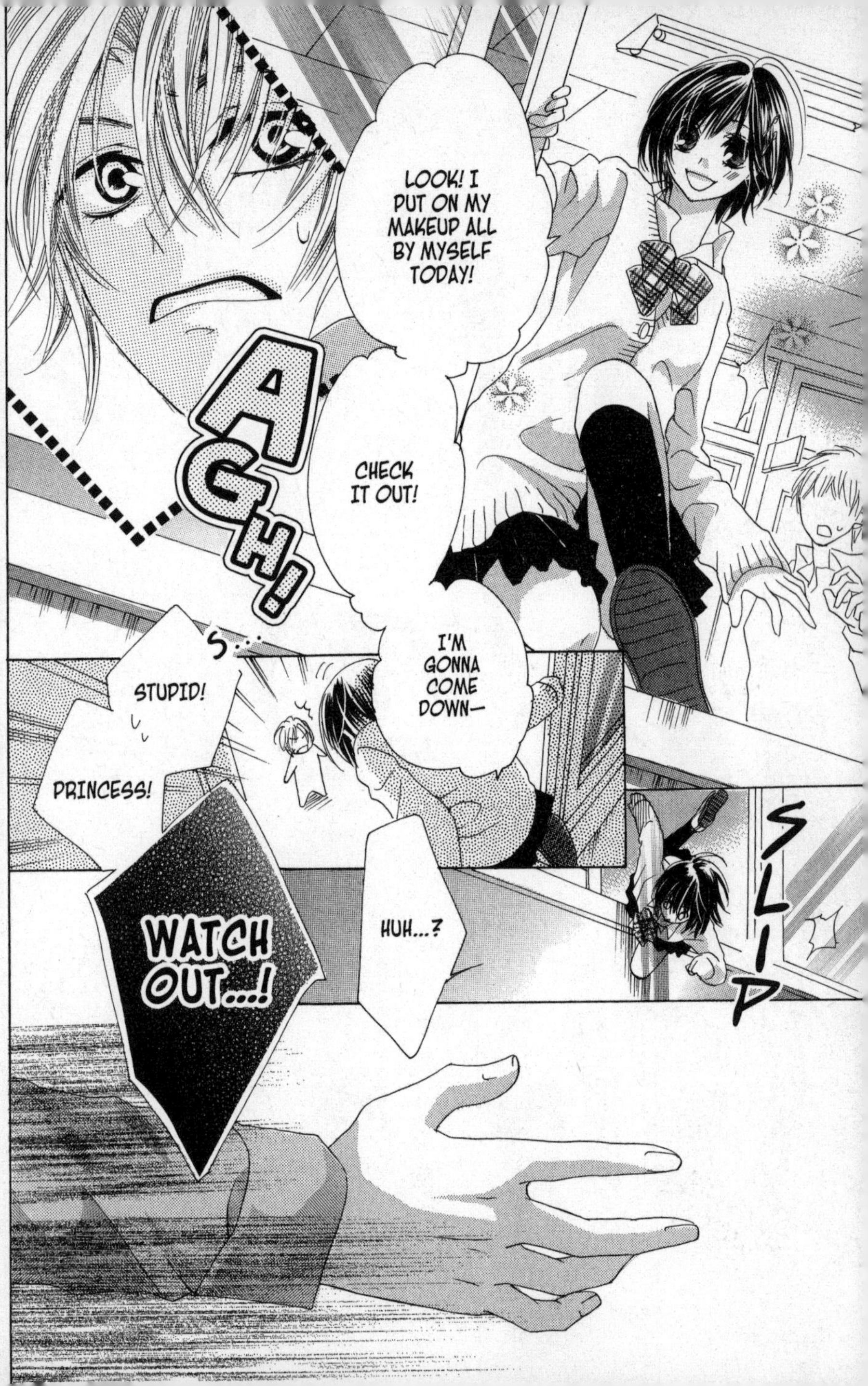
LOOK! I PUT ON MY MAKEUP ALL BY MYSELF TODAY!
CHECK IT OUT!
I'M GONNA COME DOWN—
AGH!
SLIP
S...
STUPID!
PRINCESS!
HUH...?
WATCH OUT...!

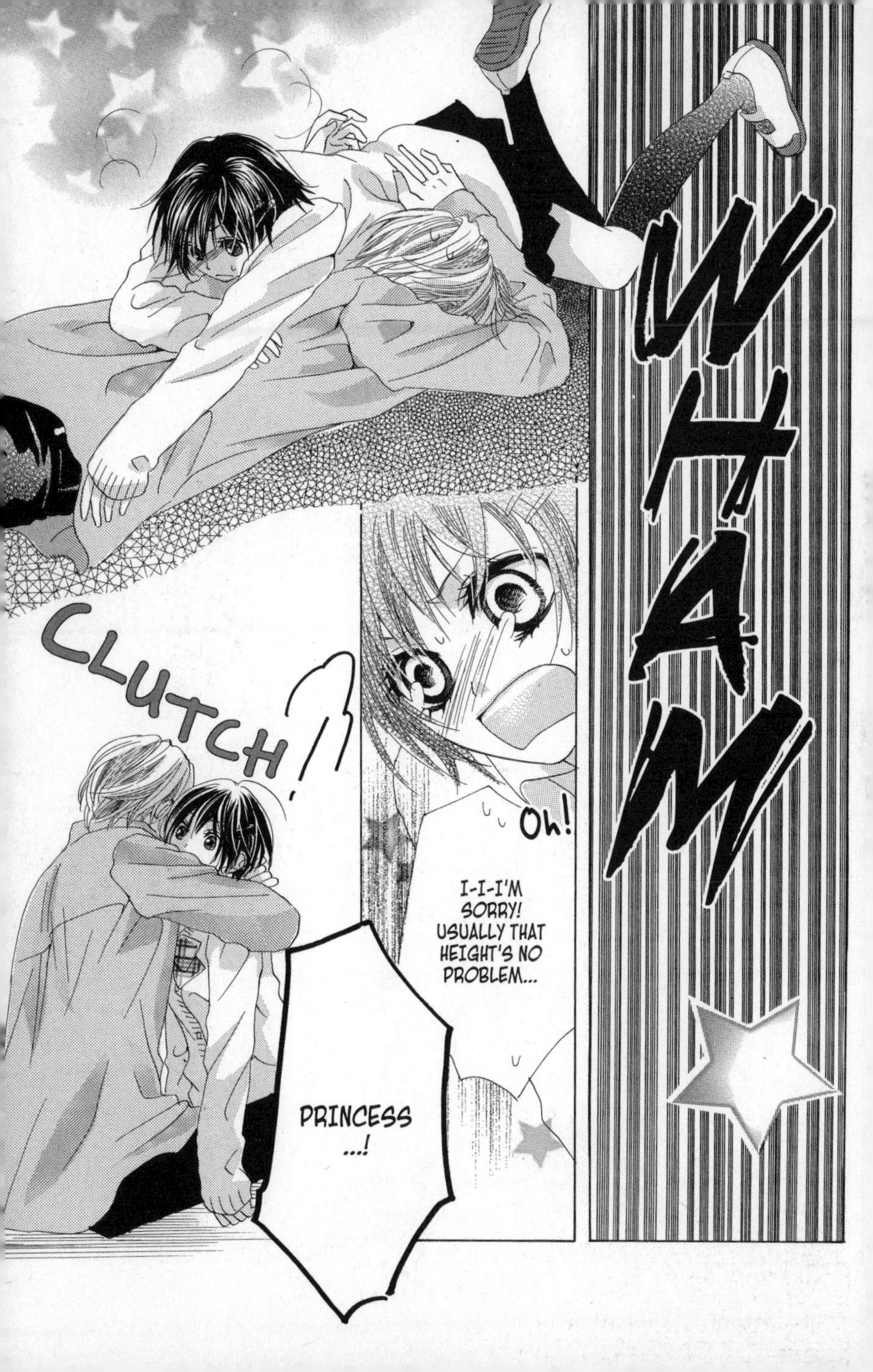
WHAM
Oh!
I-I-I'M SORRY! USUALLY THAT HEIGHT'S NO PROBLEM...
CLUTCH!
PRINCESS ...!

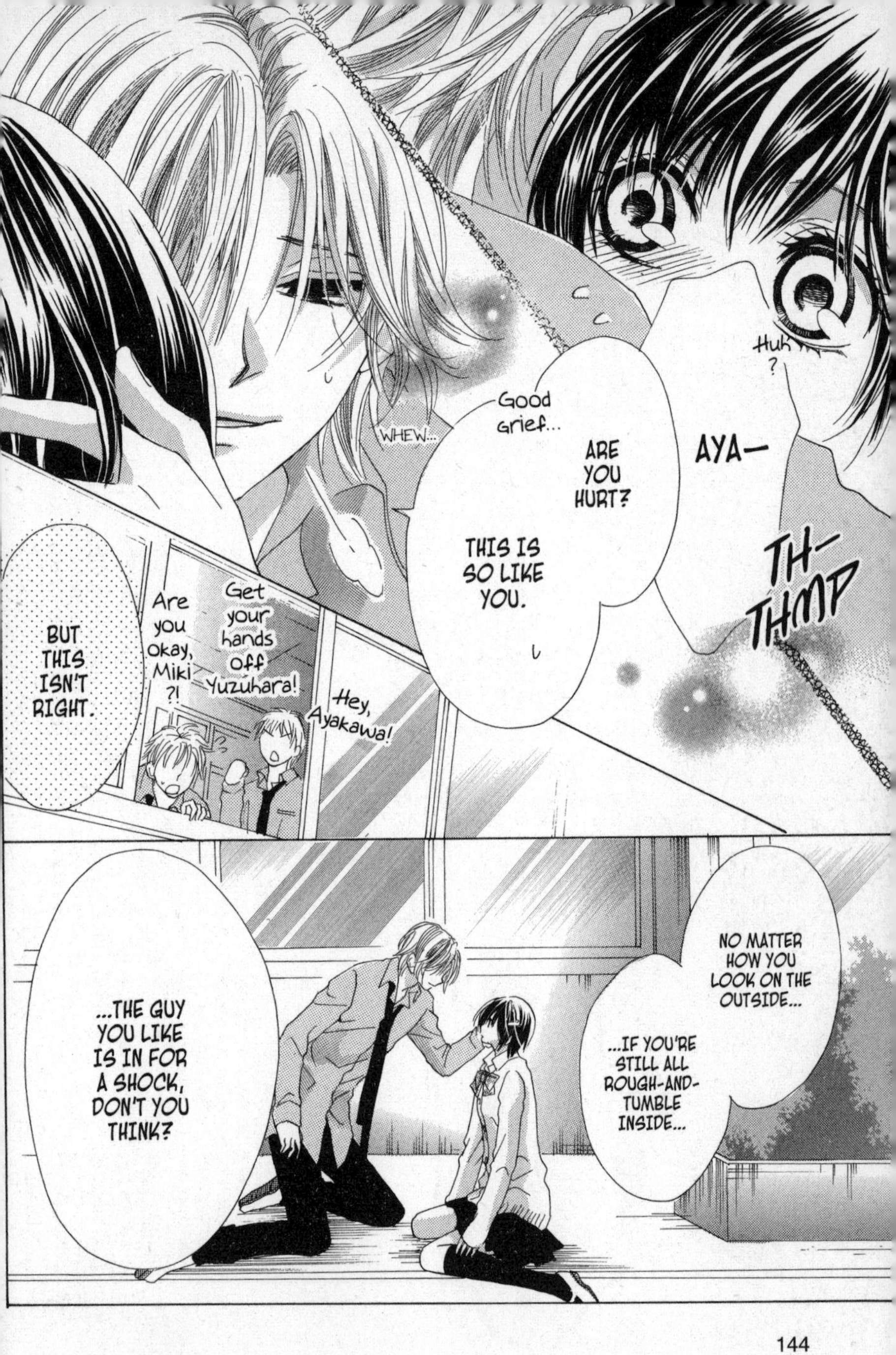
Huh?
AYA—
TH-THMP
Good grief...
ARE YOU HURT?
THIS IS SO LIKE YOU.
WHEW...
Hey, Ayakawa!
Get your hands off Yuzuhara!
Are you okay, Miki?!
BUT THIS ISN'T RIGHT.
NO MATTER HOW YOU LOOK ON THE OUTSIDE...
...IF YOU'RE STILL ALL ROUGH-AND-TUMBLE INSIDE...
...THE GUY YOU LIKE IS IN FOR A SHOCK, DON'T YOU THINK?

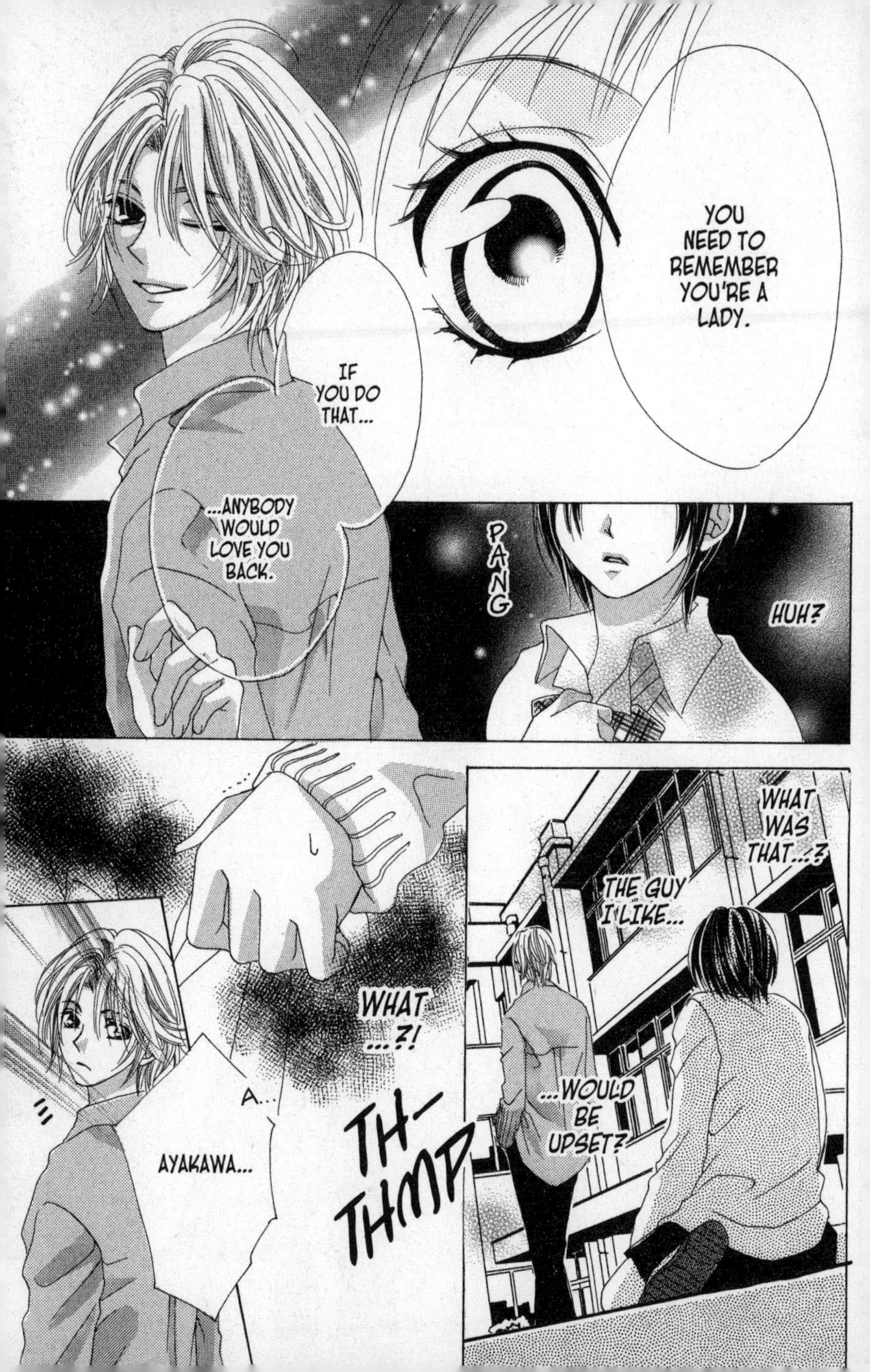
YOU NEED TO REMEMBER YOU'RE A LADY.
IF YOU DO THAT...
...ANYBODY WOULD LOVE YOU BACK.
HUH?
PANG
WHAT WAS THAT...?
THE GUY I LIKE...
...WOULD BE UPSET?
WHAT...?!
A...
AYAKAWA...
TH-THMP

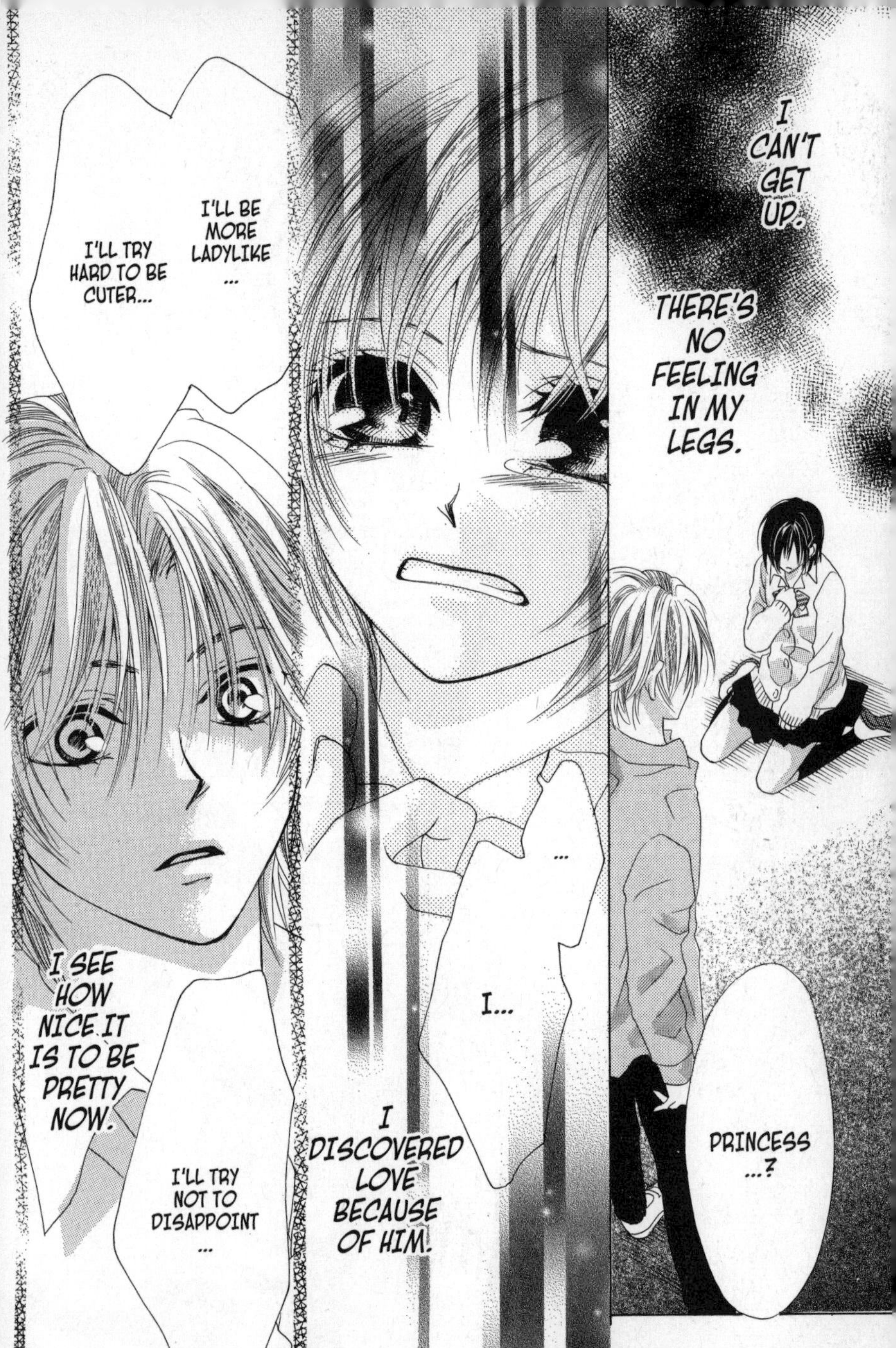
I CAN'T GET UP.
THERE'S NO FEELING IN MY LEGS.
PRINCESS ...?
...
I...
I DISCOVERED LOVE BECAUSE OF HIM.
I'LL BE MORE LADYLIKE ...
I'LL TRY HARD TO BE CUTER...
I SEE HOW NICE IT IS TO BE PRETTY NOW.
I'LL TRY NOT TO DISAPPOINT ...

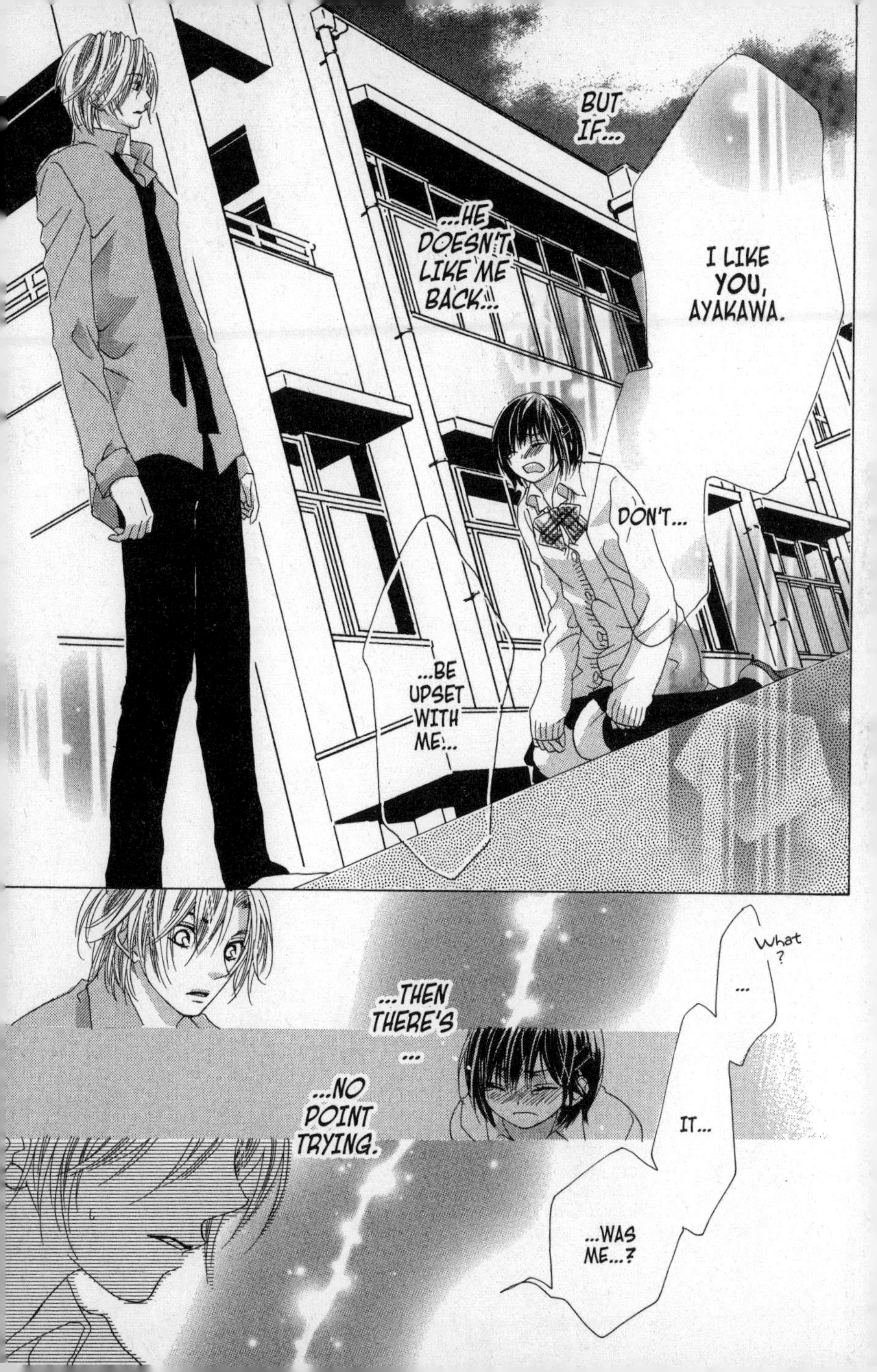
I LIKE YOU, AYAKAWA.
DON'T...
...BE UPSET WITH ME...
BUT IF...
...HE DOESN'T LIKE ME BACK...
...THEN THERE'S ...
...NO POINT TRYING.
What?
...
IT...
...WAS ME...?

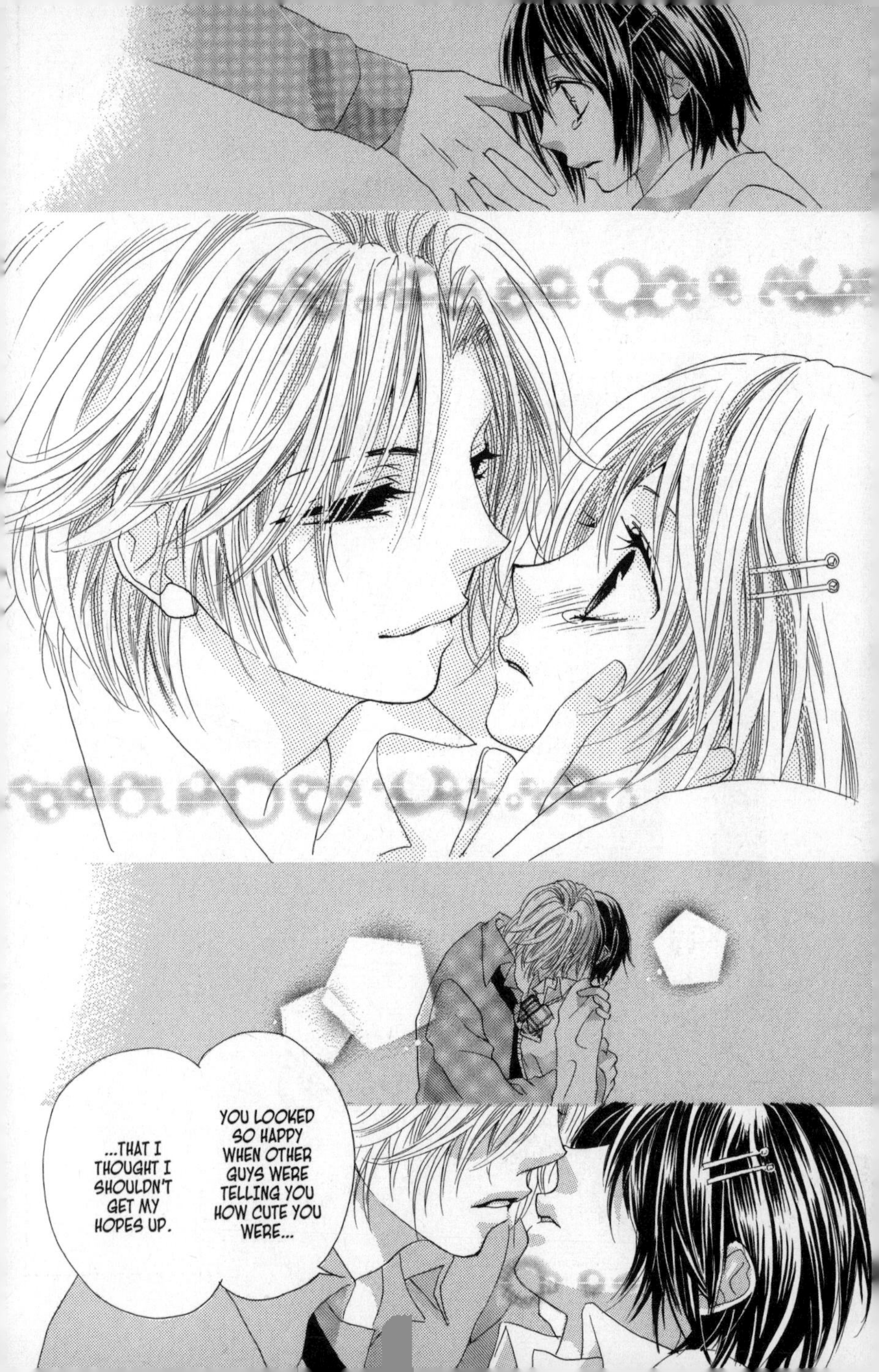
YOU LOOKED SO HAPPY WHEN OTHER GUYS WERE TELLING YOU HOW CUTE YOU WERE...
...THAT I THOUGHT I SHOULDN'T GET MY HOPES UP.

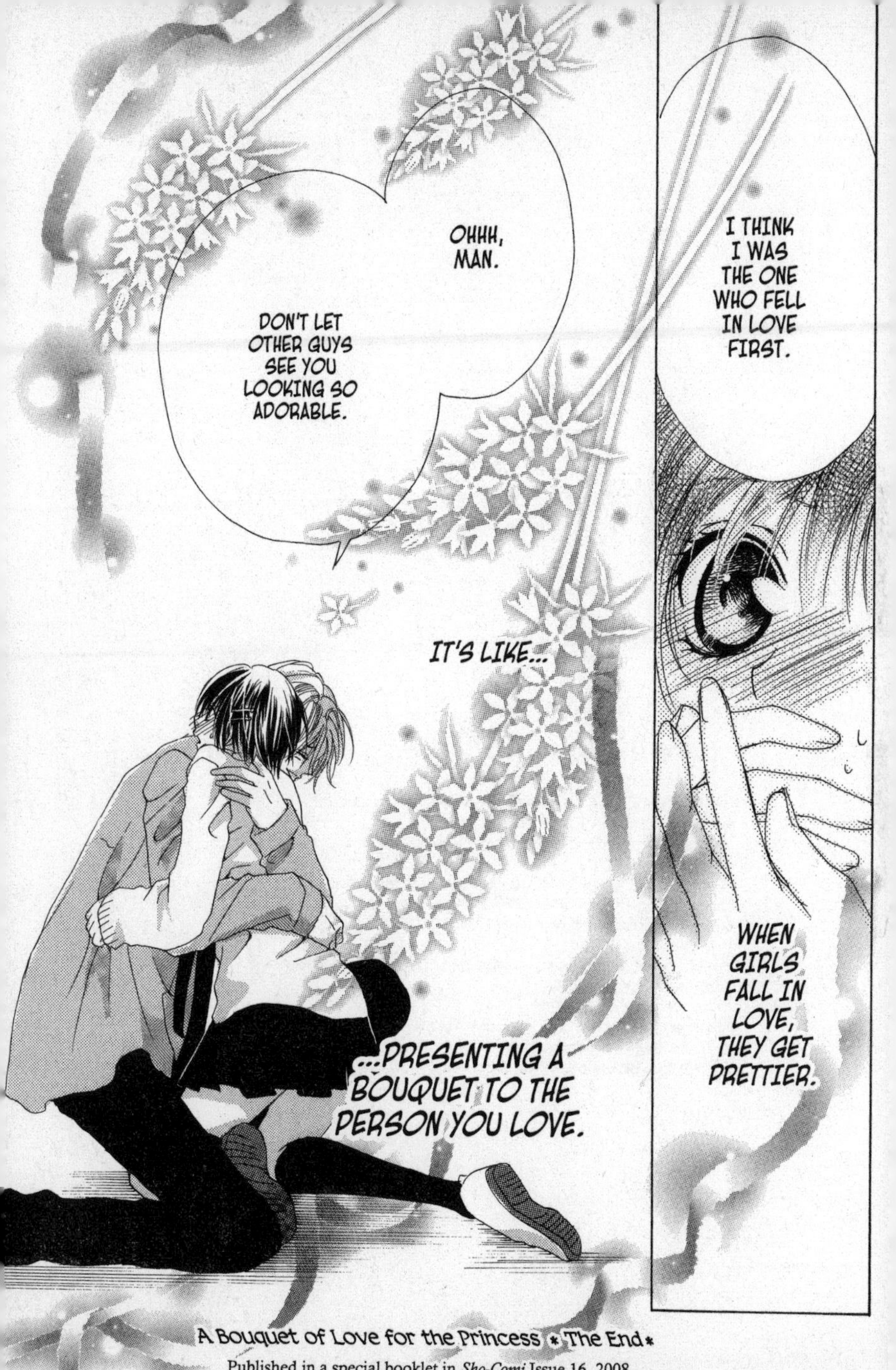
I THINK I WAS THE ONE WHO FELL IN LOVE FIRST.
WHEN GIRLS FALL IN LOVE, THEY GET PRETTIER.
OHHH, MAN.
DON'T LET OTHER GUYS SEE YOU LOOKING SO ADORABLE.
IT'S LIKE...
...PRESENTING A BOUQUET TO THE PERSON YOU LOVE.

A Bouquet of Love for the Princess * The End *

Published in a special booklet in *Sho-Comi* Issue 16, 2008

✿ "A Bouquet of Love for the Princess" ✿

This story was included in a special booklet
with Sho-Comi magazine.
My drawing style was starting to change here.

The theme was "Girls Becoming Beautiful"!
I experimented with drawing a type of girl who
wasn't typical of my work.

Even my editor was surprised that I could draw a
girl like her. ⌣ ᵇ

I like people who throw themselves completely into
things (whether they're boys or girls). I always
want to be someone like that. ⁴✦

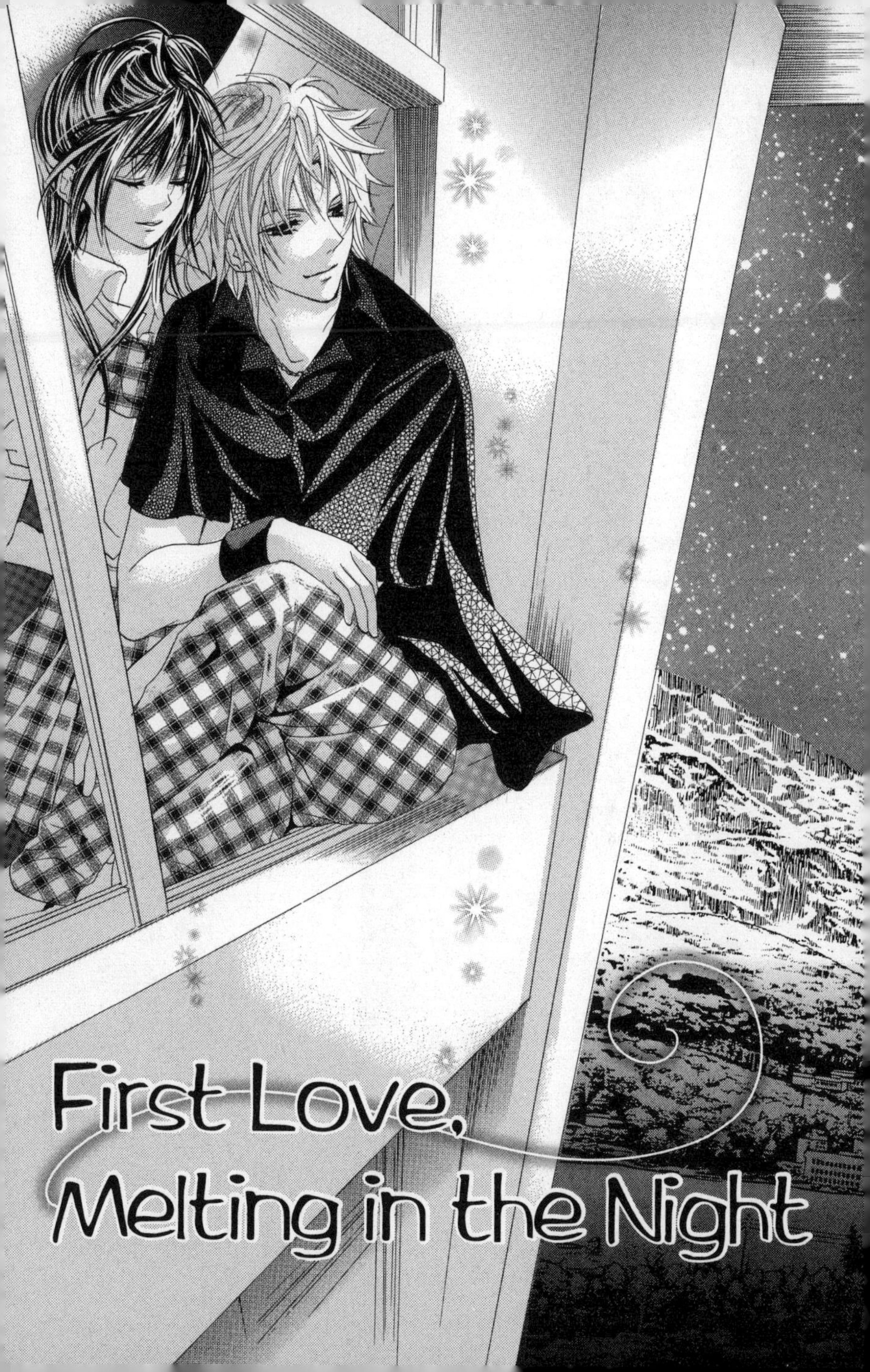
First Love,
Melting in the Night

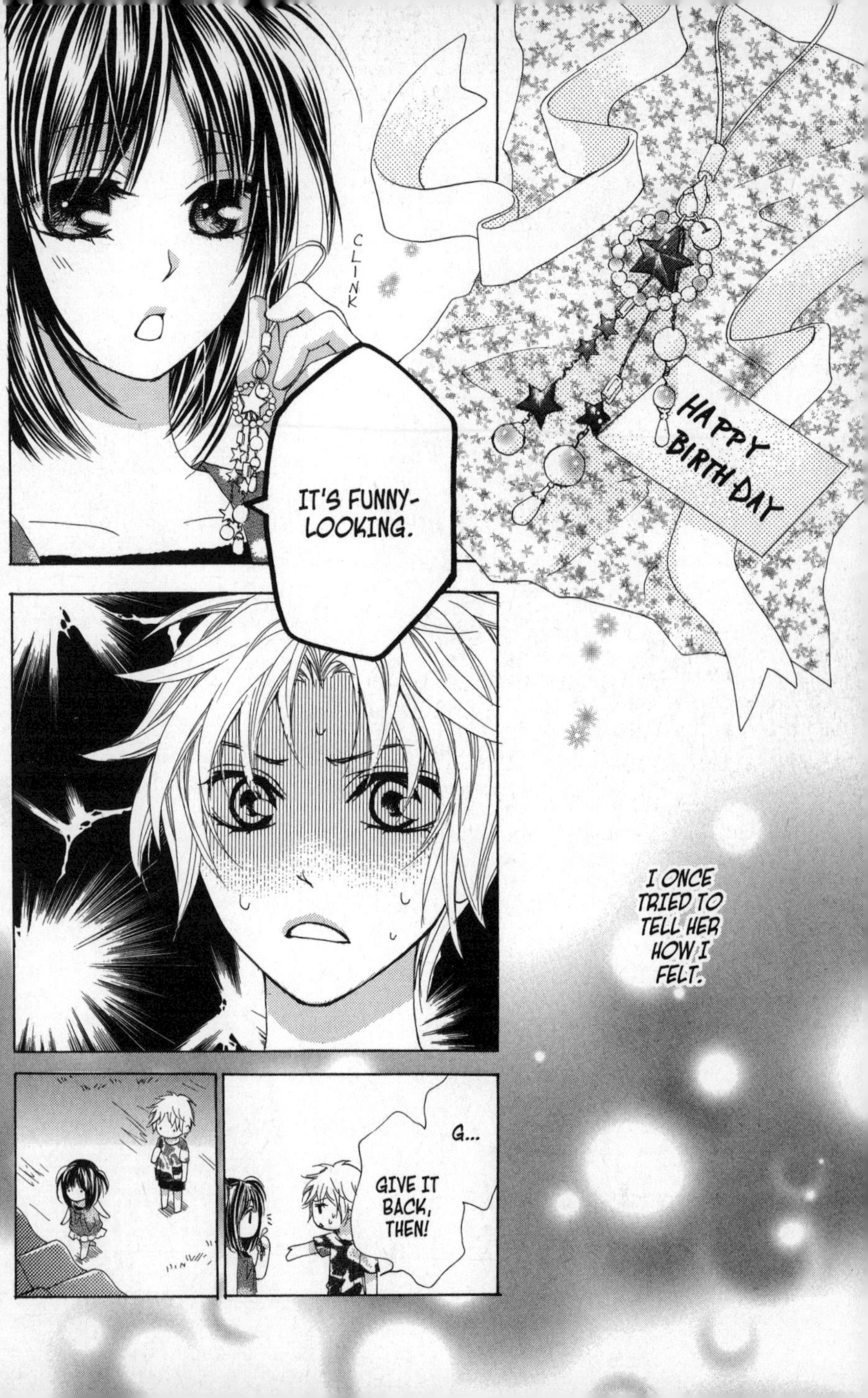
HAPPY BIRTH-DAY
CLINK
IT'S FUNNY-LOOKING.
I ONCE TRIED TO TELL HER HOW I FELT.
G...
GIVE IT BACK, THEN!

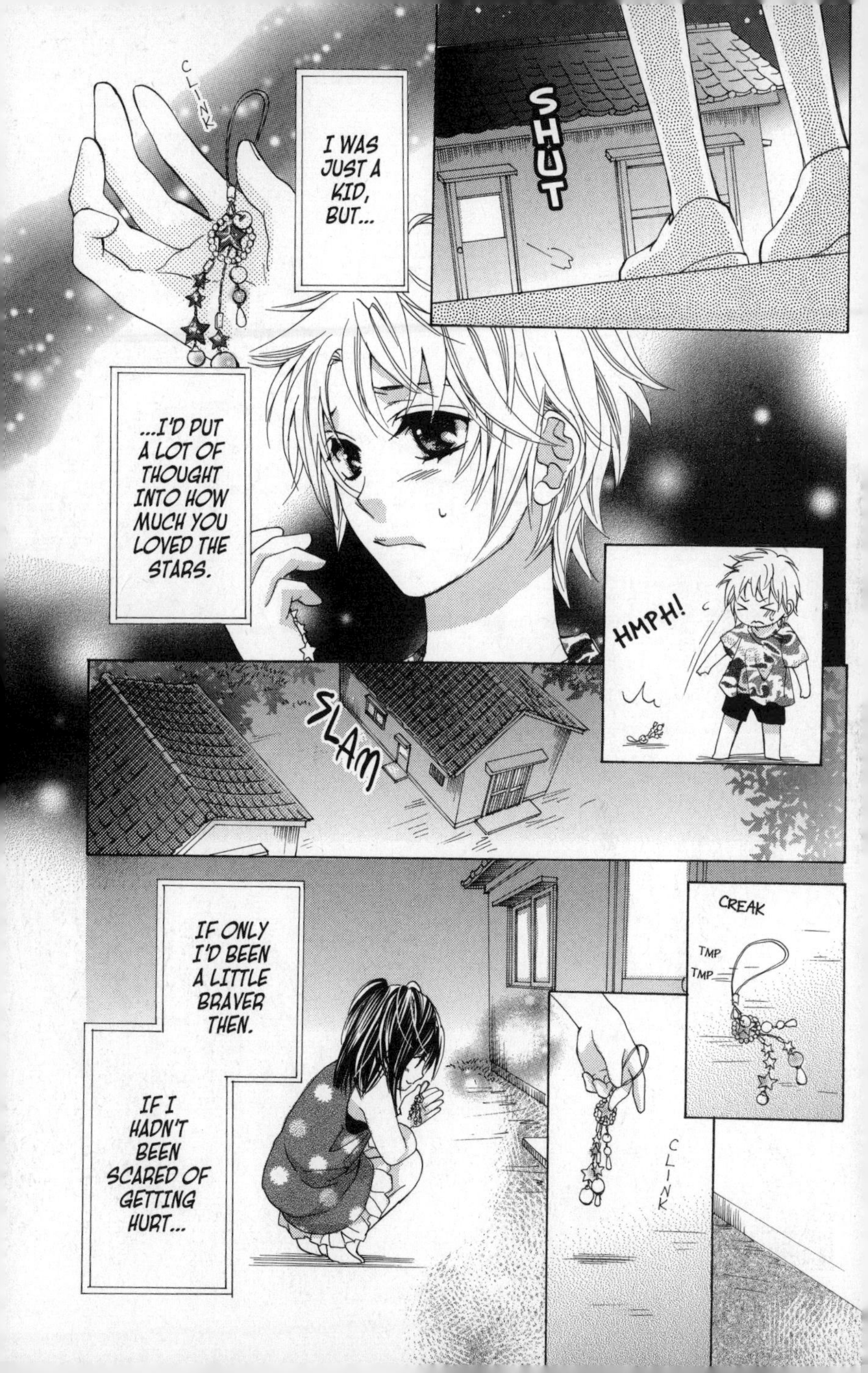
SHUT
I WAS JUST A KID, BUT...
CLINK
HMPH!
...I'D PUT A LOT OF THOUGHT INTO HOW MUCH YOU LOVED THE STARS.
SLAM
CREAK
TMP
TMP
CLINK
IF ONLY I'D BEEN A LITTLE BRAVER THEN.
IF I HADN'T BEEN SCARED OF GETTING HURT...

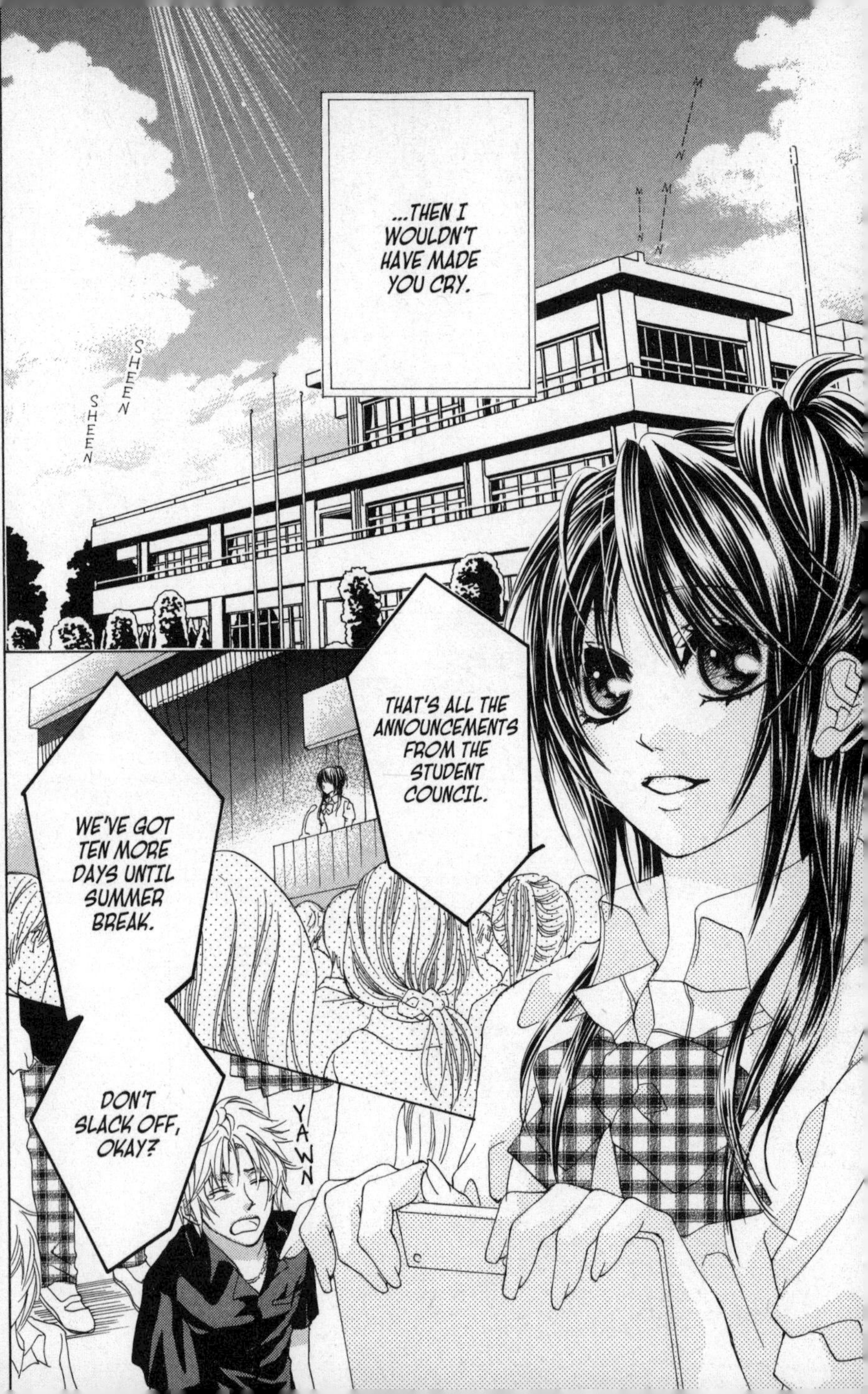
MIN
MIN
MIN
...THEN I WOULDN'T HAVE MADE YOU CRY.
SHEEN
SHEEN
THAT'S ALL THE ANNOUNCEMENTS FROM THE STUDENT COUNCIL.
WE'VE GOT TEN MORE DAYS UNTIL SUMMER BREAK.
DON'T SLACK OFF, OKAY?
YAWN

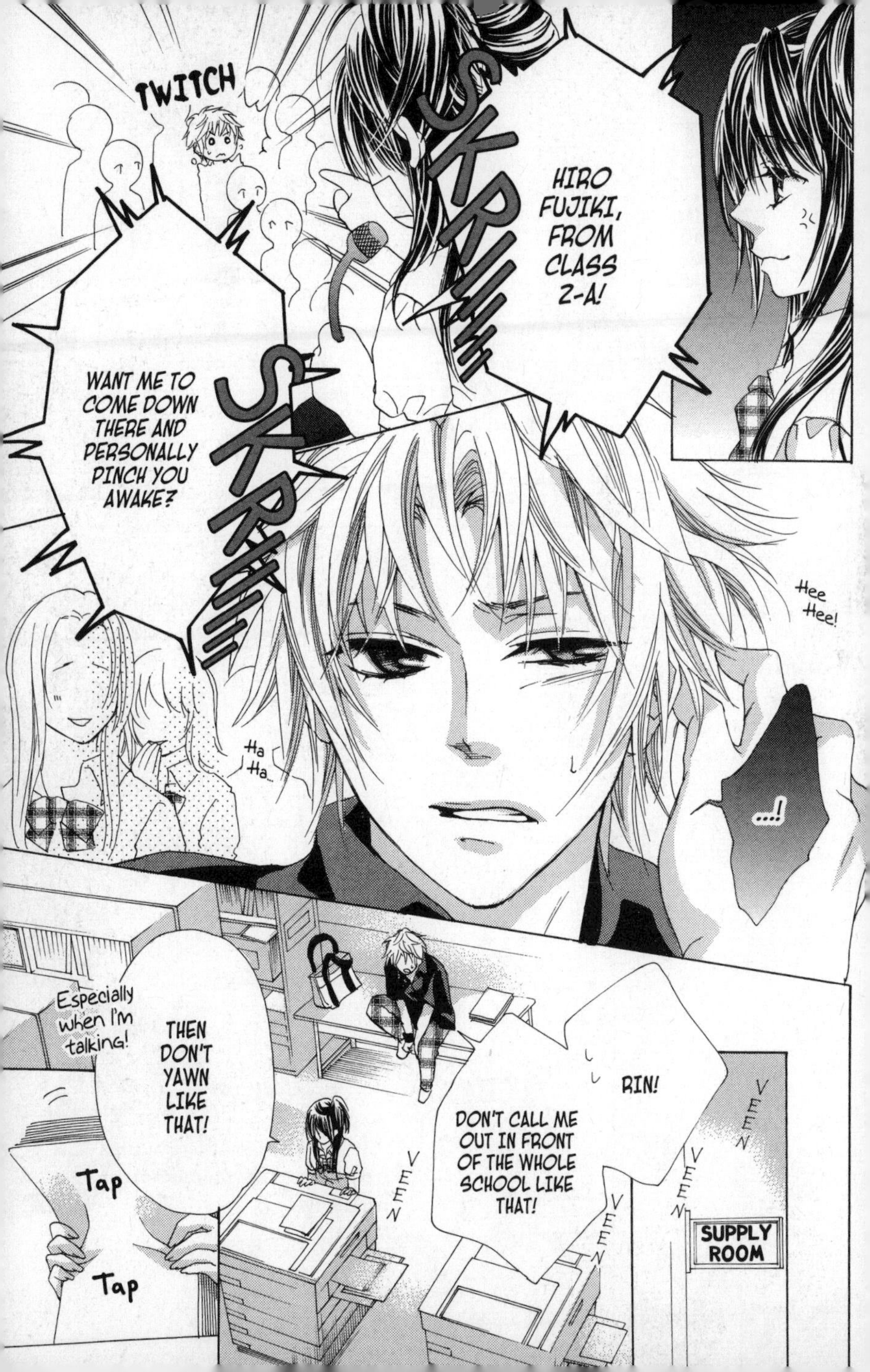
HIRO FUJIKI, FROM CLASS 2-A!
SKRIIIIII!
TWITCH
WANT ME TO COME DOWN THERE AND PERSONALLY PINCH YOU AWAKE?
SKRIIIII!
Hee Hee!
...!
Ha Ha..
RIN!
DON'T CALL ME OUT IN FRONT OF THE WHOLE SCHOOL LIKE THAT!
SUPPLY ROOM
VEEN
VEEN
VEEN
VEEN
THEN DON'T YAWN LIKE THAT!
Especially when I'm talking!
Tap
Tap

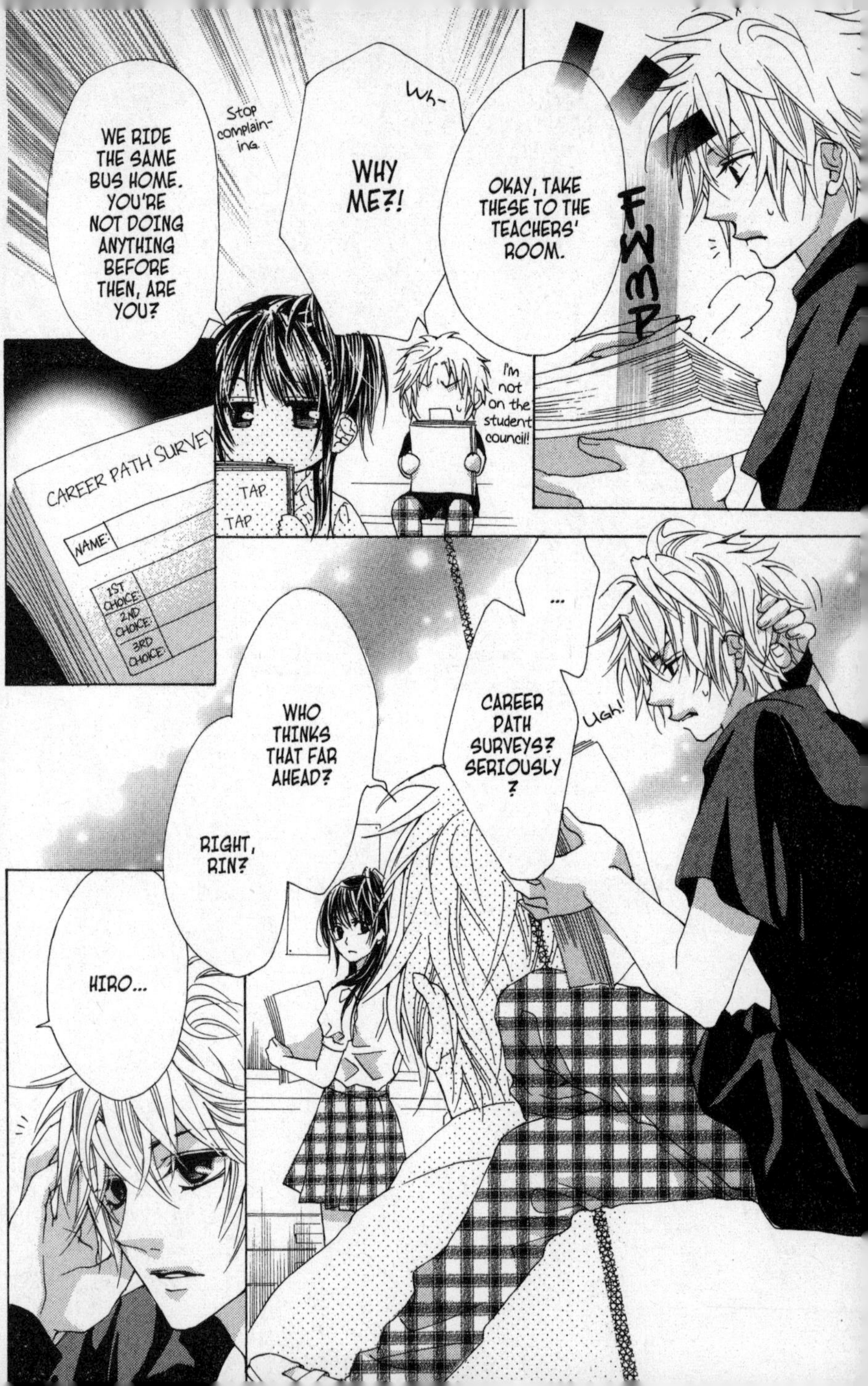
OKAY, TAKE THESE TO THE TEACHERS' ROOM.
FWMP
Wh-
WHY ME?!
I'm not on the student council!
Stop complaining.
WE RIDE THE SAME BUS HOME. YOU'RE NOT DOING ANYTHING BEFORE THEN, ARE YOU?
TAP TAP
CAREER PATH SURVEY
NAME:
1ST CHOICE:
2ND CHOICE:
3RD CHOICE:
...
Ugh!
CAREER PATH SURVEYS? SERIOUSLY?
WHO THINKS THAT FAR AHEAD?
RIGHT, RIN?
HIRO...

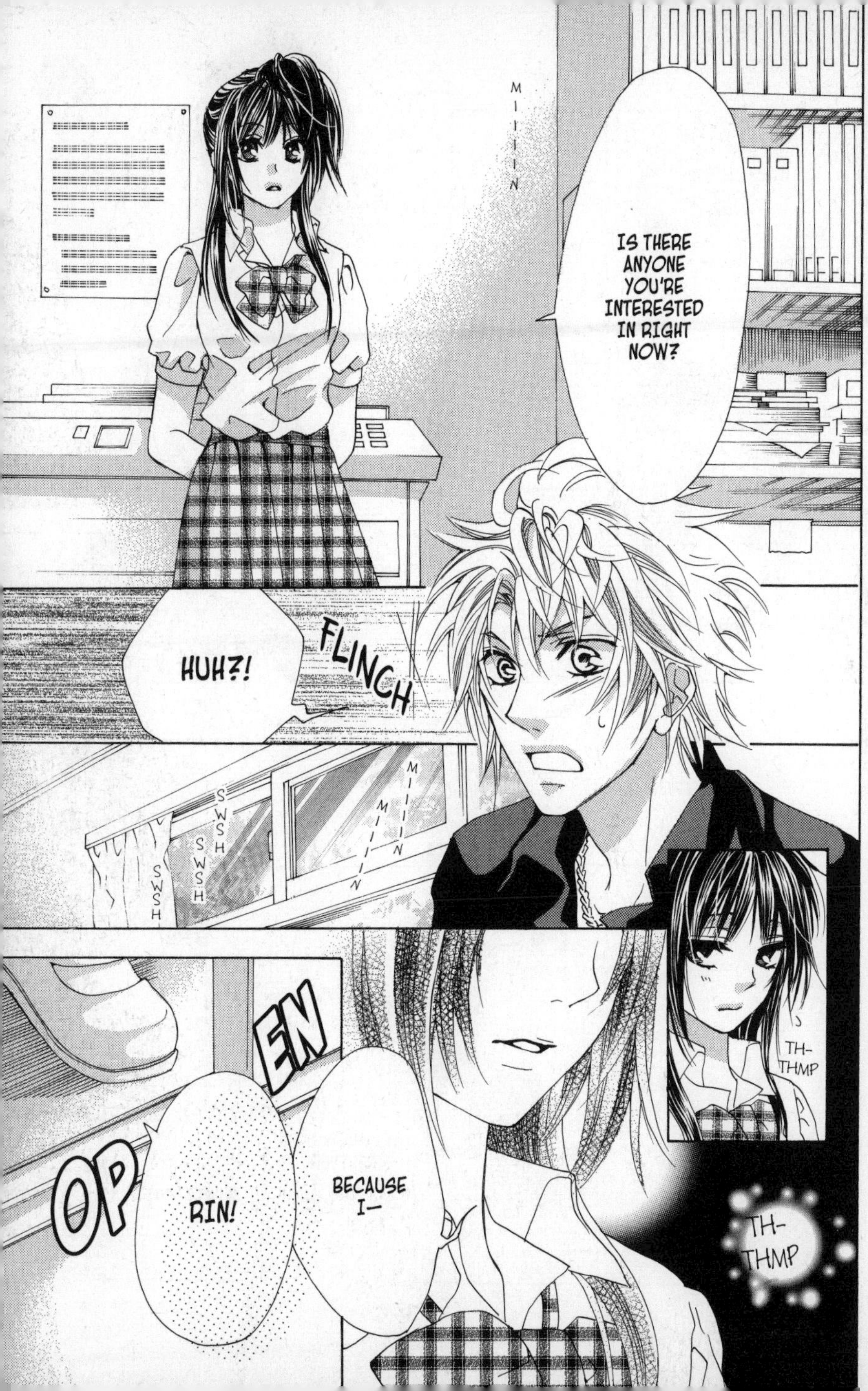
IS THERE ANYONE YOU'RE INTERESTED IN RIGHT NOW?
MIIIN
FLINCH
HUH?!
MIIIN
MIIIN
SWSH
SWSH
SWSH
TH-THMP
BECAUSE I—
RIN!
OPEN
TH-THMP

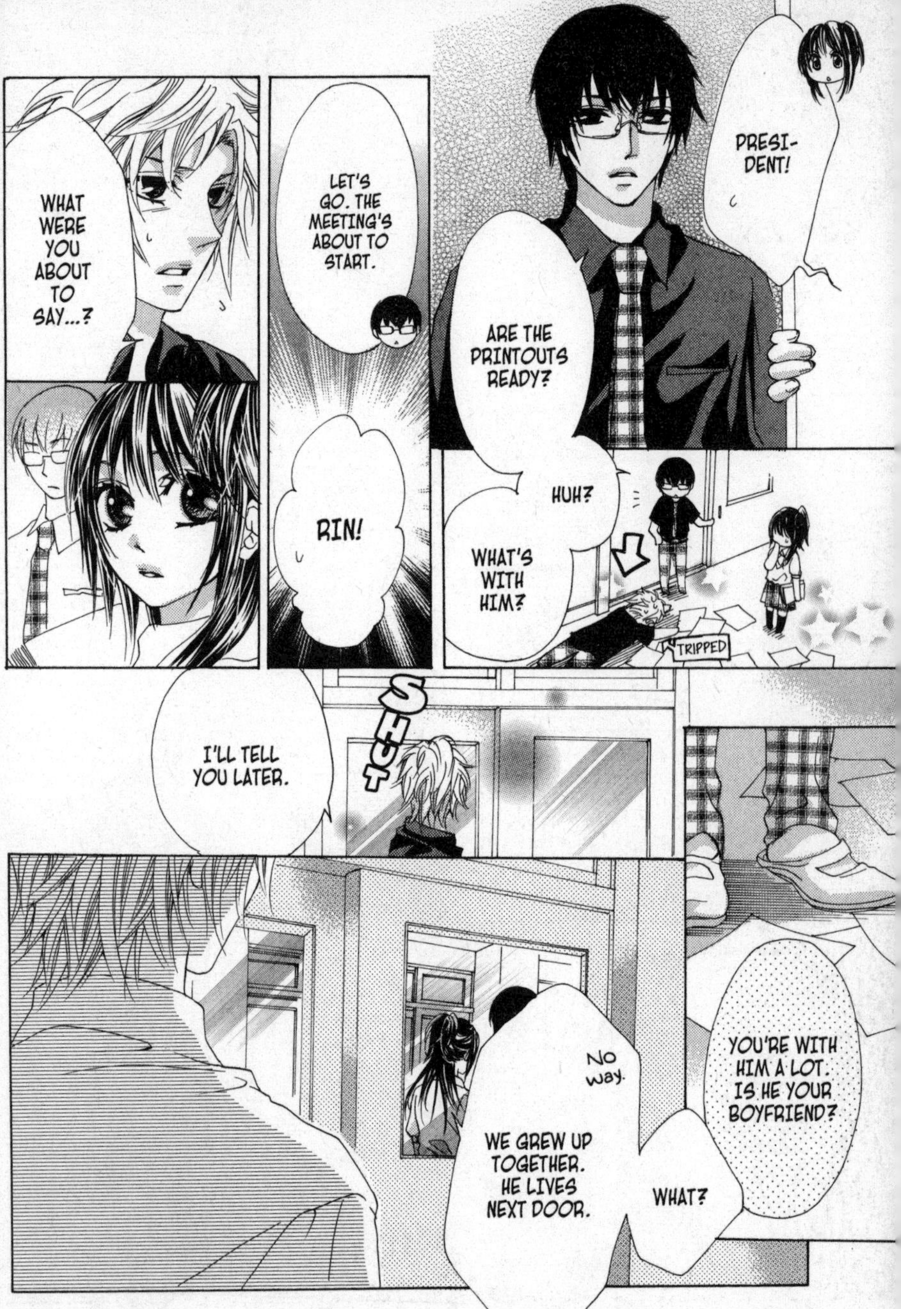
PRESI-DENT!
ARE THE PRINTOUTS READY?
HUH?
WHAT'S WITH HIM?
TRIPPED
LET'S GO. THE MEETING'S ABOUT TO START.
RIN!
WHAT WERE YOU ABOUT TO SAY...?
SHUT
I'LL TELL YOU LATER.
YOU'RE WITH HIM A LOT. IS HE YOUR BOYFRIEND?
WHAT?
No way.
WE GREW UP TOGETHER. HE LIVES NEXT DOOR.

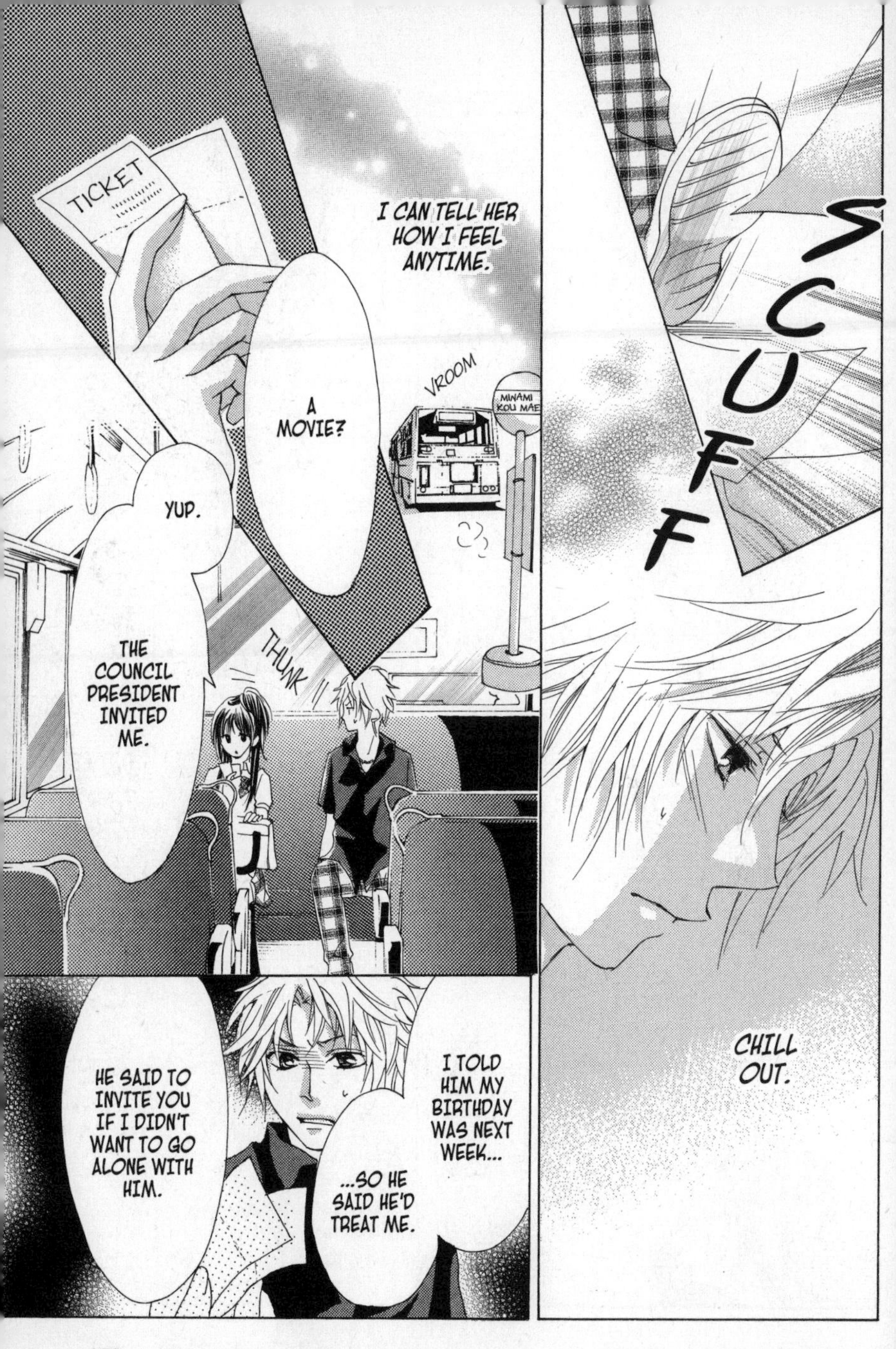
SCUFF
CHILL OUT.
I CAN TELL HER HOW I FEEL ANYTIME.
MINAMI KOU MAE
VROOM
A MOVIE?
YUP.
THE COUNCIL PRESIDENT INVITED ME.
THUNK
I TOLD HIM MY BIRTHDAY WAS NEXT WEEK...
...SO HE SAID HE'D TREAT ME.
HE SAID TO INVITE YOU IF I DIDN'T WANT TO GO ALONE WITH HIM.

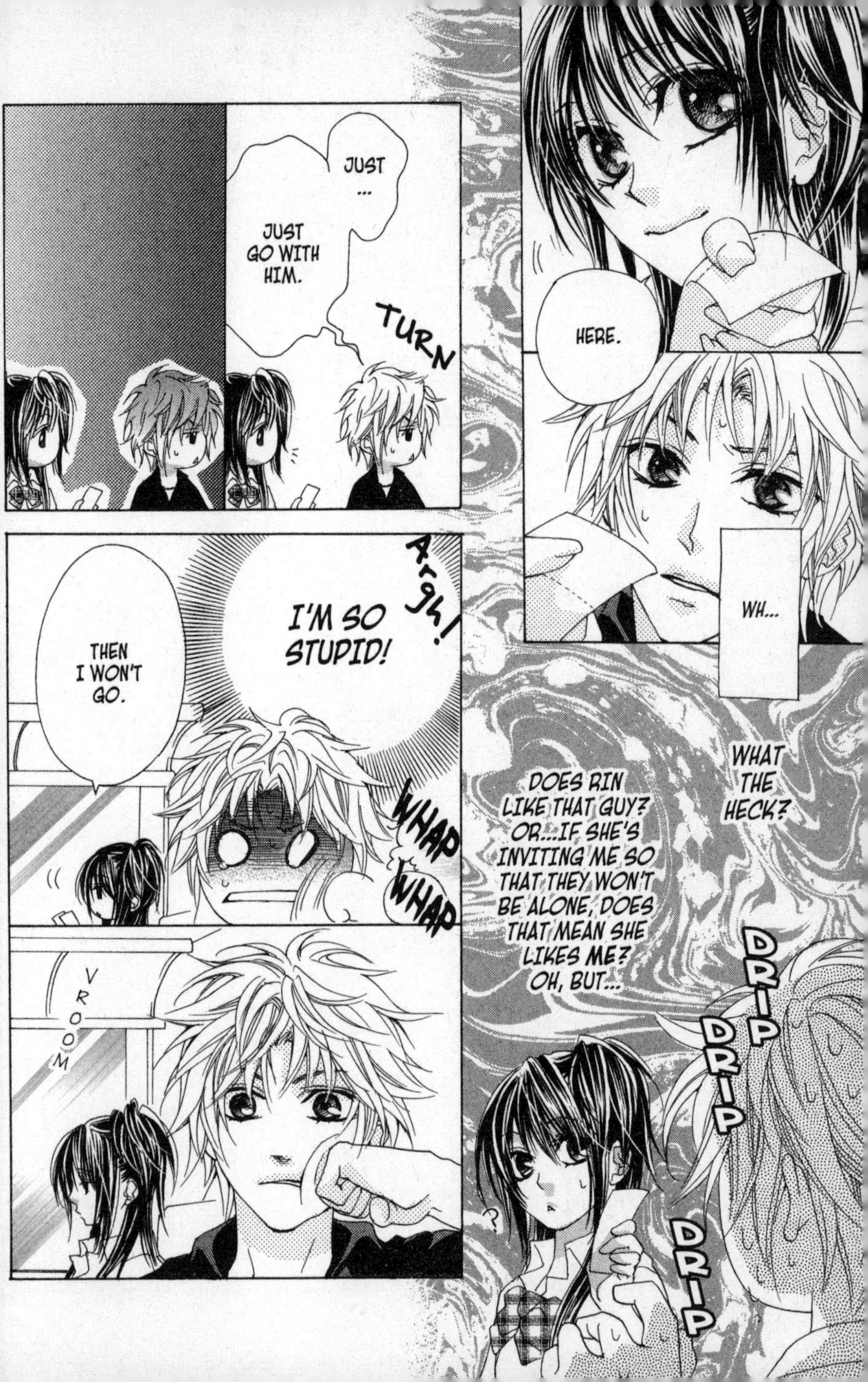
HERE.
WH...
WHAT THE HECK?
DOES RIN LIKE THAT GUY? OR...IF SHE'S INVITING ME SO THAT THEY WON'T BE ALONE, DOES THAT MEAN SHE LIKES ME? OH, BUT...
DRIP
DRIP
DRIP
DRIP
JUST ...
JUST GO WITH HIM.
TURN
I'M SO STUPID!
Argh!
THEN I WON'T GO.
WHAP
WHAP
VROOM

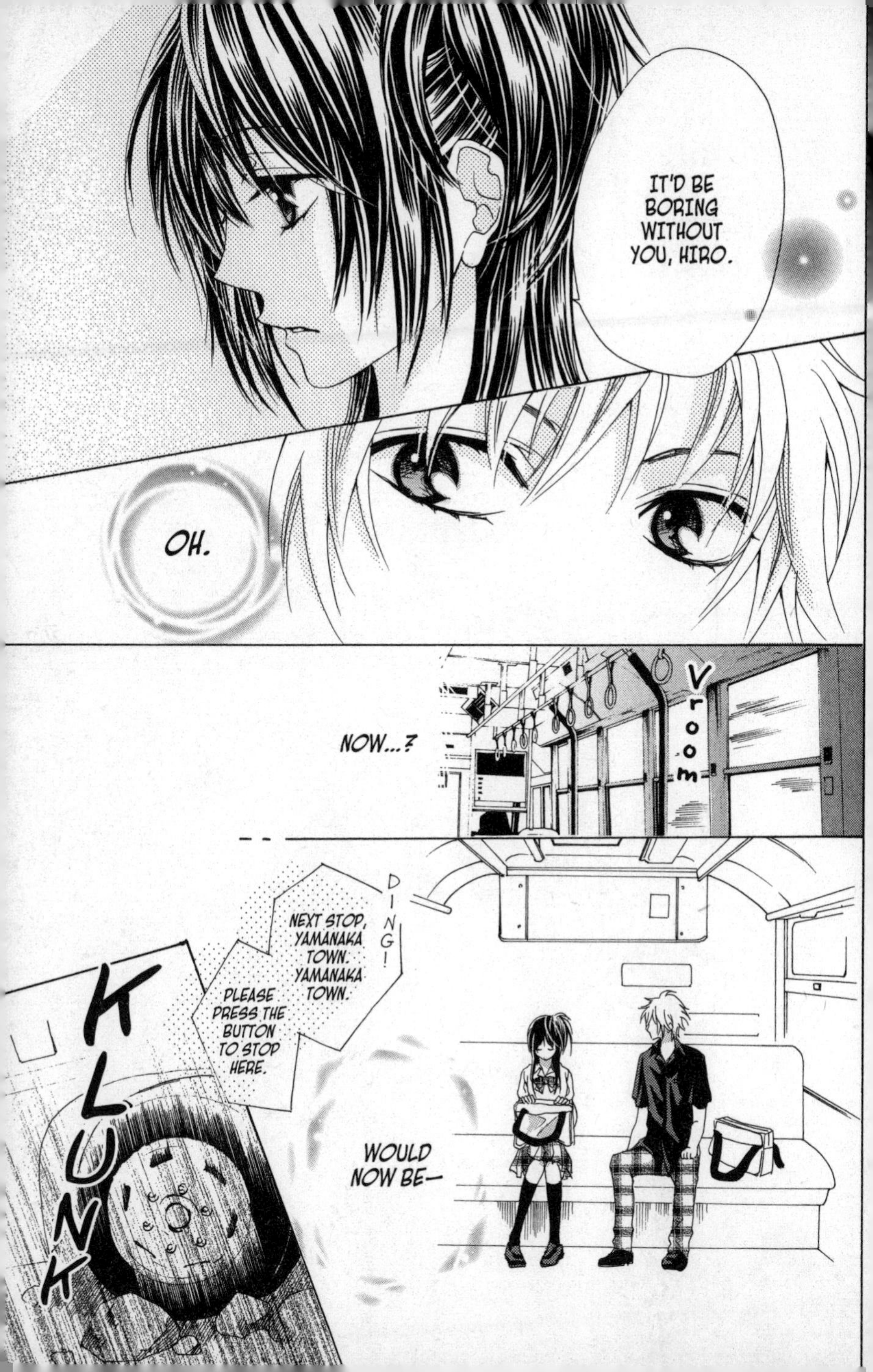
IT'D BE BORING WITHOUT YOU, HIRO.
OH.
Vroom
NOW...?
DING!
NEXT STOP, YAMANAKA TOWN. YAMANAKA TOWN.
PLEASE PRESS THE BUTTON TO STOP HERE.
WOULD NOW BE—
KLUNK

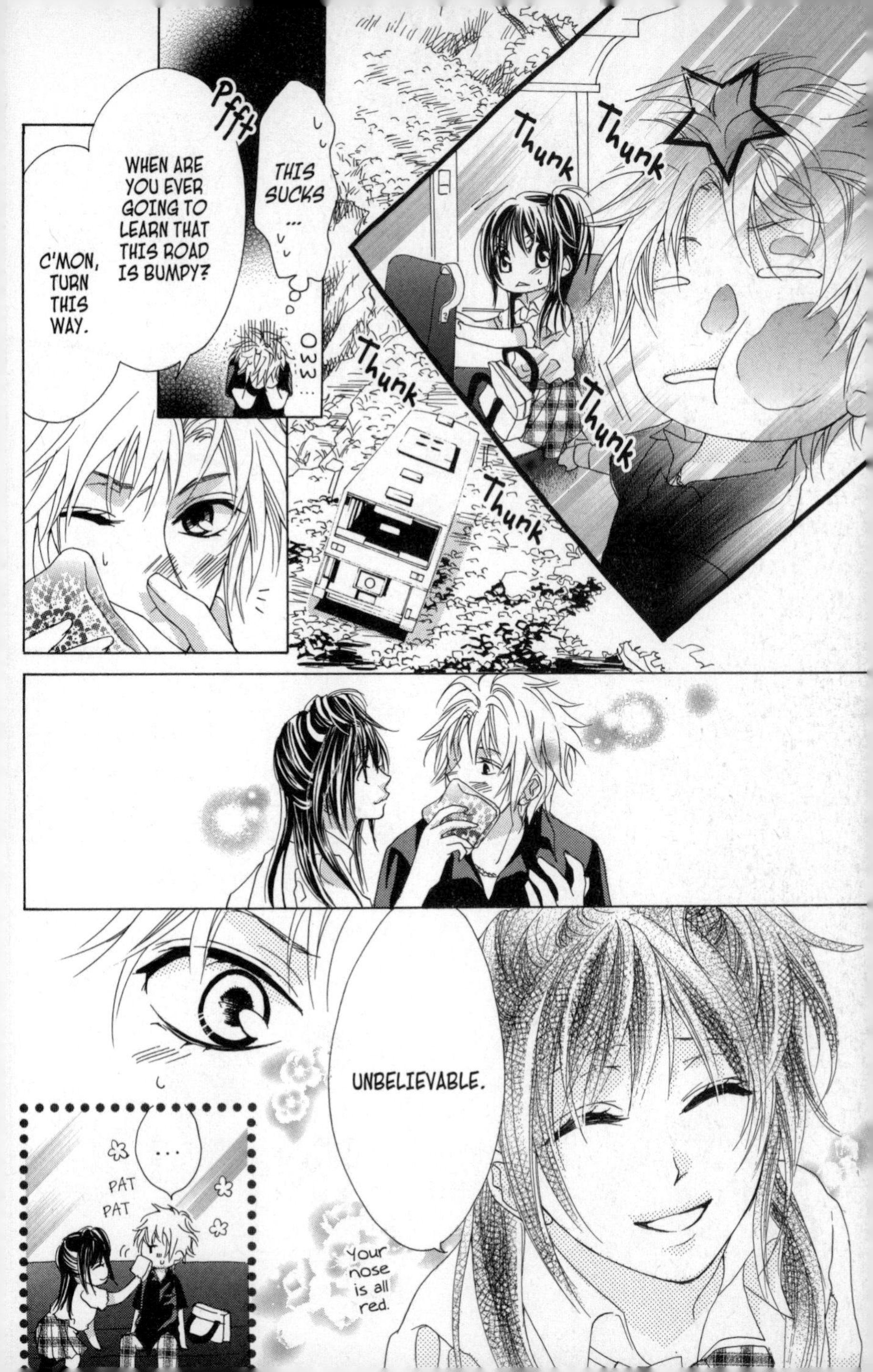
Thunk
Thunk
Thunk
Thunk
Thunk
THIS SUCKS ...
OWW...
Pfft
WHEN ARE YOU EVER GOING TO LEARN THAT THIS ROAD IS BUMPY?
C'MON, TURN THIS WAY.
UNBELIEVABLE.
Your nose is all red.
...
PAT PAT

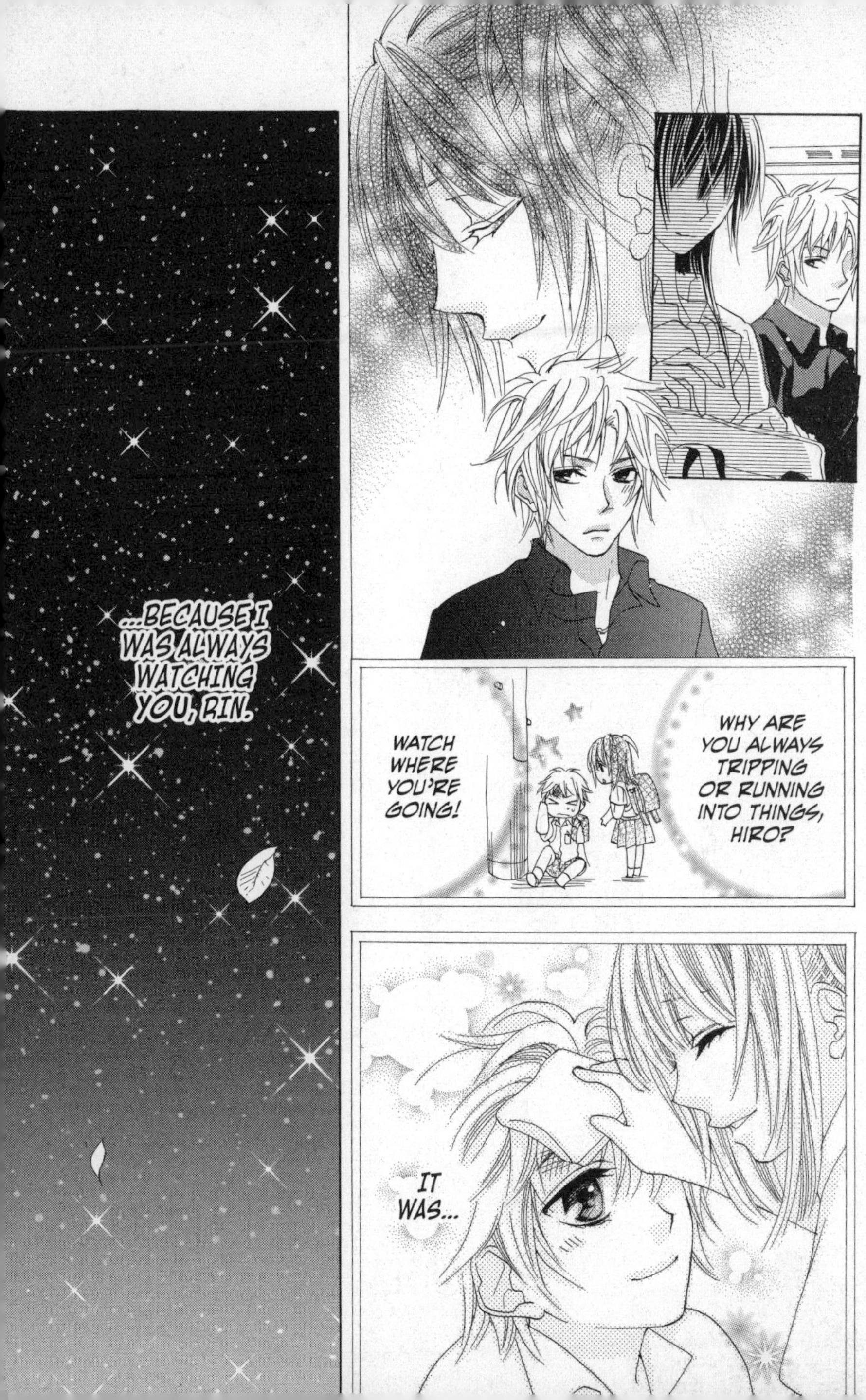
WHY ARE YOU ALWAYS TRIPPING OR RUNNING INTO THINGS, HIRO?
WATCH WHERE YOU'RE GOING!
IT WAS...
...BECAUSE I WAS ALWAYS WATCHING YOU, RIN.

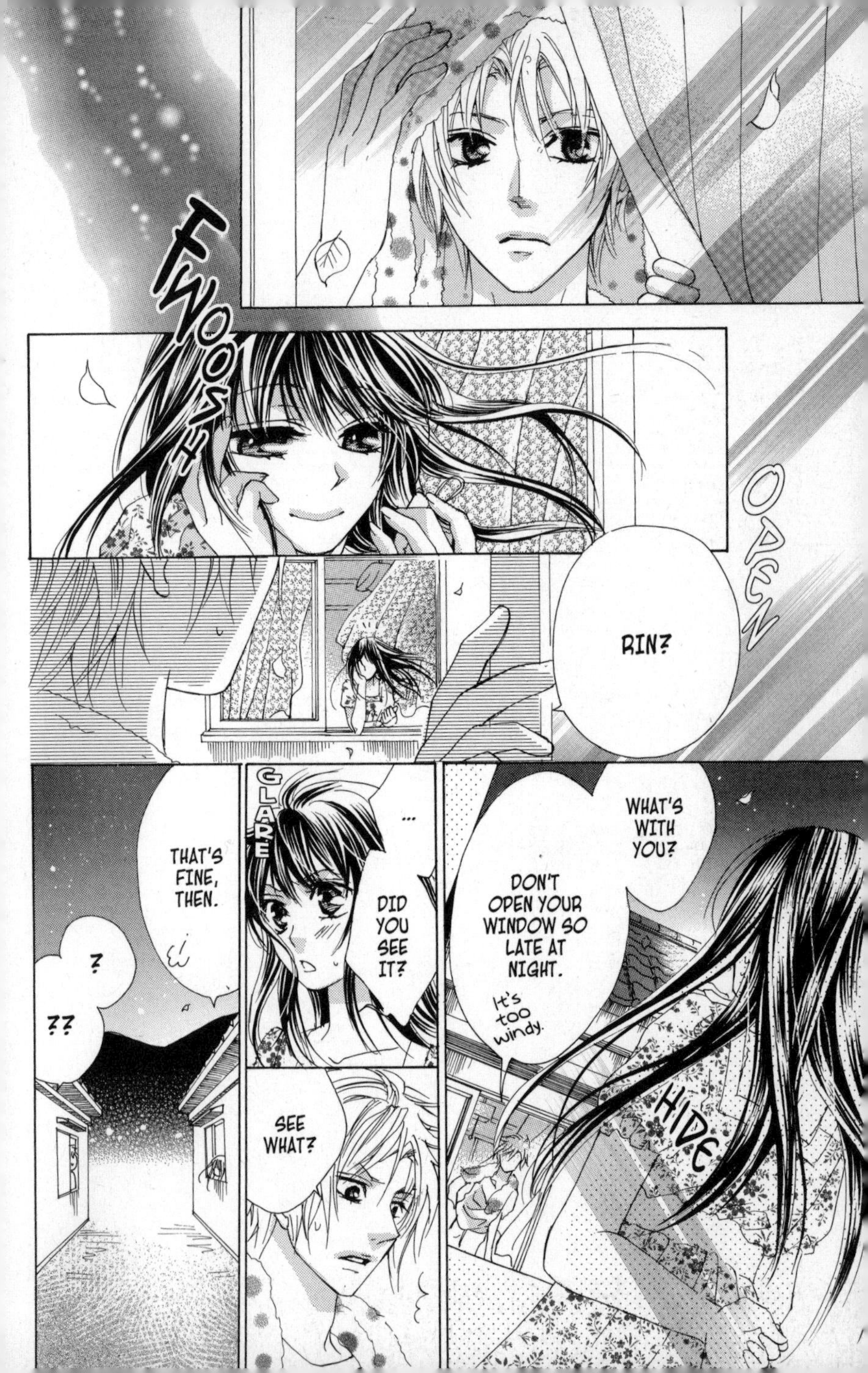
FWOOSH
OPEN
RIN?
WHAT'S WITH YOU?
DON'T OPEN YOUR WINDOW SO LATE AT NIGHT.
It's too windy.
HIDE
GLARE
...
DID YOU SEE IT?
SEE WHAT?
THAT'S FINE, THEN.
?
??

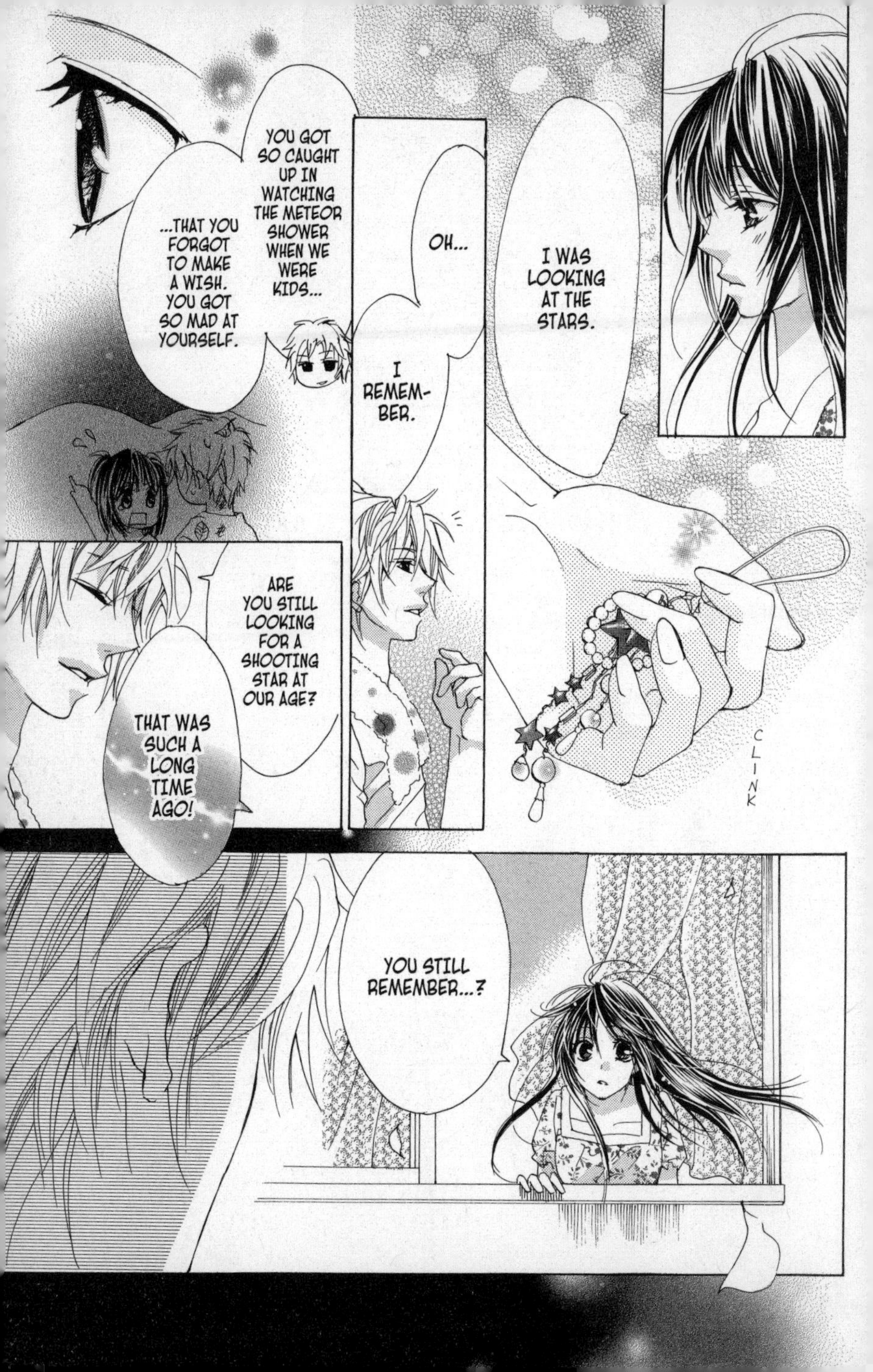
I WAS LOOKING AT THE STARS.
CLINK
OH...
I REMEMBER.
ARE YOU STILL LOOKING FOR A SHOOTING STAR AT OUR AGE?
YOU GOT SO CAUGHT UP IN WATCHING THE METEOR SHOWER WHEN WE WERE KIDS...
...THAT YOU FORGOT TO MAKE A WISH. YOU GOT SO MAD AT YOURSELF.
THAT WAS SUCH A LONG TIME AGO!
YOU STILL REMEMBER...?

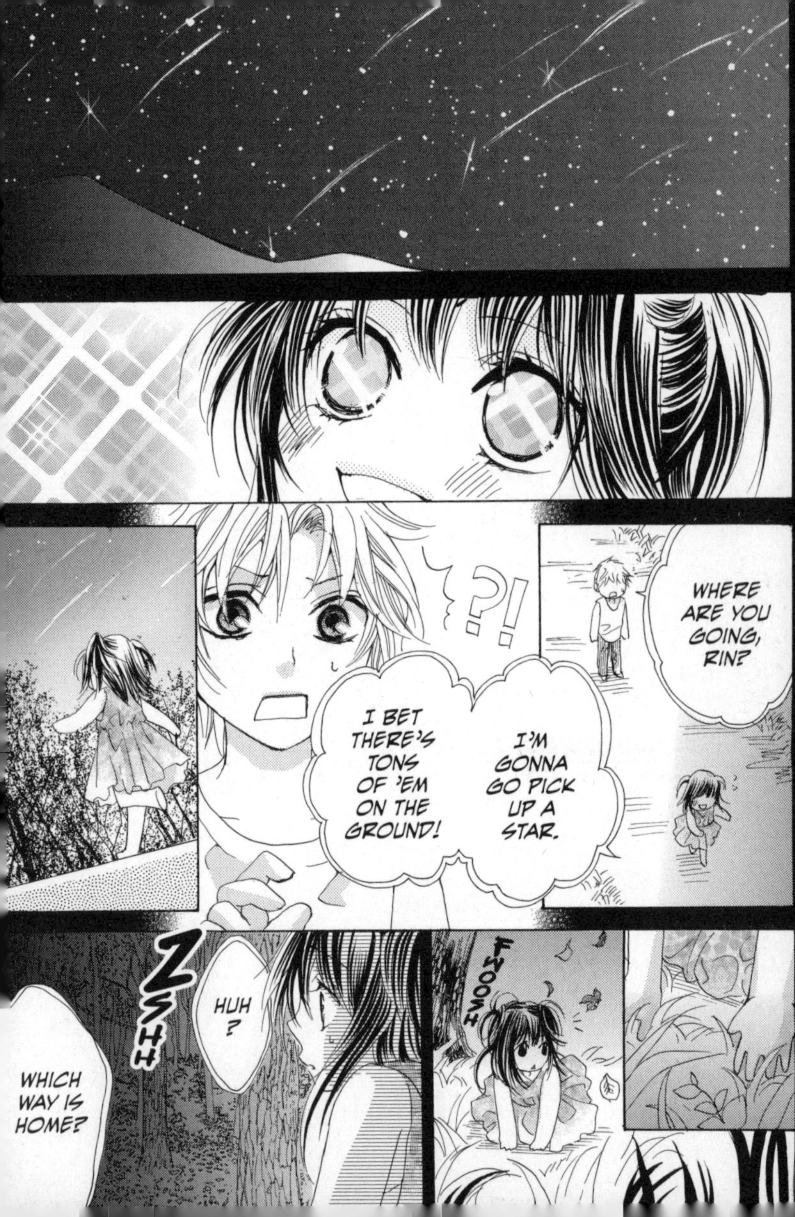
WHERE ARE YOU GOING, RIN?
?!
I'M GONNA GO PICK UP A STAR.
I BET THERE'S TONS OF 'EM ON THE GROUND!
FWOOSH
ZSHH
HUH?
WHICH WAY IS HOME?

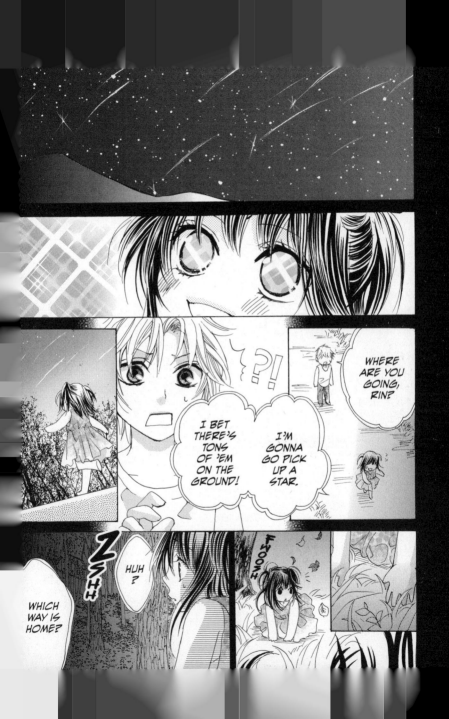

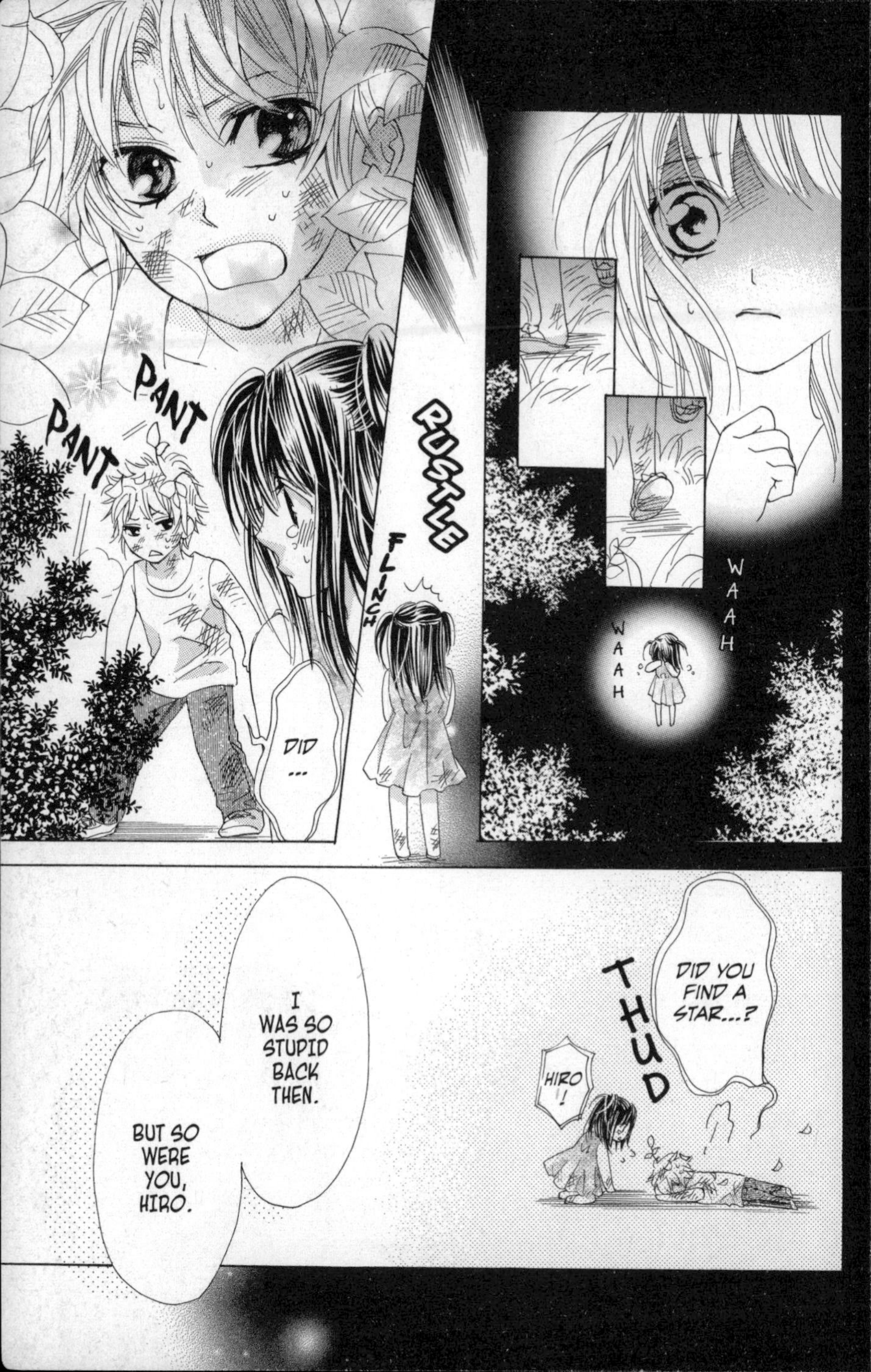
WAAH
WAAH
PANT
PANT
RUSTLE
FLINCH
DID ...
DID YOU FIND A STAR...?
THUD
HIRO!
I WAS SO STUPID BACK THEN.
BUT SO WERE YOU, HIRO.

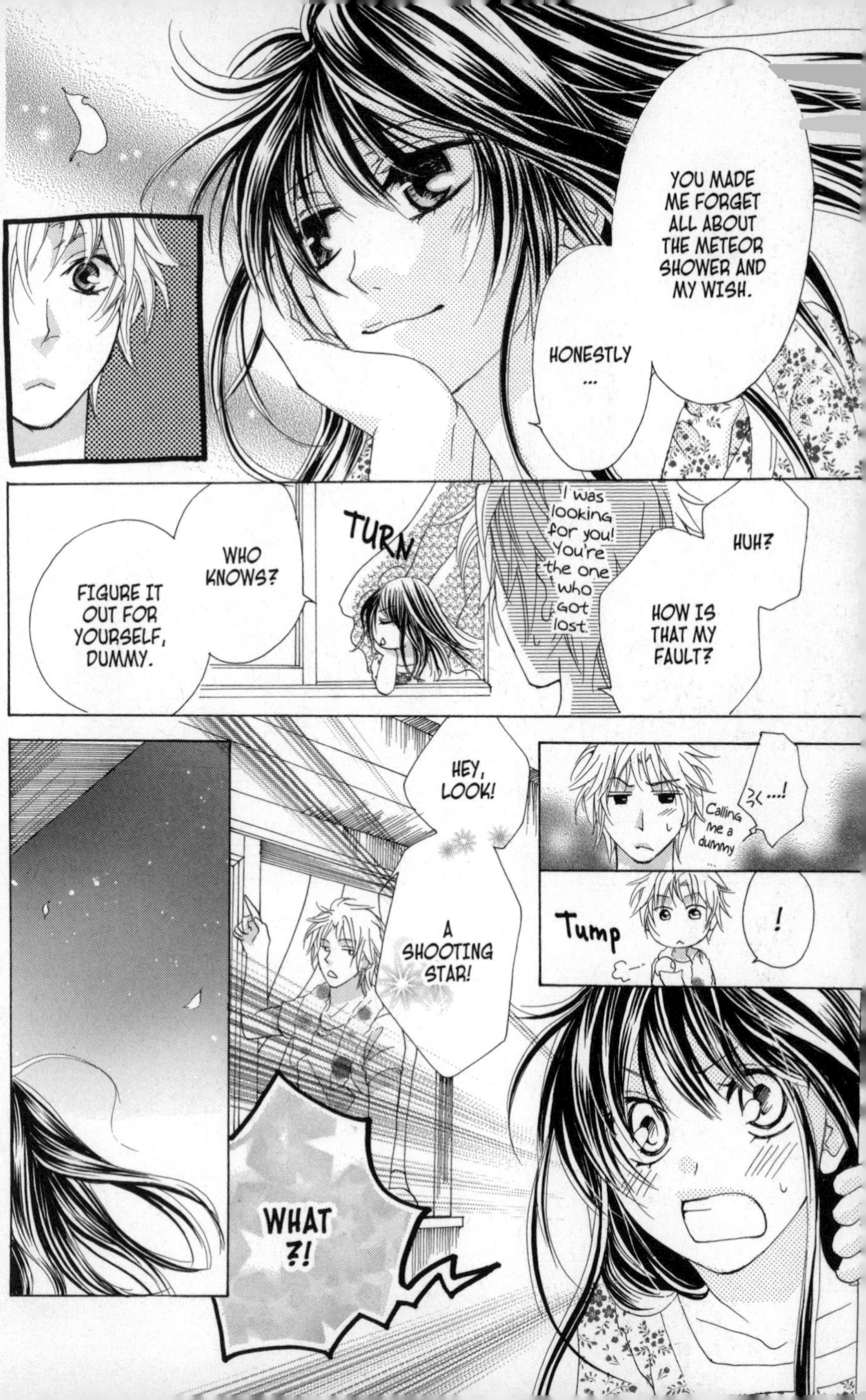
YOU MADE ME FORGET ALL ABOUT THE METEOR SHOWER AND MY WISH.
HONESTLY ...
HUH?
HOW IS THAT MY FAULT?
I was looking for you! You're the one who got lost.
TURN
WHO KNOWS?
FIGURE IT OUT FOR YOURSELF, DUMMY.
ぐ…!
Calling me a dummy ...
Tump
!
HEY, LOOK!
A SHOOTING STAR!
WHAT ?!

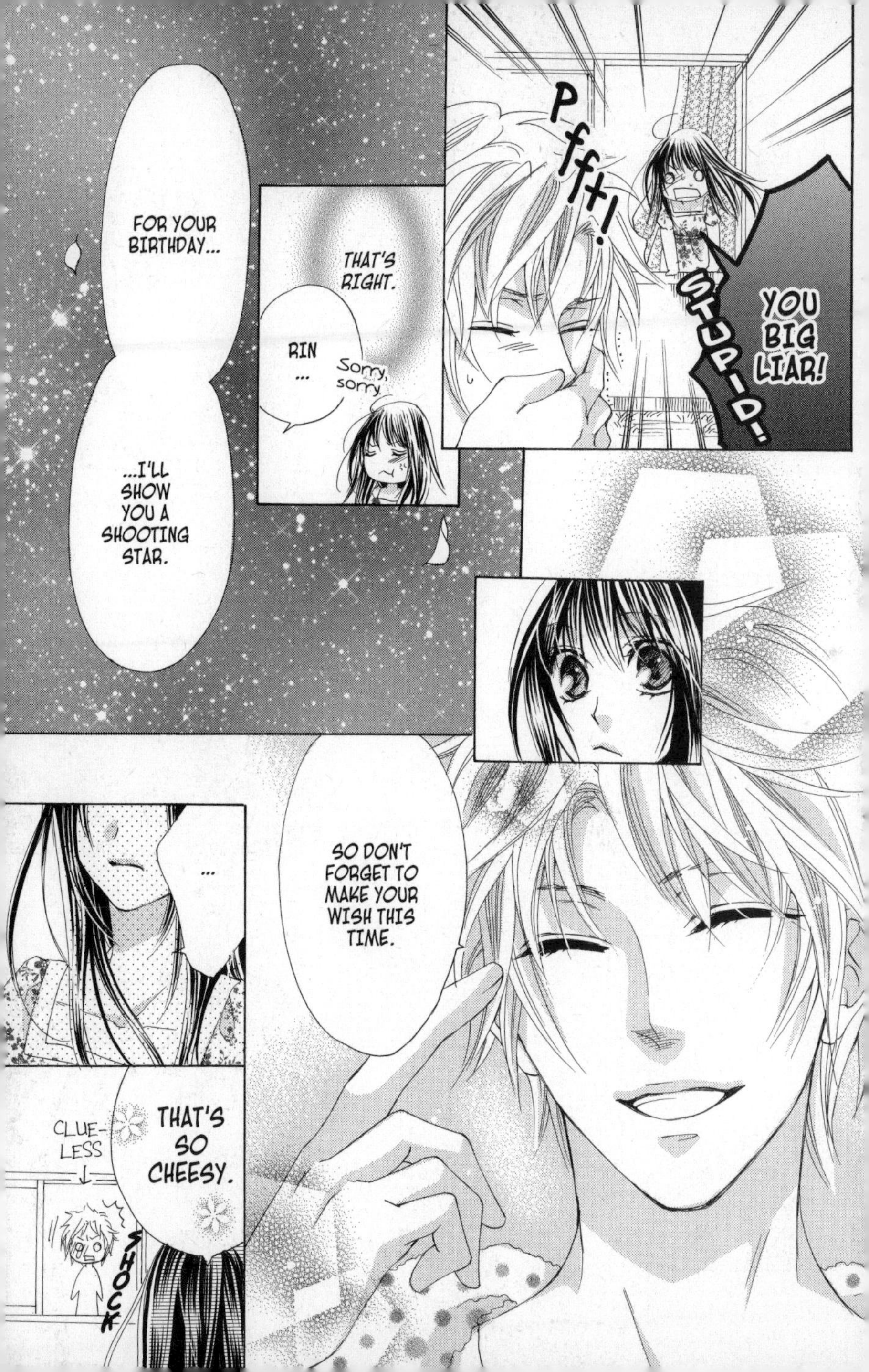

YOU BIG LIAR!
STUPID!
Pfft!
THAT'S RIGHT.
RIN...
Sorry, sorry.
FOR YOUR BIRTHDAY...
...I'LL SHOW YOU A SHOOTING STAR.
SO DON'T FORGET TO MAKE YOUR WISH THIS TIME.
...
THAT'S SO CHEESY.
CLUELESS
SHOCK

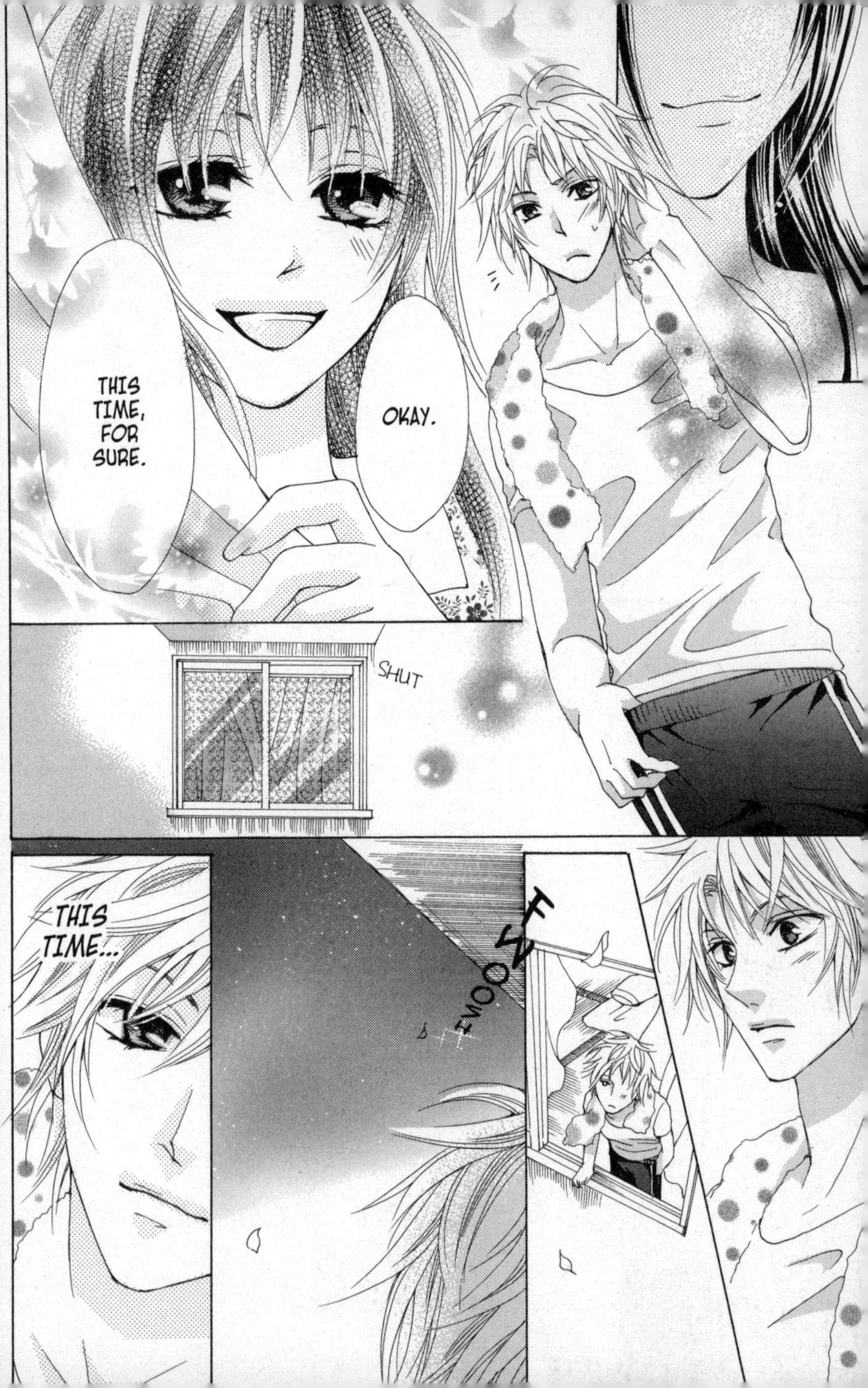
THIS TIME, FOR SURE.
OKAY.
SHUT
FWOOSH
THIS TIME...

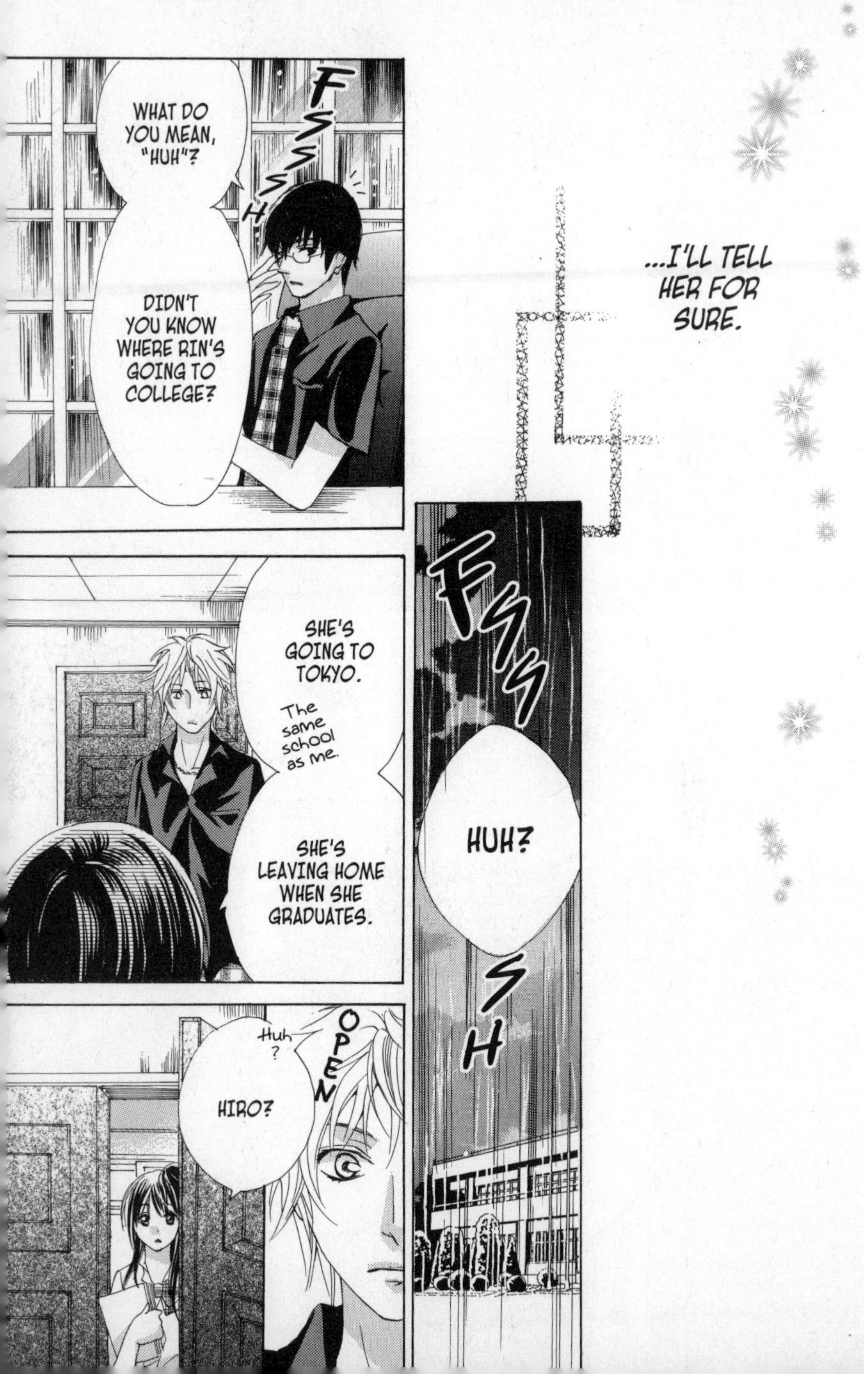
...I'LL TELL HER FOR SURE.
FSS
HUH?
SSH
FSSSH
WHAT DO YOU MEAN, "HUH"?
DIDN'T YOU KNOW WHERE RIN'S GOING TO COLLEGE?
SHE'S GOING TO TOKYO.
The same school as me.
SHE'S LEAVING HOME WHEN SHE GRADUATES.
OPEN
Huh?
HIRO?

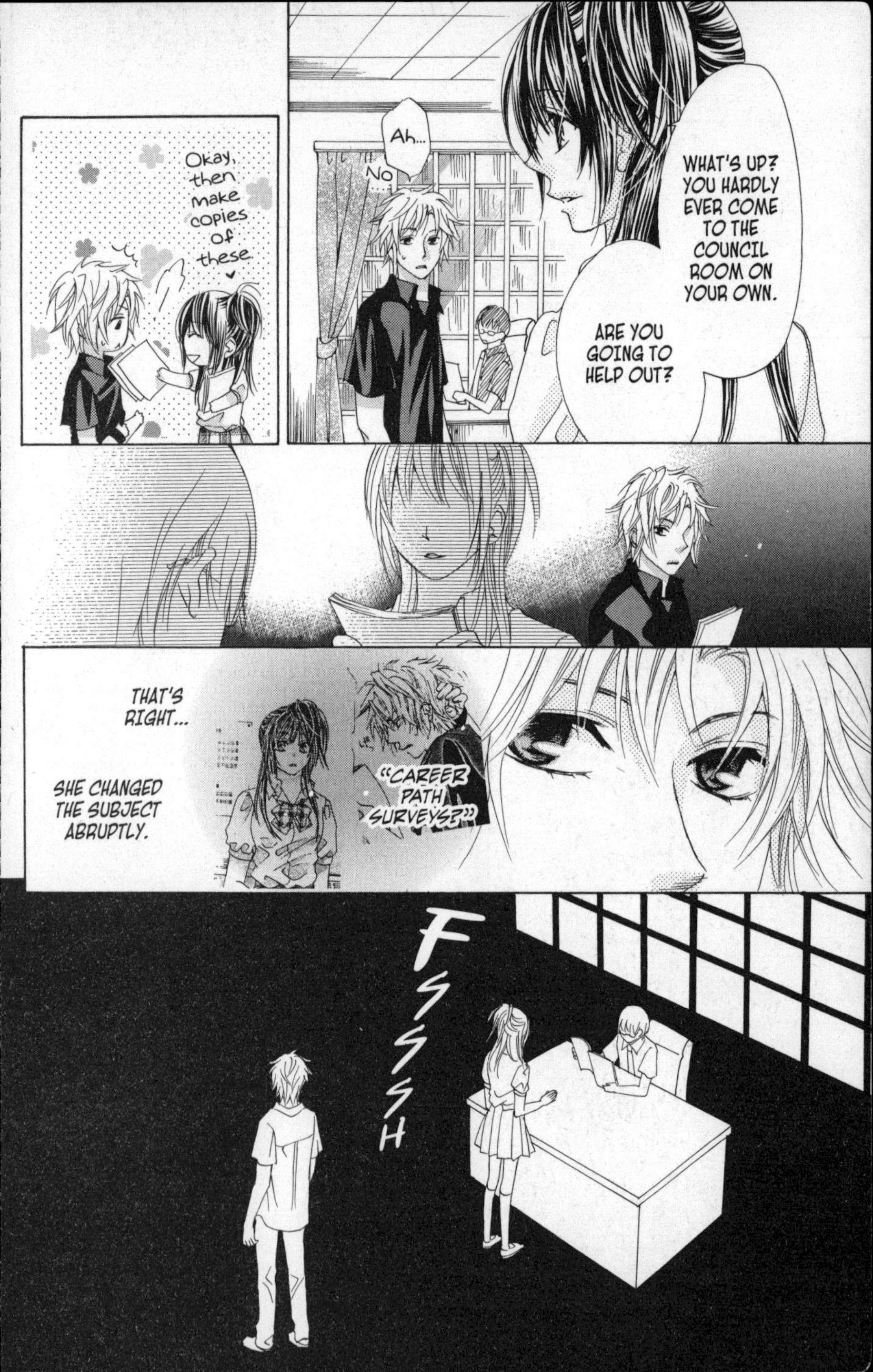
WHAT'S UP? YOU HARDLY EVER COME TO THE COUNCIL ROOM ON YOUR OWN.
ARE YOU GOING TO HELP OUT?
Ah...
No...
Okay, then make copies of these.
"CAREER PATH SURVEYS?"
THAT'S RIGHT...
SHE CHANGED THE SUBJECT ABRUPTLY.
FSSSH

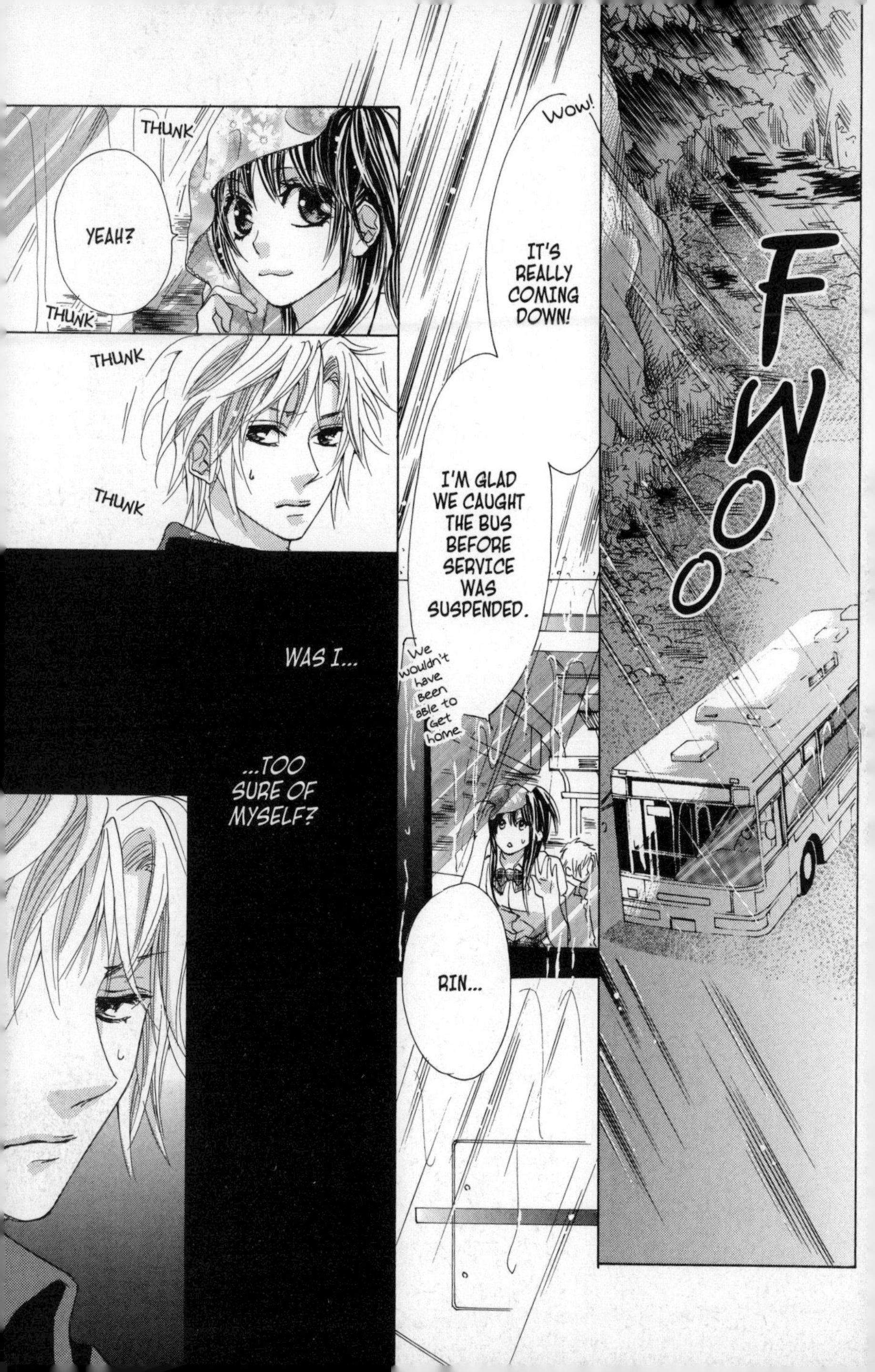
FWOOO
WOW!
IT'S REALLY COMING DOWN!
I'M GLAD WE CAUGHT THE BUS BEFORE SERVICE WAS SUSPENDED.
We wouldn't have been able to get home.
RIN...
THUNK
YEAH?
THUNK
THUNK
THUNK
WAS I...
...TOO SURE OF MYSELF?

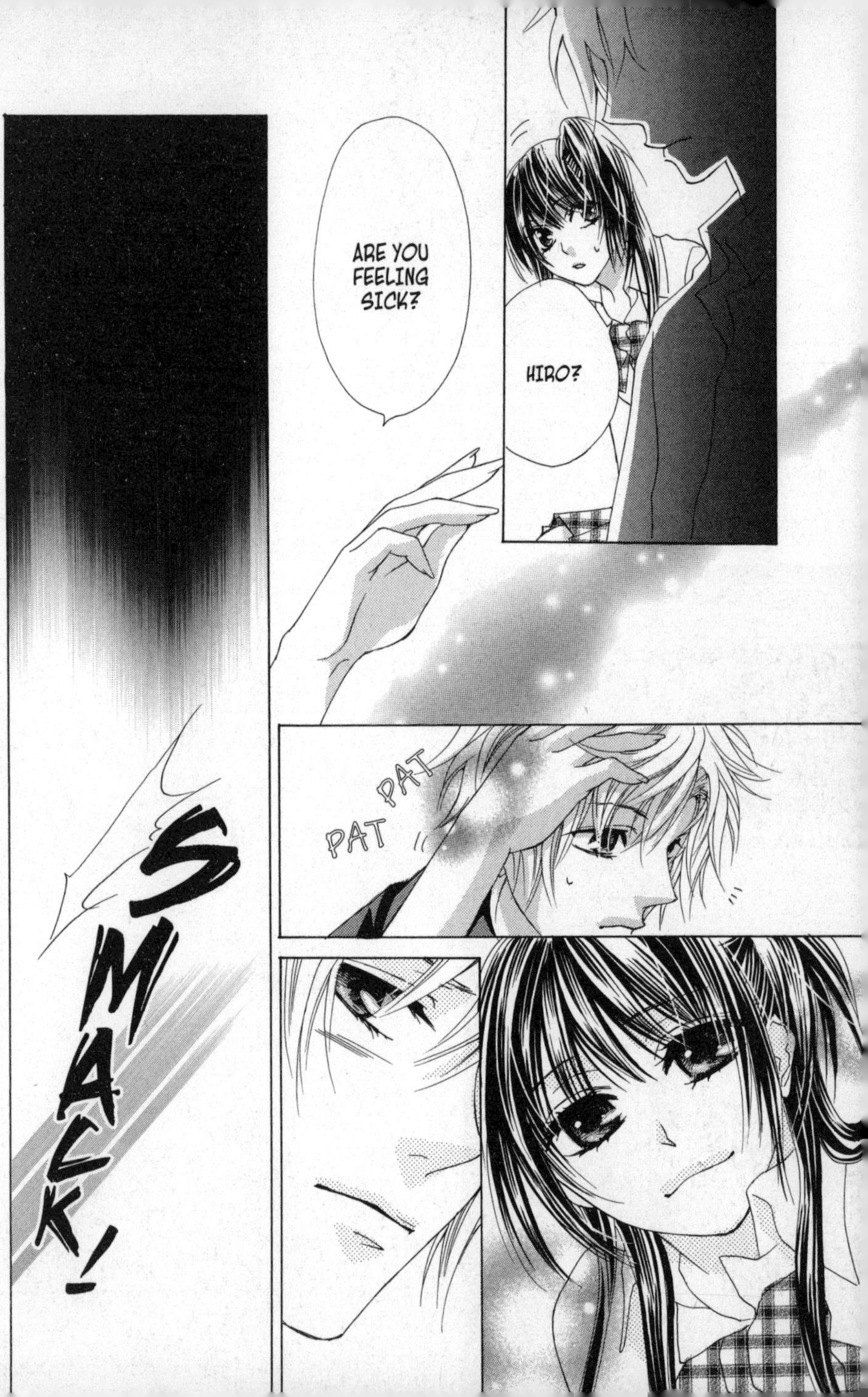
HIRO?
ARE YOU FEELING SICK?
PAT PAT
SMACK!

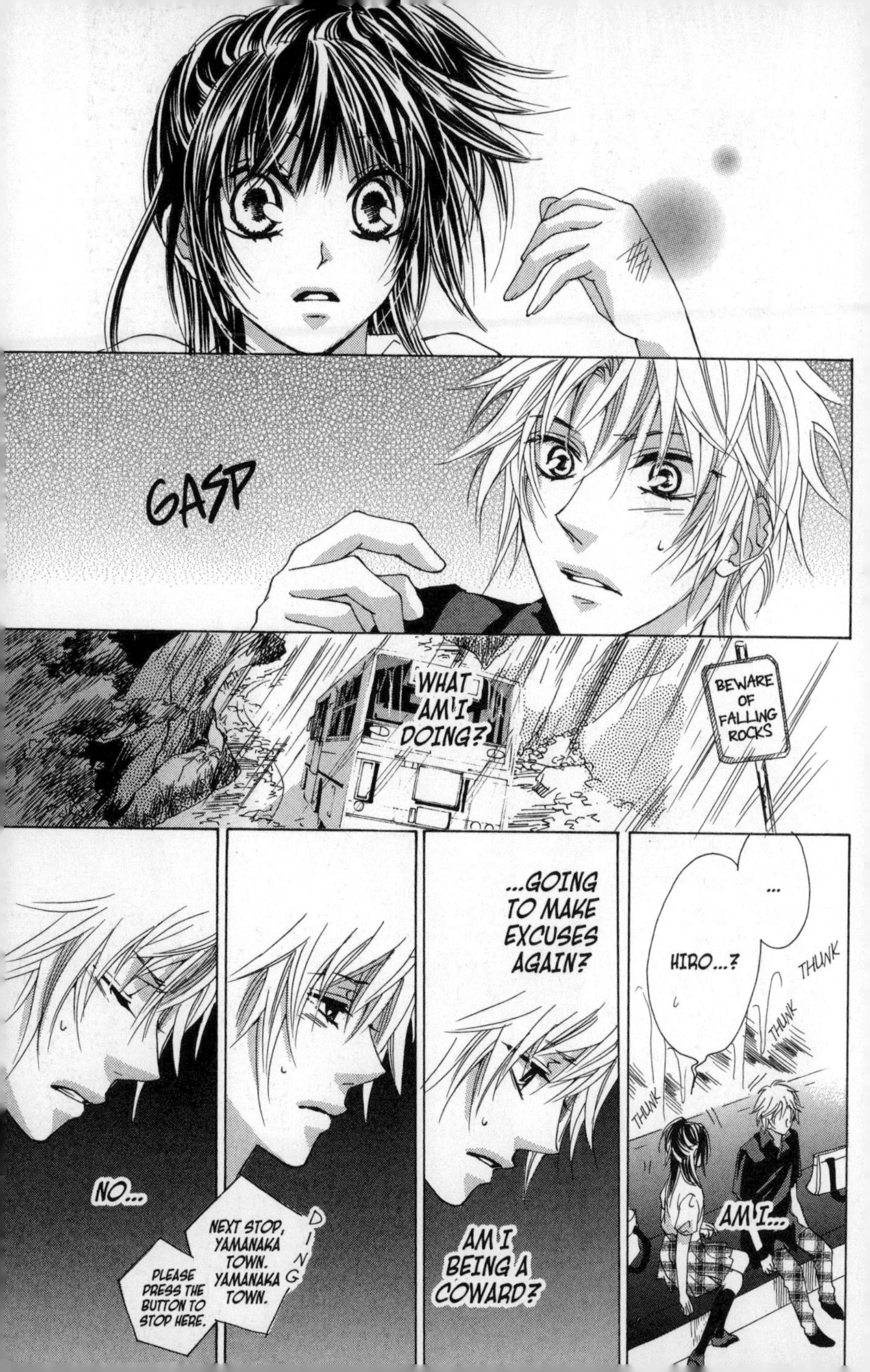
GASP
BEWARE OF FALLING ROCKS
WHAT AM I DOING?
...
HIRO...?
THUNK
THUNK
THUNK
AM I...
...GOING TO MAKE EXCUSES AGAIN?
AM I BEING A COWARD?
DING
NEXT STOP, YAMANAKA TOWN. YAMANAKA TOWN.
PLEASE PRESS THE BUTTON TO STOP HERE.
NO...

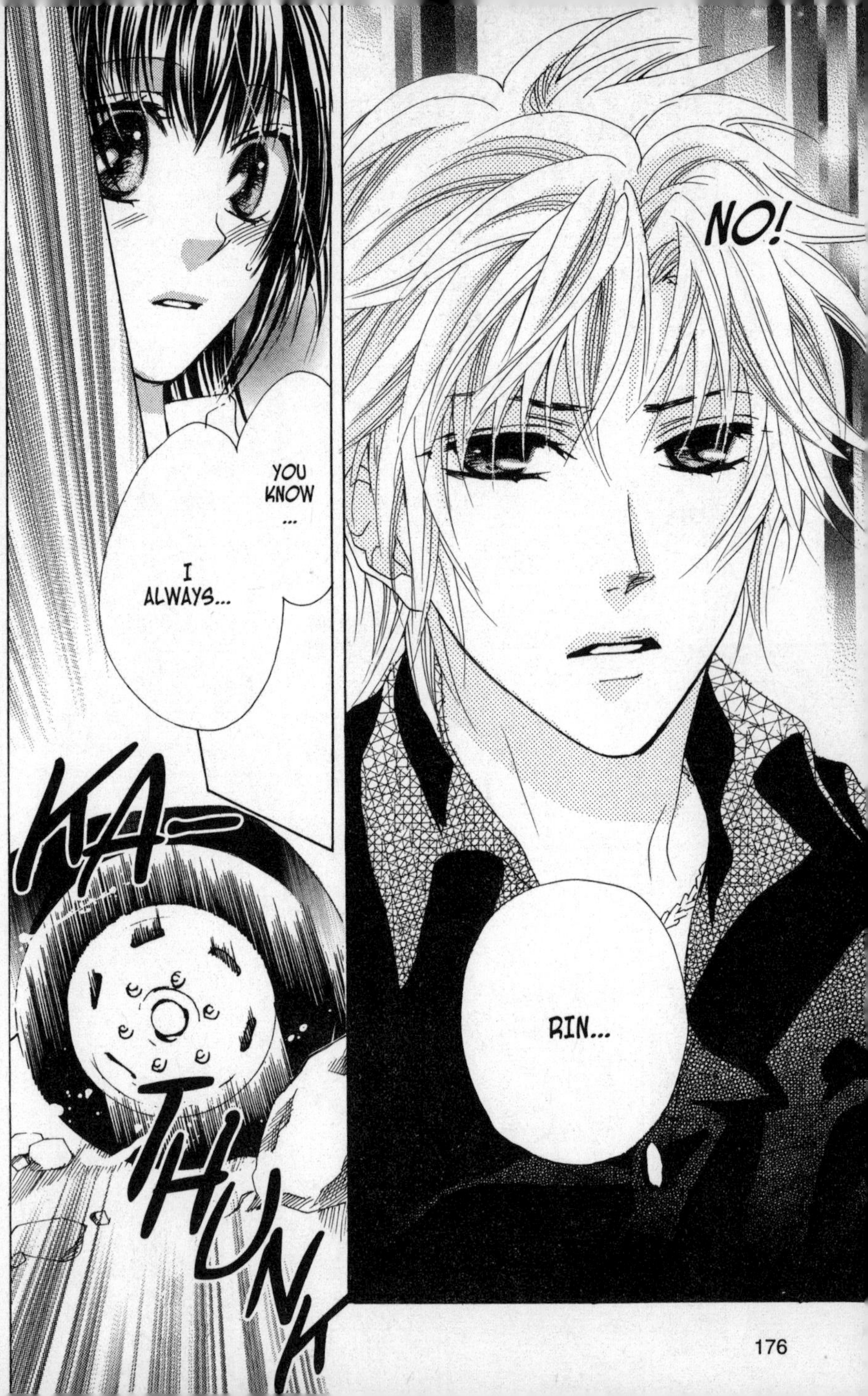
NO!
RIN...
YOU KNOW ...
I ALWAYS...
KA-THUNK

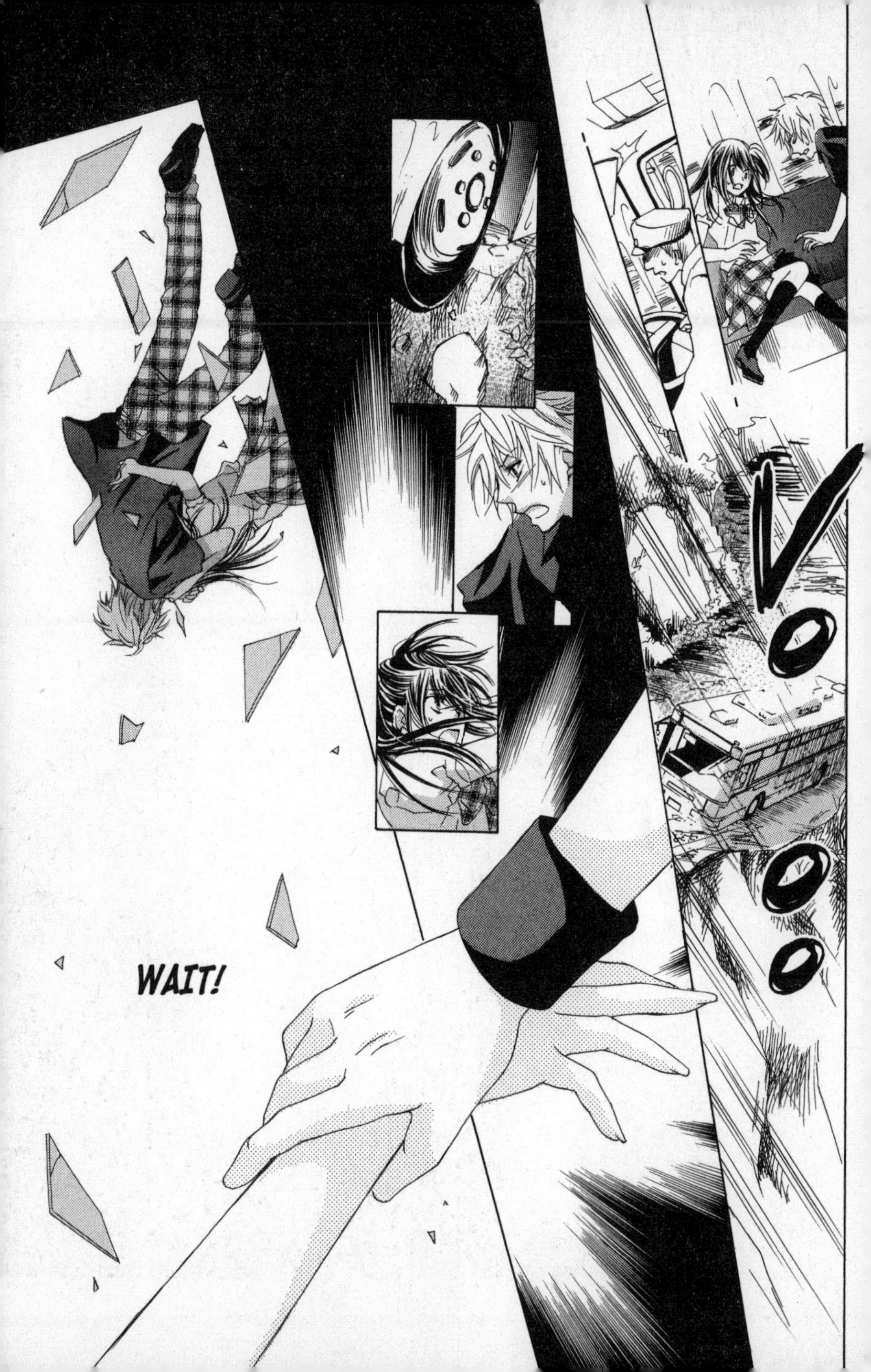
VOOO
WAIT!

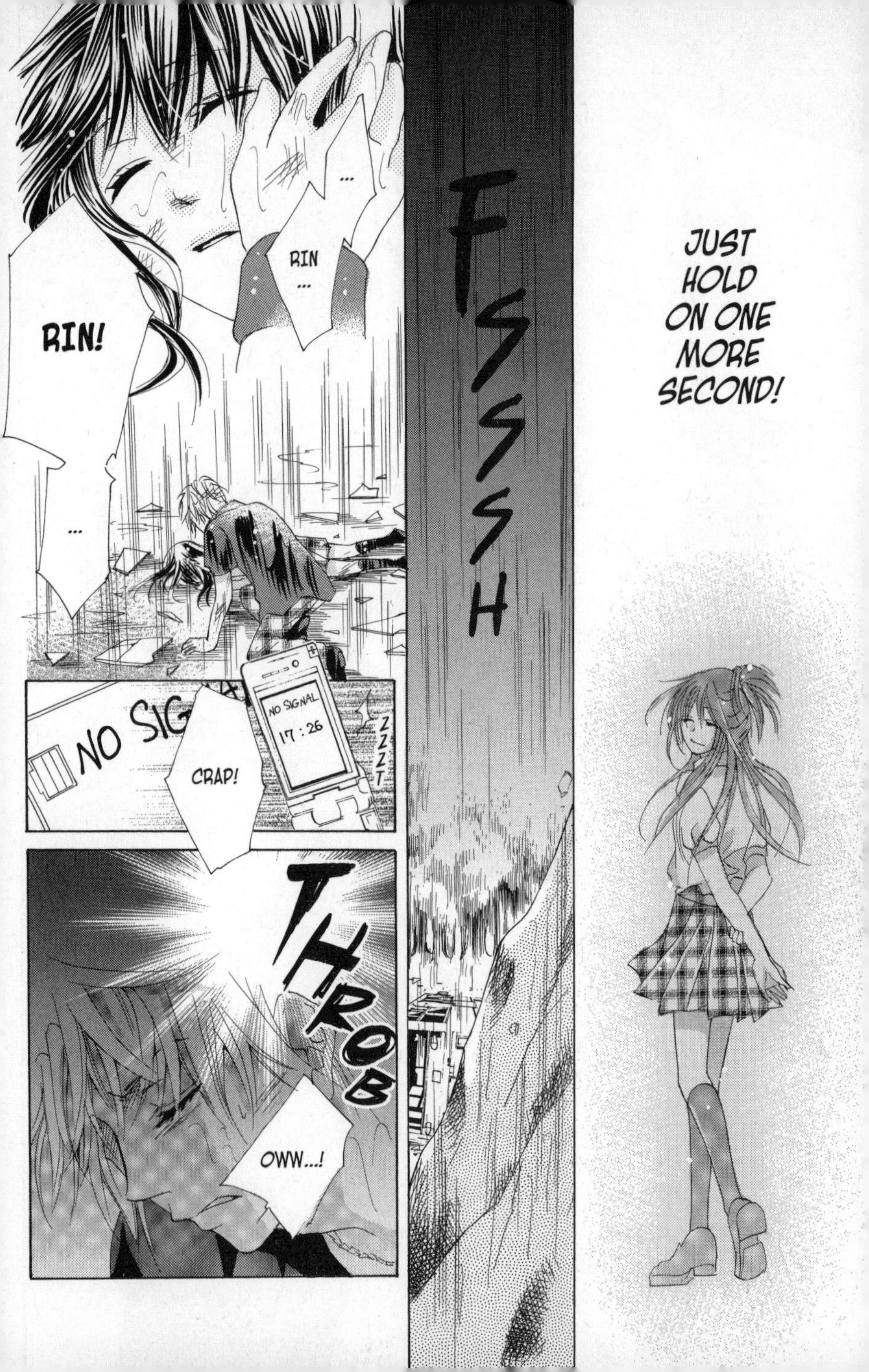
JUST HOLD ON ONE MORE SECOND!
FSSSH
...
RIN ...
RIN!
...
ZZZT
NO SIGNAL
17 : 26
CRAP!
NO SIG
THROB
OWW...!

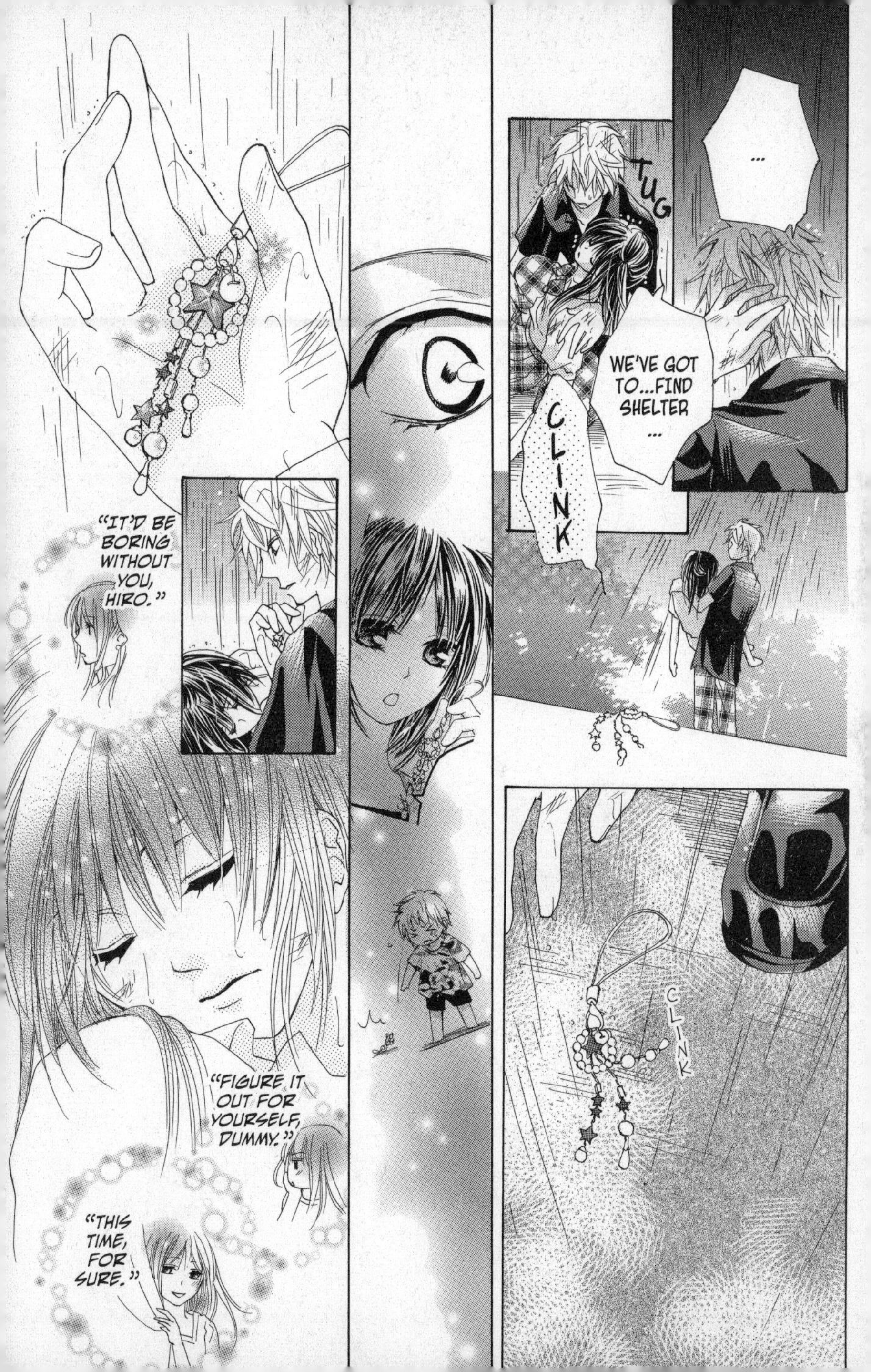
...
TUG
WE'VE GOT TO...FIND SHELTER ...
CLINK
CLINK
"IT'D BE BORING WITHOUT YOU, HIRO."
"FIGURE IT OUT FOR YOURSELF, DUMMY."
"THIS TIME, FOR SURE."

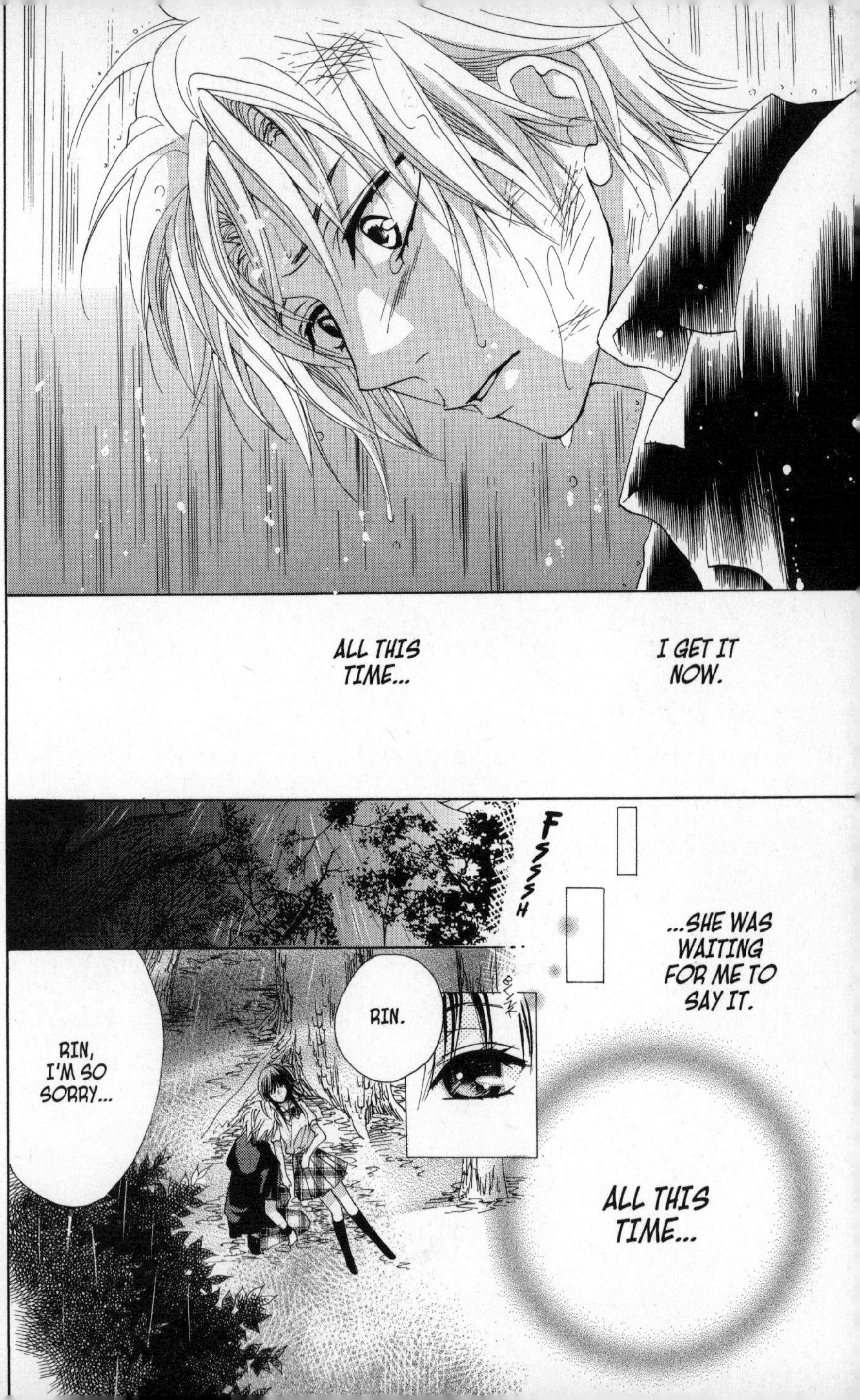
I GET IT NOW.
ALL THIS TIME...
FSSSH
...SHE WAS WAITING FOR ME TO SAY IT.
BLINK
RIN.
ALL THIS TIME...
RIN, I'M SO SORRY...

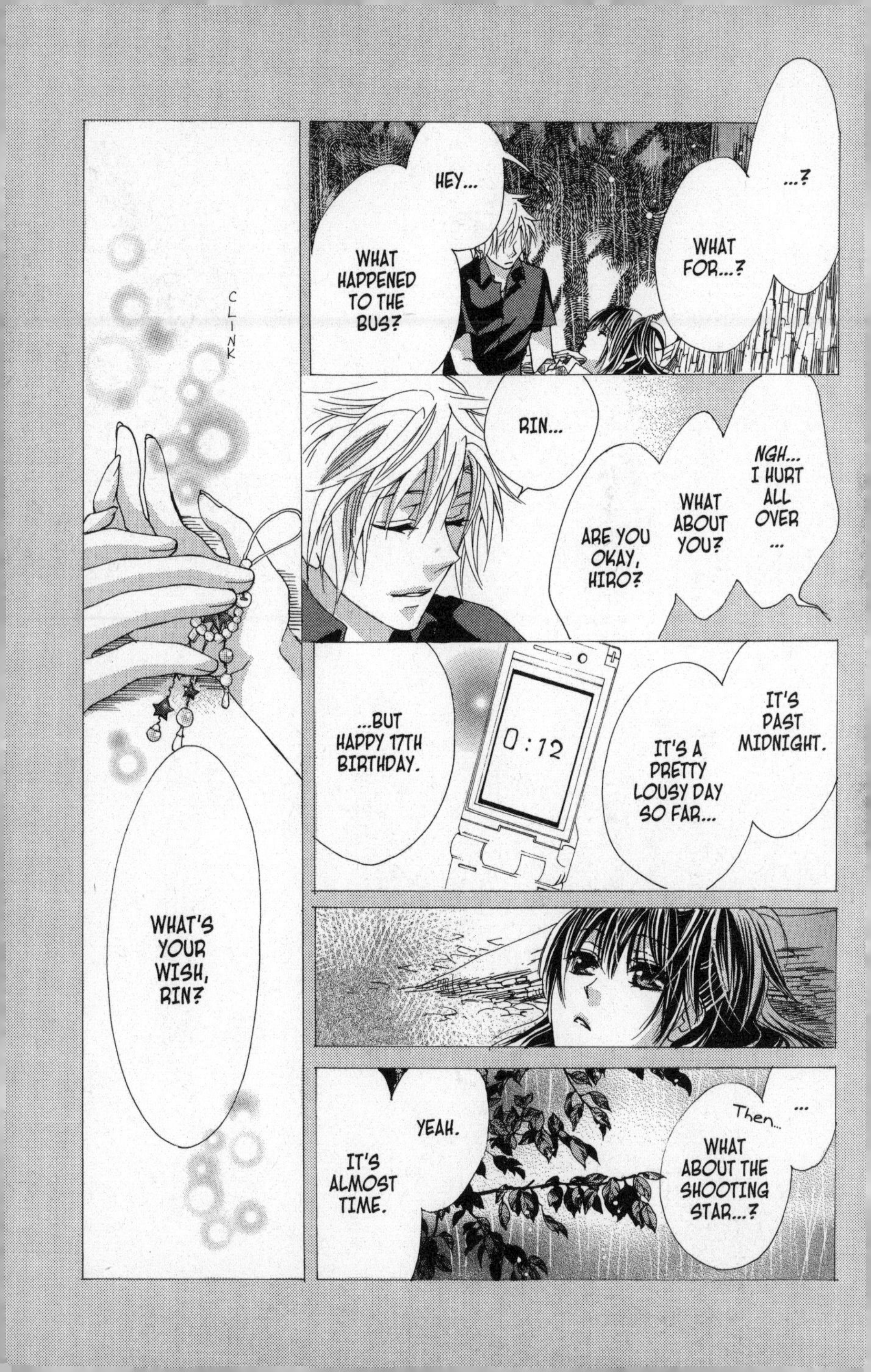
...?
WHAT FOR...?
HEY...
WHAT HAPPENED TO THE BUS?
NGH... I HURT ALL OVER ...
WHAT ABOUT YOU?
ARE YOU OKAY, HIRO?
RIN...
IT'S PAST MIDNIGHT.
IT'S A PRETTY LOUSY DAY SO FAR...
0:12
...BUT HAPPY 17TH BIRTHDAY.
...
Then...
WHAT ABOUT THE SHOOTING STAR...?
YEAH.
IT'S ALMOST TIME.
CLINK
WHAT'S YOUR WISH, RIN?

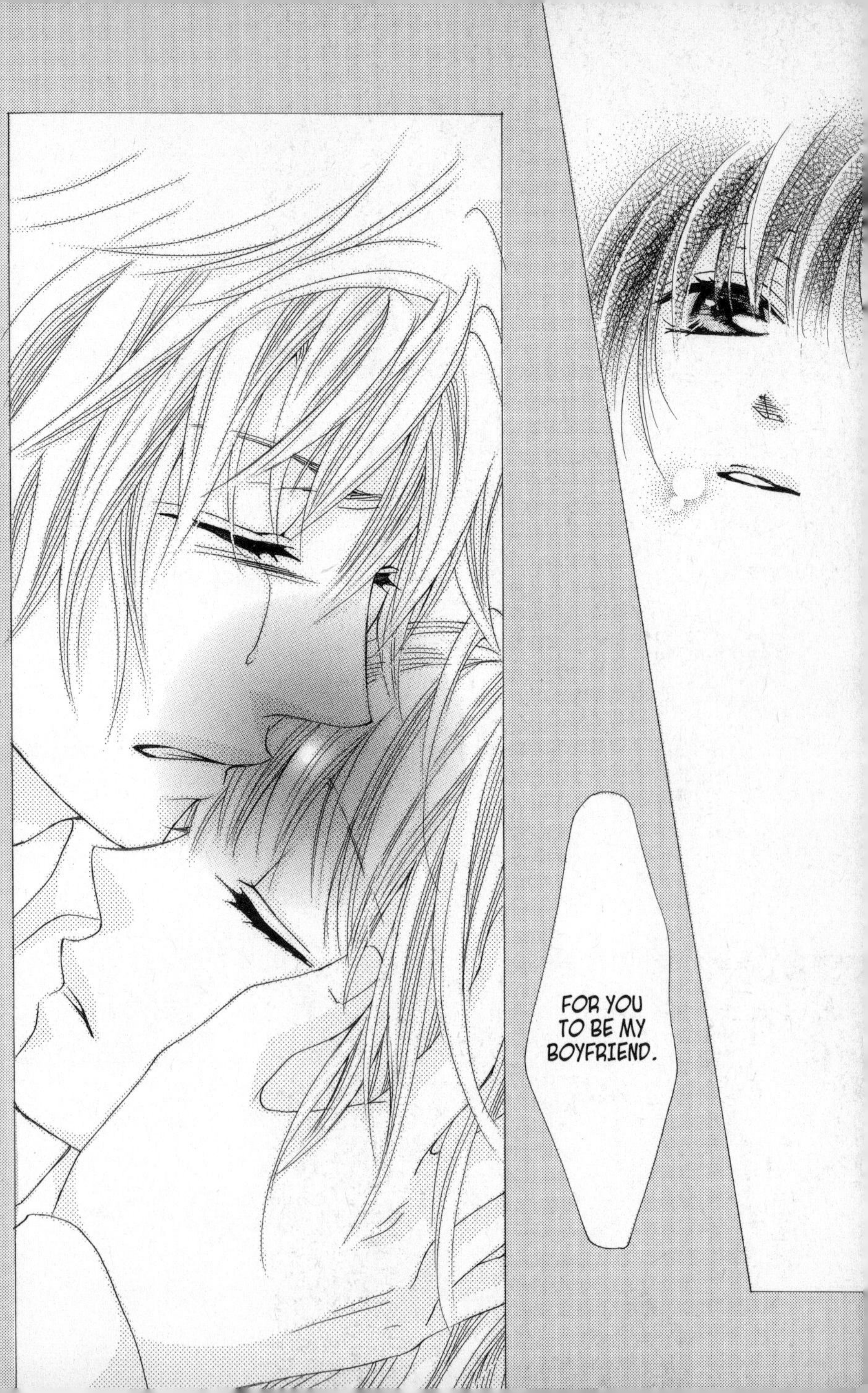
FOR YOU TO BE MY BOYFRIEND.

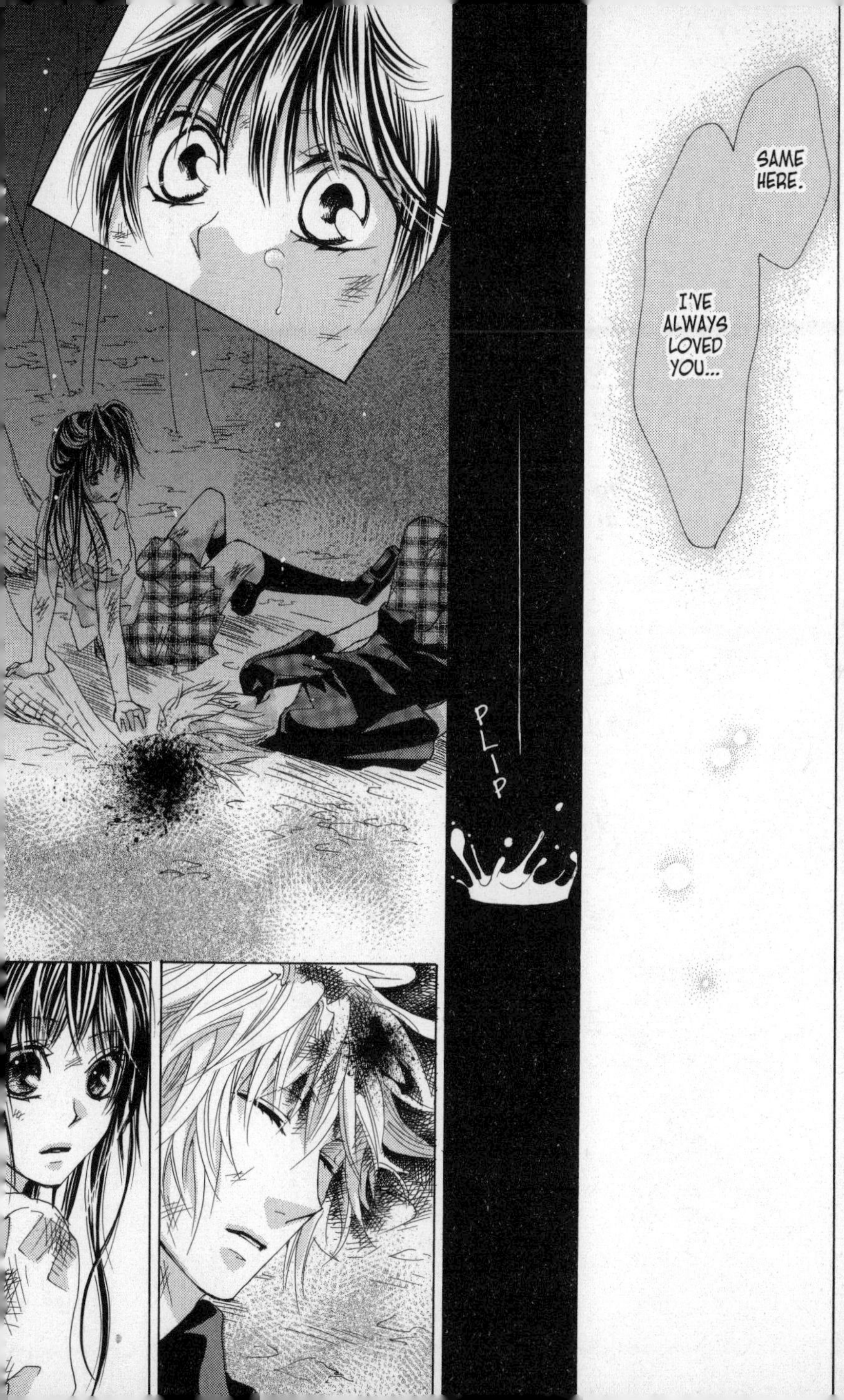
SAME HERE.
I'VE ALWAYS LOVED YOU...
PLIP

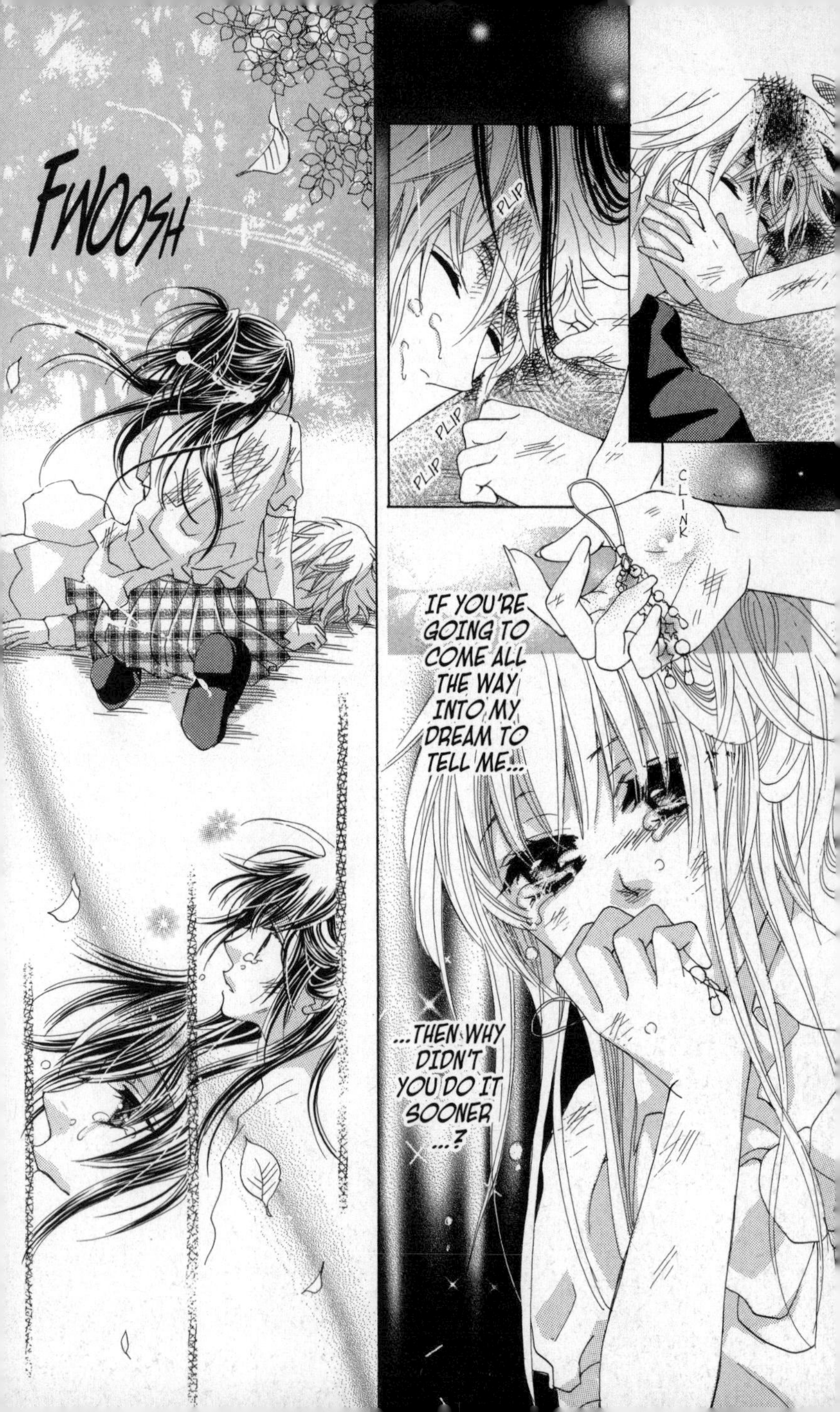
PLIP
PLIP
PLIP
PLIP
CLINK
IF YOU'RE GOING TO COME ALL THE WAY INTO MY DREAM TO TELL ME...
...THEN WHY DIDN'T YOU DO IT SOONER ...?
FWOOSH

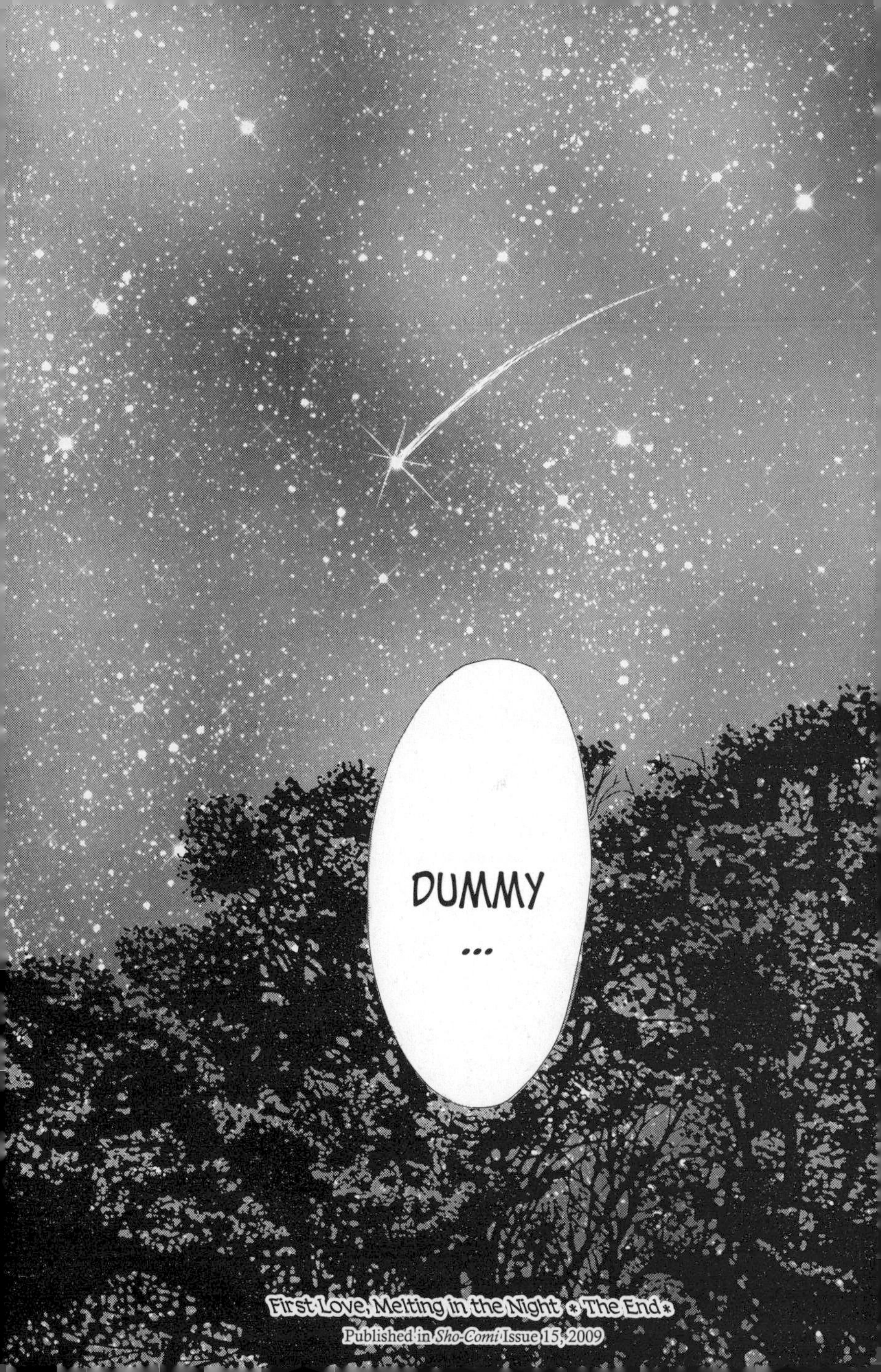
DUMMY
...

First Love, Melting in the Night * The End *

Published in *Sho-Comi* Issue 15, 2009

✿ "First Love, Melting in the Night" ✿

I hadn't had a one-shot story in the main magazine in a while. It was the first time my main character was a guy, and it also ended sadly (for a *Sho-Comi* story), so it was really challenging.

Guys don't like discussing things, do they? They think we should understand them from how they act. But girls worry about stuff all the time. Girls want things said and are waiting for guys to say them. So I wanted to write about missed signals and how irritating they can be... But judging from the readers' reaction, people didn't really get that from the story. I was reminded of my shortcomings. I'm sorry I couldn't do a better job, but I'm really glad that I was able to try it.

✿ Thank you for sticking with me for so long! The three "*Honey Blood*" stories are the basis for the serialized *Honey Blood* (Vols. 1 & 2). If you're curious, please be sure to check them out too! I hope to meet you again.

Miko Mitsuki, November 2009

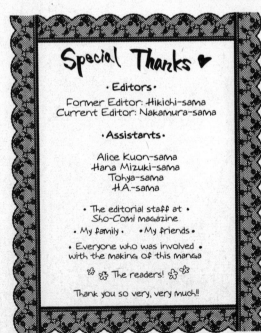

Special Thanks ♥

• Editors •

Former Editor: Hikichi-sama
Current Editor: Nakamura-sama

• Assistants •

Alice Kuon-sama
Hana Mizuki-sama
Tohya-sama
H.A.-sama

• The editorial staff at *Sho-Comi* magazine •

• My family • • My friends •

• Everyone who was involved with the making of this manga •

✿ ✿ The readers! ✿ ✿

Thank you so very, very much!!

Miko Mitsuki
c/o Honey Blood Editor
Viz Media
P.O. Box 77010
San Francisco, CA 94107

I'd love to hear from you!

Author Bio

Born on October 10, Miko Mitsuki debuted with *Utakata* in 2003. She is currently working on projects for *Sho-Comi* magazine. Mitsuki is from Kagoshima Prefecture in Japan, and her blood type is O. She loves cats the most but loves dogs as well.

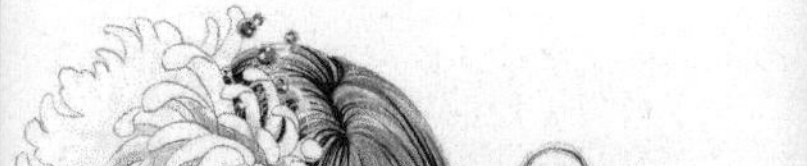

Honey Blood

Tale 0
Shojo Beat Edition

**STORY AND ART BY
MIKO MITSUKI**

MITSUAJI BLOOD TALE ZERO
by Miko MITSUKI
© 2009 Miko MITSUKI
All rights reserved.
Original Japanese edition published by SHOGAKUKAN.
English translation rights in the United States of America,
Canada, the United Kingdom,
and Ireland arranged with SHOGAKUKAN.

English Adaptation/Ysabet Reinhardt MacFarlane
Translation/pinkie-chan
Touch-up Art & Lettering/Joanna Estep
Design/Izumi Evers
Editor/Amy Yu

Printed in the U.S.A.

Published by VIZ Media, LLC
P.O. Box 77010
San Francisco, CA 94107

10 9 8 7 6 5 4 3 2 1
First printing, February 2015

www.viz.com   www.shojobeat.com

⋁I⊇MΛΠGΛ
Read manga anytime, anywhere!

From our newest hit series to the classics you know and love, the best manga in the world is now available digitally. **Buy a volume*** of digital manga for your:

- iOS device (**iPad®, iPhone®, iPod® touch**) through the **VIZ Manga app**

- Android-powered device (**phone or tablet**) with a browser by visiting VIZManga.com

- **Mac or PC computer** by visiting VIZManga.com

VIZ Digital has loads to offer:

- 500+ ready-to-read volumes
- New volumes each week
- FREE previews
- Access on multiple devices! Create a log-in through the app so you buy a book once, and read it on your device of choice!*

To learn more, visit www.viz.com/apps

* Some series may not be available for multiple devices.
Check the app on your device to find out what's available.

viz.com/apps

This is the last page.

In keeping with the original Japanese comic format, this book reads from right to left—so action, sound effects, and word balloons are completely reversed. This preserves the orientation of the original artwork—plus, it's fun! Check out the diagram shown here to get the hang of things, and then turn to the other side of the book to get started!

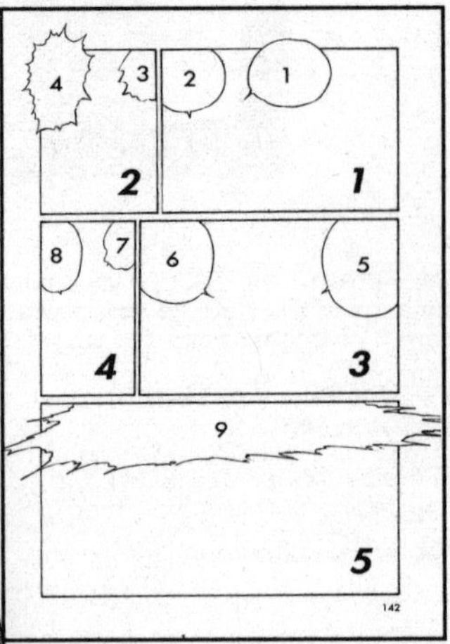

1
2
1
3
4
2
5
6
3
7
8
4
9
5
142

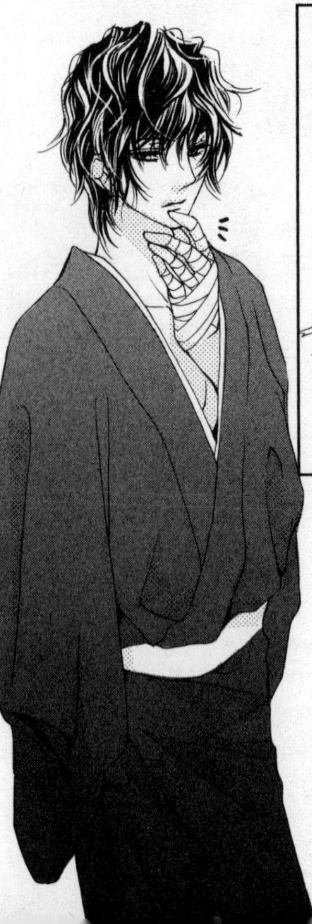